The American Historical Association

THE
MISSISSIPPI QUESTION
1795-1803

A Study in Trade, Politics, and Diplomacy

BY

ARTHUR PRESTON WHITAKER

PROFESSOR OF AMERICAN HISTORY
CORNELL UNIVERSITY

Gloucester, Mass.
PETER SMITH
1962

PREFACE

The supreme importance of the Mississippi Question is established by the testimony of two eminent authorities, and their testimony is all the more weighty because they observed the scene from such widely different points of view. "Since the question of independence, none has occurred more deeply interesting to the United States than the cession of Louisiana to France." Thus wrote Alexander Hamilton in February, 1803, at the height of the crisis provoked by the news that Spain had ceded Louisiana to France and suppressed the Americans' valuable right of deposit at New Orleans. Hamilton's chief rival, Thomas Jefferson, was in complete agreement with him in regard to the gravity of the situation. In January, 1803, he wrote James Monroe informing him that he was to be sent on a special mission to France and Spain for the purpose of protecting the interests of the United States which had been placed in jeopardy by these measures; and he solemnly assured Monroe that "on the event of this mission depends the future destinies of this republic."

So important a problem deserves careful historical study. That is what I have undertaken to provide in this book. The title that I have chosen for it seems to me an appropriate one since, in 1803, the dual problem created by the closing of the deposit and the retrocession of Louisiana to France was commonly referred to in the United States as "the Mississippi Question." The time limits of any such study are, of necessity, more or less arbitrary. In the present case I hope they are rather less so, since 1795 is the year in which France began the negotiation for the recovery of Louisiana and the United States obtained the right of deposit at New Orleans together with the closely related right of free navigation of the Mississippi River; and 1803 is the year in which France, having recovered Louisiana, sold it to the United States and thereby rendered the rights of deposit and navigation unnecessary.

As its subtitle states, this book is concerned with trade and politics as well as diplomacy. Strictly speaking, the Mississippi Question, as the term is used here, was merely a diplomatic question between Spain and the United States regarding the interpretation and enforcement of those clauses in the treaty of San Lorenzo which dealt with navigation, limits, and Indian relations in the Mississippi Valley. This, however, is too narrow a definition, as I hope the following pages show. Commercial and political developments conditioned the work of the diplomats and in large measure determined the outcome of their negotiations. The Louisiana Purchase, which brings the history of the Mississippi Question to a close, was not simply an accidental result of Jefferson's effort to solve that question. It was rather the inevitable consequence of the growth of American interests (and interest) in Louisiana; and the reader will see that in all probability even Napoleon's decision to sell Louisiana to the United States was influenced by the existence of these interests as well as by his failure in St. Domingue and the renewal of war with Great Britain.

The purpose of this book is therefore to show how Spain lost its hold on Louisiana and how the United States fell heir to the province. Contrary to the common assumption, Spain was not reluctant to part with Louisiana but was willing to cede it to France, for a price, as early as 1795. Spain's experience during the controversy over the Mississippi Question not only increased its willingness to do so but also prevented it from resisting Napoleon's fraudulent sale of Louisiana to the United States. The schemes for the invasion of the Spanish borderlands that are associated with the names of Alexander Hamilton, William Blount, and William Augustus Bowles brought home to the Spanish government, as nothing else could have done, a realization of its impotence and of the necessity of shortening its lines of defense in North America. Those schemes are therefore discussed in considerable detail.

I have spoken of American interest (as well as interests) in Louisiana. The economic penetration of the province by the United States is, of course, an important part of the following story, but it is by no means the whole story. Nations do not desire to annex each other merely because trade springs up between them. A certain mental attitude is required before economic expansion can give rise to the desire for territorial aggrandizement. In the present case, the appropriate mental attitude was the result of the growing antagonism of the American people towards France and still more towards Spain—an antagonism which found its principal nourishment in the controversy over the Mississippi Question. In this latter connection it is interesting to note that leading Federalists, among them Alexander Hamilton and Gouverneur Morris, were the most tireless disseminators of propaganda against Spain and in favor of territorial expansion at Spain's expense, and that they thus unwittingly prepared the way for the most signal triumph ever won by their arch-enemy, Thomas Jefferson.

After returning the page proofs of this book to the printer, I have just received a copy of Professor E. Wilson Lyon's *Louisiana in French Diplomacy, 1759–1804* (Norman, Oklahoma, 1934). I am happy to find in Professor Lyon's book additional reason for believing that the most important factor in the history of the Mississippi Question was not French policy, or even Spanish policy, but the commercial and political developments in the United States and Louisiana that—without neglecting diplomacy—I have described in the following pages.

In the preparation of this work I was aided by grants from the American Council of Learned Societies (1928), the John Simon Guggenheim Memorial Foundation (1929), and Western Reserve University (1929). Professors Carl Becker and J. P. Bretz of Cornell University read the manuscript and made many useful suggestions. The latter also supplied valuable information regarding the post roads shown on the accompanying map. I am likewise indebted to Professor J. P. Baxter, 3rd, of Harvard University for criticism of my chapter on the retrocession of Louisiana, and to Professor Frederick Merk of the same University for an important suggestion regarding Spanish policy towards Louisiana.

Ithaca, N. Y.   A. P. W.
March 23, 1934

CONTENTS

PART ONE

Two Frontiers

CHAPTER I

THE AMERICAN VANGUARD

I

At the end of the eighteenth century almost all the settlers in the American West lived in the Ohio Valley. There were two main avenues of approach to this region from the Atlantic coast. One lay along the roads from Philadelphia and Baltimore to Pittsburgh and Wheeling on the upper Ohio. The other led down through southwestern Virginia and East Tennessee to Cumberland Gap, where the traveler might take either the Wilderness Road to Kentucky or an equally rugged road to West Tennessee. While the southern route was followed by thousands of emigrants from the Southern States, the northern route was not only an emigrant trail for pioneers from the Middle Atlantic States and New England but also the principal commercial highway between East and West.

Kentucky and Tennessee contained two thirds of the total population of the West, but there were two other thriving communities on the waters of the Ohio. One of these consisted of the settlements in the Pittsburgh-Wheeling region of western Pennsylvania and Virginia, which were the first founded by English colonists beyond the Alleghenies. The other, situated in the eastern portion of the Northwest Territory, was of more recent origin, but it was growing so rapidly that it achieved admission into the Union as the State of Ohio in 1803. West and north of the Ohio lay a vast stretch of Indian country dotted here and there by an isolated settlement or military post, such as the old French towns of Vincennes on the Wabash, Kaskaskia and Cahokia on the Mississippi, Detroit and Michillimackinac on the Canadian border, and the infant towns of Connecticut's Western Reserve on the southern shore of Lake Erie. The region south of Tennessee and north of Spanish Florida presents a similar picture; but, since a large part of it was in the possession of Spain until 1798, it will be described more fully in later chapters.

The development of the Old Northwest, like that of the South-

3

west, was profoundly influenced by the course of international relations in the period with which we are dealing. Because the British
Lord Grenville feared that the neutral powers might embarrass England in its war with France and because the Spanish Prince of the
Peace feared that England might resent the treaty of peace which he
had concluded with France, American pioneers found new regions
north of the Ohio opened to them for settlement and facilities for
their commerce created at New Orleans. In 1794, Grenville signed
the treaty with John Jay whereby Great Britain at last agreed to
evacuate the posts within United States territory which it had retained since the end of the Revolution. Thereupon the long-sustained
resistance of the northern Indians collapsed. Beaten by Wayne at
Fallen Timbers in 1794, they signed a treaty with him at Greenville
(1795) which extinguished their title to most of the land in the
present State of Ohio. In the same year the United States obtained
from the harassed Spanish government the treaty of San Lorenzo,
which gave American citizens the right of free navigation of the
Mississippi and the privilege of trans-shipping their cargoes at New
Orleans.

These diplomatic successes were followed by a rush of emigrants
to the West; and while many of them sought that earliest Eden of
the pioneer—Kentucky—an increasingly large number found the
country north of the Ohio more to their liking. There slavery was
prohibited, a newer society offered larger opportunities to win fame
and fortune, and the soil was reputed to be richer than on the Kentucky side. Though until 1800 the United States government sold
land for cash only, private owners had large tracts which could be
bought on credit and paid for in produce.[1] Thanks to the orderly land
system established by the Ordinance of 1785 and the Act of 1796,
there was less litigation about land titles north of the Ohio than
south of it, where the chaotic systems of Virginia and North Carolina
prevailed. Finally, the immigrant who desired to settle among people
from his own section had no difficulty in finding them in Ohio, for
there were New Englanders at Marietta and Cincinnati and in the
Western Reserve (then commonly called "New Connecticut"),
Southerners in the lower tier of counties around Chillicothe, and
people from the Middle States almost everywhere.

The influx of immigrants to Ohio did most of the towns little
good. Some of them were actually depopulated when the termination
of the Indian war made it safe to live in the country. Thus John

Cleves Symmes wrote of North Bend in 1795, "The cabins are of late deserted by the dozens in a street." [2] A few of the river towns withstood the lure of country life. Among these were Marietta, the center of Western shipbuilding, and Cincinnati, which the English traveler, Francis Baily, described in 1797 as "the metropolis of the northwestern territory." Containing about four hundred houses in 1803, Cincinnati was one of the largest towns in the Ohio Valley.[3]

The Pittsburgh-Wheeling region, with its narrow valleys overtopped by rugged mountains and swept by frequent freshets, found little favor with the immigrant who came west in search of a farm; and besides, the publicity agents of companies owning land further west had done their work well. As early as 1789, when the Indians were still on the warpath, an immigrant wrote from western Pennsylvania: "Land does not raise much at this place owing to the great immigration down the River. It seems as if people were mad to git afloat on the Ohio. Many leaves pretty good liveings here sets of[f] for they know not where but to often find their mistake." [4]

Yet this region too shared in the general expansion and prosperity of the period. Even if few of the immigants stopped, it was profitable to have them pass through. Most of those who came from the Middle and North Atlantic States reached the Ohio by way of Pittsburgh or Wheeling, where they bought boats and provisions for their journey down the river. These towns also served as distributing centers for merchandise brought over the mountains from Philadelphia and Baltimore, sending out boats to sell their wares on the Ohio and its tributaries; [5] and with the vast stores of timber, coal, and iron surrounding them, they soon began to engage in manufacturing on their own account. Nor was their remoteness from the Mississippi any impediment to their engaging in the export trade in produce. Pittsburgh and Wheeling boats, laden with flour and pork, regularly joined in the semi-annual race to the New Orleans market; and Monongahela whisky enjoyed a wide patronage and just renown throughout the Ohio Valley.

The economic trend of the whole region is indicated by the development of Pittsburgh, which was in the process of rapid transformation from a frontier outpost to an industrial center. Although it was still little more than a village in 1803, the end of the process was already in sight. From the Seven Years' War to the American Revolution, Fort Pitt, built on the site of the French Fort Duquesne, was an important military and fur-trading post; but the westward movement of the frontier soon deprived it of its significance in relation to both warfare and the fur trade. In 1784 it was laid out in town lots, and for the next fifteen years it throve on the immigrant business and the river traffic, its population increasing from 1,350 in 1795 to 2,400 in 1800.[6] By the latter year it had begun to realize its destiny as an industrial center. Thaddeus M. Harris, a New Englander who visited the place in 1803, wrote that it contained "many mechanics, who carry on most of the manufactures that are to be met with in any other part of the United States." [7] Among these he mentioned two glass works, a furniture factory, tin-plate and nail factories, smiths' shops for making axes and other farm implements, and shipyards. A childhood likeness of the modern Pittsburgh can be discerned in a description of the place written not long after Harris's visit: it was a town, said the writer, in which the clangor of mill and workshop resounded from dawn to dusk and over which hung a perpetual pall of smoke.

The Northwest and Southwest were developing along divergent lines, but in 1800 they were not far apart. In the former, the mass of the people as well as the leaders were drawn from many quarters of the United States and Europe, whereas the North Carolina-Virginia element far outweighed all others in Kentucky and Tennessee. In western Pennsylvania, Albert Gallatin, member of Congress and Secretary of the Treasury, hailed from Geneva; Hugh Henry Brackenridge, judge, politician, and author of *Modern Chivalry,* was born in Scotland; and James Ross, twice United States senator, was a native of Pennsylvania. In the Northwest Territory, some of the men prominent in business and political life were Governor Arthur St. Clair of Pennsylvania; John Cleves Symmes of New Jersey; and William Henry Harrison, Nathaniel Massie, and Thomas Worthington, all of Virginia.

This list of Virginians suggests that the difference between Northwest and Southwest was one of degree rather than of kind. The same elements, though in different proportions, were to be found in both regions. The Southern upland stock was numerous in Ohio; Scottish and Scotch-Irish Presbyterians had a way of forging to the front in East Tennessee as well as in western Pennsylvania; and Germans, though seldom conspicuous, were to be found scattered throughout the West. The frontiersmen were not Northerners or Southerners, but Westerners. Slavery, which was soon to become the touchstone of sectional division, was to be found in some degree everywhere in the West, although nowhere was it the basic form of labor. In the Northwest Territory there was still a handful of slaves, despite the Ordinance of 1787. In Pennsylvania gradual emancipation was in progress, but the services of slaves for a term of years were frequently advertised for sale in Pittsburgh newspapers. In Kentucky and Tennessee slavery was established by law, but hardly more than one person in ten was held in servitude. If we examine the state of opinion in the West with regard to slavery, we find again a difference of degree rather than of kind. In the Northwest, pro-slavery sentiment was widespread as late as 1820, and in Kentucky a formidable antislavery movement had developed as early as the 1790's.

In short, the frontier of 1800, like that of 1650, was undifferentiated, and the Old Northwest and the Old Southwest resembled each other even more closely than did the Massachusetts and Virginia of the mid-seventeenth century. Whether the trans-Appalachian pioneers lived on the Scioto or the Kentucky, on the Monongahela or the Holston, they were the "men of the western waters." At that time most of the Western settlements were situated upon the waters of the Ohio, which were at once a symbol and an instrument of Western unity. The pioneers all lived much the same kind of lives and they were all animated by common interests. Foremost among these interests were Indian relations and the navigation of the Mississippi—Indian relations, because the neighboring tribes were still formidable in themselves and also, it was believed, had the backing of Great Britain in the North and Spain in the South; the navigation of the Mississippi, because that river was one side of the triangle along which the commerce of the West was carried on.

II

Hundreds of men, women, and children, barefoot and clad in rags, struggling along through ice and snow to Kentucky—this was the spectacle that met the eyes of Moses Austin as he passed along the Wilderness Road in December, 1796.[8] It was such a winter as to wring a complaint from the lips of Austin himself, tough-fibered son of Connecticut though he was, well mounted and warmly clad. His prudent mind could not grasp the enthusiasm that swept this stream of ragamuffins on to what he called mockingly "the promised land, the land of milk and honey." True, he himself was at that very time riding westward in search of El Dorado, in the shape of a lead mine on the Missouri; but he was doing the thing sanely, prudently, as if he were making a business trip from Hartford to Boston, taking with him a servant, a packhorse, letters of introduction, and plenty of money. This swarm of emigrants, traveling the same road so improvidently yet so courageously, made his common sense look a little ridiculous. Penniless, half-starved, without the slightest knowledge of the country they were going to, without land or the means of acquiring it, refusing offers of land "on any terms" from proprietors along the road—stubbornly they fought their way to Kentucky. "And why Kentucky?" asked the outraged Austin. "Because," they answered, "everybody says it's good land."

The good land of Kentucky drew within its borders the larger part of the great westward migration of this decade, trebling its population, which grew from 73,000 in 1790 to 220,000 in 1800. According to the *Kentucky Gazette,* 9,010 immigrants entered the State by way of the Wilderness Road alone in 1795. In November of the same year a despatch from Pittsburgh reported that "the banks of the Monongahela, from McKee's Port to Red Stone, are lined with people intending for the settlements on the Ohio, and Kentucky." [9] Political unrest and hard times, both accentuated by the European war, disposed thousands in the Atlantic States to try their fortune in a new country, and there were many reasons, aside from its fertile Blue Grass lands, why most of them preferred Kentucky. It had already attained statehood (1792), its numbers and situation offered the greatest security against Indian attacks, and its products were beginning to find a market at Natchez and New Orleans and even on the Atlantic seaboard.

Kentucky was the resort of the well-to-do emigrant as well as of the rabble. Already in the 1780's men of family and substance had settled there, and now, as conditions were stabilized and life and property made more secure, these aristocrats, as they were called by their less fortunate neighbors, became proportionately more numerous. A rough indication is furnished by the growth of the slave population. In the last decade of the century the number of slaves increased even more rapidly than that of the whites, rising from some twelve thousand to forty thousand, or in a ratio of 3.33:1 as against 2.95:1 for the whites. While Kentucky attracted immigrants from all parts of the Union, the men of influence came for the most part from Virginia—John Breckinridge, Harry Innes, George Nicholas, Humphrey Marshall, Henry Clay.

John Breckinridge is an excellent representative of the new type of leadership which was developing in the West, for he was not of the rough-and-tumble, Indian-fighting, hard-drinking breed so common in the earlier pioneering stage but a prudent, energetic lawyer who went West in order to better his fortune. It was not until 1793, when Kentucky had already achieved statehood and he had given hostages to fortune by getting a family, that he moved across the mountains from Albemarle County, Virginia, to the Blue Grass Country. Two considerations, he said, induced him to make the move. One was the prospect of a better law practice; the other, the opportunity of providing "good lands" for his children.[10] Though he had not belonged to the charmed circle of the Virginia gentry, he was a man of culture and had read widely and carefully in Coke on Littleton, Robertson's *Charles V,* the works of Rousseau, and many other books prized by the intelligentsia of that generation.[11] He corresponded frequently and on equal terms with such men as Thomas Jefferson, James Madison, and John Taylor of Caroline. It is not surprising that, with such an equipment, he soon built up an extensive law practice and, plunging into politics, established his leadership among the triumphant Western Republicans. His election to the United States Senate in 1800 to succeed the Federalist, Humphrey Marshall, gratified the members of his party not only in Kentucky but also in the neighboring State of Tennessee where it was hailed as a "subject of exultation"; and a year later a Tennessee correspondent wrote: "Our republican friends General Smith, Judge [Andrew] Jackson & others expressed great gratitude & attachment to you. This country are proud of you." [12]

The key to Breckinridge's conduct in national affairs is furnished by a newspaper article which he wrote in 1794, and in which he declared that Kentucky would be the "Eden of America" but for the neglect and oppression it suffered at the hands of Washington's Federalist administration.[13] The remedy he sought was not the secession of Kentucky but the overthrow of the Federalists. When that was achieved in 1800, he and his fellow Westerners were content; for now that the reign of witches was over the exploitation of America's Eden could go merrily on. The same Breckinridge who proposed nullification in the Kentucky resolutions of 1798 was a valued lieutenant of the federal government after 1800.

Tennessee was Kentucky's poor relation in this decade. For many reasons it was less attractive to the immigrant than its northern neighbor. Admitted to the Union as a State in 1796, it was still a frontier community perilously exposed to Indian attacks. More than half of its soil was still in the possession of the Cherokee and Chickasaw tribes under a perpetual guarantee by the United States government; and while no one expected perpetuity to endure very long in the case of an Indian treaty, the proximity of the Indians and their stubborn resistance to eviction were at least a temporary hindrance to the State's development. The settlements were cut in twain by the Cumberland mountains, and East and West Tennessee had less in common with each other than they had respectively with Virginia and Kentucky. Isolation, remoteness, and the transportation problem kept down immigration to Tennessee so long as Kentucky offered a fair field to the pioneer. A population of 77,000 in 1795 had grown to only 115,000 in 1800, despite the opening of the Mississippi and the temporary cessation of the Indian wars. This was an average annual increase of only 7,600 a year for the quinquennium, as against Kentucky's average of 14,700 for the whole decade. The Kentuckian, John Breckinridge, owed his preëminence in the West to his place of residence as well as to his undeniable talents.

And yet from this time on Tennessee played a more prominent part than Kentucky in the development of the Old Southwest. The American frontier was moving southward as well as westward, and Tennessee was the corridor through which a host of pioneers poured into the new country. In both the civil and the military history of the region Tennesseans were conspicuous actors. Nearly every territory established within its limits had a Tennessean as governor. W. C. C. Claiborne, territorial governor of Mississippi and Orleans (lower Louisiana), and Andrew Jackson, territorial governor of Florida, came from that State, as did also Sam Houston, first President of the Republic of Texas. It was the Tennessean Jackson who, with the support of troops from his home State, drubbed the Creek Indians into making a magnificent cession of land in 1814, beat the British at New Orleans, and invaded Florida. In the acquisition of the Spanish borderlands from St. Augustine to the Rio Grande and in the formation of society in that region, the Tennesseans were not outdone by any group of men in the United States.

In Kentucky and Tennessee, as in the seaboard South, population was spread out thinly over the countryside in farms and villages. In 1800 there was not a city in either State. Lexington, with 1,795 inhabitants, was the metropolis of Kentucky. Nor had the growth of population in the towns kept pace with that of the rural districts. Since 1790 Lexington had only doubled in size, while the State had trebled its numbers. The second largest town, Washington, had received an accession of only 108 inhabitants in ten years. Frankfort, the State capital, was a village of sixty houses at the end of 1796; and in 1800 Louisville still had only 360 inhabitants, despite its advantageous location at the "Falls of the Ohio" and the great increase in the volume of commerce down the river since 1790. Nashville and Knoxville, the chief towns of Tennessee, were also mere villages which served as markets to meet the simple needs of largely self-sufficing communities.

When Moses Austin traveled through Kentucky in the winter of 1796–1797, he recorded the number of houses in each town and noted the materials used in their construction. Passing judgment on their æsthetic quality, he found Kentucky an eyesore. At Danville he counted thirty-six houses, mostly of logs and all badly built. At Frankfort, he thought the state-house convenient but not elegant, and the other public buildings "not worth notice." The further he went the worse things got, until finally at Louisville his patience was exhausted. This place, he wrote indignantly, was by nature beautiful, "but the handy work of man has insted of improving destroy'd the works of Nature and made it a detestable place." [14]

Samuel Forman of New Jersey, who visited Louisville somewhat earlier than Austin, described it as "a beautiful little village"; but Forman wrote from memory many years after his visit. [15] Perhaps Austin's was the better judgment. It is certainly the more interesting, for, whether or not it did Louisville justice, it was substantially true of the frontier as a whole. When the pioneer set about his task of making the wilderness blossom like a rose, the instrument that he employed was an ax. He had nothing to offer in place of the beauty he destroyed, and to the sensitive eye of many a traveler besides Austin the frontier was "a detestable place." A clearing granulated with the stumps of trees, muddy crossroads (or dusty ones, according to the season), hogs rooting in the litter about the general store, a blacksmith shop and a grog shop, a few plain houses straggling out to the edge of the forest—such a dreary spectacle was enough to make the traveler pine for the neat comfort of home and more than enough to set the pioneer dreaming of the mansions of the blest in that happier land where the streets are paved with gold.

In Kentucky, as in Tennessee, this spectacle was as yet unrelieved by the spacious country houses, with their graceful lines and pleasing proportions, which could be found on many a plantation in the sea-board South. Austin found even Isaac Shelby, Governor of Kentucky and, it was said, a man of means, living in a "plain but neet Stone Hous." Many of the most prosperous pioneers had to content themselves with log or clapboard dwellings such as a Virginia gentleman might have built for his servants.

The simplicity of their habitations was, of course, a matter of necessity and not of choice. As soon as possible, those who had been thrown to the top in the tumult of frontier life began to reproduce the forms of polite society with which they were familiar. There were, for instance, the Winters brothers of Lexington, Kentucky, who could boast a "Two-storey brick house on Main Street"; but this exotic flower was produced by an uncommonly extensive commercial plant. The brothers also owned a "merchant mill," equipped with a sixteen-foot pitchback water wheel, double-geared, with French burr-stones; a grist mill with a twelve-foot water wheel, overshot and double-geared, and a four-story house, forty by fifty feet, attached; a sawmill, a hemp mill, a 250-foot covered rope-walk, a fully equipped distillery with a capacity of 375 gallons, a river-landing and stocks for the construction of boats for the Mississippi trade.[16] Few of their fellow Kentuckians could rival this display. For the present, poverty, lack of building materials, the scarcity of skilled labor, and preoccupation with the struggle for existence forced most of the pioneers to build simply.

III

Throughout the Ohio Valley the principal occupation at this time was farming. The professional hunter had been forced out to the edge of settlement, up into the backwaters of the hill country, or across the Mississippi. Tobacco, wheat, corn, hemp, whisky, salt beef and pork were the chief products. The cultivation of cotton was just beginning to gain a foothold. A market for these products was found either in the settlements themselves, where they were sold to the swarms of newly arrived immigrants; at the army posts in the West; or at Natchez and New Orleans, where they might be consumed or forwarded to the West Indies, the Atlantic coast, or Europe.[17] Herds of cattle were driven across the mountains to South Carolina and Georgia.[18]

In so far as the prevalent household economy failed to satisfy the demand for manufactured articles, these were generally packed over the mountains from Baltimore and Philadelphia. Stores in the principal towns offered a fairly wide range of choice. In Nashville, though it was one of the remotest outposts of settlement, the purchaser had at his command assorted dry goods, hats, glassware, saddlery, pepper, and spices.[19]

To East Tennessee, walled in between the Smoky mountains and the Cumberland plateau, goods had to be brought by wagon from the Atlantic seaboard; and the heavy expense of this overland transportation (usually one third of the prime cost of the goods) was one of the chief impediments to the growth of the region. If they were consigned to the Northwest Territory, Kentucky, or West Tennessee, goods from Baltimore and Philadelphia were first hauled to Pittsburgh. There they were loaded on flatboats, keelboats, or barges and floated down the Ohio to the mouth of one of its tributaries (such as the Kentucky River or the Cumberland) up which they were towed, poled, and rowed to Lexington, Nashville, or whatever town was their destination.

When Andrew Jackson made such a journey in 1804, he was five weeks on the road from Philadelphia to Nashville. At the end of three weeks he had arrived at Pittsburgh. Another week took him down the Ohio to Louisville and the last week to Nashville. From Louisville a pilot guided him over the rapids and down to the mouth of the Cumberland. There another pilot from Nashville met him with two boats and a crew of thirteen men, for the rest of the journey was upstream. The provisions laid in for the crew consisted mostly of bacon, biscuit, bread, and coffee. Occasionally the diet was varied by the purchase of butter, milk, and chickens from farms lying along the river. A barrel of whisky was bought at Pittsburgh for the remaining two weeks of the trip, although apparently only three hands accompanied Jackson. When the steersman and his crew of thirteen came down the Cumberland to meet the flatboat, they brought twenty gallons of whisky—enough to give each boatman nearly a pint a day on their sixteen-day jaunt.[20]

The financing of this transmontane trade was accomplished in a variety of ways. In 1795, commerce down the Mississippi was so small in volume and so precarious that it was not, as it soon afterwards became, a satisfactory basis for trade with the Atlantic seaboard. Until 1795 the heavy expenditures made by the federal government on account of the war with the Northern Indians provided the Northwest and Kentucky with currency of a kind in the form of drafts on the War Department. For the next few years the chief dependence was upon circulating notes issued by millers and merchants.[21] In Tennessee there was no currency in circulation that could be employed for purchases outside the limits of the State. Domestic payments were usually made in kind, and the only thing that resembled a currency was the militia certificates issued for service against the Indians and accepted by the merchants in settlement of accounts. Consequently, when Andrew Jackson wished to obtain a supply of merchandise for his store at Nashville in 1795, he did so by selling some of his Tennessee lands at Philadelphia. As the century drew to a close, the development of the Mississippi export trade provided more adequate facilities. Entries of gold and silver coins— French guineas and anonymous Spanish and German pieces—began to appear in the merchants' ledgers,[22] and regular connections were formed with correspondents and agents on the Atlantic seaboard and to a less extent at New Orleans. The development of the export trade to Spanish Louisiana, which often made payment in coin, brought its inevitable concomitant. A gang of counterfeiters, who specialized in the making of Spanish milled dollars, operated extensively in Kentucky; but in 1801 the ringleaders were caught with "the necessary apparatus" and "several counterfeit coins," and that gang was broken up.[23]

Land-jobbing was not merely a basis of trade in the early pioneer days; it was a business in itself. When Andrew Jackson went to Philadelphia in 1795, his first care was to sell a 50,000-acre tract in which he owned a half-interest and another tract that he had on commission for a client in North Carolina.[24] To his chagrin he was able to get only twenty cents an acre and was compelled to guarantee the title; but twenty cents was not a bad price at Philadelphia, when land could be had at ten cents an acre in Tennessee.[25] As long as the salesman could dispose of his lands at an advance of one hundred per cent he could afford to stay in the business. Many others in Tennessee and Kentucky were engaged in similar operations—notably William Blount, whose extensive and disastrous speculations caused one of the greatest political scandals of that generation. Jackson also suffered a severe reverse in his land-jobbing, for one of the titles which he guaranteed was worthless, as were so many of the Western titles acquired under the haphazard land systems of Virginia and North Carolina.[26] However, the litigant's poison was the lawyer's meat, and John Breckinridge owed a large part of his extensive practice to the host of controversies occasioned by conflicting land claims.

IV

The Western economy had its critics, and even the export business to New Orleans, though it brought to the West a shower of Spanish gold, did not meet with universal approval. In July, 1801, the Frankfort ladies and gentlemen at an "elegant barbacue" might toast "The *way to wealth*—Ship building & the Mississippi trade"; [27] but no less a person than the Governor of Kentucky, Thomas T. Davis, could say shortly thereafter, "However great our expectations may have been, experience does not encourage the hope of a speedy and advantageous trade to Orleans." [28]

A writer who made a comprehensive survey of the situation in Kentucky in 1803 found no redeeming feature in any part of it.[29] "The majority of the farming interest," he wrote, "emigrating from Virginia, the most dissipated state in the union, brought with them all the vices of that misguided policy in economy," consuming all they produced, accumulating no capital, and progressively impoverishing the State. The merchants were no better than the farmers, for they showed no enterprise in opening markets. They sold for cash and packed the money over the mountains for goods, retaining only enough to maintain themselves with an ostentation of "flourishing opulence" in their town houses. The result was poverty among the real producers of wealth, the farmers, who "have verged but little beyond their original settlement and improvement. The balance of our territory is still in a state of savage uncultivation. The cabin that was built, the furniture with which it was stocked, and the forests that surrounded it when the proprietor first emigrated to the country, still retain their stand."

Perhaps there were not many Westerners who would have subscribed to this wholesale indictment of the most flourishing community in the West; but all felt that there was room for improvement, and various remedies were proposed. It was urged that Congress should raise the import duty on hemp, lest, as one writer said, the "Dispots of Urop suck our wealth from us" by selling in America, at fifty per cent less than its "real value," hemp raised by the downtrodden peasants of "Rushey." [30] Many favored the improvement of communications with Georgia and Carolina in order to increase the already extensive sales of Western live stock in those markets. "Hundreds, & I believe thousands of horses," wrote a Kentucky correspondent to John Breckinridge, "are constantly going to the Southward"; and he added that he was about to send his own "crop" of horses to Charleston. The high price of salt and the cost of transportation discouraged the exportation of salt meat by way of the Mississippi, but the construction of a good road to the head of navigation of the Savannah River would enable the Kentuckians to drive their cattle to market. Such a road, he suggested, might also induce the river boatmen to return to Kentucky after their descent to New Orleans, and thus diminish a serious drain upon the State's population. It has been said, concluded the writer, that the man who introduced the seed of Irish potatoes and red clover into England rendered it a more essential service than all the prime ministers who ever served its monarchs. He fervently hoped that John Breckinridge would render a similar service to Kentucky.[31]

All agreed that the nub of the problem was the draining of specie from the West to pay for Eastern goods. The American West was only a corridor through which Mexican silver dollars flowed from New Orleans to Philadelphia. A Kentucky congressman declared in 1798 that, while everybody in his State had an abundance of the necessities of life, almost nobody had any money and that there was not as much as ten thousand dollars in coin in circulation in the whole State.[32] The rapid growth of the export trade to New Orleans in the next few years merely increased the volume of the silver current without damming it up for the West's own use. In 1802 a writer in the *Pittsburgh Gazette* [33] complained that the money was frequently "swept up and carried out of the country by waggon loads or brigades of pack-horses." The reason for this was obvious. According to a "rough calculation" made by another Pittsburgher in September, 1803, merchandise valued at $250,000 had been imported into that place within the past twelve months, whereas its exports for the same period (whisky, flour, bar-iron, castings, etc.) were worth only $180,000, leaving an unfavorable balance of $70,000.[34] "The debts of this country," said the former writer, "have accumulated, through the course of many years past, to an amount that is scarcely creditable. Is it reasonable to believe, that there has been cash enough in this country to pay for the immense quantities of store goods, salt and iron which has been consumed in it for many years[?]"

An obvious way out of the difficulty, he continued, would be for the Western people to lead a simpler life, denying themselves imported luxuries; but he admitted that there was no hope of establishing such a Spartan régime, for many of the pioneers were accustomed to European goods and would have them at any cost. This comment possesses considerable value for the student of frontier society. It suggests that, at least in the particular region and period with which we are dealing, there were many frontiersmen who were by no means satisfied with a simple, self-sufficing, agrarian type of society. They had come West so that they might lead more successful lives, and success meant, among other things, the possession of certain commodities, which were also the object of a nostalgic longing for familiar things. In order to obtain these symbols of success, these Lares and Penates of American home life, the pioneers surrendered the independence which the soil might have given them and embarked upon the troubled sea of foreign commerce, thereby making their welfare the plaything of world politics and the world market. At the time, the development of this trade through the opening of the Mississippi was generally regarded as a blessing, for it gave the Westerners the means to buy the imported goods which they prized so highly. During the continuance of the European war all went well enough; but as Henry Clay pointed out, in 1824, in a speech supporting the "American system," the termination of that war gave the West ample reason to regret its excessive dependence upon an artificially stimulated trade with foreign nations.

About 1800, many Westerners were urging the development of domestic manufactures as a means of providing the section with a better balanced economic system. There was a solid foundation to build on, and before the steamboat age domestic manufactures throve mightily in the Ohio Valley. The Appalachian barrier was not without its advantage to the West, for it served as a protective tariff wall against Eastern competitors; and the Mississippi River was still for most purposes a one-way route. Within the region thus isolated from the outside world, the Ohio and its tributaries furnished an excellent transportation system. Natural resources and raw materials were abundant, and technical experts soon answered the call of opportunity. Hard on the heels of Indian fighter and axman came iron worker and spinner. Although Kentucky was still a howling wilderness in 1774, by 1790 its inhabitants were manufacturing "a greater variety of things than were the people of New York in 1765." [35]

Many of the pioneers whom tradition remembers only as heroes of the westward movement had by the end of the century evolved into steel kings; or perhaps it would be more accurate to say iron chieftains, for their product was not steel but iron, and their market was rather narrowly circumscribed. Many of the leaders of the new order were found in Tennessee. William Cocke, who had blazed the Wilderness Trail with Daniel Boone in 1775, was, by 1801, the owner of iron works from which the United States government bought hoes and ploughs for donation to the Indians.[36] John Sevier, famous for some thirty-five battles and skirmishes against the Indians, was, by 1797, part owner of King's Iron Works, whose blast furnace and forge turned out bar iron and castings. About the same time James Robertson, the "founder of Nashville," established a furnace and forge in Middle Tennessee.[37] As early as 1795, five boats left Sumner County, Tennessee, for the lower country with cargoes which included not only whisky and bacon but also bar and cast iron.[38]

The principal industrial centers in the West, however, were those which developed in the districts surrounding Lexington and Pittsburgh. In 1787, the first paper mill was established in Kentucky; in 1791, the first furnace. A manufacturer of "boating crackers and biscuit suitable for travelers" advertised in the *Kentucky Gazette* in 1789. By 1800 the State had establishments for making nails, shot, shoes, leather, cordage, flour, linen, cigars, snuff, furniture, hats, clocks, stoves, mill-irons and kettles, not to mention boats for the river traffic.[39] We have already had occasion to speak of the rapid growth of Pittsburgh as an industrial center.

Western products were usually sold in the domestic market. According to the New England traveler, Harris, who wrote in 1803, Pittsburgh furniture, made of black walnut, wild cherry, and yellow birch, was already finding an extensive sale in settlements on both banks of the Mississippi and the Ohio.[40] In rare cases goods were shipped even as far as the Atlantic seaboard. More commonly they found a sale at Natchez and New Orleans, thereby increasing the unfavorable balance of trade against Louisiana. The latter development disappointed the expectations of the Spanish authorities of that province, who had hoped to supply the American West with manufactured goods through New Orleans and thus lay an economic foundation for their secessionist intrigue with the Westerners.

Even before Kentucky was admitted to statehood the development of a diversified, self-sufficing economy had been the goal of many prominent Kentuckians, among them Judge Harry Innes and Congressman John Brown. The plan was pressed with increasing determination as the century drew towards its close, and in 1799 the legislature passed an act for the encouragement of manufactures. In 1800, the Bourbon Association was formed for the purpose of averting "as far as possible the total ruin of our inhabitants" by refusing to purchase, except in exchange for the products of Kentucky, any "imported" articles such as woolens, linens, cottons, hats, shoes and saddles, or any liquors except such as were used for medical or religious purposes; and by encouraging the raising of sheep, the cultivation of cotton, hemp, and flax, and home manufactures of all kinds.[41] Henry Clay was a rising young Kentucky lawyer at this time, and many of the ideas that he championed in his later career were already abroad in the West. The most advanced of the Western communities had already bidden farewell to the day of rude plenty, of simple self-sufficiency. Civilization was overtaking the frontiersman with all its complications and perplexities. Ten years before Abraham Lincoln's unhasting father came to the conclusion, many a pioneer underdog had already decided that Kentucky "wasn't a place for a poor man no more" and had moved on to newer Edens—across the Ohio, out to Missouri, or down the Mississippi.

v

This is not the place for a detailed study of Western society; but certain features of it require some notice, since they seem to have a bearing upon the behavior of the frontiersman in relation to the Mississippi Question. In the first place, although there were still many survivals of a more primitive day, a large part of the Ohio Valley was passing out of the early pioneer stage of development. The original leaders—such as Isaac Shelby, John Sevier, and James Robertson, who had scaled the political heights by their ability to kill Indians—still retained much of their prestige; and occupations were still in a rudimentary state of differentiation. Such banking facilities as existed were furnished by millers and merchants; and a single individual often performed all the functions of the Mississippi trade, from sowing and harvesting the crop to building the flatboat, navigating it to New Orleans, and marketing the produce there or even taking it on to the West Indies for sale. The frontiersman was a Jack-of-all-trades; or if one prefers, resourceful and versatile. Andrew Jackson was by turns or simultaneously planter, lawyer, distiller, storekeeper, land-jobber, militia officer, judge and Congressman.

New ways and new values, however, were replacing the old ones. The expanding traffic on the Ohio and Mississippi was beginning to develop a special class of merchants and, though more slowly, of river boatmen, as well as regular transportation lines and insurance companies.[42] The professions were gradually gaining ground. One of them, the legal, had progressed so far that its members had not only overcome the initial hostility of the frontiersmen but were actually wresting the reins of political power from the Indian fighters. Men who were primarily lawyers and had never won distinction in Indian warfare—John Breckinridge and Henry Clay of Kentucky and Andrew Jackson of Tennessee—were the leaders of the rising generation in the West.

Whether these new leaders were lawyers or not, they were generally men of substance, owning a stake in society. Albert Gallatin too far excelled most of them to be taken as a representative of the group; but his well-informed mind and cool, judicious temperament did at least represent the type towards which Western leadership was tending. It appears, moreover, that most of these leaders had smoothly running political machines and that small groups of local dignitaries were frequently able to determine whom the sovereign people should elect to office and what measures they should adopt. In short, the political leaders of the West were for the most part a prudent, conservative group, exercising power out of all proportion to their numbers and acting as a brake upon the more impetuous and relatively ignorant mass of their fellow backwoodsmen.

Religious developments in the West were also a sign of the approaching maturity of the section.[43] This statement may seem paradoxical, since one of the most notable of those developments was the rise of the camp-meeting, which, with its emotional excesses and intellectual poverty, strikes the modern mind as a singularly primitive institution. In reality, however, the rise of the camp-meeting, which occurred at the very end of the eighteenth century, was a function of the growing security of the West. The coincidence of its rise with the cessation of the Indian wars suggests that the camp-meeting was the emotional equivalent of the border warfare just terminated. Again, however primitive the behavior of the faithful may have been, the very fact that thousands of them could assemble from miles around and spend a week or more in religious exercise indicates that a considerable degree of leisure had been achieved and that roads and transportation facilities were rather easily found. Finally, the sweeping success of the revival, despite the opposition of the more decorous elements of Western society, affords one more proof of the hopelessness of the Spanish intrigue with the frontiersmen, for it would be difficult to find a variety of religious experience more offensive to Catholic Spain than that flower of evangelical Protestantism, the camp-meeting.

Newspapers were one of the most important of the trappings of civilization acquired by the West in the closing years of the eighteenth century.[44] Journalism in the West began with the *Pittsburgh Gazette,* established in 1786 under the patronage of Hugh Henry Brackenridge, who subsequently parted company with the Federalist *Gazette* and aided in planting the Republican *Tree of Liberty* at Pittsburgh (1800). Except in Connecticut's Western Reserve on Lake Erie, Ohio was well supplied with newspapers. Two of these, the *Centinel of the North-Western Territory* and *Freeman's Journal,* both of Cincinnati, had a comparatively brief existence (1793–1796 and 1796–1800 respectively) ; but the *Western Spy,* established at Cincinnati in 1799, the *Scioto Gazette* (Chillicothe, 1800), and the *Ohio Gazette* (Marietta, 1801) lived long beyond the end of the period under consideration here.

Kentucky's first newspaper was the *Kentucky Gazette* (for a short time spelled "Kentucke"), established at Lexington in 1787 in order, as the promoters said, to insure unanimity of opinion on the subject of separation from Virginia. Tennessee's first paper was the *Knoxville Gazette* (1791). In 1795 Kentucky got its second paper, and in 1797 its third. In 1798, a year of feverish excitement over the Alien and Sedition Acts, the Virginia and Kentucky Resolutions, and the crisis in relations with France, two more were established, one of which was the Frankfort *Palladium.* These were soon followed by the *Knoxville Register* (1798), the *Knoxville Impartial Observer* (1799), and the *Tennessee Gazette* (Nashville, 1800).

All of these papers appeared once a week. The story that some of the type used by Kentucky's first paper were cut from dogwood in that State is very picturesque, but in reality the press and type were both bought at second-hand in Philadelphia and packed over the mountains by way of Pittsburgh. After 1793 the paper that it used was made at a mill built shortly before at Georgetown, Kentucky. A great deal of the news as well as the paper and type of these Western journals was imported. Items relating to trade on the Mississippi were comparatively rare before 1800; but as a result of its rapid expansion, they appeared with increasing frequency from that time until the acquisition of Louisiana in 1803. Such items were sometimes of local origin and sometimes taken from other Western papers. If they related to New Orleans or the lower Mississippi, they were often clipped from journals on the Atlantic seaboard. In general, the Western newspapers compared not unfavorably with their Eastern contemporaries, which they resembled in most respects. Perhaps Western editors were a shade more reticent in their comments on controversial questions, but that was the part of prudence. It has been said that when the frontiersman laid down his gun he picked up his newspaper. It might be added, without much exaggeration, that when the frontier editor delivered his paper he picked up his gun. The editor of one Kentucky paper was slain on the field of honor by a reader whose susceptibilities he had offended, and nothing but superior marksmanship saved his successor from the same fate at the hands of the same sensitive gentleman.

VI

The provincialism of the periphery still prevailed in the Ohio Valley. From the Holston and the Cumberland to the Wabash and the Allegheny, pioneer opinion of the federal government was marked by much the same suspicion bordering on hostility that the farmer feels for the county seat and the villager for the city. The West had its grievances, and resentment was aggravated by the fact that the national government was in Federalist hands while most of the frontiersmen were Republicans. Or perhaps most of the frontiersmen were Republicans because the national government was in Federalist hands. It was probably inevitable that the fierce democracy of the backwoods should prefer the national party which professed faith in the common man and that agrarians of the West should join hands with those of the East; but it was certainly fortunate for the Jeffersonian party that its Federalist rival was in power during the trying years just before the close of the century. The sufferings of the Western people might be no greater than those endured by every other frontier community since the founding of Jamestown, and they might proceed from international complications which no man or set of men in America could control; but, like most other short-sighted human beings, the Westerners were quick to lay the blame at the door of "the government," and the government was then in Federalist hands. Therein lay the good fortune of the Republicans; for most of

the Western people probably shared the conviction of John Breckinridge that Kentucky, or whatever locality they lived in, would be the
Eden of America but for the neglect and oppression which they suffered at the hands of the Federalist administration.

In western Pennsylvania the resentment which had broken forth
in the Whisky Rebellion of 1794 had by no means subsided, but Albert Gallatin and his Republican associates were conducting it into
legal channels with quiet effectiveness. The Northwest Territory
too was growing restive under the rule of Governor Arthur St. Clair
and his secretary, Winthrop Sargent. It was, however, in Kentucky
and Tennessee that Western discontent found most frequent and
emphatic utterance. The Tennesseans resented most keenly the aristocratic pretensions of the Federalists, their supposed subservience to
Great Britain, and their solicitude for the welfare of the Indians
whose hunting grounds covered so large a part of the State. In 1794,
Andrew Jackson declared that, unless Congress took more effective
measures to stop Indian attacks, the Cumberland settlers would either
have to abandon the country "or seek a protection from some other
Source than the present." The following year he roundly denounced
the "unconstitutional" negotiation of Jay's treaty and its ratification
by the "aristocratic neebobs" of the Senate. In 1797, he found the
administration's unfriendly attitude towards France most reprehensi-
ble and asserted his firm belief in State sovereignty. John Sevier,
then Governor of the State, wrote in 1798 that aristocracy was drunk
with power and that "fleebottomry" (meaning phlebotomy, blood-
letting) would be a good remedy. About the same time he described
as "infamous" an act of Congress for regulating the Indian trade, declaring that it had "given more umbridge to the people of this State
than ~~the Stamp Act itself~~ [sic] any act ever passed since the inde-
pendency of America." [45]

The Kentuckians also had their grievances—the whisky tax, the
Indian policy of the federal government, and, above all, the conviction that the failure to obtain the free navigation of the Mississippi
River was due to the ill will of the dominant East. It was taken as an
ominous sign when John Jay, champion of the mercantile interest on
the Atlantic seaboard and the "evil genius of Western America," was
sent on a special mission to England in 1794. When his treaty with
Grenville was published the following year, the Kentuckians believed
that their worst fears were justified. It was charged that once more,
as in 1786, Jay had sacrificed Western interests, for the British were

given privileges on the Mississippi which were more extensive than those accorded them by the treaty of 1783 and which would enable them to monopolize its commerce. Worse still, the treaty apparently made it more unlikely than ever that the river would be opened to the Americans, for Spain, whose consent to its opening was necessary, had just broken with Great Britain and would hardly make concessions to a power that had given such striking proof of its subservience to the British. Washington, it was said, was in his "political dotage"; and Humphrey Marshall won this tribute from one of his constituents by voting for the ratification of the treaty: "I do sincerely believe (from a knowledge of the man) that the senator from Kentucky . . . was actuated by motives the most dishonorable—that he is a stranger to virtue, either private or public, and that he would sell his country for a price, easily to be told." [46]

Governor Shelby urged the legislature to protest against the unconstitutional portions of the treaty, and in its reply the House did as he advised, though the Senate was silent. As usual in that day, public sentiment found pithy expression in toasts. At a Lexington dinner in August, 1795, the following were offered:

"May there be an universal *change* in the foederal Executive, from the highest officer, down to the lowest Maggot of Administration."

"The free use of the Mississippi by constitutional means, if shortly; if not, by *any means*." [47]

It was a fortunate thing for all concerned that the treaty of San Lorenzo arrived just at this juncture. The jubilation of the West was as great now as its wrath had been when Jay's treaty was received. Reporting the event, the *Kentucky Gazette* said: "The general joy of all ranks and descriptions of citizens, was never so conspicuous [as] upon the above occasion; of which, the firing of artillery, tolling of bells, bonfires &c, &c, were evident testimonies!" [48]

President Washington knew full well what the opening of the Mississippi meant to the Westerners, and in his Farewell Address he made much of the treaty of San Lorenzo as a proof that the federal government was solicitous for the interests of the West and able to provide for its welfare. It does not appear that the Western people saw the same lesson in the happy ending of the tedious, twelve-year-old controversy with Spain. The winter of their discontent lasted until the "evil genius of western America" and his fellow Federalists lost control of the federal government in the election of 1800.

In view of these circumstances, the adoption of the well-known

Kentucky resolutions of 1798 and 1799 and the support accorded them in Tennessee tempt one to read into these declarations a serious threat of disunion, despite the disclaimer published by Senator George Nicholas in 1798.[49] At least a few of the Western leaders, however, were not implacable in their hostility to the federal administration. When the Hamiltonian plan of campaign against France began to take shape in 1798 and it was understood that war with France would involve an assault on Spain's dominions in North America, some of the frontiersmen were won over, though many of them preferred peace, fearing that war with Spain would ruin their export trade down the Mississippi.[50]

Thomas Jefferson once declared that, while many people believed it impossible to maintain a republic in a large country, the very magnitude of the United States and the sparseness of its population had proved the salvation of republican government in the crisis of 1798–1799. That dictum provides a key to the history of the Ohio Valley in the whole period of strain and stress from the Revolution to the Louisiana Purchase. For one thing, the magnificent distances which separated village from village and farm from farm acted as a deterrent to concerted action of any kind. Writing in 1799 from a county in western Kentucky, one of its principal inhabitants said: "Though there are many people in the County yet they live in groups over an immense tract of Country. They cannot be gotten to the election. Hunters, & Beaver-Catchers care nothing about Government or the manner of it." [51] Such massive indifference, bred of isolation, made it easier for a handful of men of means in the West to gain control of the local governments; but it also rendered more difficult the use of this power for any purpose except the performance of the routine functions established by law and custom. The society was one which responded far more readily to the emotional appeal of the camp-meeting than to any political argument, no matter how simple the reasoning might be. Even had the leaders made a sustained effort at secession, the Kentucky resolutions did not offer the battle-cry that would have galvanized such a people into action.

Neither unionism nor disunionism was deeply rooted in the West at the end of the century. Patriotism ebbed and flowed with almost every act of the federal government and every turn of international affairs. There were a good many people in the West who took literally the assertion of the Declaration of Independence that governments are instituted among men in order to secure certain unalienable rights and that they may be overthrown if they fail to serve this purpose. There were also in the West many veterans of the recent war who, having taken part in one revolution, might not balk at another. There is, however, no evidence of any concerted movement towards secession, though the moribund Spanish intrigue was occasionally revived by injections of Spanish gold. Had the British or the French held New Orleans and exerted the pressure of which they were capable, the Union might have yielded to the strain ; but the conflict of interest between the frontiersmen and Spain in commerce, religion, Indian affairs, and government was so palpable that, as long as the latter power controlled the lower Mississippi, disunion would have been the sheerest folly. Thomas Jefferson might well pray for Spain's retention of the Floridas and New Orleans until the United States should be ready to acquire them, for that was the surest guaranty of continued union.

CHAPTER II

The Spanish Fringe

I

The southern and western limits of the United States were fringed with colonies under the sovereignty of Spain. These colonies were Louisiana, which no one could define much more accurately than to say that, except for the island of New Orleans, it lay west of the Mississippi River; West Florida, which extended from Baton Rouge on the Mississippi to St. Marks on the Gulf of Mexico; and East Florida, which consisted of the peninsula east of St. Marks. By the treaty of San Lorenzo (1795), the boundary between these provinces and the United States had been established as a line running along the middle of the channel of the Mississippi from its headwaters to the thirty-first parallel, thence eastward along that parallel to the Apalachicola River, thence to the headwaters of the St. Marys, and thence along the middle of its channel to the Atlantic. The international boundary thus formed a right angle, with its vertex at the intersection of the Mississippi River and the thirty-first parallel.

Louisiana and the Floridas were intended by Spain to serve as a barrier between its more precious possessions around the Gulf of Mexico—especially New Spain—and the Anglo-Americans of Canada and the United States. Yet it would have been difficult to find a position in North America more exposed to armed attack and economic penetration. Following the current of the Mississippi and its tributaries, the British from Canada and the Americans from the Ohio Valley had far easier access to the bulk of Louisiana than did the Spaniards themselves. To maintain a large army in the province was out of the question. In case of attack, reinforcements would have to be drawn from distant Cuba and Mexico. Even after reaching the mouth of the Mississippi, they would have to be brought up-stream a hundred miles—often a week's voyage for a sailing vessel—before they arrived at New Orleans and the settled portion of lower Louisiana. An expedition from that region to St. Louis, the capital of upper

Louisiana, which was wide open to British and American invasion, would then require two or three months to reach its destination; and by that time any attempt at reconquest would probably be futile. Lower Louisiana and the Floridas were less vulnerable to overland invasion; but their long coast line offered the invader every opportunity he could desire, unless Spain retained control of the seas. As relations between Spain and Great Britain became progressively more unfriendly throughout 1795, the prospect of maritime invasion became more alarming.

Foreign economic infiltration would have been difficult to prevent, even if the commercial and industrial resources of Spain had equaled those of the United States and Great Britain. The proximity of Canada and the United States to the border colonies made it likely that trade would develop between them; the length of the international frontier rendered it impossible to regulate this trade effectively; and the current of the rivers, together with other conditions, rendered it more profitable to the British and the Americans than to the colonists and Spain. Had the latter power succeeded in its effort to monopolize the navigation of the Mississippi, the task of regulating foreign commerce and keeping it within bounds might have been accomplished; but the effort ran counter to economic and political tendencies which were irresistible.

II

If the situation could have been saved by the adaptation of its venerable colonial system to the peculiar needs of the border colonies, Spain would have saved it.[1] Among the most notable modifications which the court made in favor of Louisiana were the toleration of heretics, the admission of foreign immigrants, and the granting of a considerable degree of commercial freedom. Of the commercial cedula of 1782 a Spanish historian of colonial commerce wrote that its extensive privileges were unparalleled in the history of Spanish legislation; and still more liberal concessions were made in 1793.[2] There can be no question that the government intended ultimately to convert Louisiana into a colony of the prevailing Spanish type; but the fact remains that an extensive and intelligent adaptation of the system was made in the hope of meeting the peculiar requirements of the border situation. If the ultimate purpose was to make these colonies Spanish, the immediate purpose was to foster their growth. The colonists were to serve as a living hedge for the protection of the game preserves of New Spain

from American and British poachers. The defensive system in Louisiana was inspired by the ancient principle of monopoly, but the means
employed were modern. The Spanish government at least recognized
that the old devices of presidio and mission, which had served it well
enough elsewhere, would be useless in these border provinces; and it
had some reason to hope that what priest and soldier could not do
might be accomplished by trade and toleration. By the end of the
eighteenth century, Spain had at last caught up with Colbert.

The governmental system established in these colonies had many
merits. The geographical unity of Louisiana and West Florida was
recognized by their union under the authority of a single governor,
with New Orleans as the capital. East Florida, which was quite distinct from the other two provinces, had a governor of its own, with
his residence at St. Augustine. In order to obtain unity of policy, both
governors were subordinated to the captain-general, who resided at
Havana and was also captain-general of Cuba. This was a reasonable
arrangement, for Havana was the military and naval base to which
the border colonies would naturally look for reinforcements in case
of attack, as well as the Spanish colonial port with which they carried
on most of their commerce. Since the captain-general was immediately
responsible to the court at Madrid, and since Havana was one of the
chief terminal points of the regular mail service between Spain and
the colonies, there was not likely to be—nor in normal times was there
—any serious loss of time in the administration of border affairs
through Cuba. It was urged by several officials, including the captain-
general and, of course, the governor of Louisiana, that the captaincy-
general of Louisiana and the Floridas should be separated from that
of Cuba and that the governor of Louisiana should be appointed
captain-general.[3] While this arrangement would probably have conferred some benefit upon Louisiana and West Florida, it would have
operated to the disadvantage of East Florida, which had much better
communications with Havana than with New Orleans. Nor would it
have increased appreciably the despatch of business between the
former provinces and Spain, for any ship going from one to the
other must necessarily pass by Havana. Moreover, the governor already possessed extensive discretionary power, as well as the privilege
of direct correspondence with the court in regard to certain important
matters, such as the intrigue with the American frontiersmen.[4]

There was one serious defect in the governmental system of these
border provinces. Their annual subsidies, which defrayed the greater

part of the expenses of government, came not from Havana, where the captain-general resided, but from Vera Cruz in New Spain, whose viceroy had no authority in Louisiana and the Floridas and consequently took little interest in their problems of defense. The result was that in times of stress nothing short of the most peremptory orders from Madrid could obtain the funds necessary to meet extraordinary expenses in the border provinces.[5] The arrangement was defensible, however, for Cuba itself was a parasite province supported by subsidies from Mexico. More important still, the court feared that the establishment of regular, direct communication between New Orleans and Vera Cruz would lead to the growth of smuggling between Louisiana, where foreign commerce was permitted by special dispensation, and New Spain, which had an abundance of the silver and gold so eagerly coveted by foreign nations.

The governmental system within Louisiana and the Floridas was simplicity itself, for the governor was the supreme military and civil authority. Though petty tyrants in their own jurisdictions, the post commanders—all of whom were army officers—took orders from the governor, as the governor took orders from the captain-general and the court. The only one of these subordinates who could correspond with the court directly was the governor of Natchez. There were two lieutenant-governors, one for lower and one for upper Louisiana; but these offices carried with them little but titular dignity. Provided he was willing to take the responsibility, the governor could override any official in the province, including the intendant himself, and could suspend any law or regulation whatever.

The intendancy was a new institution in Spanish America, and Louisiana was one of the first provinces in which it was established.[6] Though he exercised other functions as well, the intendant of Louisiana and West Florida was primarily a fiscal agent, collecting and disbursing the revenues of the province. Certain powers which might naturally have been entrusted to him were here reserved to the governor. Chief among these were control of the fur trade and (until 1798) the granting of lands. The intendancy owed its importance mainly to its control of the customs administration—a matter of great importance to the inhabitants of a colony which gained its livelihood through oversea commerce.

Though the intendant was normally independent within his own sphere, the unlimited discretionary power vested in the governor enabled a strong-willed official such as Manuel Gayoso to play ducks and drakes with the intendant's autonomy. Despite the abundant opportunity for controversy under this system, Louisiana was, until the closing years of the century, free from those scandalous brawls between governor and intendant which often occurred in the other Spanish colonies. From 1782 to 1788 Governor Miró and Intendant Navarro, from 1794 to 1796 Governor Carondelet and Intendant Rendón, coöperated harmoniously in the exercise of their coördinate and often overlapping authority. From 1788 to 1794 the intendancy and government were consolidated and entrusted successively to governors Miró and Carondelet. The separate intendancy was then reëstablished in order to insure the successful operation of a new commercial system promulgated the preceding year.[7] It was only after Rendón's departure in 1796 that the era of good feeling between governor and intendant came to an end. Its termination seems to have been due partly to the contentiousness of Juan Ventura Morales, who occupied the intendancy—with one brief interruption—from that time until the transfer of Louisiana in 1803; and partly to the incompetence of all the governors of that period save Gayoso. Perhaps the fundamental cause of the trouble was that Morales held the intendancy on an *ad interim* appointment.[8] If he had been confirmed as permanent intendant, he might not have been so ready to convince the court of his own zeal, integrity, and fitness for promotion by impeaching the honesty of his fellow officials in Louisiana. However that may be, the system itself does not seem to have been at fault.

Both the governor and the intendant exercised judicial functions within their respective jurisdictions; both were required to take the advice of their legal counselors (*asesores*) but not to follow it; and from the decisions of both, appeals lay by various channels to the king, whose decision was usually made in conformity with the recommendation of the Council of the Indies.[9] Since the pacification of the province by Governor O'Reilly (1769–1770), Spanish law had supplanted that of France, and all legal proceedings were in the Spanish language. In these far-flung provinces, most of whose inhabitants knew not a word of Spanish and had no lawyers to consult, it was inevitable that such a system should work many hardships. An inhabitant of St. Louis, involved in a suit concerning a flour mill, was faced with the alternative of carrying his case to New Orleans and thereby incurring expenses greater than the amount of the damages he could expect to win if he were successful, or of abandoning the suit. This was the kind of hardship that had long been suffered by inhabitants of the Atlantic Piedmont and of trans-Appalachia both before and after the independence of the United States; but in Louisiana and Florida it was aggravated by linguistic difficulties. An individual at New Madrid, where there were no lawyers or interpreters, submitted a petition in his own (and probably his only) language, English; and the Spanish commandant endorsed it: "Let this person speak in Castilian, since we are in Castile, and he will be heard." [10]

Only the wealthy could afford to take an appeal to the king, for there was little hope of success unless one had an agent at Madrid to jog the memory of clerks and judges at that leisurely court. A post commander who had been summarily dismissed by Governor Carondelet went to Spain to conduct his case in person; and, though he was finally successful, it required two years for him to obtain a decision. In another case, certain merchants of New Orleans, who had been convicted of attempting to smuggle specie out of the province, petitioned for pardon on the ground of mitigating circumstances. The Governor and the Intendant supported their petition warmly; the case was pressed by the merchants' agent at Madrid; and the chief minister, Godoy, himself urged a speedy determination of the case. Yet it was two years before a decision was reached and another five years before the decision (which was in favor of the merchants) became known to the officials of Louisiana.[11]

III

Justice in Louisiana was often delayed. Whether it was often sold is not easy to ascertain. The charge was made that one of the high officials, Nicolas María Vidal, one of the principal judges of the province and for a time acting Civil Governor, openly auctioned his decisions to the highest bidder. Berquin-Duvallon, who visited the colony in 1802, wrote of Vidal: "A zealous partisan of monarchical government, he has for it a devotion so respectful and so submissive, that the likeness of his sovereign stamped on a little metallic plate is, in his eyes, a sacred idol, and so worthy of his homage, that there is nothing that can not be obtained from him by means of that talisman. . . ." [12]

Similar charges were made by foreign travelers against other Spanish officials in every department of the government. Prefect Laussat wrote in 1803 that Intendant Morales was the only official in Louisiana not suspected of venality.[13] Such sweeping judgments must be accepted with reservations. Most of them were fathered by French visitors who had little opportunity to obtain accurate information and little disposition to judge fairly and who, moreover, visited Louisiana shortly before its transfer to France. Conditions at that juncture should not be made the basis of generalizations about the whole Spanish period.

It is almost impossible at this time to arrive at the truth of the matter. The administration of Louisiana and Florida presents a highly unedifying picture, if one accepts unquestioningly all the charges preferred by all the high officials of Louisiana against one another. As for the minor colonial officials, their shameless corruption was frankly admitted by Governor Carondelet himself. Underpaid, these subordinates employed the usual means of piecing out their slender wages. Perhaps they were only imitating their superiors. Intendant Navarro, it is said, lured a French ship to New Orleans and then confiscated it—to his own profit, under the fee system—for unlawful entry.[14] It was also asserted that Governor Miró connived at the peculations of his nephew, Vicente Folch, then commandant of Mobile, besides embezzling on his own account two thousand dollars a year in connection with tobacco purchases from James Wilkinson for the royal stores.[15] It was likewise charged that Governor Gayoso appropriated to his own use a fund of seven thousand dollars established for the care of orphans.[16] All the governors and intendants were believed to have accepted bribes from smugglers.

One of the most notorious cases was that of the *contador de ejército,* José de Orué. According to a report made by Intendant Rendón in 1795, this man had engaged in contraband trade for many years, had defrauded the royal treasury of large amounts in the purchase of medical and other supplies, and had acquired a fortune of one hundred thousand dollars in Louisiana. Though he was penniless when he first came to New Orleans, and though he received a salary of only two thousand dollars a year, he lived with the greatest ostentation throughout the period of his residence in the colony.[17] Orué, who seems to have been a thorough scoundrel, was punished; but the charges against the other high officials were not substantiated. Miró's *residencia* brought out only one serious charge against him—the one relating to the tobacco purchases from Wilkinson—and that was not proved. If a general impression is worth anything, the higher officials of Louisiana before the end of the century seem to have been for the most part honest, able, and well intentioned. The scandalous tales of their corruption which were current in Louisiana and elsewhere may have had some basis in fact, but they were more probably the result of a misunderstanding of the motives which led these officials to tolerate contraband trade in various forms. Their complaisance was popularly attributed to venality, but in fact it proceeded from a conviction that strict enforcement of the commercial regulations was impracticable and, that if it were attempted, it would only retard the development of the colony. This is almost certainly the explanation of Governor Carondelet's course, and there is reason to believe that other governors and intendants were guided by the same considerations.

Whether the charges of corruption were true or not, it can not be doubted that, with all its merits, the government failed to command the respect of the people of Louisiana. There was hardly a suggestion of the traditional Spanish tyranny in it, and the worst abuse committed by the colonial officials was the manipulation of the paper currency. There was no Inquisition. The slave code was comparatively humane. The Indians, instead of being enslaved and worked to death, were given annual presents to the value of more than fifty thousand dollars, and they were often wined and dined by the post commanders and the governor himself. Heretics and foreigners were tolerated, and the creoles suffered little at the hands of arbitrary officials. On the whole, the administration deserved its reputation for mildness. Perhaps that was its worst failing. It seemed scarcely credible that the countrymen of Alvarado and Torquemada and Philip II could be mild from choice. In them the virtue seemed a vice, a confession of weakness, a proof of timidity. In fact, whether from over-indulgence to their relatives and friends (many of the colonial officials had found wives in the creole families) or from fear that rigorous measures would provoke a revolution, the officials were far more lenient than the court wished them to be. Even the power of an absolute monarch was unable to get the Spanish will done in these border provinces; and even with the extensive modifications introduced by intelligent ministers of the king, the Spanish colonial system was unworkable in them. The surprising thing is not that Spain finally lost Louisiana and the Floridas, but that it retained possession of them so many years. Perhaps the explanation is that most of Louisiana and Florida was an untenanted wilderness.

IV

Neither Spain nor any other power could have provided adequate military defenses for so vast a region. As Godoy put it, "You can't lock up an open field." [18] In 1795, a military commission formally advised the court that nothing more should be attempted than the fortification of the capital, New Orleans, so as to enable it to resist an incursion of filibusters from the American West; [19] and that was in effect the plan which was followed. The whole frontier from St. Marks (at the eastern extremity of West Florida) to New Orleans, and from New Orleans to St. Louis, was normally covered by a single regiment. At the end of 1796 this regiment numbered only 1,386 effectives, of whom 442 were concentrated at the capital, 92 at Plaquemines (between New Orleans and the mouth of the Mississippi), and 237 at Pensacola. The rest were distributed in various tiny garrisons— St. Marks, 50; Mobile, 51; Natchez, 54; Chickasaw Bluffs, 117; New Madrid, 32; St. Louis, 110; Natchitoches, 30; and so on. [20]

The defenders of Spanish authority did possess one weapon of some value. This was the fresh-water navy, which, in 1799, consisted of eleven boats (four galleys, one *bombardera,* three galliots, and three gunboats), [21] and patrolled the whole course of the Mississippi south of St. Louis, as well as the lakes between New Orleans and Mobile. On occasion they would even venture out into the Gulf and creep along the coast as far as St. Marks. According to Daniel Clark, Jr., a New Orleans merchant, most of them carried only a twelve- or eighteen-pounder in the bow and a few swivels in the gunwales. "They are neither calculated for expedition or burden," he wrote, "and will be totally unmanageable at Sea or out of smooth Water, as I have myself had experience of, and if met with even by a British Privateer out of shoal water must fall an easy Prey to her." [22] While not so formidable as some of their names (*Achilles, Vengeance, Thunderbolt*) might suggest, they were more useful to Spain than Clark thought. The mere knowledge of their existence was a check upon turbulent elements within the province and on its borders, and they demonstrated their usefulness in the reconquest of St. Marks from Bowles and his banditti in 1800. They were essentially a river fleet, and their chief value lay in their ability to coöperate in the defense of the posts on the Mississippi. Such coöperation was sorely needed. The flimsy ramparts, rusty guns, and vulnerable positions of most of those posts would have made them an easy victim to any respectable force of invaders. For instance, St. Louis, the metropolis of upper Louisiana, had for its citadel a staked enclosure normally garrisoned by about thirty men. [23]

It was out of the question for such meager and widely scattered forces to defend the province against invasion, and indeed they were not expected to do so. Though they could not maintain Spanish sovereignty, they could at least assert it, and they could preserve order among the king's subjects. For the latter purpose they were fully adequate. Viewed as any army defending a fifteen-hundred-mile frontier, the fourteen hundred regulars of Louisiana and West Florida might look ridiculous; but as a police force for a colony of 45,000 inhabitants (one policeman to thirty-two inhabitants) they were rather impressive.[24]

v

The colonists were the easier to control because four fifths of them were concentrated in lower Louisiana, south of the Red River, and in that portion of West Florida which lay west of Mobile Bay. They were a fairly compact mass, within easy reach of Spanish sea power; and in this period Spain possessed a navy superior to any but those of Great Britain and France. The economic and social system of these colonists indisposed them towards rebellion, for the slave population was almost equal to the white, and the extensive overseas commerce of the planters and merchants was a hostage in the hands of Spain. In other parts of Louisiana and the Floridas, where these checks upon sedition did not operate, the colonists were too few, too poor, and too widely scattered to resist Spain's superior resources and facilities for military concentration.

Far the greater part of Louisiana north of the Red River was still the haunt of Indians and buffaloes. The few clusters of white settlements, such as those at St. Louis and New Madrid, clung timidly to the shifting banks of the Mississippi. In 1799, there were some six thousand inhabitants in this region, most of whom were French and Americans.[25] Except for this fringe of river settlements, the aspect of upper Louisiana had changed little since the first French and Spanish explorers visited it in the sixteenth and seventeenth centuries; but forces were already at work which were to revolutionize it within a generation. Americans were beginning to cross the Mississippi into what is now Missouri—some of them were farmers; some, like Daniel Boone, hunters; and some, like Moses Austin, lead miners. Austin, who visited St. Louis in 1797, predicted that "the large settlements makeing on the Missouri by the Americans will be of great advantage" to it. "Land have already been granted to 1000 Famelies," he said, "Near four Hundred of which have arriv.d from different parts of the United States." The town was "Prettily Situated, on a riseing spot of ground, . . . [with] a commanding prospect of the Mississipi." It was "better built than any town on the Missisipi, and has a Number of wealthey Merch^t. and an Extensive [fur] Trade, from the Missouri Illinois and upper parts of the Missisipi. its fast improveing and will soon be a large place; the town at this time Contains about 200 Houses, most of which are of Stone, and some of them large but not Elegant." [26]

The exportation of flour and corn as well as of peltry had already become a considerable business in upper Louisiana. In 1795, large quantities of flour and corn were shipped out of St. Louis, Ste. Gene-viève, and New Madrid, most of it to New Orleans, and mills were being built to improve the quality of the flour. According to Austin, the exports from St. Louis alone were supposed to amount to twenty thousand pounds per annum.

Though remote and thinly peopled, this region had not been forgotten by the authorities at New Orleans or by the court. When British interlopers from Canada threatened the hold of St. Louis on the fur trade of the Missouri Valley, a Spanish company was organized to drive them out, and the government prepared actively for overland explorations to the Pacific. [27] The British infiltration seemed to the hypersensitive Spaniards a menace to their hold on Santa Fé and the Pacific coast, and this fear played a not unimportant part in the development of Spain's foreign policy. [28] Though its political implications were probably not so serious as the court thought, the infiltration was subtle and apparently irresistible. Like the merchants who, with Spain's consent, controlled the Indian trade of the Floridas, the head of the company organized in 1794 was British; and General Collot, who visited St. Louis in 1796, reported that the merchants of that town had to buy Indian trading goods from their British rivals. In the very effort to protect its border provinces against Anglo-American penetration, Spain had to make use of British goods and services.

East of Mobile Bay, Ponce de León, Narváez, and Menéndez de Avilés would have found little that was unfamiliar to them. Since their day Pensacola and St. Marks had been established in West Florida, but in 1795 these towns had respectively a population of only six hundred and one hundred. In the whole of East Florida, which embraced the peninsula east of St. Marks, there were not more than two thousand inhabitants, including both whites and negroes, and most of these were concentrated in the region lying between the ancient presidio of St. Augustine and the St. Marys River.[29] There too were the only military posts in the province and the single battalion which held the peninsula for Spain. A few scavengers, called *wreckers,* hovered about the Florida keys, preying on the luckless ships that ran afoul of the treacherous reefs. Otherwise the peninsula was a howling wilderness. Even Tampa Bay was left in the undisturbed possession of the neighboring Indians, the memory of whose ferocity two centuries earlier still struck terror to the hearts of Spanish soldiers. When Vicente Folch led a reconnoitering party to the bay, in 1794, his men were so frightened by the call of night birds, which, in the lonely forest, they took to be Indians, that they were ready to mutiny rather than remain on shore.[30]

The northern boundary of West Florida, which ran along the thirty-first parallel from the Mississippi to the Apalachicola, was at several points only a few miles distant from the Gulf. North of this line lay the Natchez and Tombigbee settlements, composed for the most part of emigrants from the United States before and after the American Revolution. Between these settlements and those of Georgia, the Carolinas, and Tennessee lay the four principal tribes of Southern Indians —Choctaw, Creek, Chickasaw, and Cherokee. Part of the region had been occupied by Spanish garrisons. The rest of it, up to the Tennessee River, had been a Spanish sphere of influence. According to the treaty of San Lorenzo, it was to be handed over to the United States within six months; but for one reason or another the last Spanish troops were not withdrawn until 1798.

VI

It was lower Louisiana that was the heart of the Spanish borderlands at the end of the eighteenth century. Here was the focus of population, commerce, administration, and defense; here, the region most eagerly coveted by the great powers; and here, as varied and picturesque a society as could be found in North America. Every post on the Spanish border, except St. Augustine, was governed by orders received from New Orleans. The whole Mississippi Valley, American as well as Spanish, had to export the greater part of its produce through this port, and through it the lower half of the valley received most of its imports. Both in the city and in the country were to be found men of many races and nationalities—French, German,

Dutch, Spanish, Italian, American, British, Negro and Gipsy. In the last few years of the century the planters and merchants enjoyed unparalleled prosperity and lived with an ostentation that bankrupted the Spanish governors who tried to imitate it. In 1788 the population of New Orleans was 5,300. By 1803 it had increased to 8,000,[31] and the city was said to contain some 1,200 houses. The strategic importance of the region was already appreciated; its new-found prosperity soon became known, and before the end of the century France, Great Britain, and the United States were planning to wrest it from the Spaniards.

The improvements and social pretensions of New Orleans kept pace with its growing population and wealth. Partly in order to cope with the crime wave which accompanied the rise of American commerce on the lower Mississippi, a municipal force of night watchmen was created and a street lighting system installed.[32] Work was begun on a canal which would connect the Mississippi River at New Orleans with Lake Pontchartrain and the Gulf. In 1794 the *Moniteur de la Louisiane,* established by a French refugee from St. Domingue, gave New Orleans the distinction of being one of the very few cities of Spanish America that could boast a newspaper.[33] In 1793 a bishop was appointed for Louisiana, and in this decade were constructed many of the buildings, secular as well as ecclesiastical, that still give this American city an exotic flavor. There was even a theater, which Louisiana owed to the disasters of St. Domingue. In one of the favorite pieces, amateurs joined with professionals in reproducing on the banks of the Mississippi scenes from the history of the eternal city on the Tiber; and Julius Caesar, in the person of a portly creole, was nightly slain for the edification of a people who were soon to pass under the yoke of the Lutetian Caesar.[34]

As might have been expected, the increasing wealth of the town found expression in pious works. In 1791 a Holy Week procession was held. Only two figures were carried in it—a Christ crucified and a *mater dolorosa* dressed in black velvet adorned with gold braid, provided by Catalonians living in New Orleans and by Don Andrés Almonester.[35] Though a modest procession, it was a notable one, for, according to the Governor, it was the first ever held in the province. This same Don Andrés was a generous benefactor of the church, spending in all some $300,000 in building at his own expense a parish church (which later became the cathedral), a rectory, hospital, convent, and chapter hall. The church alone, which was first occupied in 1794, cost him $98,000, and he spared no expense, using brick and the best cypress in its construction and adorning it with sculpture and paintings. Feeling that his zeal deserved recognition, he petitioned the king for a Castilian title of nobility as Marqués de Almonester, but he had to be content with such minor rewards as the privilege of sitting in the choir with the clergy, the patronage of the hospital, the small cross of the Order of Charles III, and a private chapel in which he might be buried.[36]

Don Andrés made the most of the ceremony that accompanied the presentation of the small cross. After it was over, he went in state from the cathedral to his home wearing the great mantle of the order. Three lackeys in red carried the train. An immense crowd followed. Arrived at home, Don Andrés, still enveloped in his mantle, stood at the door of his drawing-room, where he affectionately kissed on both cheeks all who approached to greet him. There were about three hundred who did so. About eight o'clock he sent up from the plaza a balloon, accompanied by a display of fireworks. Then followed a collation of sweetmeats, after which they played cards until ten o'clock.[37]

While, as late as 1797, St. Augustine was supplied with only one elementary school teacher, whose monthly salary had just been raised from eight to fifteen dollars, and while Pensacola was not provided with any teacher at all until that year, New Orleans had had a superintendent of schools since 1771. By 1788 he was receiving a salary of one thousand dollars a year and had four teachers under him in the school system.[38] That, of course, was for the creole boys, for whom there were also some private schools. The girls could attend the school kept in the convent of the Ursuline nuns at New Orleans.[39]

For those who craved some other form of display than pious works and more excitement than they could find in newspapers and plays, there were hunting, gambling, the daily promenade along the levee, and balls. The promenade was a function as religiously observed in New Orleans as in the cities of Western Europe. In the late afternoon, all who could turned out with the regularity of clockwork for a ride in carriage or on horseback, or even a walk, along the levee. Balls were most frequent in the pre-Lenten season. Since they were open to the public, an officer with a squad of soldiers was always present to keep order among the excitable creoles and insolent Spanish officials. Experience justified the precaution.[40]

For all its prosperity and pretentiousness, New Orleans seemed to many observers a sorry place, in which health and life itself were in constant peril and morals had hardly a sporting chance. Laid out with narrow streets on the rectangular plan, it was neither paved nor drained. Indeed, drainage was hardly possible, since the city, protected from inundation by a levee, lay four feet below the normal level of the river. In wet weather each family was marooned in its house, and, when the waters receded, stagnant pools and dead fish were left to taint the air. The dry season brought relief tardily, for the sun released foul odors from the ground until it was baked dry. The cypress swamps surrounding the city added their peculiar perfume and bred swarms of mosquitoes to spread disease.

In 1796 came the first serious visitation of yellow fever, which was supposed to have been brought by ships from Philadelphia. The creoles and their doctors were helpless in the presence of this strange disease. They burned tar, sprinkled themselves with camphor, drank tisane, and tried a prescription which had cured Charles III of another disease; but it did not occur to them, any more than it did to their contemporaries in other lands, that killing the mosquitoes might help. When the epidemic was at its height, fifteen or twenty people were known to have died every day, though the priests and physicians concealed as many of the fatalities as possible. The only safety seemed to lie in flight. Some of the people of quality, imitating Boccaccio's Florentines, took refuge in a country house, cut themselves off from the city and its affliction, and sought an anodyne in pleasure; but they amused themselves in their own frontier fashion. "This afternoon," a visitor recorded in his diary, "they all went out on horseback, ran races and committed all sorts of extravagances." Not until November came with its frosts was the first epidemic ended.[41]

This city-under-the-river was hardly in greater danger of drowning than of burning. Before 1788 it was for the most part a wooden city roofed with shingles. After the disastrous fires of that year and 1794, which swept away half its houses and several government offices, the walls of the newer buildings were screened with brick, coated with plaster and given a covering of tile; but the danger was still great. Now and then a hurricane would ride up from the Gulf, slap houses over, and play havoc with the city's shipping. After the first servile insurrection in St. Domingue, the planters of Louisiana and even the townsmen lived in constant terror of an uprising among their own slaves, who constituted more than a third of the population of lower Louisiana; and long before the Dominican outbreak the creoles had begun to dread an incursion of American frontiersmen who would repeat the Revolutionary atrocities of Captain Willing. Altogether, life in Louisiana at the end of the century possessed a certain zest.

The shepherd of this hybrid flock found its spiritual perils quite as grave as those of a grosser kind. Though born and bred at Havana, which was certainly not a model of holy living, Bishop Peñalvert was shocked by the moral relaxation which an episcopal visitation to the four corners of lower Louisiana revealed. The people were idle and godless; at best, indifferent to religion; at worst, vicious. The Spanish officials themselves were no better. To make matters worse, the moral collapse seemed to be accompanied by political disaffection.

There were only twenty-four priests, most of them French and Irish, to serve the thirty-nine districts into which the province, with its population of some 45,000, was divided. These priests, though inadequately provided for, had to entertain their parishioners at Sunday dinner, for otherwise, explained the Governor, there would have been no congregation. By way of remedy, it was proposed that a competent instructor in logic, dogma, and morals should be provided for Louisiana, the Governor suggesting that he should be supported by a tax on powder, the Bishop preferring a tax on rum. The establishment of a seminary was also considered, but the Bishop himself opposed it on the ground that there would be no students, since the creoles, parents and children alike, had no interest in any occupation but hunting, fishing, sailing and mechanics; and that if students were found, there would be no career open to them in Louisiana after graduation. An effort was made to obtain more missionaries from Spain; but, though supported by the king and his ministers, it came to nothing. The Capuchin order, which was responsible for filling vacancies in Louisiana, could not be spurred into action. No volunteers could be found, and a controversy between the order and the Bishop of Havana led to the abandonment of the effort. Formerly, Irish priests had been sent to Louisiana, but by 1794 no more were available, since the French Jacobins had destroyed the colleges in France and all the graduates of the Irish College at Salamanca were needed for service in Ireland. After six years of disheartening struggle with the people and climate of Louisiana, Bishop Peñalvert threw up his hands in despair, protested that he had never aspired to anything more than a prebend in the Havana cathedral, and begged to be transferred to another diocese.[42]

Other writers who, as laymen, were free from the Bishop's professional bias towards pessimism in matters of morals, found lower Louisiana corrupt, and—what was worse in the opinion of some of them—intellectually stagnant. French travelers were particularly severe critics. They complained that the men were ignorant and boorish; the women, ignorant and haughty; that the balls were intolerably monotonous affairs; that there were no libraries, public or private, nor ten well educated men in the city's population of nearly ten thousand; that the average creole would take to his heels at sight of a book; and that, if the city did have a newspaper, the paper had never had as many as eighty subscribers and was kept alive only by government patronage.[43]

Americans who visited New Orleans on business were more indulgent critics than churchmen and French travelers. William Johnson of New Jersey, who was there on a flour "speck" in April and May, 1801 thought the houses "elegantly built," and was impressed by the organ and the "rich statues and vessels of gold and silver" in the church built by Almonester. The boarding-houses were "full as good" as any in the United States, though their rates (from six to twelve dollars a week) struck him as high. When he attended a ball one Sunday evening (merely from curiosity, he assures us), he found that "the room was elegant, the ladies very beautiful, the music good, and everything that could render the evening amusing and agreeable was well adapted." Apparently his only unpleasant impression was one of a political nature. After relating how a creole captain had had his nephew put in the calaboose for calling him "uncle," Johnson philosophized: "I should think it extremely inhuman if either of my uncles was to put me in gaol for calling him by that name. But away with monarchical governments, I say." [44]

In March of the same year an anonymous gentleman who had gone from New York to New Orleans on a trading venture wrote for the benefit of his friends in the States what he called a "short sketch of a place which one day must rank among the most important emporiums of the commercial world." [45] Like all the city's visitors, he found the streets abominable. They were "strait, intersected at right angles, about 40 feet wide, raised in the center, with narrow side walls and gutters; but entirely unpaved except the foot walks in places. The soil being of clay renders the walking after a rain not only muddy, but so slippery that you can scarcely keep your feet." Otherwise he had little but praise for the creole capital. The buildings, though made of "very bad" bricks, were "covered with white lime mortar, which gives a neat appearance." Most of them were only one or two stories, but there was one three-story building "which is superb, and would not disgrace even Washington." That, in 1801, was scant praise; but, raising his standard of comparison, he continued: "I know no private building in New York or Philadelphia as splendid in its exterior, said to have cost 60,000 dollars and not yet finished. Much taste is displayed in the fronts and battlements of the roof, which are generally flat and tiled." He too commented on the promenade along the levee, which, extending "many leagues on each side" of the river, and "sufficiently broad to serve as a high road," was "crowded with people of all tongues and complexions—French, Spanish, Dutch, English, Americans, and Indians by hundreds, with their nakedness scarcely covered by a short waist cloth and blanket."

Judging by William Johnson's table of rates, this anonymous gentleman stayed at one of the best houses in town, for he was "boarded at 12 dollars per week." For this sum he had "seldom less than 8 dishes elegantly dressed; and wine & claret at breakfast, dinner and supper, without limitation; a neat room, bed & curtains, and servant to brush clothes & boots." "The market," he wrote, "is abundantly supplied with but indifferent beef and veal, but plenty of fish, oysters, and some of all kinds of vegetables in the greatest luxuriance. We have had green peas and asparagus ever since my arrival— Oranges very fine for half a dollar a hundred.—The orange trees are now in full bloom, and the odour is most exquisite. The inhabitants all dine at 1, and fare sumptuously. . . . This is a very hospitable place; I have scarcely dined at my lodgings since I have been here; we sup at eight, retire at 9 and rise with the sun. I find little intellectual society, all is commercial that is worth cultivation; gambling is very frequent, and our foolish Kentucky men spend and lose their money in this place most infamously. The inhabitants are temperate, as their wine, being very small, of which however, they swallow immoderately at meals, they cannot hold enough to intoxicate them; but our northern folks will not relinquish grog, which is poison in this climate. . . . The inhabitants, men & women, are universally as hale, fair and fresh colored as our own people.—They say themselves that this is the Paradise of the world."

VIII

French travelers' indictments, as well as Bishop Peñalvert's jere-
miads, must be taken with a grain of salt, for when they were not
tendentious there was often a personal bias. In any case, whether they
approved of Louisiana or not, foreign travelers generally missed certain less obvious but more significant aspects of provincial life. Hardly
one of them noted that the lower Louisiana of 1800 was a region in
which the equality of the frontier was rapidly giving way before the
rise of an aristocracy of wealth. The occasion of this change was the
concentration of the colony's new-found prosperity in the hands of
the fortunate few who possessed the means of production and distri-
bution. Conditions were singularly favorable to such a development.
By the end of the century, sugar planting and commerce were among
the chief sources of wealth, and both lent themselves to monopoly control. When foreign connections and credit were prerequisites, it was
no easy thing to set up as a merchant at New Orleans; and those who
reaped the harvest of prosperity at the turn of the century were the
merchants already established there when the halcyon days began.
Similar difficulties faced the would-be sugar planter, for the supply
of both labor and land was strictly limited at this time. Only a small
region extending along the banks of the Mississippi from the Iberville River to New Orleans was suitable for the growth of sugar-
cane,[46] and this region was in the possession of a handful of planters.
Even if more land were made available, it would be very difficult to
obtain laborers, for the prohibition of the slave trade with the French
West Indies since 1793 had created a serious labor shortage.[47] Through
this monopolistic control, established planters and merchants such as
Julien Poydras, Étienne Boré, and Daniel Clark skimmed the cream
off the new prosperity, while, as in Kentucky at the same time, the
mass of the people lived on in the same rough simplicity as of old.

An obvious result, and one not missed by any foreign traveler, was
a state of affairs that recalled St. Domingue before the great insurrection—a corrupt aristocracy of wealth, in which the white men of
means frequently kept mulatto women as concubines, the white women
avenging themselves by treating all negroes with haughty contempt
and racial antagonism reaching a dangerously high pitch.[48] A less
obvious result, but one that was probably quite as important, was the
creation of a privileged class which, realizing its indebtedness to Spain
for its privileges, had no desire for incorporation in the United States.

This class provided some of the raw materials for the Burr conspiracy in its more dangerous phase and, even when reconciled to the union, retained a view of life at variance with the democratic dogma. The lower South of Jefferson Davis's day numbered among its forbears the particularistic gentry of Spanish Louisiana.

If this pleasure-loving society was less bookish than bourgeois French travelers would have liked, there was at least some precedent for it in the history of Europe itself. Not very many years had passed since European princes patronized men of letters as they patronized clowns and mimes. The Louisiana creole who took to his heels at the sight of a printed page might have quoted against his critics the advice of the Italian courtier's handbook that gentlemen should leave books to the clerks and spend their time in the more becoming exercises of arms and horsemanship. Privileged classes have very seldom in the world's history resolved themselves into learned societies, and local conditions made it very unlikely that Louisiana would prove an exception to the general rule. The novelty of wealth was not favorable to the cultivation of the intellectual life, while the heavy hand of the Spanish government and the Roman Catholic Church suppressed discussion of the most engrossing problems of the day in both politics and philosophy.

The last few years of the Spanish régime in Louisiana should have witnessed an extraordinary outburst of political controversy, for it was commonly believed that the destiny of the province was hanging in the balance and that it would soon pass into the hands of some other power, probably France or the United States. At New Orleans, however, there was but little discussion, and that little was mostly concerned with such commercial regulations as might be decreed by the new master. Except for the handful of American merchants in the city, the people of the province were not politically minded. That is not surprising, for the Spanish colonial system, under which the people had lived for the last three decades, gave them almost no share in the government. The creoles indeed held most of the offices in the militia and the local governments, but they were given no discretionary power. Their duties were purely military or ministerial. Such appointments accustomed them not to the exercise of power but to blind obedience.

The only institution that was even in the smallest degree representative was the *cabildo,* a kind of town council, whose twelve members were inhabitants of New Orleans. They were chosen, however, by the governor and not by the people. Quite naturally the test of their fitness for office was not ability, integrity, or popularity but devotion to the Spanish crown.[49] Appointed for life, their position was chiefly honorary, and their only important function was the supervision of the municipal police.

In politics as well as in business the creoles were at the same time more cosmopolitan and more colonial than the Kentuckians and Tennesseans. With wider contacts and more constant intercourse with the outside world, they seem never to have given a serious thought either to economic self-sufficiency or to political independence. They accepted both a foreign market and foreign domination as a matter of course. In the critical period of transition from Spanish to French and from French to American rule, they remained incoherent and left the initiative to the small group of Americans at New Orleans.

PART TWO

THE AFTERMATH OF SAN LORENZO

CHAPTER III

THE BORDER POSTS

I

By the treaty which Manuel de Godoy signed with Thomas Pinckney at San Lorenzo in 1795, Spain made some highly important concessions to the United States. Several of the most important of these concessions related to the Louisiana-Florida border region. Taken together, they marked an abandonment of the policy of frontier defense which the Spanish government had been pursuing for more than a decade. It had insisted long and stubbornly upon its exclusive right to navigate the lower Mississippi and upon its sovereignty over territory on the east bank of that river as far north as the Tennessee and the Ohio; and it had labored patiently, through trade and treaties, to extend its influence over the Indian tribes inhabiting the disputed region.[1] Now came Godoy's treaty, which gave the Americans the free navigation of the Mississippi throughout its course and a place of deposit at New Orleans for the convenience of their river traffic; recognized the thirty-first parallel as the southern boundary of the United States; agreed to withdraw the Spanish garrisons from the region thus relinquished; and resigned the effort to create a Spanish sphere of influence in the Indian country.

It was not until two and a half years later that the last of the provisions of the treaty was carried into effect. The long delay not only provoked an acute crisis in relations between the two countries; it also gave rise to a misunderstanding of Spanish policy which has persisted to the present day. The misunderstanding arose in a very natural way. The terms of the agreement were so disadvantageous to Spain that, when the court interposed obstacles to its execution, many people suspected that Godoy had acted in bad faith at San Lorenzo, assuming obligations which he never intended to discharge. The suspicion seemed to be confirmed when Timothy Pickering, Secretary of State under Adams, triumphantly demolished the tissue of lies woven by Spain's American agents in an effort to defend their government's course. The simplicity of the explanation suggested by these circumstances gained general acceptance for it in the United States; but it was wide of the mark.[2]

Further confusion in the accounts of this episode arose from the fact that the various clauses of the treaty were executed at widely separate intervals. The right of free navigation of the Mississippi was first exercised by an American vessel in December, 1796. Some of the border posts were evacuated in March, 1797; others were held by their Spanish garrisons until March, 1798. The deposit at New Orleans was formally established in April, 1798; and Spain maintained its Indian relations with little change until the same period. It is therefore impossible to fix upon a given day and say, "This is the day when the treaty of San Lorenzo was executed." It was carried into effect piecemeal; and, to make matters worse for the patient student, the considerations which induced Spain to comply with one stipulation of the treaty led it to refrain from complying with another. Only after a careful study of the Spanish records of the period has it become possible to clarify this confused question.

II

Godoy's policy towards the United States at this period was intimately related to his negotiation with France regarding the retrocession of Louisiana.[3] By the beginning of 1795 experience had shown that, as a colony, Louisiana was worse than useless to Spain; but it was still valuable as a diplomatic pawn. The crisis which confronted the court in that year forced it to employ every resource at its command. The alliance concluded with Great Britain in 1793 had proved highly unsatisfactory, the armies of France had conquered a large part of northern Spain, and the United States was threatening to go to war unless Spain agreed to a favorable settlement of the long-standing controversy over the navigation of the Mississippi.

To save his country from ruin, Godoy determined upon a diplomatic revolution. The first stage was completed when he made peace with France at Basel in July, 1795. In the course of the negotiations leading up to that treaty, the French made a determined effort to obtain Louisiana, but Godoy resisted stubbornly and made them accept Santo Domingo instead. He was willing enough to part with the continental colony, but he must first use it to effect the second stage of his diplomatic revolution by converting the United States from a potential enemy into a friendly neutral. Otherwise, Great Britain,

offended by Spain's desertion of the alliance, might easily persuade
the Americans to join in an attack on Spanish America. For Godoy's
purpose it was essential that he should have Louisiana at his disposal until he had gained the Americans' friendship by giving them
the free navigation of the Mississippi, a place of deposit at New
Orleans, and the southern boundary claimed by them. This he did in
the treaty of San Lorenzo.

After that treaty was signed he had no further use for Louisiana.
Accordingly in December, 1795, he offered to give it to France in
return for Santo Domingo, thus reversing the position which he had
taken in the negotiations at Basel six months earlier. France rejected
the offer, but the negotiation continued, and on June 27, 1796, a
treaty was signed which stipulated the retrocession of Louisiana to
France. The Directory refused to ratify it on the ground that its
plenipotentiary had agreed to pay too high a price for the province.
Two months later another treaty was concluded and duly ratified
which provided for an alliance between the two powers and a guaranty of all of Spain's possessions in America, but left the Louisiana
business for further negotiation. The subsequent history of the affair
will be told in a later chapter.

Since Spain was about to part with Louisiana, Godoy had no motive for sabotaging the treaty of San Lorenzo; and all the evidence
indicates that until October, 1796, he proceeded in perfect good faith
to fulfil Spain's obligations under that instrument. Ratifications of
the treaty were exchanged on April 25, 1796. A month later Godoy
laid it before the King and the council of state with an exposition
of the advantages which Spain had already derived from it. The King
expressed his complete satisfaction with the treaty, and there was no
dissent on the part of the council. On June first, Godoy despatched
orders to Louisiana for its execution; and on August twenty-seventh,
replying to the discreet but forceful remonstrance of its Governor,
Baron de Carondelet, against the extensive concessions made to the
Americans, he repeated the order to execute.[4] In the meanwhile the
treaty had been duly registered by the Council of Castile.[5]

Regretfully but energetically Governor Carondelet proceeded to
carry out the orders from Madrid. His regret arose from a conviction
that Godoy's surrender at San Lorenzo was unnecessary and would
prove disastrous to Spain—unnecessary, because he still believed that
his intrigue with James Wilkinson and other Kentuckians would split
the Union in twain and put the American West at the mercy of

Spain; disastrous, because the treaty, by giving the Americans possession of the free navigation of the Mississippi, a place of deposit at
New Orleans, the Southwest posts and the Southern Indian country,
would convert the Indians from friends into foes of Spain, defeat
his separatist intrigue, and establish American supremacy in the
Mississippi Valley. Louisiana and Florida would then fall an easy
prey to the United States, and Spain's other possessions on the Gulf,
including Mexico itself, would not be safe. Carondelet was as incessantly haunted by the specter of "Yankee imperialism" as any
Latin American of more recent times.[6]

Orders were orders, however, and the Governor prepared to do as
he was told. Indeed, as soon as he was convinced that the court would
not listen to his protests against the treaty, he determined to execute
it as quickly as possible. In his opinion, the article which involved
the greatest immediate peril to Louisiana was the one relating to the
surrender of the Southwest posts to the United States. Four of these
posts (St. Stephen, Confederation, Walnut Hills, and Chickasaw
Bluffs) had been erected by Spain a few years before on tracts of
land obtained from the Indians with the promise that the forts would
be used to protect the Indians against American aggression. Their
surrender by Spain to the very power against which they had been
raised would, Carondelet feared, be regarded by the tribes as an un-
forgivable act of treachery. Accordingly he directed that these posts
should be evacuated speedily and secretly, in order to protect their
garrisons from the resentment of the savages, and that the fortifications should be destroyed so that Spain might not seem utterly ob-
livious of its promises to its Indian allies. Immediately thereafter
would follow the evacuation of Natchez, the seat of Governor Gayoso
and the capital of the only considerable settlement in the region about
to be surrendered.

Disagreeable as it was to the pugnacious Governor, this retreat would
at least enable him to reinforce one of the most exposed outposts of
the province. As a result of the treaty of San Lorenzo and of Spain's
treaty of peace with France (Basel, July, 1795), Great Britain had
supplanted France and the United States as the most likely invader
of Louisiana; and the New Orleans officials soon had reason to fear
that an invasion from Canada would be attempted. In this connection,
two decisive developments occurred in November, 1796. The first
was the receipt of two royal orders addressed to the Governor. One
was Godoy's note of August 27, 1796, repeating the injunction to

proceed to the punctual execution of the treaty of San Lorenzo; the other directed Carondelet to attack a British post recently established in the Missouri Valley. The second development was the arrival at New Orleans of the French general, Victor Collot. Fresh from a tour of the West which had carried him to St. Louis, he brought alarming news of the encroachments of British fur traders in upper Louisiana, confirming the Governor's worst fears on that score. Carondelet's mind was made up. One of the royal orders just received had closed the last loophole by which he might escape compliance with the terms of the treaty of San Lorenzo; the other order and Collot's information deprived him of the desire to escape it.

The center of gravity of Spanish defense was accordingly shifted from the Tennessee-Georgia frontier in the Old Southwest to upper Louisiana. There was of course the danger of British invasion by way of the Gulf and the lower Mississippi, but that was a matter for the attention of the Spanish navy. With the resources at his command Carondelet could add little to the preparations already made in this quarter—the concentration of the river fleet, the strengthening of Fort Plaquemine, and the fortifications of New Orleans itself. In upper Louisiana, on the other hand, every man and gun that he could spare would count heavily; and the responsibility for the defense of this region could not be shared with the naval officers or any one else, but rested squarely on his own shoulders. He therefore gave orders that the troops and material from the three posts on the Mississippi which were about to be evacuated—Natchez, Walnut Hills, and Chickasaw Bluffs—should be taken up the river to St. Louis. The command of the united force was entrusted to the Irish-born Carlos Howard, lieutenant-colonel of the Louisiana Regiment and one of Spain's best officers in this whole border region. Carondelet, who evidently believed that the best defense was to attack, planned an offensive against the British along a front extending from the Missouri Valley to Lake Michigan.[7]

On February 13, 1797, he took measures which were intended to put the plan into execution at once.[8] The immediate occasion was the receipt of a letter from General Anthony Wayne, commanding the United States Army in the West, in regard to the surrender of the border posts. Carondelet thereupon instructed Governor Gayoso of Natchez to proceed at once with the evacuation of that post and Walnut Hills and to demolish their fortifications, urging him to hasten the work so that it might be completed before the arrival of

Wayne's troops. This he said, was necessary in order that the Indians might not be able to charge Spain with failure to keep its agreement with them. Replying to a personal letter in which Gayoso had expressed the belief that Spain might yet escape from the obligations entered into at San Lorenzo, Carondelet wrote: "I observe your doubts about the execution of the treaty, but I assure you that they are unfounded." [9] It was his expectation, he continued, that Natchez, the last of the border posts to be evacuated, would be turned over to the United States by the end of March (1797), and that the surveying of the international boundary along the thirty-first parallel would be commenced by the middle of the same month. Similar orders were sent to Forts Confederation and San Fernando, and a letter promising compliance with Wayne's request was promptly started up the river on its way to the American general.

III

Before the month was out Carondelet was busily engaged in undoing the work of that February day. Express riders hurriedly left the capital with orders to Gayoso and the other officials concerned to suspend the dismantling of the border forts, which were to be retained until further notice. These riders were, if possible, to overtake the messenger with the letter for Wayne and return it to New Orleans. The Governor's efforts were in the main successful. The Wayne letter was recovered, and Natchez, Walnut Hills, and St. Stephen remained in Spanish possession. Only the more remote posts at Chickasaw Bluffs and Confederation were abandoned, for their lonely garrisons had shown unexampled alacrity in executing the original order to dismantle them. Reconstruction did not seem advisable, and the troops were transferred to other posts.[10]

In place of the original letter to Wayne, Carondelet now drew up another bearing the same date but of a totally different tenor. Instead of the earlier assurance that Spain was ready to comply with the terms of the treaty, the Governor now expressed regret that the difficulty of interpreting certain of its clauses made it necessary to postpone compliance until he had had an opportunity to consult his government. Though by this time he had learned of Wayne's recent death, he nevertheless addressed the antedated letter to the defunct general, ostensibly as a duplicate of the original, and despatched it to the United States by way of the Gulf. This procedure, he explained confidentially to his superiors, would convince the American government that the original letter (which, it was a matter of common knowledge, had been sent up the river) had been duly delivered and then lost in the confusion attending Wayne's death.

The reason for the Baron's reversal of orders to the post commanders and the elaborate hocus-pocus about the letter to Wayne was simply that the court had reversed its orders to him. In the new order, dated October 29, 1796, Godoy had directed him to delay the evacuation of the Southwest posts on plausible pretexts while Spain came to an understanding with the United States in regard to certain conflicting provisions in the treaties which the latter power had concluded with Great Britain, Spain, and France.[11] The issuance of the order was likely to have serious consequences, for it marked the abandonment of Godoy's policy of conciliating the United States, and it was certain to bring on a bitter controversy with the government of that country. The circumstances, however, seemed to justify him in running that risk. The treaty of San Lorenzo had not won the good will of the United States, as he had expected it to do; on the contrary, recent events convinced him that the Federalist administration at Philadelphia was the tool of Great Britain, which was at war with Spain. At the same time, information from Paris led him to believe that the majority of the American people were devoted to France and indignant at their own government's subserviency to England. Since a controversy over Jay's treaty was already in progress between France and the United States, Godoy determined to make common cause with Spain's ally and have it out with Pitt's minions at Philadelphia. It is not certain what he hoped to gain by doing so. Perhaps he expected to obtain a revision of the treaty of San Lorenzo, for France was unable or unwilling to pay the price Spain had set on Louisiana and the province seemed likely to remain in Spanish possession for some time to come; or perhaps he only desired to force the adoption of a more friendly policy towards France and Spain by the United States government.

The order to the Governor of Louisiana was, of course, a secret one; but by March, 1797, its effects were apparent to all the world in the altered conduct of Spain's agents in North America. The expected controversy soon developed hurricane force, and during the twelvemonth period of its continuance, it threatened to sweep the two countries into war. A minor center of the disturbance was Philadelphia, where the Spanish minister, Carlos Martínez de Irujo, engaged in a wordy battle with the American Secretary of State,

Timothy Pickering. The full force of the storm, however, was felt at Natchez, the largest of the towns in the disputed region, to which the Louisiana authorities had admitted a representative of the United States government before they received the countermanding order from Godoy.

In the course of this year almost every thread of frontier history was gathered up at the tiny post on the lower Mississippi. Spanish conspirators of Tennessee and Kentucky, promoters of land speculation at Muscle Shoals and in the Yazoo country, officials of the rival governments, Indians and Indian agents, and ringleaders of the Blount conspiracy—all met in the little town that lay between the river and the worthless Spanish fort on a hill nearby. Though the population of the town and the surrounding district was not large, the behavior of the people was of vital importance; and they were so heterogeneous a mass—Spaniards, Frenchmen, Britons, and Americans from many States—that public opinion was unpredictable from one week to the next. If, as Daniel Clark wrote somewhat later, these people were always "restless and turbulent," the events of 1797 gave them plenty of the action that they found so congenial.

There can be little doubt that the conduct of the commissioner appointed to represent the United States in the transfer and to survey the international boundary, contributed handsomely to the chaos at Natchez. That commissioner was Andrew Ellicott, Quaker, member of the American Philosophical Society and a surveyor of long experience. His conduct seems to have been strongly influenced by a conversation with President Washington on the eve of his departure for Natchez. Writing from memory twelve years later, Ellicott gave the following account of the admonition which he received on that occasion: ". . . President Washington communicated to me, in the most confidential manner possible, that *suspicions* had been signified to him of certain citizens of the U. States, improperly connecting themselves with the Spanish government, among whom you [James Wilkinson] were particularly noticed. He thought it a business of so much importance, both to the honour and safety of the country, as to merit a thorough, though private investigation, and directed me to pay a strict attention to that subject." [12]

Warned by the President himself that neither the Spaniards nor all of the Western people were to be trusted and that "the honour and safety of the country" were at stake, Ellicott proceeded with taut nerves to his task of saving the Union and surveying the southern boundary. He was not reassured even when, upon his arrival at Pittsburgh in October, 1796, General Wilkinson, traveling eastward, placed his river boat with its "new and spacious cabbin" at the commissioner's disposal; nor when Philip Nolan, "so well known for his athletic exertions and dexterity in taking wild horses" and not so well known then as later for his dexterous exertions in support of the Spanish intrigue, joined the party at the mouth of the Ohio.[13] At Cincinnati, Ellicott heard rumors of Wilkinson's corrupt dealings with the Spaniards. At New Madrid the Spanish commandant tried to dissuade him from pursuing his journey down the river. At Chickasaw Bluffs he received a request from Governor Gayoso to leave his military escort behind, and the request only made him the more determined to keep the escort—some thirty men [14]—with him.

When at last he reached Natchez (February 24, 1797), he was fully prepared to meet with duplicity and evasion on the part of the Spaniards. Neither Gayoso's courtesy nor the actual dismantling of the fort increased his trust in Spain. He never believed, either then or subsequently, that the Spaniards had the slightest intention of executing the treaty in good faith. He was convinced that French influence, if nothing else, would embroil the United States and Spain, for France and Spain were allies and war between France and the United States seemed imminent. In case hostilities should break out it was his duty, he thought, "not only to retain the post we then occupied, but to extend our limits. . . ." [15] With the chief representative of the American government in such a frame of mind, it was almost inevitable that a tempest should have been stirred up in the Natchez teapot.

Ellicott was quite mistaken as to the intentions of Gayoso, who was actually proceeding with the work of evacuation under Carondelet's first orders; but shortly after the commissioner's arrival came the countermanding order from New Orleans. On March 22 the cannon which had been taken from the fort to the river landing were hauled back to the fort. A week later Gayoso issued a proclamation declaring his intention to retain possession of the district until assurance was given by the United States that the inhabitants would be protected in their real property and until the neighboring Indians were pacified. He further declared a moratorium for debtors during the planting season and reminded the people that the liberty of conscience granted by Spain did not carry with it the right of public worship.

We may agree with Ellicott [16] that this was a clever proclamation, appealing as it did to the inhabitants' fear of the Indians, love of property, and disinclination to satisfy creditors. It was not for nothing that Gayoso had studied the people of his district during his eight years' residence among them, and no one could have made a more persuasive apology for the continuance of Spanish authority at Natchez; even so his proclamation was disconcerting to his restive charges. Many of them, thinking that the Spanish régime was at an end, had openly declared themselves republicans, and they now feared reprisals. Protestants resented the persistent denial of freedom of public worship. British sympathizers were encouraged by rumors of an invasion from Canada. And there was Andrew Ellicott!

Hitherto the commissioner had been making and recording frequent "astronomical and thermometrical" observations, but under March 23 (the day after the guns were brought back from the landing and remounted in the fort) he made this entry in his journal: "From this time I was too much occupied in other concerns, occasioned by the different commotions in the country, to attend to a regular series of observations till October. . . ." [17] The Spaniards always maintained with a good deal of truth that these "different commotions" were "occasioned" by Ellicott himself. Against Gayoso's vehement protest he began to raise recruits in the district—a measure that was both improper and impolitic. Still worse, he induced Lieutenant Percy Smith Pope, familiarly known as "Crazy Pope," to violate his instructions from General Wayne and descend to Natchez with a detachment of United States troops. It certainly looked as if the commissioner were trying to provoke the hostilities which, in his own words, would make it his duty to "extend our limits."

IV

If Ellicott was determined that the Spaniards should get out, Gayoso was quite as determined to stay. The fight was on, and for the next three months the district was in a turmoil. Neither side controlled a large military force. What forces they did possess were nearly equal in strength, and both accordingly appealed to the people of the district for support. The American commissioner's confidence in the issue is easy to understand, since he estimated that seven eighths of the inhabitants were Americans by birth or sympathy, and that there were only "about eight persons, including some officers," who were "attached to the Spanish interest." [18] Gayoso's confidence may seem surprising, but there was some reason for it, as we shall see.

The bid for popular support made by these two representatives of rival governments possesses considerable interest, since it put to the test the Spanish immigration policy adopted in 1788—a policy which was unique in the annals of the Spanish colonial system and was the keystone of its defense in the Mississippi Valley.[19] With an amazing confidence in its powers of assimilation, Spain had invited immigrants from the heretical, republican United States to settle in Louisiana and Florida, believing that they could be converted into dutiful subjects of his Catholic Majesty and made a living barrier against the very country from which they had come. Natchez District was the region favored by Spain for this experiment, and Gayoso had been sent from Spain for the express purpose of conducting it. Now an American agent was endeavoring to stir up these immigrants against Gayoso himself, and so put an end to the Spanish domination. A more direct test of the Spanish defensive system could hardly have been devised even in a research laboratory.

Several factors in the situation were favorable to Spain. The growth of the district under its care had been rapid. In 1787, the year before the new immigration policy was adopted, its population was 1,926. Within the next five years it had more than doubled, standing in 1792 at 4,300.[20] Its first town, Natchez, established by Gayoso in 1791, soon became an important junction point in the growing river trade. About 1795 an added stimulus was received from the spread of cotton cultivation. Unmolested in the private exercise of their religion, the Protestants—according to Governor Gayoso—were gradually being won over to Roman Catholicism. Their conversion, he thought, would have progressed more rapidly but for the character of the Irish priests at Natchez, one of whom did not preach a public sermon in the whole period of his ministry, while the other preached only too often on the grievous sin of tolerating heretics.[21]

Above all, Spanish influence was maintained by the personal magnetism of Gayoso. Even Ellicott confessed his admiration for the public and private virtues of his antagonist, and John Pope, an American traveler who was no admirer of Spain, reported that Gayoso "has a majestic Deportment, softened by Manners the most engaging and polite." [22] His reputation for honesty—a reputation enjoyed by few of his colleagues in these border provinces—excited the admiration of all who knew him. His excellent command of the English language and his marriage to an American woman enabled him to make many friends, whose number was increased by the mildness of his administration and by his protection of the debtor planters against their creditors at New Orleans. That his open-handed hospitality was bankrupting him only added to his popularity with these insolvent planters, whose life seemed to at least one traveler a continual round of visiting, eating, drinking, dancing, card-playing, and horse-racing. Gayoso gave society the tone that they desired, and they were grateful.

Their loyalty to Spain had been demonstrated on more than one occasion. When Georgia's Bourbon County commissioners presented themselves there in 1785, inviting the Spaniards to leave and the people to drive them out, the clarion call to liberty fell on deaf ears. When the Genêt-Clark expedition was impending in 1793 and 1794, the militia of the district took up arms to repel the invaders; and when, at the same juncture, New Orleans was seething with sedition and Jacobin sympathizers were actually singing a local version of the Carmagnole in the city streets, a battalion of Natchez militia aided in suppressing the ebullient creoles. At a time when the United States government was cordially disliked in that part of the Mississippi Valley which it already held, it was not unreasonable to suppose that the Natchez settlers, many of whom were British loyalists, would have little desire to pass under the American domination. It was rumored—and Gayoso gave the rumor a helping hand—that if the treaty of San Lorenzo were executed, the district would be incorporated in the State of Georgia, which would then annul all grants of land made by Spain.[23]

On the other hand, recent developments had turned many of the people against their Spanish masters. The society of the district was so constituted as to favor the American cause. Most of the inhabitants were either small farmers or slaveholding planters. The small farmers were then a very numerous class, for their increase was fostered by the Spanish land system with its free grants to actual settlers and its impediments to the resale of granted lands. These farmers, however, felt no debt of gratitude to Spain, and the enforced simplicity of their lives disposed them to abhor aristocracy and monarchy and love democracy. The disposition was strengthened by their religious affiliations, which were largely Protestant. The Baptists were particularly numerous and active. In 1795, when Gayoso went up the river for an interview with some Kentucky conspirators, three Baptist preachers took advantage of his absence to exhort the faithful. One observer, a Connecticut Presbyterian who held a contract to supply the Spanish garrison with beef, wrote Gayoso that these Baptist preachers were "weak men, of weak minds, and illiterate, and too ignorant to know how inconsistent they act and talk . . . too weak and undesigning to lay any treasonable plans . . . but . . . they would call any chastisements from Government for their disobedience, persecution, and suffering for Christ. . . ." [24]

As for the slaveholding planters, their debts made them pro-American. Spain, they held, was responsible for their insolvency. [25] Many of them had been attracted to the district by the liberal price paid at the king's warehouse for their tobacco. As early as 1787 the crop reached 500,000 pounds, and the government was paying eight cents a pound. In the belief that the purchases would be continued indefinitely, the planters went into debt in order to purchase slaves and tools and clear lands. In the five years after 1787, the slave population trebled, while the white population only doubled. Then the Spanish government abruptly reduced its tobacco purchases to the vanishing point. That the inferior quality of the tobacco and their own negligence and frauds justified the reduction made no difference to the planters, for they were ruined. [26] Their plight became still worse with the simultaneous decay of their other business, the cultivation of indigo. [27] Though cotton had brought prosperity back by 1800, most of the planters were still in dire straits in 1797, and Spain was to blame. Gayoso's moratorium of that year, repeating a similar measure adopted to 1794, gave them some relief; but incorporation in the United States might free them of the debts altogether. One of these insolvent planters, Peter Bryan Bruin, was a most active supporter of the American faction in this critical period, though it was not many years since he had willingly taken the oath of loyalty to Spain; and he had subsequently received many favors from Gayoso. [28] It may also be that Spain's alliance with antislavery France had something to do with the disaffection among these slaveholding gentry.

V

Great as it was, Gayoso's influence was not equal to the task of pacifying all these turbulent elements. In May, 1797, Governor Carondelet offended the loyalists by proclamations in which he took the rumor of impending invasion from Canada as a text for denouncing Great Britain. [29] On their part the American faction branded the rumored attack as a Spanish fabrication which was simply another pretext for the retention of the Southwest posts. In June, Gayoso made one of the recalcitrant Baptist preachers "suffer for Christ," and the storm broke.[30] Threatened with personal violence, he and the other officials, with their families, took refuge in the fort. The American faction then threatened to storm it, and on June 22 the Governor capitulated, agreeing to four articles drawn up by a committee consisting of Ellicott, Pope, and seven other members representing the inhabitants. According to these articles, Spain agreed to respect the "neutrality" of the district pending the settlement of the controversy with the United States; the militia was not to be called into service except to repel an Indian attack or to quell a riot; Spanish law was to remain in effect, but was to be administered mildly; and offenders were not to be taken out of the district for trial. In due course the agreement was approved by Carondelet, whose ill-advised proclamations had done so much to bring the revolution to a head. That was the end of the controversy so far as Spain was concerned; but it was also virtually the end of the Spanish régime in the district. While Gayoso retained the title of governor and the Spanish garrison still held the fort, a permanent committee, elected by the people early in July, was the real governing body.

At the end of that month Gayoso was rescued from his humiliating situation by promotion to the governorship of Louisiana and West Florida,[31] which had just been vacated by Carondelet's promotion to a post in Quito. After Gayoso's departure for New Orleans hardly a trace of Spanish authority was to be seen in the disputed region. The garrisons at Natchez and Walnut Hills were happy to remain unmolested in their forts. There was, to be sure, an acting Governor, Stephen Minor of Natchez, an American immigrant who for more than a decade had been a zealous servant of his Catholic Majesty. Minor continued his faithful service but was unable to restrain the republican neophytes who now set to work Americanizing the district. Factions developed and each group vilified the others in the most approved manner of frontier communities. Anthony Hutchins, leader of the British sympathizers, dispatched a messenger with a memorial to Congress denouncing Ellicott, and Ellicott's men promptly set out after the messenger and took the memorial away from him. Hutchins then threatened to publish a story about "old Ellicott, young Ellicott and a housekeeper," and the Quaker's friends chased the scandalmonger to the woods. "God send a speedy determination of things," wrote Minor, "otherwise they will all run mad, with memorials, certificates, circular letters &ca." [32]

Another element of uncertainty was introduced by the arrival of George Mathews from Kentucky. All sorts of rumors were spread regarding his object, for he was a man of extensive connections in the United States. In order to find what he was about, Minor invited him to dinner and "pushed about the bottle"; but after a strenuous evening he concluded that while "[Mathews] loves his glass . . . I believe all the wine I have coud not make him drunk." [33] And after all, it appeared that Mathews, who as Governor of Georgia had approved the notorious Yazoo grants of 1795, had come to Natchez partly in the expectation of being appointed governor and partly in order to look after the interests of the New England Company, an association of persons who had purchased from the original grantees.[34] So far was he from making trouble that he visited Gayoso in New Orleans and came back loud in his praise of the Governor, swearing "by G—d that if any have not been treated with politeness [by Gayoso] it must have been their own faults." [35]

The final demonstration of Spanish impotence came in November, 1797, when it was announced that Colonel Carlos Grandpré, commandant at Natchez before Gayoso's appointment and now stationed at Baton Rouge, was to return as Governor of the district. The citizens' committee immediately declared that any attempt on Grandpré's part to take possession of the government would be regarded as a breach of the "neutrality" established by the articles of June 22, and would be resented accordingly. This plain language had the desired effect and Grandpré remained at Baton Rogue, though curiously enough he continued for several years to draw his salary as Governor of Natchez.[36]

By the time that news of the June revolution at Natchez reached Madrid, Godoy had once more changed his mind and had again ordered the evacuation of the Southwest posts.[37] His comment on the creation of the citizens' committee was, "A very good means of pacifying them. Proceed with the surrender as directed." [38] The considerations which led him to issue the order can only be conjectured from the circumstances. In the opinion of Timothy Pickering, Spain realized that it would soon have to cede Louisiana to France and wished to "do a grateful thing" by the United States before giving up the province.[39] This explanation, however, can hardly stand in the face of the fact that, as the records show, the Louisiana negotiation had come to a complete standstill at this time and there was not the slightest prospect that the retrocession would take place at any time in the near future.[40] It is more likely that Godoy gave the order because he feared that the Americans would invade Louisiana, knew that Spain could not send reinforcements to the aid of the colony, and had learned that France would not coöperate in the defense of Spanish America. The situation with regard to the United States was very grave. Not only had Godoy been disappointed in his hope that the American people would overthrow their supposedly Anglophile government at the behest of France and Spain, but he had also learned from the recent exposure of the Blount conspiracy that Spain had a host of enemies in the Mississippi Valley. The continuance of the trouble at Natchez might start a conflagration which would sweep over all the Spanish dominions in North America. After his one brief gesture of defiance Godoy apparently decided that it would be wiser to return to his policy of conciliating the United States.

Whatever his reasons may have been, the order was issued. This time there was no miscarriage. By the end of March, 1798, the beleaguered garrisons at Natchez and Walnut Hills had dismantled the forts and taken passage in Spain's river fleet for a more congenial clime. On March 30 Andrew Ellicott watched the departure of the Natchez garrison, and the pleasure was the more exquisite because the Spaniards had tried to slip away unobserved: "I rose . . . at four o'clock," he wrote, "and walked to the fort, and found the last party, or rear guard just leaving it, and as the gate was left open, I went in, and enjoyed from the parapet, the pleasing prospect of the gallies and boats leaving the shore, and getting under way: they were out of sight of the town before daylight. The same day our troops took possession of the works." [41]

Ellicott was now able to proceed with the principal part of his mission, which was to join the Spanish representative in a survey of the boundary between the United States and the Floridas. Spain's commissioner was soon appointed, and the work which was to occupy the surveyors for the next two years was begun. Though the Spaniards were now with Ellicott instead of against him, he was more sorely tried than ever. Mosquitoes, malaria, canebrakes, torrential rains, and incompetent helpers made his life a nightmare. Some precious pills, specially prepared by the learned Dr. Rush of Philadelphia, had fortified him from the time of his first arrival in the Natchez district; but no one had provided him with an antidote for

Indian bullets and scalping knives. Threats of violence became more and more alarming as he worked his way eastward towards the Creek and Seminole country. At last on the Apalachicola River occurred an assault that sent him flying off around the Florida peninsula to St. Augustine. After making some observations on the St. Marys he set sail for Philadelphia and safety. Even then his troubles were not at an end. Timothy Pickering, who had paid scant attention to Ellicott's warnings against Wilkinson and other Western conspirators, watched his expense accounts with an eagle eye, made some caustic remarks on their magnitude, and left a heritage of skepticism to plague Ellicott through the next administration.

CHAPTER IV

The Indian Country

I

Several stipulations in the treaty of San Lorenzo related to the Indian country. It provided that the southern boundary of the United States should run along the thirty-first parallel from the Mississippi to the Apalachicola; prohibited either power from entering into any treaty, except of friendship, with the Indians inhabiting the territory of the other; required each power to restrain its Indians from attacking the Indians or the citizens or subjects of the other; and established "the most complete reciprocity" in the Indian trade. These provisions destroyed at a single stroke the system so painstakingly built up by the officials of Louisiana and Florida, under the direction of the court, since 1783. They gave the United States unquestioned jurisdiction over nine tenths of the Southern Indians, nullified a whole flock of treaties of alliance and commerce concluded on behalf of Spain with those tribes, and threatened with ruin the trading firm of Panton, Leslie and Company, which had been the main avenue of Spanish approach to the Indians for a decade past.

The four principal tribes inhabiting the region which Spain had formerly claimed but was now obligated to relinquish were the Creek, Cherokee, Choctaw, and Chickasaw. At the end of the eighteenth century their total population was probably in the neighborhood of 60,000, of whom 13,000 were warriors.[1] While all of the tribes engaged extensively in hunting, they had all passed out of the nomadic stage and were living in fixed villages and tilling cornfields. The most advanced in civilization were the Cherokee, an offshoot of the Iroquoian group, who dwelt mainly along the streams that came tumbling down out of the Smoky Mountains to the Tennessee River. Far to the westward, in the present western Tennessee and northern Mississippi, lived the Chickasaw, the smallest of the tribes and also the friendliest towards the Americans. South of them were the villages of the Choctaw, whose five thousand warriors had the reputation of being too proud to fight and too lazy to hunt.

The storm center of the Spanish-American frontier lay in the Creek country west of Georgia. These Indians were at least as numerous [2] as the Choctaw and far more warlike, and they were the only Southern tribe which was in close and constant contact with both Spaniards and Americans. Courted by the traders and governments of both powers and never badly beaten in war by their white neighbors—as the Cherokee had been during the Revolution—they seem to have had an exaggerated sense of their own importance. Their loose tribal organization made the preservation of order difficult, for the upper Creeks (on the Coosa and Talapoosa Rivers), the lower Creeks (on the Chattahoochee and the Flint) and the Seminoles (in Florida) were bound together by the most tenuous ties. Many British and French adventurers lived among them and helped to keep them in constant turmoil, and their proximity to the Atlantic and Gulf coasts gave foreign interlopers comparatively easy access to them. Described as a "proud, haughty, lying, spoiled, untoward race" by Benjamin Hawkins,[3] who knew something of Indians, they had long been and were long to remain the chief obstacle to the extension of white settlement in the Old Southwest.

Already these tribes were alarmed by the iron ring of settlement closing around them. Through the only remaining gap they were escaping for an annual hunt across the Mississippi, but this only forged more securely the chain of servitude to the conquering race. The coming of the white man had not only deprived the Indian of his lands; it had also destroyed his economy, for it turned him back from agriculture to hunting, and at the same time induced him to annihilate the game which was once more his chief means of livelihood. In short the Indian was undone by firearms and the fur trade as well as by whisky, smallpox, and warfare. By the end of the eighteenth century the Southern tribes were almost as dependent upon oversea trade as were the Louisiana creoles. Furs and skins, their chief product, were sold in a world market, and in return they received from the white man the goods that had become most essential to them. Blankets, guns, knives, tomahawks, razors, and mirrors, as well as tobacco, salt, whisky, and even corn and flour, were bartered to the Indians in return for the skins of deer, beaver, wolf, and bear. The very war paint with which a Cherokee brave adorned himself, before using his English mirror and his English tomahawk, was bought from white traders who in turn got it from Europe.

The economic dependence of the Southern tribes upon their white neighbors only stimulated the zeal with which they were courted by the United States and Spain. The Indian trade could not last long in its existing form, for it was carried on with all the improvident greed characteristic of the frontier, with the result that deer, the Southern staple, were rapidly disappearing; but while it lasted it was a bonanza. Governments wrangled over it, while rival traders cut each other's throats and precipitated devastating wars for control of it.[4] More than this, the friendship and alliance of the tribes could be controlled through trade. The hand that sold the whisky ruled the tomahawk. The traders were often the only and generally the most trusted sources of information and advice in the remote Indian villages, and many of them increased their influence by marrying Indian women. Judicious distributions of presents among the chiefs, the timely increase or diminution of the supply of goods, manipulation of prices—all these means were used by American and Spanish agents to bend the Indian to their will.

As matters stood, the Indian's good will was of considerable consequence to both Spaniards and Americans. What the latter sought in this period was usually a cession of land, though filibustering schemes were sometimes involved, as in the Blount conspiracy of 1797. What the Spaniards desired was to create a buffer Indian state which would hold the Americans at bay. For this purpose the thirteen thousand warriors of the Southern tribes possessed some significance.[5] They outnumbered the Franco-American force that had humbled Cornwallis's army at Yorktown; they were four times as numerous as the whole United States army in 1795, and eight times as numerous as the Spanish troops in Louisiana and West Florida. If they could only be welded into a coherent, manageable unit, Spain would have at its disposal the most formidable military force in North America. So at least thought Governor Carondelet, who strove manfully to whip them into shape. He even believed the Indians better fighters, man for man, than the Americans and dreamed of taking the offensive with his sepoys and driving the shiftless frontiersmen back across the Appalachians; but the Spanish court, less optimistic, cut him down in mid flight with the treaty of San Lorenzo.

II

Carondelet, who was Governor of Louisiana and West Florida when that treaty was signed, and Gayoso, who succeeded him in 1797, feared that its stipulations in regard to the Indians and the border posts would prove fatal to Spanish interests in North America. William Panton, the fighting head of the firm which bore his name, might use his great influence to turn the Indians against the power that had just dealt his business a staggering blow. The Indians themselves had a grievance in the surrender of the border posts which Spain had built on their soil for the ostensible purpose of protecting them against encroachments by the people and government of the United States.[6] Above all, Carondelet and Gayoso were apprehensive that the Americans would make the most of the opportunities which the treaty afforded them for aggressive action in the Southwest, whether by worming their way into the Indians' friendship through control of their trade and then inciting them to lay waste the Floridas and Louisiana, or by annihilating the border tribes in order to clear the way for the conquest of those provinces.[7]

Since the Spaniards did not have the least faith in the justice or humanity of the American people, their only hope seemed to lie in conciliating the injured Panton so that they might retain the support of his house and its far-flung agencies. His good will was well worth a sacrifice. Though Spanish agents appointed by the governor were maintained in all the Southern tribes, these agents could accomplish little or nothing without Panton's coöperation. Since 1785 his company had got control of the whole Indian trade of the two Floridas and had driven out most of its competitors among the Southern Indians. Its sphere of influence had been extended northward as far as the Chickamauga towns of the mountain-dwelling Cherokee and westward to Chickasaw Bluffs on the Mississippi, where it was in a position to tap the fur trade west of the river.[8]

The firm's resources were so extensive and its business was so highly integrated that no private company could compete with it in the southern field. With the aid of its correspondents in England, Strachan, McKenzie, and Company, it conducted every operation on its own account. It bought trading goods in London, shipped them to Florida in its own vessels (two schooners of some 230 tons each and a brigantine of 170 tons), stored them in its own warehouses until its own traders could take them among the Indians to be bartered for skins and furs; cured and packed these with its own force of seventy laborers and thirty slaves and shipped them to London—again in its own vessels. Besides this, it owned salt works at New Providence in the Bahamas, engaged in the slave trade, exported lumber and cattle to the West Indies, sent an occasional ship to

Campeche for logwood, bought and sold real estate in Florida, supplied Spanish garrisons with beef, and carried on a thinly veiled contraband trade with the white inhabitants of the Floridas.

All this was made possible by the extraordinary privileges showered upon it by the Spanish court. Among these were exemption from import and export duties in Florida, and permission for the members of the company to retain their British nationality and to trade direct with Nassau and London. No less important was the indulgence shown by the colonial officials. Their course may have been influenced by bribes or gifts, as for instance the "complete outfit of English furniture of the latest fashion" said to have been presented by the company to the Governor of East Florida; but the conduct of the court itself must be explained by its conviction that only through the British firm would it be possible for Spain to retain the friendship of the Southern Indians and check the oncoming Americans.[9]

When Panton was able to give coherent expression to his rage at the terms of the treaty of San Lorenzo, he wrote Governor Carondelet as follows: "In respect to ourselves it seems as if we are entirely abandoned to the Mercy of the Americans, whom, by acting our part honorably to this [*i.e.,* the Spanish] Government, we have highly exasperated; & which You very well know. . . . At this present moment we have upwards of Two hundred thousand Dollars due to us in the four Nations of Creeks, Cherokees, Chickesaws and Chactaws, the greatest part of which will be sacrificed. . . . I beg therefore to be favoured with Your Sentiments on this subject, for if we have not positive assurance on this point we have no other alternative & must either submit to absolute ruin *or bow our knees to those whom we have much offended & endeavour to soften their resentment in the best manner we Can.*" [10]

This was plain speech from a man who, though Spain might crush him, could involve the Spanish Floridas and Louisiana in his ruin. There can be no doubt that Panton's warnings were one of the chief reasons for Carondelet's determined effort to dissuade his government from executing the treaty, and for his decision and that of his successor, Gayoso, to maintain Indian relations on the same footing as formerly, notwithstanding the treaty and even the explicit orders of the court directing exact compliance with its terms.[11] It was in this spirit that Carondelet ordered his French-born agent among the

Choctaw to inform them that, though it was necessary to evacuate Fort Confederation, Spain would destroy the fortifications and return the ceded land to the Indians, and that "s'ils [*i.e.,* les Indiens] se comportent bien avec nous, nous serons toujours leurs amis et les recevrons avec plaisir, et que *la ligne qui va se tirer ne regarde que les hommes blancs, et n'oblige en rien les hommes rouges.*" [12]

Gayoso was still paying the accustomed salaries to Indian agents and making the accustomed presents to the Indians themselves at the end of 1797. Even the Bloody Fellow, a chief of the remote Cherokee, was given a cordial reception when he visited New Orleans in November of that year. Lodged at Spanish expense at M. Bernard Coquet's tavern during his visit, he was given his passage back to Pensacola and was provided with a generous present for himself and his escort of twenty-five chiefs, warriors, and squaws. The present included such items as two suits of fine red cloth with silver braid, two blue redingotes, four hats, twenty-six blankets, six guns with powder and ball, twelve long knives, eleven razors, eleven mirrors, two pounds of vermilion; coffee, salt, and tobacco; a saddle and bridle; a copper kettle weighing thirteen and one-half pounds, and sixty needles.[13]

It was, however, not the Indians but Panton's firm that benefited most by this policy. Though he and his partners had retained their British nationality and, according to their agreement with Spain, were to liquidate their affairs and withdraw from Florida within a year after the outbreak of hostilities between the two powers, they continued to do business as usual throughout the Anglo-Spanish war from 1796 to 1802.[14] They not only retained all their former rights but were treated with the greatest delicacy and the utmost consideration during those troublous times, enjoying the privilege of carrying on their trade under the American flag or any other that could sail the seas in safety.

III

Fortunately for Panton and his Spanish patrons, it turned out that they had miscalculated the aggressiveness and singlemindedness of the American people and their government. The miscalculation was most evident in the case of government-conducted trade with the Indians, at the first rumor of which, in 1794, Panton had said it was time for him to withdraw from the business. Private competition he did not fear, but the United States government, trading without a view to profit and supported by the resources of the Union, would be too much for him.

At first it appeared that his fears were fully justified. In 1795, Congress, responding to the urgent advice of President Washington, appropriated $50,000 for the purchase of goods to be sold to the Indians at cost. In 1796, after the ratification of the treaty of San Lorenzo, an additional sum of $150,000 was provided for that purpose. Since, despite the treaty of Greenville (1795), peace had not yet been fully established on the Northern frontier, the first experiment with the new system was made in the South and government trading posts or "factories" were established at Colerain on the St. Marys for the Creek country and at Tellico Blockhouse on the Cherokee frontier in East Tennessee. This concentration of activity in the field of his own operations might well have alarmed Panton, but the experiment was conducted with so little energy by the American government and was so bitterly opposed by the frontiersmen that as late as 1801 little progress had been made. By that date only $90,000 (less than half the sum appropriated) had been utilized; and since the government located the factories on the outer fringe of the Indian country and required the Indians to come to them, instead of sending its agents among the tribes as did the enterprising Panton, the trade situation was changed but little among the Cherokee and Creeks, and not at all among the Chickasaw and Choctaw.[15] Even in the Creek country Panton, Leslie and Company still had many traders actively engaged in their interest at the end of the century.[16] So little attention did the federal administration pay to Southern Indian affairs that repeated representations from Benjamin Hawkins, its principal agent in that region, failed to obtain orders even for the renewal of the traders' licenses.

The government's neglect of an experiment which was supported by weighty arguments and the high authority of George Washington may be accounted for by its preoccupation with more important matters, such as the controversy with France, or by Federalist indifference to the Republican Southwest, or perhaps by unwillingness to prosecute too zealously a measure detested by most of the frontiersmen. Many of the latter were engaged in the trade, and they resented the competition of the federal government quite as much as did Panton and the Spaniards. It was this feeling which provoked John Sevier to denounce as "infamous" an act of Congress for regulating the Indian trade and to declare that even the Indians themselves would despise the government for taking up peddling.[17]

When the election of 1800 brought the Republicans to power, the frontiersmen had an opportunity to give effective expression to their disapproval of the factory system. One of their spokesmen, W. C. C. Claiborne of Tennessee, reported as chairman of a committee of the House of Representatives that, while the system might be made to produce some benefits and hence should be continued for some time as an experimental measure, the results did not warrant "any extension or increase of the capital stock." [18] The victory of the Republicans also softened the Westerners' resentment by giving them a share in the business of supplying the trading posts. Writing to an agent on June 5, 1802, in regard to the purchase of forty thousand dollars' worth of goods for the Indians, the Secretary of War said: "Colonel Cocke a member of the U. States Senate from Tennessee will contract with you to furnish Axes, Hoes, &ca, and every article of Iron or Steel which can be manufactured in that Country [i.e., Tennessee], and which will be wanted in that quarter. . . ." Accordingly Senator Cocke soon made a shipment of one hundred axes, one hundred hoes, and other implements from his iron works to the government agent among the Cherokee.[19]

So firmly entrenched was Panton's company that only the most strenuous efforts on the part of the United States government would have driven it out of the Southern Indian trade. The capital provided by the acts of 1795 and 1796 would hardly have proved adequate, even if it had all been employed immediately and exclusively in that region. The government would have had to build up a trade organization equal to the one which Panton had perfected in the course of a generation. Panton also had an advantage in the purchase of goods for the trade. Both obtained their supplies from London, but the American government bought at second hand from American merchants, who, besides their profit, added to the prime cost the duties paid upon importation in the United States; whereas Panton bought direct from London and had no duties to pay in the ports of Florida. Finally, he enjoyed superior transportation facilities, for he could make more extensive use of watercourses, and his seaports were closer to the Indian country than were those of the United States. Only by selling below cost and engaging in operations more extensive than Congress was willing to authorize could the government have eliminated Panton's company.

President Washington apparently desired to eliminate it by such means, but Congress willed otherwise. Sectional antagonism and personal interest, dignified by the principle of keeping the government out of business, reduced the President's plan to a petty, half-hearted experiment which caused hardly a ripple on the surface of Panton's operations; the depredations of privateers and freebooters were far more costly to him during this period. Ten years after the treaty of San Lorenzo was signed, his successors still valued the business at $400,000, which was the valuation that Panton himself had put upon it in 1794.

Nor did the treaty of San Lorenzo unleash the forces of aggression in the United States that the defenders of Spanish interests in Louisiana and Florida had apprehended. The Southern Indians were neither assailed by the Americans nor instigated by them to devastate the Spanish border. Whatever adventurers and filibusters may have done, neither the federal government—except for the abortive mission of John McKee, which will be discussed in a later chapter—nor responsible frontiersmen tried to make such use of the opportunities afforded by the treaty. Considerations of economy and self-interest laid a restraining hand upon both government and pioneers. Perhaps the principal cause of their moderation was that just at that juncture the Americans did not feel the pinch of land-hunger. The cessions extorted from the Indians during the American Revolution and by a series of treaties from 1783 to 1795 were more than sufficient to absorb the westward migration of the period. The problem at the end of the century was not to get more lands but to find settlers for the lands already available.

We may let that representative frontiersmen, John Sevier, speak for the West in the closing years of the century. During the Revolution and for some years thereafter, he had been a ruthless harrier of the Indians and a land-grabber of the first order; but by 1796, when he had accumulated more than sixty thousand acres of land in Tennessee and was Governor of the State, he had become an apostle to peace. "Only view the Great emigration into this state," he wrote to a friend in that year, "and you will readily perceive that peace is to be preferred to every other advantage that at this time could attend us." [20] Throughout his six terms as Governor he strove to prevent the constant friction on the border from bursting into flame. The Indians must go, but he was not in such a hurry to expel them as he had once been; and diplomacy now seemed to him a better means of eviction than armed force.[21] Whisky for the warriors, bribes for the chiefs and interpreters, and relentless pressure upon all would be cheaper and, in the long run, less harmful to the white community itself, especially to those influential gentlemen in the community who, like Sevier, had extensive tracts of land for sale.

Aside from its unimpressive experiment with the factory system, the United States government made only one noteworthy effort to utilize the control of the Southern Indians which it had obtained through the treaty of San Lorenzo. Benjamin Hawkins, formerly United States Senator from North Carolina, was appointed chief agent of the United States among the Southern Indians,[22] with the Creek country as his principal field of operations and the promotion of the "arts of civilization" as one of his chief duties. This fine phrase really meant that the Indians were to be converted to an agricultural economy supplemented by domestic manufactures, in place of the existing economy of hunting supplemented by agriculture. Thus the area necessary for their support would be materially reduced and the way paved for further cessions of land as they might be needed by the whites.

Thanks to the exertions of Colonel Hawkins and his coadjutors, President Jefferson was able to report in 1801 that "the continued efforts to introduce among [our Indian neighbors] the implements and the practice of husbandry, and the household arts, have not been without success."[23] Among Hawkins's Creek charges, it appeared, the raising of live stock was "more relished . . . than any part of the plan devised for their civilization," despite the fact that the horses were generally liable to "a distemper, called here the yellow water," and that the hogs often fell victims to the numerous "wolves, tigers and wild cats." In agriculture, "the improvements . . . are slowly progressive." Fifty of the seventy ploughs furnished by the Secretary of War were already in use; and cotton, fruit trees, and cereals were under cultivation. Even the household arts were beginning to triumph over the opposition of the chiefs, who at first feared "that, if their women could clothe and feed themselves by their own exertions they would become independent of the degraded state of connexion between them," but were reconciled to the new order when they saw that "the link is more firm in proportion, as the women are more useful, and occupied in domestic concerns." These domestic concerns were spinning, weaving, and the manufacture of hickory nut and black-jack acorn oil, "coarse earthen pots and pans, garters, ornamented with beads, basket sifters, and fans, ingeniously made, of split cane, and moccasins." Hogs, ploughs, black-jack acorn oil —if only Baron Carondelet could have read this report of the use the Americans had made of the opportunities for aggression afforded them by the treaty of San Lorenzo! But he would probably not have believed his eyes. Ever intriguing and ever suspecting intrigue, he would doubtless have seen in it a cipher message concealing sinister designs against the Spanish dominions in North America. And in a long-time view he would not have been far wrong.

A temporary relaxation of American pressure upon the Southern Indians, together with prudent concessions by Spain to Panton, Leslie and Company, saved Louisiana and Florida from the worst consequences that their governors had expected to flow from the treaty of 1795. Five years after its conclusion, the Governor of Louisiana was able to say with some justice that the Choctaw, Chickasaw, and Creeks still constituted a barrier against American aggression. That did not mean, however, that Spain had effective control over the border tribes. Down to the period of the Louisiana Purchase, the Southern Indian country remained a no-man's land where free-lance adventurers might create chaos overnight.

CHAPTER V

THE OPENING OF THE MISSISSIPPI

I

The commerce of the Mississippi Valley was completely revolutionized in the two decades between the American Revolution and the Louisiana Purchase. The changes that came with the steamboat age were hardly more profound than those which occurred in this period. The volume of commerce increased many times over, its character was radically altered, and the international implications of the readjustment were far-reaching. The explanation lies partly in the increasing population of the valley and partly in revolutions, political and economic, among peoples who seldom gave the Mississippi a thought and hardly even knew of its existence. It had long since been said that sovereignty over the region would be settled on the battlefields of Europe. It could now be said with equal truth that its prosperity was determined in the international market.

The best-known incident of this commercial revolution is the treaty of San Lorenzo, which gave the citizens of the United States the right of free navigation of the Mississippi River and a place of deposit at New Orleans. Considered as a diplomatic event, the treaty was spectacular; but read in the context of economic history it is less striking. With the consent of the Spaniards, American citizens were already using the Mississippi from the Illinois country to the Gulf before the treaty was signed; and it had hardly been executed when the Americans obtained from the officials of Louisiana another concession comparable in importance to those granted by the treaty. The economic drift in the Mississippi Valley was unmistakable; its probable consequences were not obscure, and by the end of the century the Spanish court saw that the maintenance of even a semblance of its traditional system in Louisiana was impossible.

II

Towards the close of the American Revolution, Spain tried to regulate the commerce of the Mississippi Valley by decree. In 1782 the King issued a cedula permitting a direct though limited trade to be carried on between New Orleans and Pensacola, on the one hand, and France and the French West Indies, on the other. The cedula was to run for a period of ten years, beginning in 1783, and it was intended to provide temporarily for the needs of Louisiana and West Florida until Spain itself could furnish the goods and ships necessary to supply them. Then their commercial regulations would be altered to conform to the principle of monopoly which prevailed in the rest of the empire.[1] Though limited to so brief a period, the measure was the most liberal in the history of Spanish colonial policy; but if the colonists took it as a promise of further favors they were sorely disappointed, for in 1784 Spain closed the Mississippi River to all foreign nations. The order was aimed against British and American commerce, but it injured the Louisianians as well, for they probably lost more by this restriction than they gained by the cedula of 1782.

Though the American frontiersmen in the Ohio Valley had flour to sell and though New Orleans needed flour, the exclusion was maintained for several years not only because it was in accordance with the monopolistic principle which governed Spanish policy but also because the authorities at New Orleans and Madrid hoped to destroy the American settlements in the West by closing the Mississippi, which was almost the only outlet for their produce. The exceptions to the rule against the use of the Mississippi by citizens of the United States were not important in either number or character. In 1785 one Richard Brashears of Pittsburgh obtained permission to bring forty-two barrels of flour to Natchez and sell them there; but the permission was granted only after he had declared that he was a Roman Catholic and taken an oath of allegiance to Spain.[2] Other American adventurers down the river who did not agree with Brashears that the Louisiana market was well worth a mass might consider themselves fortunate to escape from the Spanish officials with the loss of their cargoes.

The oversea commerce of Louisiana also was hampered by this system. The bulk of the colony's imports came from France. Its exports, for which there was no sale in Spain, went mainly to France and French St. Domingue in the West Indies; and the merchants of New Orleans were mere agents of French houses in Bordeaux, Havre, and Rouen, which were deterred by the insecurity of their economic privileges from giving remote Louisiana the capital and enterprise necessary for its development. As early as 1780 the Intendant of the province, Martín Navarro, warned his government that France alone would be unable to supply the wants of Louisiana; and events soon verified his prediction.

The principal export items of Louisiana at this time were tobacco, indigo, furs and skins, and lumber. Such tobacco as was not bought by the King had no regular market, for it could not be sold in either Spain or France, the only countries with which the colony could trade. Louisiana indigo suffered from competition with superior varieties produced in other Spanish and French colonies and was moreover not well adapted to the soil and climate of Louisiana. Furs from Florida could be sold in the best European market—the English —by virtue of the extraordinary privileges which Spain had granted Panton, Leslie and Company; but furs from Louisiana, having no sale whatever in Spain, were confined to the inferior French market, with the result that the fur trade of upper Louisiana fell more and more into the hands of British traders from Canada. Lumber and staves, which were sold in the West Indies, were gradually supplanted by the products of the United States, whose more extensive shipping and credit facilities made the competition unequal. Such hardships are common in all infant colonies before the trial-and-error method has had time to determine the kind of production best suited to their particular circumstances; but in Louisiana the process of trial and error was made much more painful by a system which limited the field of experimentation and discouraged the immigration of the necessary capital and labor.

Louisiana was also at a disadvantage with respect to importations. Here too the Spanish regulations were not entirely to blame. The creoles were a pleasure-loving people, with little of that ascetic devotion to business which was becoming characteristic of their northern neighbors. Instead of reinvesting their profits, they bought luxuries. According to a report made by Intendant Navarro in 1788, approximately one third of the total imports into Louisiana consisted of wines and liquors. With respect to the remainder, however, it was clear that the colonists were victimized by the system imposed upon them. Another third of their imports consisted of manufactured goods; and, since these came almost exclusively from France, monopoly prices were charged, to the great injury of the colony. The remaining third consisted of flour, for lower Louisiana was already a region of plantations worked by slave labor and producing staple crops for exportation. Some, but not all, of the planters raised their own food-stuffs, and the demand at New Orleans kept pace with the city's growing population. A part of the flour came from Vera Cruz, and there were even instances of shipments from France itself; but most of it came, by a devious and expensive route, from the United States, especially from Philadelphia. Since Spain prohibited the direct importation of American flour, it was usually brought by way of the French West Indies, where both Louisianians and Americans were permitted to trade.[3] The Louisiana officials protested on behalf of the colony that, if American flour was to be used, it might as well be brought direct from Philadelphia or the new mills on the Ohio at a more moderate cost; but their reasoning lost its force in crossing the Atlantic. Nothing but sheer necessity finally induced the Spanish court to let the colonists buy their American flour from the Americans.

For the first decade after the close of the American Revolution, the commerce of Louisiana limped along as best it could, under a system which seemed to many Spaniards as excessively generous as it seemed to the colonists hopelessly unenlightened and illiberal. During this period the annual exports of the province were valued at about seven hundred thousand dollars; the imports, at slightly over one million dollars. The unfavorable balance was apparently made up by the illegal exportation of specie, which was provided by the government's annual subsidy (540,000 pesos) and until 1790 by the appropriation for purchases of tobacco on the royal account (200,000 pesos). Most of this sum eventually found its way into the hands of the merchants, and they contrived to evade the sleepy watch-dogs of the treasury whose business it was to prevent the exportation of gold and silver.[4]

According to the customs records of New Orleans, 113 ships sailed from that port in 1786, the first full year in which records were kept.[5] This number indicates the amazing increase that had taken place in the colony's trade since the period of French rule, when six ships a year sufficed for the oversea commerce of New Orleans. The expansion had, however, occurred mainly between 1763 and 1778, when British ships, under cover of the right of navigating the Mississippi, had built up an extensive smuggling trade with the creoles—a trade which the Spanish colonial officials admitted their inability to suppress. If the shipping records are to be trusted, there was no further growth after 1786 until the closing years of the century. The number of sailings from New Orleans fell to 108 in 1787, and to 98 in 1789, probably because of the world-wide economic depression of those years. By 1791 a slight recovery had set in, and in both 1792 and 1793 the number of sailings stood at 116. Then the outbreak of war between Spain and France deprived Louisiana of its chief commercial support, with results that will be noticed in another place.

III

The first breach in the commercial system so hopefully imposed upon the Mississippi Valley by Spain was a concession to the Western Americans. When, towards the end of his life, James Wilkinson recapitulated his services to humanity, he boasted two achievements: one, that he had introduced window-glass into Kentucky; the other, that he had opened the Mississippi River to American commerce.[6] Though there is some hyperbole in the latter claim, there is less than one usually finds in his effusions. His well-known descent to New Orleans in 1787 and the memoir which he addressed to the Spanish officials in that year did in fact play an important part in persuading the Spanish court to tolerate American commerce on the Mississippi under certain restrictions. A royal order of December 1, 1788, decreed that the Western Americans might bring their produce down to New Orleans and sell it, subject to an import duty of fifteen per cent, which would be reduced to six per cent in certain cases in order to attach influential Westerners to Spain. Upon the further payment of the usual six per cent export duty, the produce might then be shipped to any of the ports with which New Orleans was permitted to trade.[7]

Under this order, issued seven years before the conclusion of the treaty of San Lorenzo, the Mississippi was partly opened to the Western Americans. The gate was at least ajar, and Western produce could now reach the West Indies and Europe, if there were no market in New Orleans itself. The duties imposed were not excessively burdensome, for they were computed on the basis of fixed valuations which were quite moderate.[8] Flour, for instance, which usually sold at from five to eight dollars a barrel in New Orleans, was valued at four dollars in the Louisiana tariff, so that in practice the duty amounted to considerably less than the percentage nominally exacted. The burden was again lightened in 1793, when Governor Carondelet abolished the fifteen per cent duty and permitted all Western Americans, regardless of their relations with Wilkinson and the "Spanish" party, to bring in their produce at the preferential six per cent rate. Slowly but surely the river trade increased. The royal order of 1788 reached the American West too late the following year for exporters to make their preparations and ride the spring floods down to Natchez and New Orleans; but by the end of December, 1789, an immigrant was writing home from western Pennsylvania: "The Mississippi trade is open at this time and all the wheat, whisky, bacon, etc., buying up by those concerned in it." [9] In the course of the following year, eighteen venturesome frontiersmen reached New Orleans with flatboats carrying cargoes of beef, tobacco, pork, flour, hemp, lard, and mill wheels.[10] Flour, which was soon to be the largest item, was represented this first year by only 319 barrels. Most of the adventurers brought little but tobacco, importing in all some 277,000 pounds. If they were lucky enough to have a letter of recommendation from James Wilkinson which would induce the authorities to buy their tobacco, they received approximately $9.50 per hundredweight for a commodity that had cost them only $2.00 per hundredweight in Kentucky. Just at this juncture, however, the Governor-Intendant of Louisiana was instructed to make a drastic reduction in his purchases of tobacco; and as a result, the next year's shipments from the American West were much smaller. In 1791, only three expeditions came down to New Orleans and they brought only one tenth as much tobacco as had been imported the preceding year. In 1792 eleven expeditions arrived with about the same quantity of tobacco as in 1791 and with many miscellaneous articles, including 2,500 pounds of cotton.

As milling methods improved, flour became the staple article of export from the Ohio Valley. As against 319 barrels in 1790, 687 barrels were brought to New Orleans in 1791, 846 in 1792, and some 3,200 in 1793 and 5,400 in 1794. Since most of the river craft were flatboats, and since at that time the average capacity of flatboats was probably not over two hundred and fifty barrels of flour, it must have required about twenty or twenty-five boats to hold the flour brought to New Orleans in 1794. As the total number of all craft arriving from the West in that year was only forty-six, it appears that approximately half of their cargo space was filled with flour. Substantially the same ratio was maintained until the end of the century, when cotton began to pour down in large quantities from Natchez.

In 1793 the Spanish government made an important change in the regulations concerning the oversea commerce of Louisiana and the

Floridas.[11] The cedula of 1782, though limited to ten years' duration, had almost from the start been under fire from conservatives in Spain, who attacked the commercial liberalism of Floridablanca in a spirit that reminds one of the simultaneous assaults of French neo-mercantilists upon the liberal measures of Turgot and Vergennes. As it happened, war with France broke out in 1793, so that the cedula, with its toleration of trade between Louisiana and France, could not have been renewed in any case; but the conservatives gained little by the change. The bald fact was that Spain was utterly unable to provide either ships, goods, or markets for the commerce of its border colonies in North America, which again had to be thrown open to foreigners. The new order (dated June 9, 1793) permitted Spanish subjects of Louisiana and Florida, as well as of Spain itself, to trade between New Orleans, Pensacola, and St. Augustine and all neutral and friendly nations with which Spain had treaties of commerce. The United States, not falling within this category, was excluded from trade with the border colonies; and it is probable that Gardoqui, who drafted the order, hoped that the exclusion would force the American government to moderate its claims to the free navigation of the Mississippi and the thirty-first parallel. The prohibition was nevertheless evaded. When American ships, masquerading as Spaniards or Englishmen, ventured up the river, they found that the colonial officials were not hypercritical of the disguise. The war had created such a dearth of shipping that, as the Governor frankly told the court in 1794, the subterfuge must be tolerated or Louisiana would face utter ruin.[12]

These facts make it clear that the foundations of American commerce on the Mississippi were laid before the negotiation of the treaty of San Lorenzo. American flour was now brought direct from mills on the Ohio to Louisiana; American ships now sailed between New Orleans and Philadelphia. This was a source of gratification to all concerned, except the Spanish court; but no one was satisfied. The Americans resented the exaction of duties and the precarious tenure of their privileges, while the creoles felt that the restrictions still imposed upon their commerce were the only obstacle to an era of prosperity.

IV

The treaty of San Lorenzo gave added impulse to the commerce of Louisiana as well as to the infant export trade from the American

West to New Orleans and, through New Orleans, to the West Indies, the Atlantic States and Europe. The treaty concessions did not become effective simultaneously, for the first American ship that claimed the treaty right of navigation entered the Mississippi from the Gulf in December, 1796, while the deposit at New Orleans was not established until April, 1798. Nor did the Spanish officials of Louisiana interpret either the right or the privilege as liberally as the Americans thought the phraseology of the treaty gave them a right to expect.

The first ship to take advantage of the right of free navigation was the *Prudent,* Captain Nathaniel Penfield, which came from New York with a cargo of merchandise and provisions.[13] When it arrived at the Balize, a Spanish post at the mouth of the Mississippi, the unprecedented character of the case brought on a controversy between the Governor and the acting Intendant of Louisiana which lasted from December 23 to January 5 and ended only after the two officials had exchanged politely insulting notes totaling several thousand words. The acting Intendant was Juan Ventura Morales, of whom we have heard something already and shall hear still more. He was one of those bureaucrats who seek to demonstrate their zeal by blackening the reputations of their colleagues. The Governor was Baron Carondelet, who was probably quite as honest as Morales and was certainly far less offensive in his rectitude. At any rate he was not one to be frightened by veiled threats from the tattling Intendant. He may rather have welcomed the opportunity to grapple with his associate and humble him, for he himself had recently been removed from the intendancy, which in the early part of his administration was united with the governorship, and he was still smarting from the humiliation.

The cause of the present controversy was a curious one. When the *Prudent* arrived at the Balize, the Spanish officer in charge found himself with two sets of instructions applicable to the case. He had been ordered by the Governor to permit any American ship to proceed without formality of any kind to Fort Plaquemine, which was situated some distance further up the river; but he had been ordered by the Intendant to detain any such vessel until that official (who resided one hundred miles away at New Orleans) could be consulted. Thrown into confusion by this conflict of authority, the poor underling at the Balize failed to carry out either instruction. After disobeying the Governor's orders by visiting the ship, examining its papers and sealing them, and putting a guard on board, he then violated Morales's orders by permitting the *Prudent* to proceed up-stream to Plaquemine and New Orleans.

Arrived at the capital, Captain Penfield asked Morales for permission to land his cargo (December 23, 1796). Since a political question—the interpretation of the treaty of San Lorenzo—was involved, Morales had to consult Carondelet; and the controversy was on. Morales expressed his surprise that Carondelet had interfered with the affairs of the intendancy by giving orders to the official at the Balize; maintained that the Americans would not be entitled to the privileges of navigation and deposit until the treaty stipulations regarding the marking of the southern boundary and the evacuation of the border posts had been carried out; and declared that even then the King's interests should be protected by placing on board every American vessel an official of the intendancy to prevent smuggling while the ship sailed up the river from its mouth to New Orleans. Carondelet promptly replied that nothing in the treaty justified the contention that the demarcation of limits must precede the enjoyment of the American rights of navigation and deposit. Those rights, he said, became effective as soon as the treaty was ratified; and he concluded with the warning that he would not permit the slightest infraction of them.

Since the Governor had the authority to overrule the Intendant, Morales was forced to yield. The result was the adoption of regulations which controlled the use of the river by the Americans for the rest of the Spanish period in Louisiana. On arriving at the Balize, the American captain must show his passport and ship's papers in order to establish the nationality of his ship. The Spanish official who inspected them would then warn him that he must stop again at Fort Plaquemine to repeat the formality, that his cargo must be unloaded at New Orleans where it could be stored pending trans-shipment in river craft to American territory, and that if he were caught trading with Spanish subjects his vessel and cargo would be confiscated. If the American captain requested it, a pilot would be furnished to bring him up the river to New Orleans; but a Spanish guard was not to be placed on board if any objection were raised. Without further formalities the ship might then proceed to Fort Plaquemine for the second inspection of passport and papers, and thence to New Orleans, where officials of the intendancy were to supervise the unloading of the cargo.

Subsequently other minor but vexatious restrictions were imposed upon the Americans. They were prohibited from entering or leaving the mouth of the Mississippi without the services of a Spanish pilot; and so many vessels came to grief at the hands of the pilot that the Americans suspected him of deliberately wrecking them under orders from his government.[14] From the thirty-first parallel to the mouth of the Mississippi, where both banks of the river were Spanish territory, the Americans were permitted to take soundings in order to avoid shipwreck, but not to record them.[15] And all Americans passing through New Orleans were required to obtain a Spanish passport, for which the fee was one dollar and a half.[16]

This cumbersome system was the result partly of Spanish fear of smuggling, and partly of jealousy between Governor and Intendant. The latter felt that control of all river traffic properly fell within his province; the former, that the regulations governing the exercise of a treaty right were his affair. Hence it was that American ships had to stop first at the Balize, which was under the authority of the Intendant, and then at Plaquemine, which was under that of the Governor. There was, however, excellent reason for the imposition of some regulations upon American shipping. Experience had shown, when the British exercised the right of free navigation from 1763 to 1778, that there were endless possibilities of smuggling along a river bordered with plantations, each of which had its own wharf. Furthermore, the Spaniards contended that the American right of navigation stood on an entirely different footing from the British; that, in short, it was not a right but a privilege graciously bestowed by the King of Spain, and therefore subject to such restrictions as, without essentially impairing its value, would prevent the Americans from abusing it.

Carondelet himself took this view, and his controversy with Morales involved not the principle but the mode of its application. Shortly before the *Prudent* arrived, he had received orders from the court to execute the treaty of San Lorenzo faithfully and to cultivate friendly relations with the United States. Hence his solicitude on that occasion for the treaty rights of the Americans. Even when he learned a few weeks later that Godoy had changed his mind and directed the retention of the Southwest posts, the American right of navigation was not disturbed. On the contrary, it was more scrupulously protected than ever. Determined, in case of a rupture with the United States, to push the Kentucky intrigue to a conclusion and convinced that the best way to win the Westerners' friendship was by liberal treatment of their Mississippi trade, Carondelet ordered the Intendant to let them navigate the river duty free and to treat them "with marked distinction and preference." [17]

Indeed, after the conclusion of the treaty of San Lorenzo the right of navigation was never called in question either by the Spanish court or by its colonial officials. Once open, the Mississippi was never again closed to citizens of the United States. From the time when Captain Penfield entered it in December, 1796, until American commerce on the river was made independent of Spain by the acquisition of Louisiana in December, 1803, no American was ever denied the free use of the river. On the contrary, throughout most of the period American commerce enjoyed far more extensive privileges than those guaranteed by the treaty of San Lorenzo.

v

It was quite otherwise with the privilege of deposit at New Orleans, which, unlike that of navigation and despite its importance, was most inadequately protected by the treaty. Article XXII stipulated that the deposit should be fixed at New Orleans for a period of three years, and continued: ". . . his Majesty promises either to continue this permission if he finds during that time that it is not prejudicial to the interests of Spain, or if he should not agree to continue it there, he will assign to them on another part of the banks of the Mississippi an equivalent establishment." From the American point of view, there were three serious defects in this article. It did not provide for the residence at New Orleans of an accredited agent of the United States with power to protect American interests. It did not give the United States the least shadow of a right to participate in the choice of the "equivalent establishment" which was to be designated in case of the removal of the deposit from New Orleans; on the contrary, it appeared that the King of Spain had unrestricted power to select the new place of deposit and to designate it as the equivalent of New Orleans. Finally, the Spanish text of the treaty afforded ground for the contention that the King might even suppress the deposit altogether. Just before the conclusion of the negotiation, William Short, minister of the United States in Spain, had protested to Thomas Pinckney, the envoy extraordinary who was conducting it, that the article was highly unsatisfactory, would lead to disputes between the two powers, and might entail heavy losses upon

the commerce of the United States; but Pinckney was more impresse
by the perplexities of his present negotiation than by hypothetic
problems of subsequent interpretation, and signed without more ad
The events of 1802 and 1803 fully justified Short's warning.

According to the treaty, the deposit should have been establishe
six months after ratifications were exchanged, that is, in Octobe
1796; but it was not formally opened until April, 1798. Carondelet
letters to Morales regarding the case of the *Prudent* expresse
the belief that the Americans were entitled to exercise the privileg
of deposit, as well as that of free navigation, whenever they d
manded it. Captain Penfield, however, did not demand the forme
and by the time the annual flood of produce began to arrive from tl
Ohio Valley, Carondelet had received the court's new orders direc
ing him to suspend the evacuation of the Southwest posts. Durir
the ensuing controversy, which kept Spain and the United States c
the brink of war for about a year, Governor Carondelet was so eag
to promote his separatist intrigue with Kentucky that he gave tl
Westerners every facility for their export and import trade on tl
lower Mississippi; but it does not appear that he had the depos
formally opened.

By the end of March, 1798, the controversy was terminated k
Spain's evacuation of the border posts. Thereupon Intendant Morale
after consulting his subordinates in the treasury department (Ap
12, 1798) resolved to establish the deposit and drew up the regul
tions governing its use.[18] Under these rules, American goods in trans
were permitted to enter and leave New Orleans duty free, but c
course they could not be legally sold there. Immediately upon ent
they must be placed in storage and could be withdrawn only f
re-exportation. No single warehouse was designated as a place c
deposit. The government buildings suitable for such a purpose we
already overcrowded, and, as Morales explained, the erection of ar
other warehouse was impossible "because of the invincible difficul
of having no funds." The Americans were therefore permitted
store their goods at their own expense anywhere they pleased in tl
city. So far, the transaction was like any other of a private natur
The difference lay in the formalities which were prescribed in ord
to prevent the abuse of the privilege. The treasury department w
to keep a list of all goods deposited and withdrawn, recording tl
number and mark of all articles, but boxes and packages were not
be opened for examination except in case of violent suspicion c

fraud. A customs officer must be present when deposits or withdrawals were made, and he must keep the key to one of the two locks with which every place of deposit was required to be equipped. With some minor changes, these regulations remained in effect for the next four years, for, contrary to a statement often made,[19] the deposit was not closed in 1798 or 1799, but remained open and was constantly in use until Morales closed it by his well-known proclamation of October, 1802.

The first entry in the books kept by the customs officials records the deposit of seventy bags of cotton by Daniel Clark on April 17, 1798. For more than five years thereafter the Spaniards kept a scrupulous and appallingly detailed record of the deposit.[20] In every case the entry shows the name of the owner or depositor, the number and character of the articles deposited, the date of deposit, the date of withdrawal, and the destination of the articles withdrawn. Thus Clark's first consignment of cotton was withdrawn on August 31, 1798, and was shipped to "Virginia"—probably to Alexandria or Norfolk. One of the principal merchants of New Orleans, Clark was the most frequent user of the deposit during this first year. Of the fifty-two entries appearing in the records for 1798, fifteen are in his name. His goods, like those of all the other depositors, were almost invariably sent to some port of the United States on the Atlantic seaboard, generally to New York, Philadelphia, Baltimore, or Charleston, though a few shipments were consigned to Hamburg. The principal items in the deposit list were cotton (from Natchez and Nashville), flour (from the Ohio Valley and the Illinois country), and Kentucky tobacco. There were also occasional entries of skins and furs, lead, iron, hams and bacon, salt pork and beef, specie, and even manufactured goods. Not even the roughest estimate of the value of the deposits can be ventured here. It may be remarked, however, that in 1802 some 70,000 barrels of flour passed through the deposit; and as the average price of flour at New Orleans was then about five dollars a barrel, this item alone represented a value of some $350,000.

Since exports from the American West had to obey the whims of the Mississippi, the business of the deposit was highly seasonal. The peak was reached in the four months from March to June. For instance, in 1801, 308 entries out of a total of 492 for the year occurred in those months. From July to November the movement was sluggish, accelerating gradually from December to March. The year of greatest activity in the history of the deposit was 1801. In the first year of its operation (1798), news of its opening reached the Western farmers too late for them to take advantage of the spring floods, and only 52 entries appear on the books for that year. Thereafter the number rose rapidly—to 201 in 1799, 356 in 1800, and 492 in 1801. In 1802 it fell to 425, because of the decline of American exports with the return of peace and because of the closing of the deposit in October.

VI

Even the privileges contained in the treaty of San Lorenzo did not provide all the necessary facilities for American commerce on the Mississippi, which might have limped along at a halting pace for some time to come, had not Daniel Clark, Jr., obtained another valuable concession in 1798. Clark was a molelike individual, who burrowed his way through the life of his generation in tne Southwest, leaving many surface indications of his activity, but seldom giving any sign of what the activity was all about.[21] It cannot be proved that he was a rascal, and yet one would hardly employ such terms as honor, probity, fidelity, in describing him. In 1786 he came to New Orleans and entered business with his uncle of the same name, who was a prosperous merchant and for a time handled the New Orleans end of James Wilkinson's commercial ventures. There is no evidence that the younger Clark was a party to the intrigue which Wilkinson was then carrying on with Spain; and yet he later showed an extraordinary familiarity with the details of the intrigue, revealing all that he knew and far more than he was able to prove about his former friend's villainy.[22] While his uncle of the same name was seeking Wilkinson's support in order to obtain a consular appointment for him at New Orleans, young Daniel was giving the American government a secret warning against Wilkinson's relations with Spain. In 1801 he finally obtained the desired appointment; and the following year he went to France, where preparations were being made for the occupation of Louisiana and where he had some mysterious conversations with French officials known to be hostile to the commercial privileges of the United States on the Mississippi. Failing to ingratiate himself with the new masters of Louisiana, he returned to New Orleans a bitter enemy of France; and when the province was sold to the United States, he valiantly championed American authority in the creole capital. On the whole, one gets the impression that he possessed unusual energy, intelligence, and pliability and was determined to get on in the world.

The privilege which he obtained for the United States in 1798 was that of trading with Spanish subjects at New Orleans. His betters, among them John Jay, Robert Morris, and Thomas Pinckney, had tried in vain to gain admission to Spanish colonial ports for American shipping. Where they failed, the obscure Clark succeeded. His export business gave him an interest in succeeding; and various circumstances combined to obtain for him what he desired. He possessed wealth and official connections at New Orleans, and the disorganization of maritime commerce at the time gave the Louisiana authorities ample pretext for complying with his wishes, regardless of what the Spanish court might think.

On May 1, 1798, he addressed to the Intendant a memorial on the subject of commerce.[23] To give the document more weight, he described himself as the American Vice-Consul at New Orleans. There was a certain note of independence in his action, for Spain did not permit foreign consuls to reside in any of its colonies, and the United States government had not appointed him to any such post.[24] But that was Clark's way. His memorial contained two proposals. The first of these was that American ships should be permitted to carry the produce of Louisiana from New Orleans to ports of the United States or foreign nations, paying only the six per cent export duty required even of Spanish ships; the second, that Spanish ships should be permitted to take cargoes from the American deposit, without the payment of export duties, to all ports except those of Spain and its colonies. In other words, he asked that exports from the American deposit and from Spanish Louisiana should be placed on the same footing.

In support of his first point, he asserted that the maritime war between France, Spain, and Great Britain had deprived New Orleans of the necessary supply of shipping and so had cut in half the price of rice, salt meat, cotton, hides, lumber, tar, pitch, and other products of the colony. American ships were already permitted to take out such cargoes on payment of the duty of *extranjería;* but that duty (twenty-one per cent) was so high as to be prohibitive. American captains preferred to sail from New Orleans in ballast rather than pay it. Nor was his proposal absolutely revolutionary, for, he reminded the Intendant, the free exportation of Louisiana sugar in American ships was already permitted by royal order. Clark merely asked that the principle be extended to all articles which might be legitimately exported. The granting of his second request, he continued, would confer a great benefit upon the subjects of Spain, for it would permit them to share in the carrying of American products.

While he was drafting the memorial, Clark wrote Secretary of State Pickering a letter explaining his proposals to Morales.[25] The letter is useful for purposes of comparison with the memorial to the Intendant; but it is valuable chiefly because it shows how inadequate to American needs were the treaty rights of navigation and deposit, unless they were supplemented by the privilege of trade with Louisiana. As described by Clark, the situation was as follows: In practice, the treaty rights made possible only one-way traffic for the Americans at New Orleans—the exportation of produce from the deposit; and even this traffic was hampered by lack of shipping facilities. "There is really no American shipping in Orleans to carry off the Produce deposited there in virtue of the treaty," he wrote. The explanation was simple enough. American ships might come to New Orleans either with a cargo or in ballast. If they brought cargoes, they must find a market in Spanish Louisiana, since there was comparatively little shipment of goods up stream to the American West. Yet goods imported at New Orleans in American ships were subject to a ruinous duty of twenty-one per cent. In order to escape payment of the duty, the Americans masqueraded as Spaniards; and as the Spanish officials connived at the practice for the good of Louisiana itself, the danger of detection was negligible. But what was gained with one hand was lost with the other. By assuming a Spanish disguise, the American ships forfeited the right to take American produce duty free from the deposit, with the result that the operation would now cost them duties aggregating twelve per cent. Nor could American vessels afford to come to New Orleans in ballast merely in order to take off produce from the deposit, especially since a large part of the produce consisted of light, loosely packed bags of cotton, which made a dangerous cargo.[26]

And so, according to Clark, the American rights of navigation and deposit were largely illusory. The ship-owner either had to pay import duties of twenty-one per cent if he came to New Orleans as an American; or, escaping this burden by the fiction of Spanish nationality, he had to pay twelve per cent export duties on American produce; or else, if he came in ballast, he not only got an undesirable cargo, but had to charge such high freight rates that the American producer lost all the profit on his crop. The necessity of remedying this situation was Clark's chief apology to Pickering for assuming the character of vice-consul.

Clark's memorial may not have been inspired by the colonial officials, but it was certainly the result of a previous understanding with them.[27] The day after it was written—extraordinary despatch for any Spaniard—Morales submitted it to the chamber of commerce for the merchants' advice. As the province was suffering greatly for lack of shipping facilities, they gave the proposal an enthusiastic welcome and urged Morales to adopt it. The Intendant next consulted the Governor, Manuel Gayoso, who also approved it warmly. Finally the memorial, together with the reports of the merchants and the Governor, was considered on June 11, 1798, at a formal session of treasury officials (*Junta de Real Hacienda*) presided over by Morales himself.

The result was a change even more extensive than Clark had suggested.[28] Henceforth all neutral vessels might engage in trade with New Orleans on the same terms as Spaniards, that is, on the payment of six per cent duties on both imports and exports; and goods might be exported from New Orleans to the territory of the United States on the Mississippi River without the payment of any duty whatever. Morales immediately enforced these new regulations, with the stipulation that they should remain in effect until four months after the restoration of peace, or until the King should direct otherwise. The latter clause was merely a perfunctory obeisance before the throne, for when the King did direct otherwise, issuing a peremptory order that the new regulations should be withdrawn, Morales made only a brief gesture of compliance and then, pleading the exigencies of war-time, revived the more liberal system.[29] As a result of his action, citizens of the United States continued to share the commerce of Louisiana on equal terms with Spaniards until several months after the restoration of peace in 1802.

There is one feature of the new system which requires a word of explanation. The abolition of the export duty on goods shipped from New Orleans to the American West had not been requested by Daniel Clark. Morales adopted the measure in order to compensate Spanish merchants of New Orleans for the opening of the deposit, for without some such compensation they could not have competed with American exports from the deposit to the settlements up the river. This may seem much ado about nothing, for before the steamboat age the volume of shipments up-stream was very small. The commercial current seemed rather to be setting the other way. In 1801, for instance, some fifty thousand dollars' worth of merchandise was exported from the Natchez customs district to New Orleans.[30] There was, however, a persistent belief among the Spanish officials that New Orleans would some day supply the whole valley with goods. The belief was shared by General Victor Collot, who had inquired into the subject on his trip down the Mississippi in 1796, and asserted that the freight rates from New Orleans to Kentucky and the Illinois country were less than half the rates from Philadelphia and Baltimore to the same regions.[31] At any rate, it was entirely possible for New Orleans to retain control of the nearer and rapidly growing Natchez market and that seems to have been the immediate purpose of the Intendant's action in 1798.

VII

On the whole, the Americans had little cause for complaint on account of their treatment at New Orleans between the execution of the treaty of San Lorenzo in 1798 and the end of the European war in 1802. While the war lasted, the Spanish border provinces were so dependent upon American commerce that the colonial officials did not dare offend their republican neighbors. The regulations governing the deposit and the navigation of the river were as liberal as could reasonably be expected, and citizens of the United States had extensive trade privileges in Louisiana which they had never enjoyed before and which they had no legal right to claim. The restrictions so vigorously denounced by the American consular agents at New Orleans were no doubt vexatious, but they were not serious impediments to commerce; and most of them were the result of a legitimate effort on the part of the Spaniards to protect their own interests. Indeed, if a balance sheet of grievances had been drawn up, the Spaniards could at least have equaled the Americans in the number and gravity of complaints.[32]

The most justifiable complaint from the American side related to Spain's refusal to recognize an American consular agent at New Orleans. Such an agent was, as the United States asserted, necessary for the protection of American treaty rights; but the Spanish government retorted with perfect truth that its settled policy forbade the admission of consular agents to its colonial ports.[33] As the treaty of 1795 did not give the United States the slightest ground for claiming that an exception should be made in its favor at New Orleans, the repeated efforts of Adams and Jefferson failed to obtain the desired permission.

On the other hand, the Spanish officials at New Orleans were not unwilling to have the assistance of American agents in the management of the swarms of their unruly countrymen who poured into New Orleans on flatboats and schooners. Though never formally recognized, several consular agents of the United States resided at the creole capital from 1798 to 1803 and were permitted to perform most of the ordinary duties of their office,[34] granting certificates of ownership to planters and masters, giving what protection they could to seamen who were maltreated by their captains, compelling French privateers to comply with all legal forms in the condemnation of American prizes,[35] and furnishing the American government with its only authentic information regarding the national commerce on the lower Mississippi. If the Spanish government had been willing to regularize the status of these informal agents, one serious cause of friction between Spain and the United States might have been removed.

PART THREE

From San Lorenzo to Paris

CHAPTER VI

The Shadow of France in the West: I

I

Early in 1797, Andrew Jackson of Tennessee was informed (erroneously, of course) that the Floridas and a part of Louisiana had been ceded by Spain to France and that the French would therefore be "masters of the mouth of the Mississippi." His pregnant comment was, "I hope they will be good neighbors." In January of the following year, Jackson, now a United States Senator, wrote to a friend from Philadelphia: "Do not then be surprised if my next letter should announce a revolution in England. Should Boneparte make a landing on the English shore Tyranny will be humbled, a Throne crushed, and a republic will spring from the wreck, and millions of distressed people [will be] restored to the rights of man, by the conquering arm of Boneparte." Two weeks later, perhaps on sober second thought, he wrote another letter which shows that democratic enthusiasm was not his only reason for regarding the projected invasion of England as a happy event; for, said he, if the Anglo-French war were terminated, France might "give america [the United States] a sweap with her tail." [1]

Andrew Jackson might impress some of his contemporaries as merely an uncouth backwoodsman who wore his long hair in an eelskin bag and choked with rage when he tried to take part in the debates of Congress, but his letters show that he had a clear conception of the crisis in world affairs through which his country and his section were passing. Briefly stated, the situation was as follows: From the publication of Jay's treaty in 1795 to the despatching of President Adams's commissioners to Paris in 1799, the United States and France hovered on the brink of war, and the outbreak of hostilities was rendered all the more probable by the fact that throughout most of this period the control of the American government rested in the hands of Anglophile Federalists. Spain, whose provinces of Louisiana and Florida bordered the United States on the south and west, and blocked the mouth of the Mississippi, soon abandoned

the conciliatory policy which had led Godoy to sign the treaty of
San Lorenzo with Thomas Pinckney in 1795. Having deserted its
British alliance for one with France, the Spanish court at the end of
1796 joined the latter power in so vehement a protest to the United
States against Jay's treaty that the outbreak of war became a distinct
possibility. Between the United States and this Franco-Spanish coalition stood the British navy, but in 1796 and 1797 England appeared
to be tottering on the verge of ruin. The bonds of its government fell
to unprecedentedly low levels, the navy was threatened with widespread mutiny, and for the first time in two centuries the island
seemed in serious danger of invasion. It was not until 1799 that the
crisis came to an end so far as the United States was concerned. By
that time France as well as Spain had chosen the path of peace, and
Adams met them half way in it.

Across the whole of this four-year period lay the shadow of the
retrocession of Louisiana to France. The recovery of the province
was one of the major purposes of the French government after 1795,
and its purpose, though shrouded in the conventional secrecy of
diplomatic negotiation, was soon a matter of common knowledge, or
at least of common surmise, in Europe and America. The success of
France would very probably unsettle the settlement of the affairs of
the Mississippi Valley recently agreed upon by Spain and the United
States, but there was a rich feast for conjecture as to the probable
course of events under the new dispensation. Would the French in
Louisiana respect the rights of the United States under the treaty of
San Lorenzo? Or would they pursue a hostile policy towards the
Eastern states while they intrigued with the Westerners to bring
about the disruption of the Union? Or would they close the river,
defying West and East alike? And would Great Britain or the United
States or both together forestall the French by seizing Louisiana and
Florida? Nowhere were these questions asked more eagerly or answered more variously than in the United States, where Federalists
and Republicans, Easterners and Westerners, adventurers and high
government officials, all undertook to read the future. There was
only one point of agreement among these seers, namely, that—as
Thomas Jefferson oracularly expressed it—the recovery of Louisiana
by France would effect a profound change in the system of the
United States.

The congenial atmosphere of uncertainty brought forth a tropical
profusion of plots. Several of these were discovered or suspected by

Andrew Ellicott in the course of his residence at that focus of intrigue, the tumultuous town of Natchez, in 1797. Ellicott had come down the Mississippi prepared to find evidences of conspiracy, but he must have been amazed at the number and intricacy of the undercurrents and cross-currents which he saw sweeping over the West. Aside from the maneuvers of rival factions at Natchez, which kept the district in a turmoil during most of his eighteen months' residence there, he noted three major plots, all affecting Spain and the United States, and each running counter to the other two.[2] From information which he gathered, it appeared, first, that, as President Washington suspected, the Spanish officials of Louisiana were conspiring with James Wilkinson and other frontiersmen to separate the West from the Union and attach it to Spain; second, that these same Spanish officials and American frontiersmen were planning to revolutionize Florida and Louisiana and make them a base for the emancipation of the rest of Spanish America; and third, that the frontiersmen and the colonists of Louisiana and Florida were concerting measures to expel the Spaniards from those provinces and annex them to Great Britain or the United States. Even this formidable inventory did not exhaust the list of projects, for in 1798 Alexander Hamilton and his henchmen in the President's cabinet added one of their own making.

To Ellicott himself the secessionist intrigue, in which General James Wilkinson was the arch-conspirator, seemed the most important, and he forwarded to the government at Philadelphia information that should have heightened its suspicion of Wilkinson's guilt.[3] The administration's failure to heed these warnings from Ellicott and other informants may not be inexplicable, but the explanation would probably bring some curious facts to light. At any rate, if a decade later Jefferson seemed unaccountably indifferent to grave accusations against Wilkinson, it must be remembered that he was only following the precedent set by Washington and Adams. In spite of charges that he was engaged in treasonable dealings with Spain, Wilkinson was first appointed to a commission in the army by Washington (1791) and subsequently promoted and singled out for high commendation. Though Anthony Wayne, Wilkinson's superior, was convinced of his guilt and though certain sinister occurrences of 1794 and 1795 pointed in that direction, Wilkinson was, at Wayne's death, placed in command of the United States army in the West. Though Ellicott's letters strengthened the case against him, and though blunt John Adams wrote Wilkinson that ugly rumors about him were pouring in from the West,[4] he was nevertheless kept at his post, receiving every mark of favor from the government, and in 1799 was called into consultation by Major General Alexander Hamilton when the latter was planning an invasion of the Spanish border provinces.[5] It was not the alertness of the federal government that saved the United States from the consequences of Wilkinson's treasonable activities.

II

The twilight movements of James Wilkinson were scarcely more alarming to Ellicott than the filibustering designs of American frontiersmen and British agents. Foremost among these designs was one that is associated with the name of William Blount, United States Senator from Tennessee and former Governor of that territory before its admission to statehood.[6] Again, as in the case of the Spanish intrigue, Ellicott industriously gathered information for Secretary of State Pickering, and again Pickering read his communications with apparent indifference. The information furnished by Ellicott was distasteful to the Secretary, for it tended to establish a connection between Blount and various British sympathizers, whereas Pickering was straining every nerve to prove that Great Britain was in no way implicated in the affair.

It seems more than likely that the turmoil at Natchez in 1797 was intimately connected with the Blount conspiracy and that this conspiracy was in turn related to the notorious Yazoo land speculation. Full documentary proof is lacking, but conspirators have never been considerate of the historian. There is at least enough evidence to establish the probability of the relationship; and the explanation here offered accounts better than any other for many enigmatic facts of the border history of this period.

Contemporary observers often interpreted the Blount conspiracy in terms of foreign intrigue. Their interpretations were as various as their prepossessions. The Anglophile Pickering declared that it was due to French influence among the American frontiersmen. The Spanish envoy, Irujo, charged that it was a British scheme of conquest and that the Federalists, including Pickering himself, were implicated in it.[7] Most people on the Atlantic coast were inclined to take one of these two views, Federalists following Pickering, Republicans Irujo. Both of these diagnosticians were mistaken, for Blount's conspiracy was a flower of native frontier growth. While the ring-

leaders undoubtedly worked with an eye on the international situation and probably hoped for British aid, the plan was conceived and
matured by men of the southwestern border, and it was intimately
connected with land speculation, which was at once the favorite
pastime and the only form of big business known on the frontier.

Other contemporaries, closer to the springs of the conspiracy,
analyzed it more successfully than did Pickering and Irujo. Two of
them pointed out the connection between the Blount plan and the
Yazoo land companies. James Jackson, who was Governor of Georgia
at the time of Blount's exposure and who was an eminent authority
on the ramifications of the Yazoo speculation, declared on the floor
of the United States Senate in 1803 that there was "an intimate connexion" between the two enterprises.[8] Similar testimony came from a
well-informed resident of Blount's home country on the Holston.
This was Arthur Campbell, who, living in that part of southwestern
Virginia that borders on East Tennessee, had long taken a deep interest in its affairs, partly because his brother, Judge David Campbell,
was a citizen of Tennessee. Writing to Timothy Pickering in the latter
half of 1797, Campbell confessed that no one was acquainted with
Blount's "plans and views," but he suggested that they revolved about
Muscle Shoals, which was included in the grant of one of the Yazoo
companies. What is more important, Campbell named as Blount's
"confederates" men who had long been associated with the enterprise
for settling that region. Among these confederates were George
Mathews, Zachariah Cox, Lachlan McIntosh, and John Sevier. Except as to Sevier, the evidence tends to corroborate Campbell's statement and only adds to the list of confederates.[9]

The conspiracy very properly takes its name from William Blount,
and his implication in the affair shows how powerfully the frontier
wrought upon those who came within its reach. Judging him by his
record before he first crossed the mountains as Governor of the
Southwest Territory in 1790, one would say that until then he was
a good Federalist in the making. He came of a respectable mercantile
family in eastern North Carolina and at an early age distinguished
himself as a land speculator. In 1787 he was a delegate in Congress
and at the same time a member of the constitutional convention at
Philadelphia. When the constitution was submitted for ratification,
he was one of the minority in his State who from the outset favored
its acceptance. In 1790 his constancy won him the appointment of
Governor of the new Southwest Territory and Superintendent of

Southern Indian affairs. For several years he zealously guarded federal interests in that region without neglecting his own; but the steady pressure of local opinion had its effect, and by 1795 he was as determined an enemy of the administration as any backwoodsman. Indeed he outdid the backwoodsmen at their own game, for his official position and his more ample means had enabled him to identify himself with a greater variety of frontier interests than it was possible for many of his fellow westerners to do.

Overshadowing all else was his interest in land speculation. The records show that his activities along this line began at least as early as the end of the Revolution and continued until his death in 1800. The ramifications were many and widespread. They reached into the legislatures of Georgia and South Carolina, into State and federal negotiations with the Indians, to the Spanish legation at New York and the colonial governments of Cuba and New Orleans. He exploited his own office of territorial governor and Indian superintendent, writing with unusual candor just after it was bestowed upon him: ". . . My Western Lands had become so great an object to me that it had become absolutely necessary that I should go to the Western Country to secure them and perhaps my Presence might have enhanced their Value—I am sure my present appointment will." [10] Even the American legation at Paris was not exempt from his influence, for one of the attachés was Colonel James Mountflorence, who sold Blount's lands to the citizens of the sister republic and did his best to improve the real estate market by seeking to enlist French support of the American claim to the free navigation ·of the Mississippi.[11]

Blount was literally a land-jobber, for he bought land in Tennessee for ten cents an acre for resale in France through Mountflorence and in England through a Dr. Nicholas Romayne of New York; [12] but he aspired to be something more than a land-jobber. For many years he had been engaged in a notable effort to establish a colony at Muscle Shoals, which would be both a farming community and a fur-trading center.[13] More than this, the construction of a canal from the Tennessee to the headwaters of the Tombigbee River would, it was thought, provide a highway to the Gulf superior to the Mississippi itself and make the Shoals region the commercial capital of the Ohio Valley. It was so seductive an idea that many influential Southerners on both sides of the mountains embarked in the enterprise. Together with other groups of Yazoo speculators, they made a raid on the Georgia legislature in 1795 and, through the efforts of Zachariah Cox, obtained a grant of lands lying in the "Great Bend" of the Tennessee River at Muscle Shoals. This was only the beginning. Until the Spaniards were expelled from Florida the full execution of the plan was impossible, for Spain had long supported Indian resistance to the extension of the American frontier, vetoing this very enterprise in 1789, and the Spanish garrison at Mobile blocked the outlet of the projected waterway to the Gulf.

In 1796 several circumstances combined to convince Blount that filibustering was the only way out. Rumors were flying thick and fast that France was about to recover Louisiana and the Floridas. Once entrenched there, it would raise a barrier to the Gulf that even the boldest frontiersman could hardly hope to penetrate. A quick thrust, however, might save the day, for the despised Spaniards were still in possession; and in October of that year Spain was further enfeebled by going to war with England. The desperate state into which Blount's finances had fallen induced him to grasp at the opportunity, for it might never come again.[14] The bottom had fallen out of the market for Western lands. European as well as American investors had become fastidious, for both purchasers and emigrants, such as the Gallipolis colonists, had been bitterly disappointed in their expectations. The crash sent Robert Morris to a debtor's prison and involved Andrew Jackson so deeply that years passed before he extricated himself. Blount too was threatened with ruin, but his response was not that of either Jackson or Morris. Instead, he planned a theatrical coup that would clear the way for the establishment of his colony along with those of the other Yazoo companies, sweep the Spanish impediment from the mouths of the southern rivers, and put new life into the sagging prices of western lands. It is not likely that he had any such vision of empire as had Aaron Burr, for at the very same time that he was hatching the conspiracy he was also maturing his plans for reëlection as United States Senator from Tennessee. He was merely an overbold frontiersman playing international politics in order to bolster up a desperate speculation.

III

Towards the end of 1796 a garrulous adventurer by the name of John Chisholm arrived at Philadelphia fresh from the Cherokee country. He was one of a swarm of British loyalists who had remained among the Southern Indian tribes after the close of the

American Revolution and had given no end of trouble to the neighboring Americans and Spaniards and to the Indians themselves. One
of their favorite projects was the conquest of Spanish Florida, and
they seem to have been parties to the plots hatched by William
Augustus Bowles in 1788 and 1792 with that end in view. It was
alleged—with how much truth we can not say—that Governor Blount
and General John Sevier agreed to join them. Their plans went awry,
and these parasites of the border made a precarious living by plundering the Indians under the guise of trade and by obtaining occasional
employment as the Indian agents of Spain and the United States.
Chisholm himself had acted as interpreter at some of Blount's conferences with the Cherokee and as Blount's agent on a mysterious
mission to sound out the Southern Indians in 1795.[15] When he arrived at Philadelphia in 1796 he came in company with a troup of
hungry, curious savages.

According to Chisholm, he himself was the originator of the grandiose scheme known as the Blount conspiracy, and Blount stole it
from him.[16] His story was that he came to Philadelphia as the representative of twenty-five loyalists of his own stripe, intending first
to demand of the United States government the same liberal treatment that they claimed to have received formerly from Great Britain,
and, failing that, to organize an assault on Florida. Spain, it seemed,
must suffer for the parsimony of Washington. Failing dismally to
interest the federal administration, he proceeded with the second part
of his plan. Then it was that he revealed it to William Blount, seeking his coöperation.

The tale does not ring true, but that makes little difference. Certain
it is that, whoever was the author of it, Blount soon made the plan
his own. He permitted Chisholm to unfold his simple freebooting designs to the British minister, Robert Liston, who was glad to pay his
passage to London in order to rid himself of the importunate Scot
and escape the responsibility of a decision. Meanwhile, Blount himself got in touch with his New York friend, Romayne, and, through
Romayne, with Liston; enlarged the scope of the plan, enlisted the
services of many agents, and sent them out to put the plan in operation—though Arthur Campbell was probably right in saying that
Blount did not take any one completely into his confidence. The plan
of conquest was extended to Spain's Mississippi posts in both upper
and lower Louisiana; but the main objective appears to have been
the establishment of the long-desired colony at Muscle Shoals.

It can hardly be a mere coincidence that Dr. James White of Tennessee put in his appearance at Natchez at the end of 1796, for he had visited Havana and New Orleans in the interest of the Muscle Shoals adventurers in 1788 and 1789, and as late as 1798 he was closely associated with Zachariah Cox, their titular leader. His conduct at once aroused the suspicions of Governor Gayoso, for, though he posed as a trader, he sold his wares at such ridiculously low prices that his peddling seemed only a screen to hide an intrigue with the widely scattered people of the district.[17] Gayoso's uneasiness was all the greater because many of the inhabitants were British loyalists,[18] and Blount was supposed to have obtained British patronage for his scheme. It was suspected that George Mathews, who came to Natchez a few months after White, was also an agent of Blount;[19] but, while we may share the suspicion, we cannot verify it. Another person widely regarded as a ringleader in the conspiracy was John McKee, who was an agent in the Southern Indian department and in that capacity had been a subordinate of Blount until 1796. Early in 1797 McKee passed through Natchez on his way to the headquarters of the Indian trading firm of Panton, Leslie and Company at Pensacola. William Panton, the head of the firm, gave him a warm welcome. Their intimacy excited the fears of both Ellicott and Gayoso,[20] for Panton was still bitterly resentful against the Spanish government for its sacrifice of his interests in the treaty of San Lorenzo. In 1796 one of his partners had visited Knoxville, the home of William Blount, for the ostensible purpose of closing out the firm's Cherokee business, which had been ruined by the treaty. Now, in the half-light of McKee's mysterious intimacy with Panton at Pensacola, the earlier visit seemed to take on sinister significance, for no man had more power to turn the border Indians against Spain than William Panton. As we shall see, however, rumor was probably mistaken as to the purpose of McKee's mission.

Among the persons who were associated with Blount at this juncture were Zachariah Cox and Lachlan McIntosh. Cox was the chief promoter of the Tennessee Company, which had obtained the Muscle Shoals grant from Georgia in 1795.[21] McIntosh, an influential Georgian, was one of the original grantees under the Georgia act of that year and was now an attorney for the company. While Cox busied himself on the frontier, McIntosh worked with Blount in the East, and after the exposure of the plot accompanied the latter in his flight to Tennessee.[22] There is also another name, the most notorious of them all, that flits tantalizingly across the records of the affair. While the plot was thickening, Blount's New York agent, Romayne, wrote him of conversations with "your friend Aaron Burr." [23] What the conversations were about we do not know, nor is there any evidence that Burr was one of the conspirators; but it may be significant in the development of Burr's own ideas that he was the friend of Blount and the intimate of Romayne at this juncture.

Romayne's interest was naturally in the national and British aspects of the undertaking, and he gave Blount some shrewd advice. The frontiersmen, he said, must be told that France would soon recover Louisiana and Florida and would immediately shut the Mississippi River to American commerce, for a report of this sort would "put things in such a situation as will make our plan when it takes place appear as a salvation to the people." That, it may be remarked, was not hard to do, for the rumor of the retrocession of Louisiana was already widely circulated and widely believed. Romayne also urged that Senator Blount should be careful to conceal his agency in the enterprise, in order that by preserving the appearance of a "pure, dignified, political character" he might have more influence when the time came for him to act. [24]

This consideration no doubt explains why Blount refrained from holding any direct communication with Liston, who was given to believe that Chisholm was the real leader of the conspirators and that he and Blount were not on friendly terms. Another consideration was doubtless the British minister's intimacy with Pickering, who was Blount's sworn enemy. It was left to Romayne to approach Liston, and this he did with skill and success. Liston replied (April 28, 1797) that while Chisholm had impressed him as "illiterate and unfit to assume command," he believed that "if a person of confidence, with proper authority from home, were to accompany him [Chisholm] something might be effected," invited a "full expression of your [Romayne's] sentiments on the subject," and promised "secrecy and discretion." [25]

It is impossible to say just what the plan of operations was. Our chief source of information on this point is a statement made by Chisholm in London after the exposure of the conspiracy. [26] From this it appears that three separate expeditions were to attack the Spanish posts simultaneously. One column, consisting of northern Indians and frontiersmen of New York and Pennsylvania, was to attack New Madrid and seize the silver mines at the head of the Red River. Another column, which Blount himself was expected to lead, was to fall upon New Orleans. It was to be recruited in Tennessee, Kentucky, and Natchez, and was to have the coöperation of the Choctaw. The third objective was Pensacola, which was to be taken by the Cherokee and Creeks, together with a body of white men from Florida. Great Britain was expected to provide a subvention and six frigates to blockade Pensacola and the mouth of the Mississippi. In the division of the spoils, the British were to have Louisiana and the Floridas, while the invading force was to be rewarded with one half of the public funds and private property within the conquered provinces, as well as land grants at the basic rate of one thousand acres for each private soldier. In order no doubt to lessen the danger of controversy with the federal government, the posts within the territory of the United States, still occupied by Spanish garrisons (Natchez, Walnut Hills, Confederation, and Chickasaw Bluffs), were not to be molested. There was no suggestion of the coöperation of a British force from Canada. Such a force could hardly have reached Spanish territory without crossing that of the United States, and the conspirators were trying to avoid giving more offense to the federal government than was necessarily inherent in the nature of their plan.

It is possible, though not probable, that this plan never existed except in Chisholm's imagination. While he may have concocted it in order to satisfy his interrogators at London, drawing on his knowledge of the recent Genêt project, his statement seems credible because it agrees in its main outlines with what other sources indicate was in the mind of Blount and his associates. The plan was certainly feasible. Besides the Indians whose coöperation was expected, there were some 300,000 Americans living on the western waters, of whom a large proportion were trained and willing fighters, and the West had a long-standing grudge against Spain. True, they had little love for Great Britain either, but they were not likely to quibble over the nationality of the ships that would help them fling open the gates of the Mississippi. It was only a few months later that Alexander Hamilton, who usually knew what he was about, was planning a somewhat similar campaign—an attack upon Louisiana and Florida with troops drawn to a large extent from the southern and western border and with the coöperation of a British fleet.

IV

Rumors that a plot against Spain was on foot in the West began to fly thick and fast. As early as December, 1796, the Spanish ambassador in distant Paris warned his government that the British were preparing to invade Louisiana from Canada and were counting on the coöperation of the Southern Indians.[27] Similar information was given to Minister Irujo by General Collot, who had recently returned from a tour of the Mississippi Valley; and in March, 1797, Irujo laid it before the American government.[28] Such gossip did Blount's cohorts no harm, for it diverted attention from their project. It is not unlikely that they had a hand in raising this smoke screen so that they might carry on their preparations undisturbed behind it.

An incredibly thoughtless act brought his fine scaffolding crashing down about Blount's ears, and caused an uproar that reverberated from New Orleans to London, Paris, and Madrid. Fresh from his conferences with Romayne, he set out for Tennessee about the end of March, 1797, as Chisholm was sailing for England. Upon his arrival at Colonel King's iron works just south of the Virginia line, he was overtaken by word that President Adams had convened Congress in special session. Unable to continue on his way, he was guilty of the supreme folly of writing out his instructions in a letter to one James Carey, an agent in the Southern Indian department. As superintendent of that department before he became senator, Blount had been Carey's chief, and now Carey was evidently an important factor in Blount's preparations among the Southern tribes.

Some of the more significant portions of the letter follow:

"Dear Carey:

". . . Among other things that I wished to have seen you about, was the business Capt. Chisholm mentioned to the British minister last winter, at Philadelphia.

"I believe, but am not quite sure, that the plan then talked of will be attempted this fall, and, if it is attempted, it will be in a much larger way than then talked of; and if the Indians act their part, I have no doubt but it will succeed. A man of consequence has gone to England about the business, and if he makes arrangements as he expects, I shall myself have a hand in the business, and probably shall be at the head of the business on the part of the British. . . . You must take care . . . not to let the plan be discovered by Hawkins,

Dinsmoor, Byers or any other person in the interest of the United States or Spain.

"If I attempt this plan, I shall expect to have you and all my Indian country and Indian friends with me. . . .

". . . When you have read this letter over three times, then burn it. I shall be at Knoxville in July or August." [29]

Instead of burning the letter, Carey celebrated the good news by getting drunk, and gave the game away. The very men against whom Blount had warned him got possession of the letter, and one of them took it to Philadelphia.[30] The original was given to President Adams and a copy sent to Washington. Senator Blount's course was run.

The letter was not immediately made public, possibly because the administration wished to gather quietly as much corroborative evidence as possible before disclosing its knowledge of the affair. The delay may also have been due to pressure from the British minister, for Pickering informed Liston of the existence of the letter before he did the Senate, and Liston used all his influence to prevent its publication.[31] He argued very sensibly that, although the innocence of the British government could be proved, widespread antagonism to Great Britain would be aroused by the publication of the letter; and, since Pickering's faction based its whole policy on Anglo-American solidarity, its own cause would suffer. Liston's argument fell on deaf ears. As he said, Blount was an anti-administration Senator, and the Federalists could not forego this opportunity to humble the opposition. Pickering did what he could, however, to soften the blow. In advance of the publication of the letter, he gave Liston an opportunity to disavow the plan on behalf of his government; and after its publication he made a strenuous but futile effort to prove that France, not Great Britain,[32] was the power from which Blount really expected to receive aid. The Federalists also tried to implicate James Wilkinson, Thomas Jefferson, and through Jefferson, the Republican party, in the conspiracy.[33] Again no evidence of any value was presented, and vociferation was required to supply the lack of proof.

Finally on July 3, 1797, the letter to Carey was communicated to the Senate, and Blount was immediately expelled from that body. Impeachment proceedings were also instituted but subsequently dropped, for there was some difficulty in impeaching a person who no longer held office. Arrested shortly after his expulsion from the Senate, Blount was admitted to bail and promptly absconded, re-

turning as precipitately from Philadelphia to Tennessee at the end of
July as he had returned from Tennessee to Philadelphia at the end
of April. Pickering tried to procure his arrest at Staunton, Virginia,
on the road to Tennessee, but failed.[34] The Senate's sergeant-at-arms,
who was then sent to bring him into court, met with no better success, for the frontiersmen would not let one of their number be
dragged away for trial in what they regarded as a foreign court.

V

The aftermath of the affair in Tennessee was peculiar. On the one
hand, some of Blount's closest friends betrayed no indignation at his
treatment by the administration; yet, on the other hand, they did not
condemn the course that had led to his expulsion from the Senate.
Conduct that George Washington denounced as "nefarious" seemed
to John Sevier, Governor of Tennessee, merely "very imprudent." [35]
While General James Robertson of Nashville expressed grief at his
friend's reverses, he could find nothing more to say in his defense
than that he himself did not find the Carey letter so criminal as did
Blount's enemies.[36] On the whole, the opinion in Tennessee seems to
have been that Blount was very much to blame for having been
found out. After his unimpressive homecoming he had the effrontery
to seek reëlection to the United States Senate, but was defeated.[37]
He found some consolation in election to the State Senate, which
by a close vote chose him as its presiding officer.

The Muscle Shoals enterprise proved a hardy perennial. It weathered the wintry storm of 1797, bursting into bloom again under a
genial Tennessee sky in 1798. Blount still supported it with might
and main, saying it was a pity that such a respectable company, composed of many men of worth, could not get possession of property
honestly bought and paid for.[38] Zachariah Cox, its active head,
visited Nashville and, although the settlement was prohibited by the
federal government, got from Governor John Sevier a statement
that he could find no objection to the company's occupying its grant.[39]
Once more the project met with a reverse. In August, 1798, Cox arrived with a party of men at Natchez, now an American post. At the
instance of General James Wilkinson he was arrested, but soon
escaped and fled to New Orleans. Even this was not the end, for
if the Spanish minister was correctly informed, Blount and Romayne
were still laboring to revive the filibustering project up to the time
of the former's death in 1800.[40]

The Blount affair was not—as one writer has asserted [41]—responsible for the delay in the evacuation of the Southwest posts, for the Spanish government had decided upon that course nine months before the conspiracy was exposed. On the contrary, the exposure probably played an important part in determining the Spanish court to surrender the posts. The agents of Spain in America did, however, use the episode to justify a measure that had already been adopted, for they argued that the retention of the posts was necessary to safeguard Louisiana and Florida against the danger of invasion revealed by the publication of Blount's letter to Carey. And for a time it did seem that a rupture was inevitable, for the affair added acrimony to the bitter dispute already in progress between Irujo and Pickering.[42] Fortunately for Spain, the war fever in the United States, which was to reach its highest pitch the following year, was only in an incipient stage in 1797, and the result of the brawl between these two officials was merely a demand for the recall of the Spanish minister. Even that demand was evaded by the court, and Irujo remained in the United States to try the temper of the next administration.[43]

CHAPTER VII

The Shadow of France in the West: II

I

On February 22, 1798, Thomas Jefferson wrote his friend Madison from Philadelphia: "The news from the Natchez, of the delivery of the posts, which you will see in the papers, is to be relied on. We have escaped a dangerous crisis there." [1] Jefferson was correctly informed about the intentions of the Spanish court, but he was very much mistaken in his belief that the danger of war with Spain had passed. Just as the court proceeded to fulfil its obligations under the treaty of San Lorenzo by evacuating the Southwestern posts, beginning the boundary survey, and opening the deposit at New Orleans, relations between the United States and Spain's ally, France, took a turn for the worse with the publication of the X Y Z correspondence. A group of Americans whose guiding spirit was Alexander Hamilton welcomed the call to arms. War with France would in all probability mean war with Spain too, and that was what made the prospect of fighting so attractive. As the war aims of the Hamiltonian clique developed, it appeared that Louisiana and Florida were to be invaded and that, with the aid of the British navy and a band of Spanish colonists represented by Francisco de Miranda, the field of operations would be extended to Mexico and South America. [2]

The scheme was ingenious as well as grandiose. The coupling of Spain with France was evidently expected to win support in the South and West, where there would have been serious opposition to a war against France alone. In so far as it related to Spain's possessions in North America, it also provided war aims that could be attained, for while hardly any exploit of military importance or of value for domestic political purposes could be performed at the expense of France, the conquest of the Spanish borderlands offered just that dash of difficulty which was necessary to make its certain success glorious. [3]

Though Hamilton had retired to private life and was practising law in New York, the war would afford him an opportunity to win the military distinction which he craved, for early in 1798 his influence in the right places was so great that he could reasonably expect to obtain any post he might desire in the army. John Adams seemed to be President in name only. "Whether he was chastened by his wife's illness," says Channing, "or whether he was mellowed by the responsibility of his high office," he left the conduct of the administration almost entirely to his cabinet, which was dominated by Hamilton. George Washington, whose universal popularity had long since gone up in the smoke of party battles but whose military prestige was still unequaled in the United States, could be counted on to support his trusted counselor and friend.

It has long been a matter of common knowledge that Hamilton was the prime mover in this enterprise, and yet, as it has been generally understood, the scheme was so chimerical that an air of unreality envelops his participation in it. In spite of the evidence, we are tempted to ask if he ever seriously thought of undertaking the conquest of Spain's far-flung empire in America. We can hardly picture the little New York lawyer and former Secretary of the Treasury as another Alexander the Great establishing his satraps over creoles, Aztecs, and Incas from St. Louis to the Straits of Magellan.

In the opinion of the present writer, there can be no question that Hamilton threw himself heart and soul into the plan of conquest in 1798 and 1799; but there was nothing chimerical about it. Mexico and Peru lay doubtfully on the outer fringe of his designs. At the heart and center lay Florida and Louisiana. It was the acquisition of these border provinces that formed the principal purpose of his martial preparations. They could be taken without great difficulty and, for reasons that will soon appear, he and his associates believed that their immediate seizure was essential to the welfare of the United States. After that was accomplished he might be willing, to use his own phrase, to "squint at South America," but this was never more than a remote possibility. His full gaze was fixed upon the neighboring colonies of Spain in North America. It was doubtless in order to obtain British aid for his own darling project that he expressed an interest in the remoter and rather fantastic enterprises which might yield benefit to Great Britain. Neither are the documentary sources for the history of this affair misleading, nor was Hamilton suffering from a brainstorm. His conduct in it was part and parcel of his whole career. On this occasion, as on others, he was both the patriot who thought in continental terms and the Federalist who feared and detested France. If Spain, not France, was the immediate victim, that was the penalty it must pay for its subserviency to the Jacobins.

It is impossible to say precisely when visions of conquest began to float through the heads of the Hamiltonian group, but they probably had their plans ready as early as January, 1798. On the twenty-fourth of that month President Adams addressed a series of questions to his cabinet asking if, in their opinion, war would necessarily result from the failure of the negotiation which Pinckney, Marshall, and Gerry were conducting in Paris. The faithful Secretary of War, James McHenry, went to Alexander Hamilton for advice. Hamilton replied that he preferred mitigated hostility to open war with France and coöperation with Great Britain to an entangling alliance with that power. Then followed what, for our present purpose, is the most important part of the letter. If the rupture should extend to Spain—"as is probable," said Hamilton—the United States should point its coöperation with Great Britain to the Floridas, Louisiana, and the South American possessions of Spain. "All on this side the Mississippi must be ours," he declared, "including both Floridas." [4]

Hamilton's assumption that the rupture would extend to Spain was justified when he wrote, for "very acrimonious altercations," as Jefferson described them, were then going on between the United States government and Minister Irujo. Within another month word reached Philadelphia that Spain was about to terminate the controversy by surrendering the disputed territory, and Jefferson breathed a sigh of relief that the "dangerous crisis" had passed; but he reckoned without the Federalist war hawks. Hamilton and Pickering were so enamored of the plan of conquest which they had conceived while Spain was defiant that they could not bear to abandon it merely because Spain had given in and agreed to execute the treaty. Indeed the very submission of the court was converted into a reason for attacking Spanish Louisiana and Florida.

Late in March, 1798, as Pickering was about to transmit the X Y Z correspondence to Congress, he was authoritatively informed that Spain was at last going to surrender the Southwestern posts. This action was probably designed by the court to disarm the hostility of the war hawks, of which it had been warned repeatedly by Irujo; but if that was the purpose of the measure, it had an effect precisely opposite to the one intended. On March twenty-fifth, the day after the news reached him, Pickering wrote Hamilton: "What ought we to do in respect to *Louisiana?* . . . Perhaps these orders [to evacuate the posts] may have resulted from Spain's seeing or fearing the necessity of ceding Louisiana to France, and hence concluding that she might as well do a grateful thing to us before the surrender. . . . The Spanish force in all Louisiana is small, probably not rising to a thousand men, from the Balize [at the mouth of the Mississippi] to the Missouri." [5]

"The necessity of ceding Louisiana to France"—in that phrase probably lies one of the chief explanations of the Federalist war party's plan to pick a quarrel with France and Spain. Americans of all shades of political opinion were profoundly alarmed at this juncture by the prospect that France would obtain Louisiana and the Floridas from Spain. To the Federalists, however, the prospect was doubly alarming, for they believed that the possession of those provinces by France would at least strengthen the Republican party, whom they were denouncing as a "Gallo-American faction," and might even lead to a revival of the secession movement in the West.

The fears of the Federalists seem to have proceeded mainly from a conjectural interpretation of circumstantial evidence; but it is possible that they were inspired by two despatches written by Minister Fauchet at Philadelphia in 1795, intercepted by the British, and communicated by them to Secretary of State Pickering at a date which still remains uncertain.[6] Discussing the unsatisfactory state of relations between France and the United States, Fauchet argued that his government could remedy the situation by recovering Louisiana, which would enable it to build up a party of French sympathizers in the United States, and, in case of necessity, to bring about the separation of the West from the Union. The despatch was, of course, only an exposition of the envoy's own views and not an authoritative statement of French policy; but such a distinction was no easier to make in 1795 than it had been in the analogous case of Marbois's intercepted despatch on the fisheries in 1782. Pickering and Hamilton were as firmly convinced on the later occasion as Jay and Adams on the earlier, that the policy of the government at Paris was to convert the United States into a sphere of French influence.

As early as May, 1796, Federalist leaders believed that France was making active preparations to capitalize the discontent long rife in the

West. They believed that the retrocession of Louisiana had already been stipulated in a secret clause of the treaty of Basel (July, 1795); and when Minister Adet sent his fellow-countryman, General Victor Collot, on a mission to the Ohio Valley in 1796, their worst suspicions seemed to be confirmed. The administration consequently appropriated a secret service fund of five hundred dollars for the purpose of unmasking Adet's supposed accomplices in the West. An undercover agent was hired through the faithful Pittsburgh Federalist, Senator James Ross; and Governor St. Clair of the Northwest Territory and General Anthony Wayne, commanding the United States army on the Ohio, were instructed to coöperate. The results were rather disappointing. The investigation yielded more rumors about Wilkinson's intrigue with Spain, but such rumors could have been gathered in any desired number without the services of a detective. Evidences of French intrigue were not obtained.[7] Pickering and his associates nevertheless remained unshaken in their belief that France was plotting the dissolution of the Union and could count upon a numerous and enthusiastic following in the West. The government's failure to discover the conspirators seemed only to prove how dangerously clever they were in covering their tracks.

It was this fear of imminent western secession which gave point to Washington's fervent plea for the preservation of the Union in his Farewell Address (September 17, 1796); and the reader need hardly be reminded that Hamilton played an important part in drafting the message. While the plea was addressed to every part of the United States, it was directed particularly to the Western people, and it appealed not only to their patriotism but also to their interest in the free navigation of the Mississippi. "The *West*," said Washington, "must of necessity owe the *secure* enjoyment of indispensable *outlets* for its own productions to the weight, influence, and the future maritime strength of the Atlantic side of the Union, directed by an indissoluble community of interest as *one nation*. Any other tenure by which the *West* can hold this essential advantage, whether derived from its own separate strength or from an apostate and unnatural connection with any foreign power, must be intrinsically precarious."[8] The events of the next twelve months did little or nothing to allay the fears implicit in this admonition. France soon assumed an arrogant tone towards the United States; Spain took its cue from France, and Blount's conspiracy, exposed in the summer of 1797, was regarded by most Federalists as proof that the Southwest was ripe for a secessionist intrigue with France.[9]

II

As the cat's paw of France, Spain received its full share of abuse from Federalist champions in this crisis. When the controversy over the Southwest posts was at its height in July, 1797, and Minister Irujo was publicly proclaiming his low opinion of the American government, "Peter Porcupine" (William Cobbett) exclaimed in his Philadelphia *Gazette:* "Gracious Heaven! insulted by a Spaniard! Eight years of war and misery [the American Revolution], and a hundred thousand men stretched dead upon the plains of America, and all to purchase a kick from a tawny-pelted nation, which Americans had ever been taught to despise." On another occasion he denounced the Spanish King, Charles IV, as a "degenerate prince" who "seems destitute not only of the dignity of a King, but of the common virtues of a man," and declared that "every important measure" of the Spanish court was "directed by the crooked politics of France." [10] Even John Quincy Adams, who was not under any compulsion to use the violent language of a party hack, wrote from London: "Spain has promised like a Castilian—she performs not even like a Jew; she does not perform at all." [11]

It was at this time that "Peter Porcupine" trumpeted forth the war party's call to arms against Spain. Commenting on the fact that Minister Irujo seemed to be inviting a rupture, "Porcupine" urged the American people to accept the invitation, saying: "A war with Spain is absolutely necessary to the salvation of this country, if a war with France takes place, or if the Spaniards have ceded Louisiana to France. They must both be driven into the Gulf of Mexico, or we shall never sleep in peace. Besides, a war with Spain would be so convenient! There is nothing but dry blows to be gotten from the pennyless sans-culottes; but the wealth of Spanish America would be a salve for every sore. It would be the cream of the war. Everything seems to be working together for good; as Cromwell said, when the Scots were coming down upon him, 'the Lord hath delivered them into my hands.' May we treat them as they deserve!" [12]

Three months later the outbreak of war between the United States and the allied powers of France and Spain was brought appreciably nearer by the *coup d'état* of 18 Fructidor (September 4, 1797), for that overturn placed the government of France in the hands of a group of men who were even more hostile to the Federalist administration than their predecessors had been. John Quincy Adams warned his father, the President, "Everything that envy and malice, both against our country and against you personally, can suggest, they will attempt." Most alarming was the fact that among the new rulers of France was Merlin de Douai, who, young Adams believed, had "long since entered into an organized plan for dismembering our union." [13]

The Federalist belief that the Republicans, Eastern or Western, were a French party was quite as absurd as the Republican conviction that the Federalists were the henchmen of William Pitt; but it was quite as sincere. Granted this premise, the Hamiltonian group was fully justified in its fear of the consequences of the recovery of Louisiana by France. As early as 1797, Secretary Pickering began to question Irujo so persistently about the truth of the rumored cession that the Spaniard took alarm and wrote his government a cipher despatch warning it that, if Louisiana should in fact be retroceded to France, the negotiation must be kept a profound secret until the French were ready to take possession of Louisiana with a large force, since the Federalist administration would go to war rather than permit the transfer to take place.[14] Then in March, 1798, came the X Y Z despatches and the news that Spain was about to evacuate the Southwest posts, and Pickering wrote Hamilton the letter about Louisiana from which we have already quoted.

Hamilton unquestionably saw the matter in the same light as Pickering. In his reply to the latter's inquiry, "What ought we to do in respect to *Louisiana?*" he did not meet squarely the Secretary's thinly veiled hint that the province should be seized by armed force, promising instead to write a longer letter "to-morrow." [15] If he kept his promise, the letter has been lost,[16] but a newspaper article which he published three weeks later (April 12, 1798) shows how his mind was working. "The probability is," he declared, "that before this time the cession [of Louisiana to France] has been made; and Spain has learnt to her cost that the chief privilege of an ally of France is to be plundered at discretion. With the acquisition of Louisiana, the foundation will be laid for stripping her of South America and her mines; and perhaps for dismembering the United States. The magnitude of this mighty mischief is not easily calculated." [17] Hamilton could truthfully say in 1802, "I have always held that the *unity of our Empire,* and the best interests of our nation, require that we shall annex to the United States all the territory east of the Mississippi, New Orleans included." [18]

It was not until August, 1798, that Hamilton began to express an interest in Miranda's ambitious scheme of conquest, and the circumstances suggest that his interest was perhaps simulated and certainly remote. In February of this year Miranda had written him proposing a joint British and American attack on Spanish America, and Hamilton had dismissed the proposal with the observation that he considered Miranda "an intriguing adventurer." In August, however, further overtures from Miranda evoked a very different response from him. This time he wrote that he hoped very much to see the plan carried into effect.[19]

The change of tone was probably due to changed circumstances. On the earlier occasion Hamilton had reason to believe that the United States alone would provide adequate forces at once and that his own project—the conquest of Louisiana and Florida—could be executed without foreign aid. Since Congress, President and people all seemed at first to have been swept off their feet by enthusiasm for war, he might well think that his only problem was to direct their enthusiasm into the right channel and that he would have little difficulty in doing so. A very different situation faced him in August. The preparations which he had expected to be made so expeditiously were moving at a snail-like pace. Opposition to the war was beginning to make itself heard in various parts of the country. The President, who at first gave the war party vigorous support, had cooled perceptibly. Perhaps this was because he resented their effort to convert a war of defense against France into a war of aggression against Spain; perhaps because he had learned that his rival, Hamilton, was to be virtually commander-in-chief of the army. It is also likely that when Hamilton gave more careful thought to his plan of campaign he recognized the necessity of obtaining the coöperation of a British fleet, for as yet the United States navy existed largely on paper. And finally Miranda, who was now supported by the United States minister to England, Rufus King, and apparently by the English government as well, had become a more important person since February.

Whether or not Hamilton still regarded the Venezuelan as an intriguing adventurer, he was no longer unwilling to use him for his own purpose. There is, however, no good reason to believe that his purpose had changed; he had merely decided that after all Miranda might be useful to him. All his letters and all his preparations indicate that the conquest of Louisiana and Florida was still uppermost in his mind. He encouraged Miranda because he now felt the need of British aid and because he thought Miranda could help him secure it. The coöperation of Great Britain would provide the necessary fleet, stimulate the flagging war spirit in the United States, and thus enable him to overcome any resistance the President might offer to his plan of campaign. The character of his plan is shown by his declaration in December, 1798, that he was preparing for offensive operations and that, in case war should break out, France was not to be considered as separated from "her ally," meaning Spain. "Tempting objects," he said, "will be within our grasp." [20]

New Orleans was only one of those objects, but it was one of the most tempting. Its acquisition, which many people thought necessary for the protection of American commerce on the Mississippi, could be used to justify a war of conquest. Once such a war was begun, the field of operations could easily be extended to other dominions of Spain in America, if Hamilton should decide to embark on the larger enterprise; and New Orleans would serve as a valuable base of operations and supply for the whole Gulf region. On February 12, 1799, Hamilton, who had been appointed ranking major-general and inspector-general, summoned General Wilkinson from his post near Natchez to headquarters in the East. Curiously enough he suggested that Wilkinson might, if he found it convenient, come by way of New Orleans.[21] Since that was the route any one journeying from the lower Mississippi to the Atlantic coast at that time would follow if he could possibly do so, the suggestion has the appearance of an admonition to Wilkinson to keep his eyes open as he passed through Spanish territory.

Arrived at New York, Wilkinson lost no time in conferring with his superior. In the preliminary exchange of courtesies, he took occasion to say that, notwithstanding his own higher rank during the Revolution and his many military services rendered since that time, he did not resent Hamilton's sudden promotion over his head. Hamilton replied, "Upon my word, General Wilkinson, I admire this frankness";[22] and the two then got down to business. In order to facilitate their discussion of the affairs of the Western department, Hamilton drew up several "heads for conversations,"[23] two of which gave Wilkinson an opportunity to display the information he had acquired in coming by way of New Orleans. One of these heads was, "The disposition of the Spaniards in our vicinity—their strength in number and fortification"; the other, "The best mode (in the event of a *rupture with Spain*) of attacking the two Floridas: Troops, artillery, etc., requisite." After considerable discussion, Wilkinson submitted a written report on the affairs of the Western department on September 4, 1799. Three days later Hamilton made him the bearer of a letter to President Adams strongly recommending him for promotion to the rank of major-general.[24]

Hamilton's interest in the projected conquest of Louisiana is shown in another way. Upon his urgent insistence, the Secretary of War was relieved of the superintendence of the army, which was vested in the two major-generals, Hamilton and Pinckney. The army was then divided between these two on a geographical basis, Hamilton taking the Northern division and Pinckney the Southern; but in the West, instead of confining himself to the region between the Ohio and the Great Lakes, Hamilton obtained command over all the forces on the Mississippi River, which would, of course, be the main highway for any attack on New Orleans.[25]

III

In view of the meagerness of transportation facilities and the remoteness of the centers of population on the Atlantic seaboard from the Mississippi, the war party needed all the support it could get from the Western frontiersmen and the Southern Indians. One of the most important efforts made in this direction, and certainly the most singular, was the sending of John McKee to the headquarters of the Anglo-Spanish trading firm of Panton, Leslie and Company at Pensacola in 1797. Though the mission was regarded by some observers as a move in the Blount conspiracy, there is good reason to believe that it was in fact engineered by the Federalist war party in order to pave the way for the conquest of Florida by enlisting the services of Panton, Leslie and Company, whose influence was paramount among the Indian tribes on the Florida border. It is certainly not without significance that McKee, an Indian agent of the United States in the South, was under the orders of Secretary of War McHenry, and that Secretary of State Pickering was privy to the purpose of his mission. Thus, when Andrew Ellicott wrote from Natchez that McKee, on passing through that place, had been suspiciously intimate with Blount's adherents, Pickering replied that the government was informed of McKee's activities and fully satisfied of his loyalty.[26]

The real purpose of the mission is indicated in a letter written by McKee himself five years later, in which he spoke of the "promise made by the Government *thro' me* in the summer of 1797 that they [Panton, Leslie and Company] might reasonably look forward to such indulgences as would greatly facilitate the effectual and prompt collection of their debts within our Indian Nations." [27] There seems to be no reason for questioning the truth of McKee's statement, but it points to an intrigue which is almost incredible. The American government had known for nearly a decade that Panton, Leslie and Company was the chief agent of Spanish resistance to American influence among the Southern tribes within the limits which the United States claimed, and that, by stirring up the Indians to ravage the frontiers of Georgia and Tennessee, the company had stained its hands with the blood of American citizens. Yet high officials of the government were now offering the company facilities for collecting from these very Indian tribes the debts which were the most eloquent reminder of that long and cruel warfare. So important an "indulgence"—the debts in question amounted to nearly $200,000 [28]—could not have been offered without the expectation of a commensurate return; and there was only one such return that the company could make, namely, the use of its extensive influence among the Indians to draw them over to the side of the United States in the projected attack on New Orleans and Florida. The war party in the United States was willing to pay a high price for Panton's betrayal of his Spanish patrons. It is impossible to say whether he would have sold out. The canny Scot was not one to commit himself prematurely, and as the invasion never took place, he was not forced to show his hand.

It was even more important to gain adherents among the Western frontiersmen, from whom the bulk of the expeditionary force would have to be drawn. The lengths to which the war party would go to win support in that quarter were shown by the selection of John Sevier as brigadier-general in the provisional army authorized by Congress in 1798. Irrepressible land speculator and scourge of the Indians, Sevier had done more than any other person to frustrate the Western policy of Washington and Adams, as Pickering and McHenry knew to their cost. Nevertheless, Sevier was now Governor of Tennessee, where he had a large personal following, and his co-operation therefore seemed indispensable. At Pickering's suggestion and with McHenry's approval, he was chosen to be one of the new brigadier-generals. Washington's gorge rose at this choice. "What in the name of military prudence," he asked, could have induced the appointment of Sevier, who "never was celebrated for anything (that ever came to my knowledge) except the murder of Indians," and was "better qualified to *cut off Indians,* than to discipline an army and lead a Brigade to the mouths of cannon." Pickering, how-ever, held that the appointment would have a salutary effect on opin-ion in Tennessee, and the offer was accordingly made to Sevier, who quickly signified his willingness to serve. That his enthusiasm for war had its source in personal interests shared by few of his fellow Tennesseans is suggested by a letter of May 4, 1798, in which he said to the Secretary of War: "Not far from this place, and on the main river Holston I have a new and well erected set of iron works, suitable for casting almost every kind of mettle, and manufacturing of bar iron, the same shall in the shortest notice be converted to any public use that might be deemed expedient, and should be glad to be honored with any commands that might be thought necessary." [29]

On the whole, however, the response of the West must have been keenly disappointing to the Hamiltonians.[30] In the latter half of 1798 the newly established *Palladium* of Frankfort, Kentucky, conducted a vigorous campaign for the maintenance of peace. Albert Gallatin, speaking for western Pennsylvania, said in Congress in June, 1798, that a breach with Spain would be "extremely fatal" to his constitu-ents, and representatives from Kentucky and Tennessee took the same view.[31] What Gallatin had in mind was the West's export trade down the Mississippi, which had been stimulated by the opening of the river to free navigation by citizens of the United States in 1796 and had just been placed on a most favorable footing by the estab-lishment of the American deposit at New Orleans in April, 1798. The conquest of Louisiana could hardly help the Westerners and would almost certainly injure them. On the one hand, it could add little to the extensive privileges which they already enjoyed; on the other, it would at least temporarily throw their river trade into confusion, would permanently deprive them of the Spanish gold which they were now receiving for their produce at New Orleans, and would cut them off from the profitable market in the Spanish and French West Indies to which they had access through Spanish New Orleans.

Material interests aside, many of the Westerners doubtless preferred peace because they liked France, hated England, and suspected the Federalists who would be in charge of the war. Hence it was that the West did not rally to Hamilton in 1798 as it had to Genêt in 1793.

It was President Adams who administered the *coup de grâce* to the war party. He did not find it so easy as did Hamilton and Pickering to ignore the fact that Spain had executed the treaty of 1795; and when a letter from Miranda outlining the projected conquest of Spanish America was laid before him in 1798, he dismissed it with this frigid observation: "We are friends with Spain. If we were enemies, would the project be useful to us? It will not be in character for me to answer the letter. Will any notice of it, in any manner, be proper?"[32] Hamilton was wrong in saying that John Adams could not keep his temper. Chilling as they were, these restrained phrases only faintly suggest the mortal aversion that he felt for the project, which, as he explained many years later, seemed to him part of a concerted effort to involve the United States in the wars of Europe and bind it to Great Britain by a permanent military alliance.[33]

"The grand plan," in the words of Adams's grandson, "thus perished by inanition."[34] Without the President's approval it could not succeed. There was no doubt that the government at Madrid desired peace. When it appeared that France too was pacifically inclined towards the Americans and had not meant a request for a bribe as a challenge to mortal combat, President Adams accepted Talleyrand's peace overtures, nominating three commissioners to treat with France (February, 1799). Even then the Hamilton-Pickering group did not despair of getting a war with Spain by keeping open the breach with France. They strove to prevent the sailing of the envoys appointed by Adams, and as late as June, 1799, Hamilton made this significant statement of what he conceived to be the purpose of the military and naval preparations still in progress: "Besides eventual security against invasion," he wrote Secretary of War McHenry, "we ought certainly to look to the possession of the Floridas and Louisiana, and we ought to squint at South America."[35]

The efforts of the Hamiltonians to block the negotiation were unavailing, for in October Adams brushed aside their opposition and sent the commissioners on their way. This action was taken under circumstances which must have made it particularly galling to the leader of the war party. The seat of the federal government was temporarily at Trenton, New Jersey. Hamilton had just arrived there with his precious coadjutor, General Wilkinson, in the expectation of completing arrangements for the army in the Mississippi Valley, when the President, who had spent the last six months in Massachusetts, put in an unexpected and unwelcome appearance. At first he merely discussed with his cabinet the instructions which were to govern the negotiation, and the Hamiltonians breathed easier, convinced that the departure of the envoys would again be indefinitely postponed. On the following day, however, Adams, without consulting Secretary of State Pickering or any one else, abruptly ordered the commissioners to embark for France; and Hamilton's game was up.[36] Though the treaty with France was not signed until nearly a year later, Adams's action was decisive, for it took the wind out of the war party's sails by making the avoidance of war with France, and therefore with Spain, a virtual certainty.

By the latter part of 1799 the crisis that began in 1795 and reached its most acute stage in 1798 had passed. The Federalist administration continued to press for Irujo's recall, but until the closing days of 1802 relations between the United States and Spain were undisturbed by any serious controversy. President Jefferson, who was more than willing to let Irujo remain at his post, was able to say as he took up the reins of government in 1801: "With respect to Spain, our disposition is sincerely amicable, and even affectionate." [37]

CHAPTER VIII

Trade on the Mississippi, 1799–1802

I

The fear that France would recover Louisiana and shackle the increasing commerce of the West was not immediately realized. On the contrary, trade on the Mississippi grew to unprecedented proportions in the four years from 1799 to 1802, and the greater part of it was carried on by American citizens. The chief stimulus was supplied by the establishment of the American deposit at New Orleans in April, 1798, by the opening of the port to neutral shipping in June of the same year, and by a royal order of 1797 which permitted neutrals to trade with Havana and other Spanish colonial ports. Before these measures went into effect, planters and farmers of Louisiana and the American West were complaining bitterly that they could not sell their surplus produce.[1] When the bars were let down, so that sugar, flour, and cotton from the Mississippi Valley could reach the profitable war-time market in the West Indies and Europe at a reasonable rate, producers and merchants from New Orleans to St. Louis and Pittsburgh enjoyed greater prosperity than they had ever known before.

Nowhere was the new commercial system more welcome than in lower Louisiana, for the creole planters were then engaged in effecting an important economic readjustment. Before 1790 tobacco and indigo, and to a less extent rice, had been their principal money crops. In 1791 royal purchases of tobacco were reduced to an insignificant figure, with the result that thereafter only Natchitoches and a few other favored districts could raise it with profit. About the same time indigo failed the harassed planters. Increasing competition from India lowered the price in Europe to the point where its cultivation in Louisiana was no longer profitable, especially since the dampness of the soil and the ravages of a worm, as destructive to the indigo plant as boll-weevil to cotton, occasioned heavy losses even when the price level was high. The total failure of the crop in 1794 was the final blow.[2] Like the planters of Georgia and South Carolina at the same period, the creoles began casting about for a less temperamental crop. Some of them concentrated on wheat and corn, and others, taking advantage of the abundance of fine timber at their back doors, began the construction of portable houses for sale in the West Indies. The rewards, however, did not seem sufficient, and they continued their search for a suitable crop.

Cotton and sugar saved the day. Both plants had long been familiar to the Louisianians, but as late as 1788 neither was so much as mentioned in a list of the colony's exports drawn up by former Intendant Navarro. In the next few years the world market for cotton expanded under the influence of the industrial revolution and the war-time demands of British factories. Simultaneously the devastation of the French sugar islands by servile insurrection created an opening for new sources of supply and sent refugees to Louisiana who probably brought with them a technical knowledge of the business superior to that possessed by the Louisianians. By 1802 the sugar exported from New Orleans was valued at over $300,000; the cotton (much of which came from Natchez and Nashville) at over $1,000,000.[3]

A picturesque story is told about the establishment of the sugar industry in Louisiana.[4] In 1795, after many failures over a long period of time, the effort to obtain marketable sugar from Louisiana cane succeeded with such dramatic suddenness and so providentially that tradition inevitably produced a hero and placed the crystalline halo on his brow. Étienne Boré is the hero of this bourgeois epic. Other planters, it seems, were already making molasses and tafia from cane which they raised. "Why not sugar?" asked Boré, and decided to risk his whole fortune in the venture. His family and friends tried to convince him of his folly; but times were hard; something must be done; and if he succeeded, the high price of sugar would make him a rich man. Buying some cane from his Spanish neighbors, Méndez and Solís, he planted it on his estate six miles above New Orleans. In due time the crop was harvested. Then came the crucial moment—what answer would the cauldrons give to his audacious question? An eager, fearful crowd gathered round the simmering pots. Suddenly "It granulates! It granulates!" shouted the watchers. and the cry was echoed on every plantation south of Baton Rouge. Five years later Louisiana was exporting sugar worth a quarter of a million dollars.

Contemporary sources confirm the tradition that it was Boré who first made a success of raising and refining Louisiana cane and was so notoriously successful that other planters in the colony flocked to the new industry like flies to a jug of molasses. In 1797 Victor Collot wrote an account of the introduction of sugar planting into Louisiana.[5] He could speak with authority, for he had spent two days with Boré at the latter's plantation in 1796. Though the time was short, Collot, whose long residence in Guadeloupe had given him an expert knowledge of the sugar business, was able to make the most of it. According to his account, Boré attributed his success to his irrigation system, which kept the fields well watered during the dry spring season and enabled the cane to mature in the nine months that intervened between frosts in lower Louisiana. Other planters had thought it necessary to follow the West India practice of allowing fourteen or fifteen months for the maturity of the cane; but by his forcing process Boré had squeezed the season within the narrower limits fixed by the climate of Louisiana.

Though earlier writers differ as to details, it is more than likely that Boré was aided by experts from the French or Spanish West Indies, for he was intelligent enough to know the value of such aid and wealthy enough to pay for it; and Collot says that the mill he used was similar to those of St. Domingue. With the important exception of his irrigation system, originality did not, so far as we know, mark either the effort or the methods, but Boré's courage, resourcefulness, and energy were remarkable. He had his reward. With a cash outlay of four thousand dollars and with the labor of forty slaves—men and women—he constructed a complete plant, made his crop, refined his sugar, and sold the product for twelve thousand dollars. According to the Intendant of Louisiana, his profit the first year was five thousand dollars.[6] Collot states that he obtained a yield of only eight or nine hundred livres of sugar per acre, as against a normal yield of three or four times as much in St. Domingue, but that his sugar was of the highest quality and found a ready market in Europe and the United States.

II

Two facts will show how completely the commerce of Louisiana was revolutionized in the last years of the Spanish régime. In 1797, about half the ships that brought goods to New Orleans returned in ballast for lack of a cargo; but by 1802 the situation had been reversed, and probably one third of the ships that sailed from New

Orleans arrived there in ballast. Cotton, sugar, and flour had effected the revolution. As a corollary of this development there occurred a change in the government policy regarding the exportation of specie from Louisiana. Upon the urgent recommendation of colonial officials, extending over a period of several years, the king had ordered in 1797 that the exportation of specie, hitherto prohibited under severe penalties, should thenceforth be permitted, subject only to a duty of six per cent. The purpose of the concession was to enable the colony to make good its unfavorable trade balance. For various reasons the order was not received in Louisiana until January, 1802. By that time the character of the colony's commerce had so completely changed that the Intendant refused to enforce it, arguing that the increase of cotton and sugar exports had wiped out the unfavorable trade balance and so had destroyed the premises on which the order was based.[7]

As a matter of fact, it appears that, despite the growth of its exports, Louisiana still had an unfavorable trade balance to the very end of the Spanish period, and that this balance always amounted to some four hundred thousand dollars, which was nearly four fifths of the annual subvention in specie sent to New Orleans from Mexico for the support of the colonial government. In other words, whatever the exports in commodities might amount to, the local merchants were able to count upon the exportation of a fairly constant sum in specie for the purchase of an additional supply of goods from abroad. The law prohibiting the exportation of specie was almost a dead letter. Try as they might—and the evidence indicates that they seldom tried very hard—the customs officials could do nothing more than detect an occasional offender. When on rare occasions big game was caught, as in the case of the *Noah's Ark* which attempted to sail for Philadelphia in 1794 with forty thousand dollars in specie, public opinion forced the colonial officials to recommend clemency, and the fear of revolution in Louisiana compelled the court to approve the recommendation.[8]

In short, specie was simply one of the commodities regularly exported from Louisiana, and as the annual subvention remained at substantially the same figure from 1785 to 1803, the amount of specie exported varied but little from year to year. This probably explains why there was so little variation throughout the period in the unfavorable balance of trade. In 1787, with exports at $700,000, imports stood at $1,100,000. In 1802 the figures were respectively $2,100,000 and $2,500,000.[9] Much of this smuggled coin went by land and sea to the United States, where specie was at a premium and where the silver stream increased the desire of merchants and farmers for trade with Spanish Louisiana.

The statistics of commerce at New Orleans that have just been given are probably not accurate, but it is not unlikely that the element of error remained fairly constant and that the impression of the rate of growth which the figures give is substantially correct. Except for such comparative purposes, it is almost a waste of time to examine the voluminous records kept by the port officials of New Orleans and now preserved in the Archives of the Indies at Seville. The details of customs inspection were naturally left to subordinate officials, of whom the Governor himself wrote in an official letter in 1797 that their corruption must be taken for granted.[10] These poorly paid underlings had their price, and the prices were so well known as to constitute a kind of extra-official tariff, and so very low that no one could complain of them but the king, whom they defrauded. For instance, cotton was subject to a duty of about $3.25 a bale, but the payment of the duty might be avoided by bribing the inspector to look the other way at the rate of thirteen and a half cents a bale.[11] Another dodge was to export fine furs wrapped in bundles of deerskins. With the establishment of the American deposit, the facilities for smuggling were greatly enlarged, especially when the volume of traffic became so great as almost to swamp the small staff of customs officials. One of the commonest devices was to deposit, say, one hundred bales of cotton, declare that one hundred and fifty bales had been deposited, obtain a certificate to that effect from the overworked and negligent inspector, and later export the hundred bales actually deposited, together with fifty bales of Louisiana cotton. The latter thereby escaped paying either the legal six per cent duty or the modest bribe which had hitherto been the only alternative to the payment of the duty.[12] The same procedure was followed in the case of specie, until in 1801 the suspicious Intendant, discovering that two parties of Kentucky boatmen who declared they were depositing $4,300 actually possessed only $140, established a separate coffer for the deposit of American specie under his own personal supervision. To the great disgust of the Americans he charged a three per cent duty for this compulsory service; and he then wrote the court asking for a share of the revenue thus raised.[13] It was granted him.

The shipping records of New Orleans are not as open to exception as are the records of imports and exports, for, even with a well-greased palm, customs officials could not afford to ignore the presence of a schooner in port. The governors and intendants, who were generally honest men, could compel their subordinates to enforce the law to that extent at least. Even in these records, however, there is one important hiatus. After the Americans began to use the right of free navigation—the first case, it will be recalled, occurred in December, 1796—many ships that visited New Orleans were not mentioned in the Spanish records, which included only such vessels as paid duties. Hence it is that while the total number of vessels sailing from New Orleans in 1802 appears to have been 265, the Spanish records mention only 211.[14] The difference between these two figures presumably represents the number of American ships whose cargoes came exclusively from the deposit and were therefore sent out duty free. Moreover the Spanish records are quite unreliable as to the nationality of the vessels listed. Except in the period from June 11, 1798, to October 18, 1802, during which American and other neutral vessels were admitted to New Orleans on the same terms as those of Spain, there were undoubtedly many ships entered as Spanish (or, at times, as French) which were in reality English or American; and in that interval from 1798 to 1802 English ships sometimes masqueraded as Americans.[15]

With these exceptions, the shipping records may be used with the assurance that they are substantially correct; and they yield some interesting facts regarding the development of commerce on the Mississippi from 1793 to 1803.[16] As stated in an earlier chapter, the number of sailings from New Orleans fell from 113 to 1786 to 98 in 1789, creeping back up to 116 in 1793. In that year, however, war broke out between Spain and France. Since the latter, together with its West India islands, had supplied a large part of the goods consumed in Louisiana and had taken a large part of its produce, the colony's trade was thrown into dire confusion. Despite the concessions granted by the royal order of June, 1793, it languished miserably until 1798, when the opening of the American deposit and the admission of neutral ships on advantageous terms brought about a quick recovery and a remarkable expansion of commerce at New Orleans. Thus, while there were only 95 sailings from that port in 1794, the same number in 1795, 93 in 1796, and 95 again in 1797, the number rose to 102 in 1798, 119 in 1799, and, after a temporary drop to 97 in 1800, rose again with great rapidity in the following years—to

138 in 1801 and 211 in 1802. The exclusion of neutrals after October, 1802, reduced the number to 142 in 1803; but the loss was more apparent than real. In that year, as throughout the period after the establishment of the deposit, many unrecorded vessels called at New Orleans for American cargoes. If the proportion existing in 1802 may be taken as an index, the approximate number of American vessels calling at the port for that purpose in any given year after the opening of the deposit was about one fourth of the total number of sailings listed in the Spanish records for the same period.

While the commerce of Louisiana expanded rapidly at the turn of the century, the share of the United States in that commerce increased at an even more rapid rate. The trend can be conveniently illustrated by the nationality of vessels calling at New Orleans and by the destination of those leaving it. Prior to 1796, for reasons stated above, the American flag never appeared at New Orleans save under special license from the governor in very rare cases of emergency, as for instance after the great fire of 1794. In 1802, however, more than half of the ships which arrived at New Orleans were of American nationality (158 in a total of 265), and in tonnage the American ships made up more than two thirds of the total (21,-383 tons in a total of 31,241).[17] On a single day (May 7, 1802) there were, according to the vice consul, "upwards of thirty-five American Vessels in Port." [18]

There was a corresponding shift in the destination of ships leaving New Orleans. In 1787, which may be taken as a typical year for the decade from 1784 to 1793, 42 of the 108 vessels sailing from New Orleans cleared for the French West Indies and 6 for France. Of the remaining 60, 41 cleared for Havana; and none, of course, for the United States. In 1794, the first full war-year, 54 of the 95 sailings were for Havana, 12 for Philadelphia, 9 for New York, and 3 for other ports of the United States. Much the same proportion was maintained through the next three years, somewhat more than half of the ships making the short and comparatively safe voyage to Havana, and somewhat more than a quarter of them clearing for the neutral ports of the United States. With the admission of neutrals to equal privileges at New Orleans in 1798, the proportion of sailings to the United States rose sharply; and after the first year sailings to Havana were considerably reduced. New York, moreover, had by this time supplanted Philadelphia as the favorite destination in the United

States. The following table of sailings from New Orleans shows
the movement in detail:

DESTINATION

Year	Total Number of Sailings	Havana	New York	Phila- delphia	Balti- more	Charles- ton	Other Ports in U. S.	Ports not in U. S. (other than Havana)
1798	102	63	24	3	2	1	0	9
1799	119	29	35	6	12	3	10	24
1800	97	16	28	13	4	2	12	22
1801	138	16	41	14	8	21	13	25
1802	211	54	39	17	13	4	4	80

It will be noticed that the figure in the last column (sailings to
ports other than Havana and those of the United States) is much
larger for 1802 than for the preceding years covered in the table.
The explanation lies partly in the fact that in this first year of peace
Louisiana's trade began to swing back into the pre-war channel—46
ships sailed for ports of France or the French West Indies, chiefly
Bordeaux (18), Guadeloupe (11), and St. Domingue (15). Yet the
old channel was not quite the same. Before 1793 French trade with
Louisiana had been carried on mainly through St. Domingue, but in
1802 St. Domingue was rivaled by Guadeloupe and surpassed by
Bordeaux.

The tendency shown in 1802 was carried still further the following year. Of the total of 142 sailings, only one was for a port of the
United States (Baltimore). Sixty-four were for Havana and 35 for
the ports of France and its colonies, 22 ships clearing for Bordeaux
alone. The virtual disappearance of sailings for ports of the United
States is explained by the fact that under the proclamation of October 16, 1802, trade with Louisiana was no longer open to the
Americans,[19] and that the numerous American vessels which took
cargoes exclusively from the deposit were not listed in the Spanish
shipping records. The swing back to French ports was still notice-
able, for, while sailings for French ports were less numerous in 1803
than in 1802, they constituted a larger proportion of the total number
of sailings.

This movement raises an interesting question. If peace had continued, might not France have recovered its commercial ascendancy
in Louisiana as completely as Great Britain had done in the United
States after the American Revolution? Might not old commercial
habits, community of language, and the predilection of the creoles for

French goods have demonstrated that the American mastery of Louisiana commerce in the preceding few months was not a genuine economic conquest but only an essay in war relief? Napoleon certainly intended to legislate the commerce of the province into French hands, and the excellent market that existed in France for what were now the chief products of Louisiana—sugar and cotton—together with the quick reversion of the colony's commerce to France in 1802 and 1803, inclines one to the belief that Napoleon's effort might have succeeded.

III

One of the chief reasons for the growth of commerce at New Orleans was the great increase in the export trade down the river from the American West—the Illinois country, the Ohio Valley, and, after its transfer to American possession in March, 1798, the Natchez district. The Natchez cotton crop, which was negligible in 1795, was valued at $700,000 in 1801, and most of it was sent down the river to seek passage for Europe.[20] Flour shipments, however, furnish the best basis of comparison and give the best idea of the growth of the river trade, for flour had already become the chief export item before the deposit was opened. In 1794, the year before the treaty of San Lorenzo was signed, 5,400 barrels of flour from the American West paid import duties at New Orleans.[21] In 1797, the year before the deposit was opened, the number of barrels was 8,600. During the next three years, despite the diversion of American flour to an oversea market by the opening of the deposit, the number still hovered between 7,000 and 7,500. In 1802 and 1803 there was a sharp upturn to 12,000 and 14,500 respectively. The increase was probably due to the reduction of the demand in the West Indies with the return of peace, as well as to the closing of the deposit.

Here is at least one field in which the American economic penetration of Louisiana was genuine, for the peace of Amiens did not deprive the West of its recently won hold on the grain market of lower Louisiana. On the contrary, its grip tightened as the certainty of an outlet for their produce encouraged the Westerners to improve their milling methods and to develop business connections at New Orleans. In 1797, while the war was in progress, the total flour imports of New Orleans were 11,580 barrels; of this number, 8,600 came from the American West. In 1803, in time of peace, the figures were respectively 16,385 and 14,500.

Large as was the increase in the Westerners' trade with Louisiana, it was completely overshadowed by the growth of the export trade which they carried on through the New Orleans deposit.[22] Again flour is the index. In 1802, while 12,200 barrels of flour from the American West were sold at New Orleans, presumably for local consumption, the deposit received from the same source some 70,000 barrels, virtually all of which was withdrawn for exportation duty free, principally to the West Indies. For purposes of comparison the foregoing figures have been taken from the Spanish customs records. A more accurate statement of the river trade at its height is furnished by the American customs records kept at Loftus Heights, the southernmost port of entry of the United States on the Mississippi. These show that, in 1801, commodities to the value of $1,095,412 passed that place on their way down the river to lower Louisiana.[23] The chief item was 73,058 barrels of flour, which was ten times the amount imported into New Orleans from the West for domestic use in the same year. That is, in 1801 as in 1802, much the greater part of the Western flour exports passed through the deposit to the West Indies and other oversea markets. Other items in the 1801 list were: cotton, 5,923 bales (250 or 300 pounds to the bale); cordage, 147,400 pounds; iron (bar and castings), 24,570 pounds; lead, 67,900 pounds; merchandise, $22,105; peltry, 7,692 pounds; tobacco, 1,068 hogsheads. Until 1801 whisky was a frequent item in Western shipments to New Orleans. In that year the Intendant prohibited its importation, partly on the ground that it was injurious to the health of the colonists, but chiefly because it was underselling domestic rum, to the great displeasure of the Louisiana sugar planters.[24]

Almost the whole of this river trade was carried on in flatboats knocked together at any convenient place on the Ohio or its tributaries. Of the 585 craft that carried the West's million dollars' worth of produce down the Mississippi in 1801, 514 were flatboats, 50 keelboats, 19 pirogues, 1 a brig and 1 a schooner. There was the greatest diversity in the nomenclature, design, and dimensions of the flatboats. They were frequently, though by no means invariably, known as "Kentucky boats" from their principal place of origin, and as "Orleans boats" from their destination. According to a western Pennsylvanian, writing in 1802, they would generally "carry from two to five or six hundred barrels of flour." [25] Early in 1803 the well-known Pittsburgh shipbuilding firm of Tarascon Brothers, James Berthoud and Company advertised for sale "Several Mississippi Flat-bottomed boats, from 40 to 45 feet long, built in the best manner, with chimneys and pumps complete." [26] The Englishman, Francis Baily, who visited Pittsburgh in 1796, states that the boats were at that time usually thirty or forty feet long and twelve feet broad, with a draft of only eighteen inches when loaded, and that they cost from one dollar to one dollar and a quarter per twelve square feet. An extra charge was made for such accessories as pumps and chimneys. Victor Collot, who descended the Ohio and the Mississippi in 1796, advised strongly against the use of flat-bottomed Kentucky boats on the Mississippi, since they were built without nails and were too flimsy. He thought keelboats far superior for this purpose, and recommended a boat from forty to forty-five feet long, twelve broad, and four deep [27]—that is, with the sides built up to a height of four feet for protection against both the elements and marauders.

The crew of a flatboat normally consisted of five men including the "patron." The trip down the river from Kentucky required a month or six weeks; from Pittsburgh, an additional two weeks, though of course the period varied widely in individual cases. It was estimated about 1796 that 250 barrels of flour could be taken from Kentucky to New Orleans at a net cost of $360, allowing $110 for the cost of the boat, $160 for four men's wages, $50 for the patron, $45 for provisions and liquor (for five men, thirty-six days at eighteen pence per day), and deducting five dollars for what the boat would bring at New Orleans.[28] Freight rates from Natchez to New Orleans were one dollar per ton in 1801, and the newspaper at the rival town of Nashville bestowed the epithet "patriotic" upon a certain Captain Caffery when he offered to take freight from that town to New Orleans at the same rate.[29]

Much has been written of the rowdy gangs of river boatmen who, once their business at New Orleans was done, returned to Natchez-under-the-Hill for a carouse before plunging into the wilderness on their way to Nashville, Kentucky, and Pittsburgh. There is a good deal of truth in the story. The boatmen were a rowdy lot, of the same breed as the Erie Canal boatmen celebrated by Herman Melville. For many of them the carouse began long before they reached Natchez. An American writing from New Orleans in 1801 said: ". . . our foolish Kentucky men spend and lose their money in this place most infamously." [30] But there must have been many who were not so foolish, for a large stream of Spanish gold and silver poured northward along the Natchez Trace into the Ohio Valley settlements.

In 1801 a Nashville newspaper reported: "From the best calculation we are able to make, there has not less than 120,000 dollars crossed the Cumberland at this place from New-Orleans and the Natchez, destined for Kentucky, and the back parts of Pennsylvania, and horse-loads daily passing." [31] This was only three years after a Kentucky representative in Congress asserted that there was not as much as ten thousand dollars in coin in circulation in the whole of his State.

On an unpoliced road and in a society where every man fended for himself and expected others to do the same, the opportunities for plunder were too enticing and too numerous to go unimproved. Gangs of gunmen, oftener white than red, infested the highways. Cave-in-Rock on the Ohio, Chickasaw Bluffs and Walnut Hills on the Mississippi, and the Natchez Trace between Natchez and Nashville were among their favorite haunts. The most notorious of these birds of prey were the Mason gang, whose leader is portrayed in some accounts as the conventional gentleman highwayman of romance, and the Harpes, "Big" and "Little," who killed for the pleasure of inflicting pain. One gets the impression, however, that Robin Hood and Marquis de Sade had few counterparts among the highwaymen, who generally conducted their operations in a quite businesslike fashion. At Natchez, for instance, they are reported to have had confederates who informed them which parties of travelers had enough money to make a hold-up worth while; and when the victims reached the ambush, they were relieved of their valuables with as little violence as the circumstances permitted.[32]

Curiously enough, the brawling river boatmen who terrorized law-abiding citizens in the river towns fell easy victims to the highwaymen. Whether it was because of this danger or because of the tedium of the long overland journey, comparatively few of those who floated down the river to New Orleans returned through the wilderness to the Ohio Valley. As for returning by the Mississippi itself, that was possible for only a small fraction of the boatmen, so great was the excess of downstream over upstream traffic. According to a statement made in 1802, not one third of the boatmen who went down the river from Kentucky each year ever returned to it.[33] The result was that New Orleans swarmed with Americans seeking employment on ships sailing for the United States by way of the Gulf, and the American consular agents at that place found it almost impossible to protect crews from abuse at the hands of unscrupulous captains. The transients also suffered grievously for want of proper medical attention until 1802, when an American hospital was established at New Orleans with funds provided by Congress and administered by the consul.[34] Under these conditions the development of a professional class of boatmen proceeded very slowly. As late as 1811, Zadok Cramer, writing in *The Navigator*, said that Pittsburgh merchants were just beginning to employ keelboats with professional crews in place of flatboats which they manned themselves.[35]

IV

Lack of information makes it dangerous to generalize about the way in which this business was conducted. One thing that is fairly certain is that the procedure varied widely in individual cases. This was a necessary consequence of the complete lack of banking facilities and of the rudimentary development of commercial connections between the Ohio Valley and New Orleans. Sometimes the exporter had a friend in that town who would look after his interests. James Wilkinson and Philip Nolan stood in this relation about 1791, when Wilkinson engaged a certain Hugh McIlvain to take 120 hogsheads of tobacco to the creole capital, where he was to be governed by Nolan's instructions in disposing of it. If Nolan thought it advisable, McIlvain was to offer a certain Spanish official as much as $4,000 to get the tobacco purchased by the government for the royal stores.[36]

The best facilities for carrying on this triangular trade were enjoyed by Philadelphia and Baltimore merchants who had factors at Pittsburgh and correspondents at New Orleans;[37] but apparently only a small fraction of the trade passed through their hands. As we have noted elsewhere, more ships sailed from New Orleans to New York than to Philadelphia; and yet New York's share of the export trade to the Ohio Valley was still insignificant compared with that of Philadelphia. The export trade in produce from the Ohio Valley to New Orleans was indeed of too recent origin and was expanding too rapidly to lend itself to organization, and geographical factors prevented any merchant or group of merchants from getting control of it. On the Ohio and its tributaries, every river farm was a potential port, every man who could use hammer and saw was a boatbuilder, and every farmer an exporter. The Mississippi trade was a free-for-all, a mad scramble to be the first to reach New Orleans on the spring floods and sell one's flour at the fancy prices that still held over from the winter period of scarcity. The same scene was again enacted, though on a smaller scale, when the autumn rains once more raised the rivers to flood levels.

Upon his arrival at New Orleans the farmer, having played the part of boatman, proceeded to turn trader. This last and vitally important operation was carried out under the most unfavorable conditions—in a foreign city, where the language and laws were strange to the frontiersman, and where American produce was for the most part purchased for an oversea market whose wants were utterly unknown to him. Save in flush times, the results were inevitably disappointing. "It is but too well known," said a western Pennsylvanian in 1802, "what difficulty and distress our traders have suffered at that place [New Orleans] for want of storage, advice and assistance, when markets were dull, or rather no market at all." [38]

An increasingly large share of the Westerners' business fell into the hands of the American and creole merchants at New Orleans. Among these were Daniel Clark and Evan Jones, both of whom were at various times consular agents of the United States at that port; also Shepherd Brown, Cochran and Rhea, and Lanthois and Pitot.[39] In 1802 this development was accelerated by the Intendant's order requiring all deposited goods to be bonded by two merchants of New Orleans.[40] The latter seem to have operated on commission for the most part, taking no risk themselves, but selling for their clients at the market price and charging a commission of two and a half per cent whether the produce was disposed of in New Orleans or shipped to a foreign market.[41]

The proceeds of sales at New Orleans were sometimes turned into cash, which was sent northward over the Natchez Trace; and sometimes invested in cotton and sugar, which were shipped to the West Indies or an Atlantic seaport and there sold. In the latter case the transaction was usually completed by the purchase of merchandise at Philadelphia or Baltimore for the Western market. Drafts were not unknown, though their use does not seem to have been extensive before 1803. William Dunbar of Natchez made an arrangement by which he could draw on his London correspondents to the value of two thirds of his cotton exports from New Orleans, and in one such case he paid a three per cent discount for a draft in the amount of one thousand dollars.[42] It is not likely that, at that early day, less distinguished persons were able to obtain the same privilege as Dunbar, who was a well-known scientist as well as a prosperous planter, had served as Spain's representative in the demarcation of the southern boundary of the United States (1798), and corresponded with many persons of prominence in his native Great Britain and the Atlantic States, among them Thomas Jefferson.

A procedure which seems to have been rather common was employed by Ezekiel and Daniel Forman in 1790 and by William Johnson in 1801. Detailed accounts of both ventures have been preserved, and as Johnson's illustrates the hazards of the still highly speculative trade when it was at its height, we may follow his movements in some detail.[43] In October, 1800, William and his "Brother Sammy" arrived at Pittsburgh from Newton, New Jersey. Exchanging their horse for wheat, which was then ground into flour, they bought a thirty-ton boat for sixty dollars and loaded it with the flour, apples, brandy, and whisky. On February 10, 1801, they left Pittsburgh for New Orleans, which they reached on April 14 after a narrow escape from shipwreck just below Natchez. As they had beaten most of their competitors to market, their flour brought a good price; but within the next few days large quantities came down the river and the price tumbled to so low a level that they decided to rebuy and try another flour "speck" in the West Indies.

Shortly after their arrival, William, like so many newcomers from the North, fell sick, suffering from a complaint that was diagnosed as cholera morbus. A few days later, however, he was well enough to attend an oyster supper where, he recorded, "13 of us drank 27 bottles of long-cork claret." On the following day he confided to his journal that "the long-cork claret had a good effect on me," and the brothers went ahead with their business. Captain Manwarring of the *Ocean,* an American vessel, agreed to take their flour to Havana for $3.25 a barrel, but it soon developed that the *Ocean* was too small to take the whole lot. They then decided to exchange the surplus for cotton, which William was to take to New York in the *Neptune* while Brother Sammy escorted the flour to Havana.[44] Since the transaction was of such a nature that it could not be carried on through the American deposit, they had to pay the usual Spanish duties of six per cent on the produce that they had imported and six per cent on the cotton and flour that they were taking away with them.

The *Ocean,* which sailed first, took the brothers together as far as the Balize, at the river's mouth. The trip was uneventful, the *Ocean* leaving New Orleans on May 15, anchoring at dusk every evening and arriving at the Balize on May 18. There the brothers separated, and there the dangers of the voyage began. The *Ocean* went aground while crossing the bar, and its captain had to pay a passing schooner $600 to help him out of the mud. In due course the *Neptune,* accompanied by another ship, arrived at the Balize and took William on board. For several days they had to remain at anchor awaiting the proper conjunction of time, tide, and wind. On June second this came and they set sail, only to run aground, although the *Neptune's* companion had paid the same schooner $1,200 to lighter it across the bar. The *Neptune* was able to extricate itself by emptying its watercasks, which were refilled when the ship was safe across the bar in five fathoms of water; but the other vessel was still stuck fast in the mud when the *Neptune* passed out of sight.

For several days all went well, but in the cross-currents and shifting winds of the Gulf of Mexico the ship's captain lost his bearings and ran on a reef. This misfortune nearly cost the crew and passengers their lives. By throwing overboard most of the cargo, including William's cotton, they at last got the ship free. It was not until July fourth, a month and two days after leaving the mouth of the Mississippi, that the *Neptune* reached the Bahama Channel and got into the gulf stream. From that time on they had plain sailing, and arrived at New York a fortnight later. William was delighted at the outcome, for though his cotton was lost his life was saved. At a New York coffee house he had the consolation of learning from a captain just in from Havana that Brother Sammy had sold his flour at the very satisfactory price of eighteen dollars a barrel, and had invested the proceeds in sugar, which he was bringing to New York in the *Ocean.*

v

Quite aside from the justifiable fear that international complications might throw it out of joint at any moment, there was widespread dissatisfaction with the way in which the Mississippi trade was carried on. It was regarded as wasteful and unnecessarily cumbersome, with its trans-shipments at New Orleans, the dangerous return trip over the Natchez Trace, and the importation of merchandise into the Mississippi Valley by wretched wagon roads over the mountains. Both Americans and Spaniards tried repeatedly to improve the system. For obvious reasons, Spanish officials at New Orleans were eager to have that port supplant the Atlantic seaboard as the source of supply of manufactured goods for the Ohio Valley.

By way of experiment they permitted James Wilkinson to ship a consignment of goods from New Orleans to Kentucky in the *Speedwell* in 1788, but the venture turned out disastrously.[45]

As late as 1797, Victor Collot, who had just spent several months in the Mississippi Valley, still believed that it would be possible to develop a large up-stream traffic. Such shipments were sometimes made, as in 1802 when a consignment of sugar from New Orleans reached Kentucky.[46] By dint of poling, towing, rowing, and warping, a river boat using both sails and oars could be got up to Kentucky in two and half or three months. The galleys of the Spanish river fleet were constantly passing up and down the river, and commercial craft frequently plied the Ohio and the lower Mississippi in both directions. The first barge packet on the Ohio was the *Mayflower*. It was built in 1788 by Captain Jonathan Devol, a Rhode Island shipbuilder settled on the Muskingum, and served as a packet between Marietta, Wheeling, and Pittsburgh.[47] By 1801 there had also grown up a not inconsiderable traffic between upper Louisiana and the Ohio Valley, which seems to have been based in large part on the exports of lead from Moses Austin's mines near St. Louis.[48] Similarly the lower Mississippi was well served by river boats, which were generally of from fifteen to thirty tons' burden. In 1801 these boats brought from New Orleans to Natchez merchandise on which import duties aggregating $16,000 were paid.[49] The two regions, however, were separated by too extensive a wilderness to be linked by a regular up-stream service, for from Natchez to the Ohio there were only two or three settlements of any consequence.

For commercial purposes, Natchez marked the northernmost limit of the export trade from New Orleans. To that point very considerable shipments were made. Duties on such shipments rose from $16,000 in 1801 to $25,000 in 1802. They fell to slightly less than $15,000 in the first nine months of 1803, partly because of the closing of the deposit. That event was also responsible for the ascent of the first sea-going vessels to Natchez. Hitherto they had stopped at New Orleans, where goods for the up-river trade were transferred to smaller craft. The 179-ton *Mary* of Boston, which arrived at Natchez in January, 1803, was said to have been the first ship of American registry that ever performed the feat; it was certainly the largest of that year's arrivals. An incomplete list shows that thirteen ocean-going vessels came to Natchez between October 1, 1802, and September 30, 1803. Besides the *Mary* there were nine schooners of from

31 to 111 tons; a sloop of 51 tons; and a brig of 146 tons.[50] Six came from the Atlantic seaports of the United States, two from New Orleans, four from the West Indies, and one from London, and they were only slightly smaller than those which came regularly to New Orleans, the latter averaging about 120 tons.[51]

In the light of these facts, Jefferson seems to have had some ground for believing that the United States could, in case of necessity, make itself independent of New Orleans by developing the rival port of Natchez.[52] Neither port could have overcome the difficulties of up-stream navigation through the hundreds of miles of wilderness which separated them from the American West, but if either Spain or France had pursued an excessively illiberal commercial policy at New Orleans, Natchez might have supplanted it as the junction point for the West's great and growing export trade. At any rate, the 179-ton *Mary* of Boston had shown that the manipulators of tariffs at New Orleans would have to adjust their duties to the differential between up-stream and down-stream freight rates between that port and Natchez. Outright exclusion of American commerce from New Orleans would have been suicidal.

Corporate enterprise soon promised to make smooth the path blazed by pioneer traders. In 1802 a company with a capital of $20,000 was organized at Lexington, Kentucky, to insure vessels navigating "the Western Waters" as far south as Natchez and New Orleans; and in February of that year it was stated that a large number of vessels had already taken out policies at a premium of three and a half percent.[53] Another venture, "The Ohio Company, for the improvement of the Mississippi trade," was launched at Pittsburgh in September, 1802, by a number of inhabitants of Western Pennsylvania and Virginia for the purpose of exporting "the produce and commodities of that country, by the channel of the Mississippi." Such coöperation was necessary, they declared, in order to obviate the difficulties which rendered prices precarious and discouraged industry, "and which are too formidable to be any longer encountered by the limited credit and capital of individuals." Shares were to be sold at one hundred dollars each, and the company (which was to be under the management of a president and twelve directors) was to purchase commodities and export them to the best market at the joint risk and for the joint benefit of the members. Subscribers were required to pay one dollar down, and the balance at such time and place as the directors might determine, with the proviso that one fifth should be in cash and four fifths in produce. Nothing seems to have come of the enterprise, which was launched just before the receipt of news that the deposit had been closed and was attacked by Republicans as a Federalist electioneering scheme.[54]

It was from undertakings of this character and as a by-product of the Mississippi export trade that Western banking institutions first developed. As New York city had its water company, so the West had its insurance and banking companies. The charter of incorporation of the Kentucky insurance company established in 1802 contained an astutely worded clause by virtue of which the bills issued by the company were to all intents and purposes bank bills. "Thus indirectly," wrote an indignant Kentuckian some thirty years later, "was a bank forced upon our legislators." But at least he had the grim pleasure of recording that, while this surreptitious bank began in fraud, it ended (in 1818) in bankruptcy.[55] An Ohio venture which combined some of the principal features of the Pittsburgh Ohio Company and the Kentucky insurance company was launched at Cincinnati in February, 1803, under the name of the Miami Exporting Company. In obvious imitation of the Pittsburgh project, this company was designed to carry on the export trade down the Ohio and Mississippi. The extension of its activities into the banking field was a natural, almost an inevitable, consequence. The merchants and millers who were engaged in that trade and who were the organizers of the company, were already providing currency and credit facilities for their neighbors; so that with the formation of the Miami Exporting Company they only began to do collectively what they had for some years past been doing individually.[56]

A still more interesting effort to improve the facilities for carrying on the river trade was the construction of sea-going vessels on the waters of the Ohio. Built and launched at Pittsburgh, Marietta, and elsewhere, these ships carried Western produce straight to the market in the West Indies, the Atlantic States and Europe, thus avoiding the expense of trans-shipment and the petty annoyances of Spanish officials at New Orleans. As early as 1792 a sloop built on the Monongahela sailed down the Ohio and the Mississippi to the West Indies and thence to Philadelphia; but this venture seems to have been not so much a commercial gesture as a political grimace, since its chief purpose was to show Spain what the Kentuckians thought of its edict closing the Mississippi to foreign ships.[57]

At any rate this was an isolated case, for it was not until 1801 that the next sea-going ship was launched on the waters of the Ohio. In the interval a stimulus to shipbuilding had been given by the construction of two gunboats for the United States at Pittsburgh in 1798 and 1799 and by the phenomenal increase of the river traffic following the establishment of the deposit and the opening of New Orleans to American commerce in 1798. In 1801, five sea-going ships sailed down the Ohio and the Mississippi to oversea ports. The number fell to four in 1802, but rose again to eleven in 1803. In the nine days from April 27 to May 5 of the latter year, six ships passed the rapids at Louisville without mishap. One of them, the *Indiana,* left Louisville on April 29, and after stopping at Natchez and New Orleans, proceeded to New York, where she arrived safely about July 29. Her captain reported that he had left at New Orleans four ships from Marietta and one from Pittsburgh, all bound for Liverpool.[58] These Western ships ranged in size from the *Dorcas and Sally* of fifty tons to the *Pittsburgh* of two hundred and fifty tons. Most of them were rigged as schooners and brigs. Twelve of the twenty ships launched in these three years were built at Marietta, and the rest at Pittsburgh, Wheeling, Elizabeth, and Frankfort.[59]

This spectacular development was hailed with appropriate superlatives by the Western people. A ship under construction at Louisville was described as "the most arduous undertaking of the kind we have as yet heard of on the Western waters, and the first keel ever laid in the state of Kentucky." The undertaking was indeed a little too arduous, for the launching of the ship was twice postponed and, so far as is known, never took place. The *Pittsburgh,* a ship of two hundred and fifty (according to one report, two hundred and seventy) tons' burden launched at the town of the same name in February, 1803, was proclaimed "the largest vessel that ever floated on these waters." When the septuagenerian Commodore Abraham Whipple arrived at New Orleans with the *St. Clair* of Marietta in June, 1801, he was reported to have said that he "thinks it the greatest thing he ever did, and deserves more credit than his going out of Newport in a frigate with despatches from Congress, after passing seven British frigates lying on the harbour in order to blockade him there." [60]

The enthusiasm of the Westerners for the new enterprise was not unreasonable. They had all the materials for shipbuilding at hand—timber from their forests, iron from their iron works, rope and cordage from their rope-walks. Sails, though often imported from

Philadelphia and Baltimore, were sometimes manufactured on the spot. There were experienced shipwrights, such as Jonathan Devol of Marietta, and Tarascon Brothers, James Berthoud and Company of Pittsburgh. If the larger vessels could descend the river only during the period of the spring floods, the same seasonal limitation was suffered, though in a less degree, by the flatboats, for which the trip was intolerably slow except when the river was at flood stage. There was sound economic justification for the building of sea-going ships, which flourished until the embargo of 1808 and steamboat competition brought about their decline and disappearance.[61]

VI

Of the many far-reaching consequences of the commercial revolution that occurred in the Mississippi Valley between 1793 and 1803, the most striking was the economic and social penetration of Louisiana by the United States. In 1792 only a scant dozen flatboats came down to New Orleans from the American West, and maritime commerce with the United States was prohibited. The one ship that sailed from New Orleans for a port of the United States in that year did so by special dispensation of the governor-intendant. In 1802, more than 550 river craft arrived at New Orleans from the American West, and more than half of the sea-going vessels in that port flew the American flag. It has already been suggested that there is some doubt whether the contrast, striking though it is, represents a genuine economic penetration. While the war lasted, many of the nominally American ships at New Orleans were undoubtedly the property of Englishmen and other foreigners who desired the protection of a neutral flag; and after the restoration of peace, France began to recover rapidly the ascendancy that it had held in the commerce of Louisiana before 1793. Moreover, most of the merchandise brought to Louisiana from the United States consisted of reëxported British goods.

On the other hand, there are some indications that the American penetration was genuine and would be lasting. By 1801 the American West had a firm hold on the New Orleans flour market. Spanish products, under cover of the American deposit, were finding their way out of Louisiana in American ships; and as long as the deposit was continued at New Orleans and its European sovereign maintained a protective system in Louisiana, the practice was not likely to diminish. Whatever the causes of the American commercial ascendancy in Louisiana may have been, the fact remains that a powerful American interest had been built up at New Orleans. In January, 1803, Robert Livingston, American minister to France, asserted that at least half the trade of New Orleans was "carried on upon the capital of citizens of the United States"; and since he probably obtained his information from the New Orleans merchant, Daniel Clark, whom he had recently seen in Paris, the estimate may have approximated the truth.[62]

It seems reasonable to assume that the steady flow of American river boatmen and seamen through New Orleans was another instrument of penetration. In August, 1801, the acting consul, Evan Jones, estimated that in the past twelve months some two hundred American vessels, with an average crew of at least eight sailors, had come up the river to New Orleans, and that three hundred and fifty or four hundred craft, each with four men, had come down it from the West; in other words, that in a single year some 3,200 American sailors and boatmen had visited New Orleans.[63] The number was doubtless still larger during the next year; and, barring interference with the right of navigation and the deposit at New Orleans, it might reasonably be expected to increase from year to year. Certainly this floating population of Americans at New Orleans, numbering upwards of three thousand in the course of a year, could hardly fail to make some impression in a city whose resident population was only eight thousand. The Bishop of Louisiana was of the opinion that the godless American immigrants settled in Louisiana were responsible for the deplorable state of faith, morals, and patriotism in the province; but there is no reason to believe that the sailors and boatmen were any less republican or more godly than their farming and hunting countrymen. Whatever the impression they produced at New Orleans, these cohorts of commerce could not be ignored either by the people and government of Louisiana or by their own country.

Another consequence of the commercial revolution was that the United States itself had become Mississippi-minded. Less striking than the American economic penetration of Louisiana, this development was, from the point of view of international relations, more important. In the 1780's, what was known as the "Mississippi interest" embraced only the Southern States and, of course, their Western offshoots, the infant settlements of Kentucky and Tennessee, whose voice was seldom heard or heeded in Congress. Perhaps Rufus King did not accurately express the opinion of his neighbors in the Middle

Atlantic and New England States when he wrote, in 1786, that the closing of the Mississippi would be a boon to the country and that he considered every emigrant who crossed the Appalachians as lost forever to the Union; but certainly there were few Easterners who would have agreed with Hamilton, in 1790, that the free navigation of the Mississippi was essential to the welfare of the United States. Before 1795 there was abundant justification for the frontiersmen's charge that most of the people living north of the Potomac were indifferent or hostile to the West's demand for the free use of its greatest highway.

Within a few years all that was changed. By 1802, partly because of the opening of the Mississippi, the population of the West had grown to half a million—probably ten times as many as at the end of the Revolution. Two Western States, Tennessee and Kentucky, had representatives in Congress who could look after their interests; and a third Western community, Ohio, was on the threshold of statehood. The two national parties were so evenly balanced in the rest of the Union that this Western bloc had an influence out of all proportion to its numbers, as the events of 1802-1803 were to show. Moreover the West could now use statistics as well as rhetoric and prophecy to prove the importance of the Mississippi trade. Its exports down the river were nil in 1786, when Congress adopted John Jay's proposal to acquiesce in the closing of it by Spain for a generation; in 1802 Western exports by that route were valued in the customhouse at nearly two million dollars.[64]

Here was an argument that even merchants on the remote Atlantic seaboard could understand; and they had reasons of their own for abandoning their earlier views on the Mississippi question. Though the river had been wide open to American commerce since 1798, the fear that Philadelphia flour would suffer from the competition of Western flour had not been realized—the war had provided markets for all. Nor was the West doing all its trading with New Orleans, as even George Washington had expected it to. As formerly, Western consumers got what manufactured goods they needed and could afford from cities on the Atlantic seaboard; and by 1802 it was evident that the more produce the West sold down the river, the more goods it would buy over the mountains. These came chiefly from Baltimore and Philadelphia. New York had little share in that business as yet, but its merchants were already planning canals and other internal improvements which would enable it to outstrip its competitors in the Western market.

Most important of all, the Middle Atlantic seaports now had a direct interest in the West's export trade from New Orleans, and in this field the energetic New Yorkers were already supreme. In 1786, when John Jay, a New Yorker, with the support of Rufus King, a New Englander with business and family connections in New York, made his famous proposal to suspend for a generation the claim to the free navigation of the Mississippi, not a single ship from New York or any other port of the United States entered or left New Orleans; but in 1802, seventy-four American ships sailed from New Orleans to ports of the United States with cargoes consisting in whole or in part of the produce of Louisiana, besides many other ships which got their cargoes exclusively from the American deposit. Thirty-nine of these seventy-four ships cleared for New York; the next largest number (seventeen) went to Philadelphia.[65] In developing new fields and in adapting itself to novel conditions, New York was already showing the enterprise that was to carry it ahead of Philadelphia within the next generation.

The Hudson, not the Potomac, was now the northern boundary of the "Mississippi interest." With the extension of that interest into the Middle Atlantic region and with the creation of the new Western States, it had developed from a Southern, sectional interest into a national interest warmly supported in every part of the country except New England. The "Bostoneses" who were incessantly poaching on Spanish preserves in the West Indies, the South Atlantic, and the Pacific almost never turned up at New Orleans. Perhaps this lack of contact with the emporium of Western commerce explains why New England, unlike the rest of the country, remained indifferent to the West's most vital concern. As late as 1814, in the peace negotiations at Ghent, the least provincial of New England statesmen, John Quincy Adams, impressed the outraged Kentuckian, Henry Clay, as the spiritual heir of the John Jay of 1786.

One must not by any means overlook the effect of the growing Mississippi trade upon the West itself. After seven lean years the frontiersmen had thriven mightily in seven fat years, and they were not ready to submit without a struggle to an abridgment of their commercial privileges that might bring on another cycle of hard times. Rather, the prosperity which came at the turn of the century created in them a Gargantuan appetite for more. A Kentuckian probably expressed what was in the minds of most of his fellow Westerners when he wrote in 1799: "The quantity of boats laden with the various productions of the Western Country that has passed here [Henderson] would be incredible to relate, & now they are passing six or seven almost every day. With the improvement that a few years would produce, & a liberal policy in the Eastern States, & general Government, this Country would or might administer to the wants of North, & South America and their dependencies." [66]

CHAPTER IX

FIN DE SIÈCLE

I

Though nothing came of the plans of Hamilton and others for invading Louisiana, it was increasingly clear that Spain's days in the Mississippi Valley were numbered. Floridablanca's defensive system had been dealt a death-blow by the treaty of San Lorenzo, which had also given the Americans facilities for penetrating the remnant of Spanish territory in the valley.[1] Yet in sheer desperation the Spanish officials of Louisiana and Florida clung to Floridablanca's system and continued to go through the motions of promoting immigration, cultivating the friendship of the Southern Indians, and inciting a rebellion in the American West. One could look far before finding a more perfect example of strenuous futility.

Even Governor Carondelet, who had once seen the folly of settling the Goths at the gates of Rome, had by 1796 compromised with his convictions to the extent of admitting the Americans to upper Louisiana.[2] Moses Austin and Daniel Boone were among these immigrants, and for a time George Rogers Clark himself found refuge at St. Louis. Perhaps Carondelet thought that the Americans could at any rate be no worse than the French who already lived there. Thanks to General Collot's visit in 1796, he said, Jacobinism was rampant. A society called the Sansculottes had been organized at St. Louis, and on September 22 (the first day of the revolutionary calendar) had had the effrontery to serenade the curate wishing him a "Happy New Year!"[3]

If Spain had retained these border regions much longer, it might have paid a heavy penalty for permitting the barbarians to settle in them; but no great harm resulted in the brief remaining period of Spanish domination. There were indeed many Americans in upper Louisiana, as well as at Natchez and New Orleans, who were quite content to live under Spanish rule; and when it came to an end there were even some who followed the retreating Spanish flag.[4] This fact, however, is simply another proof of the disintegration of Spanish authority, which was popular because it was ineffective. It was only by being false to itself—setting up in these border provinces a system which was at variance with the most venerable traditions of the empire and the monarchy and then permitting wholesale infractions of the laws which it did profess to enforce—that Spain was able to win a measure of affection from the colonists. Americans flocked to Spanish territory during this period for the same reason that they had so often sought out regions in dispute between the colonies and states of the Atlantic seaboard—namely, because they found there an escape from authority and taxation.

Carondelet still tried to exclude American immigrants from lower Louisiana and West Florida, admitting only European immigrants, preferably Roman Catholics. Spain's land system should have attracted settlers, for it was far more liberal than that of the United States. It was a kind of homestead system, with no charge except fees for surveying and registration; no obligation except that of residence for four years, cultivation of one tenth of the grant, and the erection of a house. The size of the grant depended upon the size of the grantee's family, including slaves, and usually consisted of from five hundred to a thousand acres. Every effort was made to stimulate immigration from desirable sources. Agents had formerly been sent to Philadelphia and New York to divert the stream pouring into those ports from Europe; but since the court disliked this "public solicitation of immigrants," Carondelet then employed promoters such as Baron Bastrop and the Marquis de Maison Rouge, who were offered veritable principalities on condition that they should induce God-fearing Flemings and Germans to settle in the wilds of Louisiana.[5] It was all in vain. Lower Louisiana was too remote from the beaten track of European immigration, its future too uncertain to attract the well-to-do, its plantation system too expensive for the poor immigrant, and its reputation for unhealthfulness too forbidding for either. Maison Rouge failed and passed into obscurity; Bastrop also failed and might never have been heard of again but for Aaron Burr and the Austins, Moses and Stephen. The God-fearing Flemings and Germans found homes elsewhere, and of the handful of settlers whom Bastrop did import, nine tenths turned out to be Americans.[6] Dissatisfied with the Governor's handling of the land system, the Spanish government transferred control of it to the Intendant in 1798.[7] He issued a new set of instructions, extending the ban on American immigrants and renewing the offers to Europeans; but he was no more successful than the Governor had been, and in 1801 he sought to solve the problem by the heroic expedient of closing the land office.[8]

A striking proof of Spain's weakness in the Mississippi Valley was afforded by the continuation of the absurd Kentucky intrigue. Whatever chance there might once have been of revolutionizing the American West in the interest of Spain had disappeared with the treaty of San Lorenzo. Even before news of the treaty reached Kentucky, Michel Lacassagne, one of Spain's agents at Louisville, informed Governor Gayoso that on a recent visit to Lexington, the largest town in the State, he had found everybody ready to make war on the Spaniards.[9] After the publication of the treaty, it was evident that the majority of the people were decidedly unfriendly to Spain and that the so-called Spanish party was sick of the conspiracy and mortally afraid of exposure. When Thomas Power, one of Carondelet's messengers to Wilkinson, passed through Nashville on his way to Kentucky, he narrowly escaped being mobbed as a Spanish agent. With one voice the conspirators assured Carondelet and Gayoso that the time was not ripe for prosecuting the intrigue. Their chief anxiety was to put a stop to Spain's highly embarrassing perseverance in it. Judge Harry Innes and George Nicholas declared flatly that the Kentuckians were able to take care of themselves without any aid from Spain. Even Benjamin Sebastian, though he was willing to compromise himself publicly by visiting New Orleans in 1796 and 1798 and though in the latter year the people of his State were highly displeased with the conduct of the federal government, assured his hosts that they must play a waiting game.[10]

James Wilkinson himself was thoroughly frightened at the turn events had taken. In September, 1796, he sent Philip Nolan to obtain for him a grant of land in Louisiana "to which I may resort in case of necessity."[11] Convinced that the game was up, he buried his cipher; and, although the arrival of a subsidy of $9,000 from New Orleans, together with the promise of the continuation of his $4,000 pension, induced him to disinter the profitable code, he could not disguise his utter inability to forward the intrigue. Like the other conspirators, he could only tell the Spaniards to play a waiting game —and to be punctual with the payment of his pension while they waited. His chief concern, however, was not to keep Spanish gold flowing into his coffers but to prevent Spanish carelessness from affording proof of his corruption, and he adjured Gayoso "in the name of God" never to write or even speak his name. Otherwise his letters of this period are distinguished principally by his denunciations of his fellow Westerners, the very people whom Spain was courting. The dregs and offscourings of society, he called them, assuring Gayoso on his "word of honor" that not one of them was to be trusted. Gayoso took the advice to heart and trusted no one, least of all Wilkinson himself.[12]

Only imbecility or desperation can explain the Spaniards' perseverance in the intrigue in the face of the manifest hostility of the great mass of frontiersmen and the helplessness, demoralization, and mutual jealousy of the conspirators. With the possible exception of Salcedo, the last of them, the governors of Louisiana were not imbeciles, and yet all of them continued the effort begun by Miró and Wilkinson in 1787. The explanation must be that they were desperate. The isolation of the province, the very hostility of the frontiersmen, Indian unrest, all required them to do something; and as there was nothing better to do, they talked about revolutionizing the West. In the manner of the Eastern mystic who gazes fixedly at his navel until he sees visions of bliss, these governors contemplated their absurd conspiracy with unwavering eyes until reality yielded to desire, and they saw the Union dissolved, Spain mistress of the Mississippi Valley, and their own troubles at an end. The Kentucky intrigue was an opiate to quiet their nerves until the executioner's axe should fall.

Even the Spaniards had their lucid intervals. Governor Gayoso, who was an enthusiastic expansionist when he first came to Louisiana in 1789, had lost hope by this time. "The zeal of a good official," he wrote gloomily in 1799, "can aspire to nothing higher than to keep unchanged the people he governs." [13] Perhaps this confession of failure proceeded from ill health as well as from clarity of vision, for three weeks later Gayoso was dead. In him Spain lost one of the ablest of all the officials it ever had in these border provinces. Suave but firm, he had shown in his eight-year administration of the difficult Natchez district that a Spaniard could govern Anglo-Americans with success. He had given the court much better advice about frontier affairs than his superior, the faithful but too bellicose Carondelet. As Governor of Louisiana and West Florida from 1797 to 1799 he had at least avoided disaster in a trying period. His reputation for honesty—almost unique in these provinces—was once questioned by Intendant Morales: but Morales was a scandalmonger who never had a good word for any one. The accusation was made after Gayoso's death, and is the less credible since he died bankrupt.

II

From this time on there was a marked deterioration in the character of the higher officials of Louisiana and West Florida. In East Florida there was no such alteration, for Enrique White, an officer in the Irish Regiment, held the government from 1795 to his death in 1813 and discharged his duties with laudable though unavailing zeal. At New Orleans, only two of the five governors and intendants in the period from Gayoso's death to the Louisiana Purchase possessed even moderate ability; and not one of them was worthy of comparison with their immediate predecessors—Gálvez, Navarro, Miró, Carondelet, Rendón, and Gayoso. From 1799 to 1801, the government was divided between Nicolas María Vidal, acting Civil Governor, and the Marqués de Casa Calvo, acting Military Governor; from 1801 to 1803 it was reunited under Manuel de Salcedo. Our old friend Morales was acting Intendant from 1796 to 1800, when he was supplanted by Ramón de López y Ángulo, and again from the latter's summary removal in 1801 until 1803.

Of these five, only Casa Calvo and Morales are entitled to the slightest respect, and the respect due them is very slight. Casa Calvo was esteemed an elegant gentleman by the creoles. This is about the measure of his greatness. He was a typical Spanish bureaucrat of the old school, adorning with graceful negligence the office that gave him his livelihood. Unoriginal, unenergetic, he at least kept his subordinates from letting the business of the government fall too far in arrears. Daniel Clark wrote that "he hates application to business, is fond of company and amusement, affects to be frank and open in his manner, but is full of the consequence derived from the possession of rank and riches." Both Casa Calvo and Vidal, according to Clark, were dependent upon the Secretary of the government, Don Andrés López de Armesto, "who is famous for procrastination." [14] Casa Calvo's one claim upon our sympathy is the effectiveness with which he put the insufferable Morales in his proper place.

The latter, who probably held the Spanish record for the number of appointments and length of service as acting Intendant, possessed unquestionable talents as a fiscal agent. In 1786 he was highly recommended on that score by Governor Gálvez, who, like Morales, was a native of Malaga; and there are many evidences that he enjoyed the confidence of the ministry of finance at Madrid.[15] But despite his technical proficiency he was a heavy liability to Spain. Daniel Clark, who had known him for several years, wrote that Morales's "sole delight is, to thwart every design which does not originate with himself." [16] Perhaps repeated disappointments had soured his disposition, for, though entrusted with the acting intendancy of Louisiana time and again, he could never persuade the court to elevate him permanently to that post. Whatever the reason for his contrariness may have been, his endless squabbles with his colleagues were harmful to the credit and efficiency of the administration; and his very devotion to the monopolistic traditions of Spanish policy, which recommended him so strongly to the court, unfitted him for high office in these border provinces. His personal character was odious. Though he sought to prove his own probity by blackening the character of his associates, there is reason to believe that he was no better than the worst of his victims. At any rate the charges against him were numerous and circumstantial. It was asserted at one time that he was acting as judge in the case of a man who held a mortgage on his house and with whose wife he had committed adultery; at others, that he was engaged in extensive land frauds in Louisiana and West Florida. Certain it is that in 1812, while an inquiry into his conduct was pending, the records of his office at Pensacola were destroyed by fire. The suspicions aroused by the coincidence are not entirely allayed by the exoneration which he received from the court several years later.

The other high officials of Louisiana at this period were a sorry lot. Vidal we have already encountered as a shameless auctioneer of justice.[17] Salcedo was, from all accounts, a well-meaning nonentity who had fallen into senile decay before he took over the government of Louisiana. In 1800, after forty years in the king's service, he was transferred from the Canary Islands to Louisiana, where he arrived in July, 1801, after a journey of nearly a year. A large part of his time and energy during his thirty-month administration was expended in petitioning for an increase of salary, for rewards for his two sons which were out of all proportion to the petty services rendered by them, and for permission to retire to the Canary Islands. Routine affairs were administered by the Armesto mentioned above, whom one writer described as a "semi-literate pedagogue"—for he was superintendent of the local school system as well as Secretary to the Governor. Questions of policy, it was said, were settled by the

Governor's eldest son, in whose absence the poor old man met all problems with tearful indecision.[18]

The luckless Intendant, López y Ángulo, was, according to his own story, more sinned against than sinning; but even if that was true, his appointment, like that of Salcedo, shows how little the Spanish court cared for the efficient administration of the affairs of Louisiana at this juncture. After eight years in the diplomatic service at Copenhagen and the Hague, and six years as an undersecretary in the ministry of foreign affairs at Madrid, he found his prospects suddenly blighted, as he expressed it, by his appointment to the intendancy of Louisiana and West Florida. This he regarded as exile, and he later charged that the unmerited punishment was dictated by the king's chief minister, Don Luis Mariano de Urquijo, who had sought in vain to seduce López y Ángulo's wife. However that may be, the new Intendant had not the slightest desire or qualification for his office; and when he left it at the end of a year and a half his papers were in utter confusion.

His removal was as abrupt and unjustifiable as his appointment. His constant wife having died on the outward voyage, he soon married Marie Delphine Macarty of New Orleans, cousin of former Governor Miró's wife and member of a prosperous creole family. In violation of the law, the marriage was contracted without the king's consent; and though he plead extenuating circumstances and precedents set by Governors Unzaga, Gálvez, and Miró, by acting Intendant Morales of Louisiana, and by Minister Irujo of Philadelphia, and though the Bishop of Louisiana interceded for him, the luckless Intendant was summarily removed from office, placed under arrest, recalled to Spain and exiled to San Sebastian. It might be added by way of postscript that after his persecutor Urquijo's fall and after the transfer of Louisiana to the United States, he was finally pardoned and appointed consul at New Orleans; but as he was proceeding to his post in the American *Ulysses* from Bordeaux, the ship ran aground and he died of heart failure from the shock.[19]

The disintegration of Spanish authority in Louisiana was not confined to high official circles. In 1799 Andrew Ellicott, whom the business of surveying the international boundary had taken to New Orleans, reported it as the general opinion of the people that the province would unquestionably be annexed to the United States before many years had elapsed.[20] In July of the same year the Bishop of Louisiana, informing the court of Gayoso's death, described a moral collapse which involved almost every region and class in Louisiana. In the suburbs of New Orleans there was a masonic lodge "in which are enrolled officers of the garrison, dependents of the royal treasury, merchants, countrymen, both natives and foreigners." This was disquieting news, for in every masonic lodge the court saw a revolutionary club. "The parishes of Louisiana, though formerly religious," continued the Bishop, "are now falling away from their faith and customs." If the colonists were reprehended for their laxity, they could truthfully reply that they only followed the example of their Spanish masters, for the army officers had taken to living openly with mulatto concubines and some of the chief officials were never seen at church. It appeared to the Bishop that one of the chief causes of the trouble was the American penetration, which was undermining orthodoxy and loyalty in Louisiana and was moving on through upper Louisiana, Natchitoches, and Attakapas towards the remoter provinces of Texas and New Mexico. These American intruders would show how their minds were working by patting their more robust children on the head and saying, "You will go to Mexico." In conclusion, the Bishop urged the necessity of appointing a governor of "fervent but prudent zeal, with a decided love for the government and customs of Spain," who would coöperate with the church in correcting these spiritual and temporal disorders. The court recognized the necessity of a "most prompt reform"; [21] but the Governor whom it chose for that task was the superannuated Salcedo.

A striking illustration of one of the dangers mentioned by the Bishop was furnished by the activities of Philip Nolan. This former agent of James Wilkinson in his dealings with the Spaniards had broken with his employer and had taken to trading in horses across the Louisiana-Texas border. Suspecting him of insurrectionary designs, the colonial governments of Louisiana and Texas sent out expeditions against him simultaneously. The latter caught him first, and in March, 1801, his career came to an end by the Brazos River.[22] It was reported that one of his enemies cut off his ears and preserved them in salt as a memento of the exploit.[23]

III

An adventurer more difficult to eliminate than Nolan was William Augustus Bowles, self-styled "General and Director of the Creek and Cherokee Nations," who in 1800 captured the Spanish fort at St. Marks and for nearly three years thereafter made life miserable for the Spaniards in East and West Florida. The very embodiment of the chaotic forces that preyed upon this region, he was for a time a walking demonstration of the collapse of Spanish authority even along the coastal fringe of its border colonies. His career justified the assumption of Blount and Chisholm that the Southern Indians would join in an attack upon Spanish Florida and that the Spaniards would not be able to resist a sudden blow. At the same time, Bowles learned to his cost that, given the time and opportunity to marshal its forces, Spain could still deal with a filibuster who failed to keep open his line of communications.

Bowles was already an old hand at the game in 1799 when he began his last and most formidable attempt to drive the Spaniards out of Florida.[24] Since his previous efforts had failed utterly and since the most recent failure had cost him a long imprisonment in the Philippines, it must have been a powerful urge that induced him to risk his neck again in so dangerous a game. One very obvious explanation of his pertinacity suggests itself, for it is well known that he was the agent of a mercantile house in the island of New Providence—Miller, Bonnamy and Company—which was trying to ruin Panton, Leslie and Company and supplant it in the Florida Indian trade. But in this case, as in so many others, economic interpretation leaves the most important things unexplained. Bowles was a commercial agent—there can be no doubt of that; but surely a mere bundle of economic interests never put its neck in a noose.

There was a strong strain of romanticism in this adventurer. Perhaps his middle name had inspired him with delusions of grandeur; but it is more probable that the pattern of his life was stamped in the Indian country of semi-tropical Florida. He was born in Maryland in 1764 and served as ensign with a Loyalist regiment which was sent to Pensacola early in the Revolution. Dismissed from the service in 1779 for insubordination, he took to the woods and lived with the Florida Indians for two years at a most impressionable period of his life. The society into which he was thrown was certainly not civilized, and yet it was not utterly primitive. During the last half-century and especially after the acquisition of Florida by Great Britain in 1763, the European penetration of the Creek country had proceeded rapidly. A swarm of British traders had settled among the Indians, and they and their half-breed sons and their relatives had won a position of great influence in the tribe, accumulating slaves and live stock and building up extensive plantations. Their European connections, knowledge of the English language, and ability to read and write gave these men a hold over the Indians, enabling them to control trade and to determine what, for lack of a better term, may be called the foreign policy of the tribe. The best known half-breed of this class was Alexander McGillivray, who had made a name for himself throughout North America by 1788. That was the year of Bowles's first return to the Creek country after the Revolution. Perhaps the achievements of McGillivray, who lived among the upper Creeks, inspired him with the ambition to make a similar place for himself in the lower Creek villages on the Apalachicola River. At any rate, the way of life in the Indian country seems to have had an ir-resistible fascination for him. Neither safety nor danger was constant enough to be monotonous, and life was active without being laborious. Again and again in his later years he was drawn back to the scene of his adolescent adventures.

After his first two years with the Indians, he brought a party of Creek warriors to aid the British at Pensacola (1781) and conducted himself so creditably that he was reinstated in his commission. At the end of the war he was retired on half-pay. For a time he knocked about in the British West Indies, where he was by turns or simul-taneously musician, portrait painter, and actor; but Bohemianism must have tasted flat when he remembered the years of his youth with the Florida Indians. Then it was that he came to some sort of agreement with Miller, Bonnamy and Company of New Provi-dence, who seem to have supported every one of his incursions into the Indian country.

The activities of this British firm in Florida have been compared to those of British merchants of Canada in the American North-west,[25] but there seems little basis for the comparison. Miller, Bon-namy and Company were engaged in rivalry not with a foreign power or its subjects but with a mercantile firm of their own nation; for Panton, Leslie and Company, though trading in Florida under Spanish license, retained their British nationality and traded direct with London.[26] Great Britain had a stake in the interests of its mer-chants in the Old Northwest, but it would not have gained a farthing by the triumph of Miller, Bonnamy and Company over Panton, Les-lie and Company. Theirs was simply the cut-throat competition of two British firms.

Lord Dunmore, Governor of the Bahamas, did support the inter-lopers, but this fact does not warrant the inference that Miller, Bonnamy and Company were the agents of the British government. Great Britain had no need of such agents. Had it so desired, it could have kept East Florida in the peace settlement of 1783, and it could probably have recovered the province at any time in the next ten years without resort to a devious politico-mercantile filibustering project. Spain would have been delighted to share with so powerful a nation as the British the burden of frontier defense against the United States by the retrocession of East Florida [27]—and it was East Florida which was the scene of Bowles's activities under the patronage of Miller, Bonnamy and Company. Dunmore was no more the agent of the British government in this affair than he was in his aggressions against the Indians on the Virginia frontier in 1774. Bowles's incursions into Florida were the result not of international rivalry but of competition between two British firms, one of which he used to further his own purposes.

After two trips to Florida in 1788 and 1789 and a futile attempt to detach Alexander McGillivray from Panton, Leslie and Company, Bowles made his way to London with a troupe of Indians whom he exhibited at Vauxhall Gardens while he tried to obtain Pitt's backing for an attack on Florida. Here again he failed. Returning to the Bahamas, he soon crossed to Florida in an effort to capitalize the unpopularity McGillivray had incurred by his treaty of 1790 with the United States. Setting himself up as the defender of the Creeks against oppression by Spain, aggression on the part of the United States, and exploitation by Panton, Leslie and Company, Bowles raised a sufficient force of Indians and white adventurers to capture the store of the hated firm at St. Marks; but he soon fell an easy victim to Spanish duplicity. Trusting to the solemn assurance that he would be permitted to return within forty days to his people, as he called the Indians, he went to New Orleans for a conference with the Governor. That was in 1792. When next he returned to Florida, seven years had passed. In the meanwhile he had been sent to Havana, Cadiz, Madrid, and the Philippines. At Madrid he was kept in the city jail for more than a year. Then while the Council of the Indies was still considering his case, the King decided, on the recommendation of Diego de Gardoqui, to dispense with judicial proceedings and summarily deport him to the Philippines. After his arrival at Manila in 1795, Bowles was informed of his sentence, which was that he should be detained indefinitely at Tondo in the island of Luzon, given his liberty so that he might work for his living, and required to report daily to the local *corregidor*. The Luzon authorities soon had enough of Bowles. He refused to report to the *corregidor,* openly denounced the King and his ministers, and demanded a pension to enable him to live in a style befitting a gentleman. Fearful that he might escape or communicate with one of his lieutenants who had been captured with him and sent under similar orders to the neighboring Cavite, the Spanish governor had Bowles deported on the *Concepción,* alias the *Clive,* bound for Cadiz (February, 1797). As the ship was on its way home with a convoy by way of the Cape of Good Hope, he hatched a plot to murder the captain and passengers and make off with the ship. Through the chaplain the plot was discovered, and Bowles and twelve other conspirators were removed to another ship for safekeeping; but he soon contrived to escape. Making his way to Sierra Leone he was well received by Governor Zachary Macaulay. From that place he wrote Lord Grenville a twenty-page letter recounting his adventures and announcing his intention of sailing at once for Tobago and thence to the Creek country, his "home." [28]

For some reason he changed his mind and visited London before returning to Florida. There he got in touch with a missionary society and had some discussion with it concerning a mission to the Creeks. By January 24, 1799, the uneasy William Panton had learned of the presence of the "noted vagabond" in London. He expressed his regret that Spain had not been more careful to guard a man who "merited the gallows" rather than arrest, but found some consolation in the fact that the intriguing Dunmore was no longer governor of the Bahamas.[29]

IV

By the summer of 1799 Bowles was back in the West Indies, and he soon showed that even without Dunmore's aid he could make things hot for the Spaniards and Panton. Arrived at Jamaica, he made the acquaintance of a young man whom he tricked into joining the expedition by deceiving him (as he may also have deceived himself) in regard to its character, and who later had his revenge by betraying Bowles. When it was all over, this young man, Thomas Hugh Ferguson, wrote a narrative of his adventures which contains some curious information about his quondam chief.[30] According to this account, Bowles came to Jamaica with "the reputation of a very learned man, which added to the singularity of the indian dress he wore made him much researched by every class of people. . . ." He played his part well, and "introduced himself into the best company in the island, where every mark of respect & attention was paid him by the Governor, Sir Hyde Parker, Genl. Churchill & the other leading personnages of the place." Though Ferguson noticed that Bowles was preternaturally silent in company, he thought nothing of it at the time. Great men do not make confidants of casual acquaintances. William the Silent did however find words enough to paint so alluring a picture of Florida that Ferguson entered his service with the promise of the collectorship of a port to be built on the Ocklockonee River, which flows into the Gulf between St. Marks and the Apalachicola River.

On August 10, 1799, Bowles and his party left Jamaica for Nassau in his Majesty's schooner *Fox,* Captain Wooldridge. At Nassau, says Ferguson, the scene changed. Once Bowles had had his chief support there; but now Governor Dunmore was gone and the new governor would not receive him. "We no longer see those marks of distinction with which he was honored at Jamaica, nor is he flattered with the appelation of the indian prince." Leaving Nassau, from which so many descents upon the Florida coast have been made, they set sail in the *Fox* for the mouth of the Ocklockonee River. Just before reaching it they ran aground on the eastern end of St. George's Island. There on September 24, 1799, they were found by Andrew Ellicott, who was on his way to complete the marking of the boundary between Florida and the United States. Since the United States was neutral in the war then in progress between Spain and Great Britain, Ellicott refused their request to take them off the island, but he did give them some much needed provisions. A gale detained his ship for eight days, and he had several conversations with Bowles, whom he thought "certainly a man of enterprize, and address, added to considerable talents. . . . He speaks in the style of a king; 'my nation' and 'my people' are his common expressions." When Ellicott finally left, he accepted from the shipwrecked Bowles some charts to help him around the treacherous Florida Cape.[31]

The Indian Prince soon made his way to the mainland, leaving Ferguson and another man on St. George's Island in charge of the stores. Not until November did he send canoes to bring them over. Arrived at the fabled Ocklockonee, wrote Ferguson, "we found we were to pass our winter in the woods instead of being at his palace he had so often made mention of—we now see our folly Alas when too late —the trap is now shut," and the dupes were left with no solace but to "despise the vilain who had so scandalously trepaned us." The collector of the port and his companions spent most of the next two months building huts and gathering firewood. To add to their troubles, a force of two hundred Spanish troops surprised and destroyed their camp in February, 1800, capturing several of the invaders.[32] The collector of the port-to-be escaped by diving into the harbor, where he spent the night. For the next five days he wandered about in the woods "without fire, covering or sustenance of any kind."

Bowles also managed to elude the Spaniards, but his curiously assorted belongings fell into their hands. The chief items of his wardrobe were a green jacket and a blue cloak, both ornamented with gold braid; a fur turban adorned with glass pearls; one sheet, an empty pocketbook, and a watch. His library was more impressive, containing such works as Abbé Raynal's *Indies* in seven volumes; Milton's *Paradise* (the Spanish inventory does not state whether it was lost or regained); the *Letters of Junius,* various works of Molière and Boileau, some treatises on physics, algebra, and painting; a classical mythology; some dictionaries (English, French, and Spanish), and several English grammars. There were also some miscellaneous items—an octant, two saddles, some hydrographic plans, a pair of spurs, two fragments of a flute, a picture of Venus and Cupid, and a bar of soap.[33] With nothing more than these hastily abandoned belongings of the Indian Prince at one's disposal, it would be possible to reconstruct a fairly accurate picture of eighteenth century civilization.

The Ocklockonee rout was an ominous beginning, but Bowles was not dismayed. Taking refuge with his old friends in the lower Creek towns near the present Tallahassee, Florida, and within a day's march of Panton's store and the Spanish fort at St. Marks, he reassembled his scattered forces. Eight years earlier he had captured the store without great difficulty, and he now prepared to grasp again at the valuable prize. With some three hundred men, all but ten or twelve of whom were Indians, he swooped down on St. Marks—and the store was his.

There remained the fort. The store was the private property of Panton's company, but the fort belonged to the king of Spain. Should he attack it too? Formerly he had hesitated to make a direct assault upon a power that possessed the third strongest navy in the world and was at peace with all the world. Now Spain was at war with Great Britain, which had crippled its navy at Cape St. Vincent.

Bowles knew moreover that this time he could not afford to temporize with the Spaniards, for he was a marked man. On March 20, 1800, the head of the Spanish government issued an order to the colonial officials "to make every effort to capture him [Bowles] and to execute him on the spot." [34] Though of course Bowles knew nothing about this order, he did not need to see it signed and sealed in order to divine the court's intentions with regard to him, an escaped prisoner making his third incursion into Spanish territory. Without hesitation he invested the fort and began a regular siege.

Reinforcements soon brought the number of the attacking party up to about four hundred. The garrison numbered one hundred and six officers and men. The fort was solidly constructed of hewn stone and stood on a narrow peninsula at the confluence of the Apalachee and Wakulla Rivers. It could be approached by land from only one side, the north, and that was protected by a stone wall and a deep ditch connecting the two rivers. Several serviceable cannon were mounted on the walls of the fort, and at the beginning of the siege Bowles's men had nothing larger than a musket. There was a sufficient store of all the supplies necessary to withstand a long siege, and, though the drinking water was not very palatable, it was always to be had in abundance.[35] The fort was apparently impregnable against any attack that Bowles could launch.

Yet after a brief and perfunctory defense and with only ten per cent of his men on the sick list, Captain Thomas Portell surrendered the fort (May 19, 1800). Court-martialed for the capitulation, Portell was dismissed from the service when the case was finally settled more than five years later. In defense of his course he declared that his only hope of relief lay in the nearby galleys of the Louisiana fleet and that their failure to respond to his cry for help had convinced him that further resistance was hopeless. The prosecution met this argument with the curious assertion that, while the officers of the galleys had indeed received personal letters and verbal messages from Portell reporting his plight, he had never requested them officially in writing to come to his rescue; and that therefore their failure to relieve him was neither a dereliction of duty on their part nor a justification of Portell's surrender.

There was one point, however, at which Portell was unquestionably vulnerable. When asked to explain why, even granting that there was no immediate prospect of relief, he did not maintain his defense with the adequate resources at his command, he replied that he and his garrison knew that one of Panton's ships had just been captured by the besiegers and thought that the guns which it contained were four-pounders. For some obscure reason, they concluded that further resistance would be suicidal. As it turned out, the captured guns were only two-pounders; and Portell was cashiered.[36]

The truth of the matter seems to be that Portell and his garrison and the naval officers—and indeed every Spaniard in Florida at that time—were all in a dead funk. That is why the episode is worth recounting. The whole service, military and civil, was thoroughly demoralized. Otherwise one hundred well-armed Europeans in a substantial stone fort would never have surrendered to a rabble of four hundred Indians led by ten white men, on the mere rumor that two-pounders were four-pounders; nor would the Louisiana galleys have remained in the offing while they awaited a formal invitation to relieve a beleaguered fort to which they had direct access from the Gulf. While the traditional ferocity of the Florida Indians may have contributed to it in this case, the panic was a symptom of the general breakdown of Spanish morale in North America.

The capture of St. Marks was Bowles's flashing riposte to the Ocklockonee rout. Had he been given time to consolidate his position, it might have required another Bernardo de Gálvez to restore Spanish authority in Florida. The Creek Indians had long been a turbulent tribe, and their warlike offshoot, the Seminoles, lived in the neighborhood of St. Marks. Their British and half-breed traders had taught them to despise the Spaniards. At this juncture they were particularly hostile to the United States, for they had been thrown into a "panic terror" when the American frontiersmen hailed Jefferson's election as an assurance that extensive land cessions were to be wrested from the Indians.[37] The Creeks, who would be the first to suffer, were naturally alarmed at the prospect and ready to welcome any liberator such as the self-styled "General and Director of the Creek and Cherokee Nations." He promised them the free port on the Gulf that they had long been clamoring for. His claim that he was an agent of the British government doubtless made a strong appeal to the numerous British faction among the Indians. Even Panton, Briton though he was, could not trust his own traders in this crisis, for they and their Indian customers were perennially in debt to him and might welcome an opportunity to cancel the debts by annihilating the creditor.

Prompt reinforcements from New Providence might have en-

abled Bowles to develop these possibilities; but about the end of
April one of his ships from the Bahamas was captured by a Spanish
naval vessel.[38] Before another could be despatched, the Spaniards
had screwed their courage up to the point of attacking him in his
recently won stronghold at St. Marks. Thomas Ferguson at last had
his revenge upon the man who had "so scandalously trepaned" him.
In June, 1800, just a year after his first meeting with Bowles, Ferguson left St. Marks on a fishing trip and never returned. Boarding
one of Panton's brigs that was cruising in the vicinity, he hurried to
Pensacola and informed the commandant, Vicente Folch, that Bowles
and his men were utterly unable to resist the Spanish forces which
had already been assembled at Pensacola for the recovery of
St. Marks but which were hesitating to make the attack. It was
this authoritative revelation of Bowles's weakness, not blind heroism,
that launched the Spanish ships against the invader.[39] That very day
Folch set forth at the head of an armada consisting of five well-
armed ships of the Louisiana fleet (three galleys and two gunboats)
with a complement of one hundred and fifty officers and men, besides four schooners which served as transports for a company of
grenadiers.[40]

At three o'clock on the morning of June twenty-third the expedition
arrived before St. Marks and prepared at once for action.[41] There was
some preliminary parleying with Bowles, during the course of which
the Spanish ships moved up under cover of a white flag within point-
blank range of the fort. That position attained, it was decided that
Bowles's replies were unsatisfactory, and the Spaniards opened fire.
This was about two o'clock in the afternoon. For an hour the fort,
aided by a Spanish deserter, replied with a lively and well-directed
fire. Then the largest of the galleys, the *Luisiana,* which had run
aground earlier in the day, got into action. At 3:15 a small explosion occurred in the fort, and Folch ordered an assault. As soon as
the defenders saw what was coming, they took to their heels, Bowles
making off up the river with two boats containing powder, guns,
and the last batch of mail from Madrid. A detachment sent in pursuit
the following day was fortunate enough to recover the Madrid mail,
together with the boats, but the adventurer himself escaped. Among
the recaptured despatches were two royal orders, relating to the use
of the Indians against the Americans, which might have caused the
Spaniards no little embarrassment if Bowles had brought them to
the attention of the United States government. Altogether the ex-

pedition was well worth the $20,000 that it cost the colonial government.[42]

V

Bowles had held St. Marks only five weeks and had then been chased to the woods again; but he was by no means done for. In 1801 he received a liberal supply of goods and munitions from New Providence,[43] and with these he easily built up another party. Within the next year his depredations extended over a large part of Florida, from the outskirts of Pensacola to Tampa Bay; and he even cut off a Spanish supply ship on its way to St. Marks. Minister Irujo at Washington remarked that, while no serious injury had so far resulted from these raids, it was highly discreditable to Spain that such a freebooter should remain at large in its dominions now that it was at peace with the rest of Europe. Benjamin Hawkins, United States agent among the Creek Indians, took the situation more seriously. Writing in 1802, he admitted that Bowles's effective force consisted of only about sixty men who were "more attentive to frolicking than fighting"; but he believed that Spain's supineness invited trouble and that the time had come when the Spaniards "must give up the Floridas or fight for them." [44]

Irujo had several times invoked the aid of the United States against Bowles, citing Article V of the treaty of San Lorenzo. The Adams administration had manifested no interest in the matter,[45] but Jefferson was more obliging. On June 10, 1801, Secretary of War Dearborn wrote Benjamin Hawkins, government agent among the Creeks: "Should Bowles at any time come within the limits of the United States, every exertion must be made to apprehend him taking care only not to compromit the peace of the United States." On April 6, 1802, further representations from the Spanish minister obtained more emphatic instructions to Hawkins: "No exertion," wrote Dearborn, "should be wanting on your part for securing him [Bowles] if he should venture within our limits; if there has been one or more thousand dollars offered for him by the Spanish government, as stated by the Minister [Irujo], I should suppose that a knowledge of that circumstance among the Creeks, or some particular individuals of them would induce them to make an exertion to apprehend him. His being secured is so important to the peace and harmony of the Spanish and American frontiers that every justifiable measure should be taken for placing him in such a situation as will prevent his being mischievous." [46]

In view of Dearborn's reference to the reward said to have been offered by the Spanish government for Bowles's capture, it is a curious fact that, according to Irujo, the suggestion that the Spaniards should put a price on the adventurer's head came from Dearborn himself. However the suggestion originated, Irujo passed it on to the colonial officials and they adopted it. Commandant Folch of Pensacola named four thousand five hundred dollars as the price; but to Governor Salcedo at far-off New Orleans, Bowles was worth only one third as much.[47]

Still more striking, from the point of view of international law, was the manner in which Bowles was captured and turned over to the Spaniards. In the latter part of May, 1803, there was to be a meeting of the Southern Indians at the Hickory Ground on the Coosa River, which had once been the home of Alexander McGillivray and his Scottish father, Lachlan, and was later to be the field of Andrew Jackson's smashing victory over the Creeks. Bowles was to attend with his Seminole followers, for he was confident that he could do so with impunity and hopeful that he might even gain the active support of the united Southern tribes. This suited Hawkins perfectly. At least as early as November, 1802, he had begun to make his preparations, doubtless in response to the instructions sent him by Dearborn in April. Besides Hawkins's own deputy and some of his faction among the Creeks, John Forbes, now the head of Panton, Leslie and Company, and Esteban Folch, son of the commandant of Pensacola, were in the plot.

At the appointed time the tribes began to gather at the Hickory Ground; and on May twenty-fourth Bowles and his followers put in their appearance. By this time he knew that some intrigue against himself was on foot, but he asserted loudly that Folch and Forbes had "done very ill" to come to the meeting, for they might "find themselves caught in their own trap." The boast was not an idle one, for he still had a large following among the belligerent younger warriors. The result remained in doubt several days, and Forbes's diary reveals the misgivings he suffered until the united efforts of the British, Spanish, and American conspirators bent the Indians to their will. Perhaps the fact that the adventurer's supposed patron, Great Britain, was now at peace with Spain had something to do with his downfall. Perhaps the cession of Louisiana to France also contributed to it. Certainly his inability to produce documentary proof of his boasted British appointment made a bad impression on the assembled chiefs; and the rewards offered for his capture were seductive.[48] By May 27 his enemies had had their way. He was first separated from his Seminole followers, then arrested, and finally secured with handcuffs which were made to order by the American blacksmith maintained among the Creeks in pursuance of the government's program of civilizing the savages.[49]

So far the proceedings were legal enough; but then came a curious twist. Though he was arrested on American soil and the handcuffs were placed on him by order of Hawkins's deputy, Bowles was immediately turned over to a party of Indians who took him to New Orleans, delivered him into the hands of Governor Salcedo, and collected the reward. This was plain kidnaping, and yet it was accomplished with the active coöperation of United States agent Hawkins and his deputy.[50] There was something Napoleonic about this summary mode of extradition. Even the Duc d'Enghien was not brought to justice more expeditiously or with less respect for the laws of civilized nations.

While the Governor of New Orleans and his son disputed with the commandant of Pensacola and his son the credit for the capture,[51] the captive was sent to Havana, where he passed the short remainder of his life a prisoner in the Morro Castle. The cause and circumstances of his death are not known; but whatever they were he would have done better to die fighting, like Philip Nolan. It was a somber end for a man whose life had burned bright with adventure, and whose career is one of the most fascinating chapters in the history of the Spanish borderlands. He was not by any means a great man. He was not even, according to prudential standards, a highly intelligent man, for while he saw that Spain's days in Florida were numbered, he did not see—though it was by that time apparent to many—that just as certain a doom hung over the Indians among whom he strove so stubbornly to establish an independent state. His mind was littered with a chaotic jumble of eighteenth century clichés whose only unity proceeded from their regimentation in the service of his fixed idea. But at least his life was highly spiced with that exotic flavor so much prized in the generation of Bernardin de St. Pierre and Chateaubriand, and it was with more than average determination, courage, and resourcefulness that he pushed on towards his goal. He had none of the charlatanism of Francisco de Miranda, none of the savagery of Toussaint L'Ouverture—contemporaries of his, who also fought to liberate oppressed peoples and died in the prison of the oppressor. Bowles must have suffered more cruelly in captivity than either of the others. Miranda was a broken old man when he entered his cell at Cadiz, and Toussaint, son of the tropics, was already done with life as he knew it when he reached the bleak Jura Mountains. Bowles, still in the full vigor of manhood, was taken from the land he loved and imprisoned at Havana, which was an intenser Florida; and to add to the prisoner's torment, only a few hours' sail across the channel lay Florida itself, and freedom. Miranda could reflect that his course was run anyway; Toussaint, that he was at least the victim of the greatest soldier of the age; but Bowles found that the power which he had so utterly despised was still strong enough to break him in the prime of life.

CHAPTER X

THE RETROCESSION OF LOUISIANA

I

"Between ourselves, Louisiana costs us more than it is worth. . . . If the French could arrange a peace for us in which we obtain Trinidad and Minorca, and the House of Parma obtains, in addition to its present possessions, the Papal Legations, Modena, and Reggio or the Milanese, we could not only give the three millions to Bonaparte and Talleyrand but also Louisiana and many thanks into the bargain, and we could flatter ourselves that such a peace had never before been obtained." [1]

Thus wrote Spain's Secretary of State for Foreign Affairs, Mariano Luis de Urquijo, to an agent in Paris through whom he had recently begun a negotiation in behalf of his royal master's cousins of Parma. The letter was dated June 22, 1800. The creation of an Italian kingdom for the house of Parma had been under discussion since April, but it was this letter of Urquijo's that revived the long dormant Louisiana negotiation and linked it with the Parma business. The three millions (of *pesos* or dollars) mentioned by Urquijo constituted the *douceur, pot de vin,* or, to put it in plain English, the bribe which Spain was willing to give Bonaparte and Talleyrand in return for their aid in establishing the much desired kingdom. Within three months after Urquijo's letter reached Paris, France and Spain concluded a treaty which provided for the establishment of the Italian state and the retrocession of Louisiana.

These facts alone are enough to prove the inaccuracy of the old story, told by Henry Adams,[2] which represents the retrocession as having been wrung from reluctant Spain by the masterful Napoleon. If more proof is wanted, it can be had in abundance. The records show not only that Urquijo was amply justified in saying that Louisiana "costs us more than it is worth," but also that Spain had been willing to sell the province as early as 1795.

What did Urquijo mean when he spoke of the cost of Louisiana to

Spain? Though his letter does not develop the point at length, it does contain passages that suggest what he had in mind. These, together with the record of Spain's experience with Louisiana, enable us to reconstruct the Louisiana debit column with a reasonable degree of confidence that we are not including any items which would have escaped the attention of so intelligent a minister as Urquijo. The account was indeed a formidable one, for, as his letter indicates, we must reckon in it not only the money cost of Louisiana, which was not to be taken lightly by any government and least of all by impoverished Spain, but also the exceptions to its colonial system which Spain was forced to make in favor of the creoles, the smuggling trade which Britons and Americans were carrying on with the neighboring Spanish colonies through New Orleans, and the international rivalries in which Spain was involved by reason of its possession of Louisiana.

At the end of the eighteenth century, the money cost of Louisiana to Spain was great, was increasing, and could not be diminished. Louisiana was a parasite colony whose revenues did not amount to one fifth of its fixed expenditures. The difference was made up by an annual subsidy from Mexico. In the 1790's the expenses of the colonial government mounted rapidly with the growth of population and commerce and the need for stronger defenses in time of war. By 1795 the court was already finding the burden excessive, and it is easily demonstrable that one of Godoy's reasons for concluding the treaty of San Lorenzo was his desire to afford the treasury some relief by conciliating the United States, exorcising the danger of invasion from that quarter, and thus making it possible to reduce the cost of frontier defense.[3] Again, it was partly in the hope of collecting larger customs revenues that the government made commercial concessions to Louisiana in this decade.

In both cases, however, it was disappointed. When the treaty of San Lorenzo was signed, the court ordered the discontinuance of the annual presents which were being given the Indian tribes on the frontier between the United States and Florida; but the colonial officials protested that it would be suicidal folly to offend these Indians. The court had to acquiesce, and the presents continued to be made without appreciable diminution.[4] Nor were the commerical concessions to Louisiana much more productive of benefit to the treasury. Though the volume of commerce doubled between 1798 and 1801, revenues from customs duties increased by only a few thousand dollars and never amounted to more than one eighth of the expenses of the government. This was partly because the rates had been reduced and partly because a large share of the import and export trade now passed, legally or illegally, through the American deposit at New Orleans and thus escaped the payment of duties.

The situation can be shown more concretely by figures taken from one of the last of the colony's balance sheets received by the court before the retrocession took place. This was the report of the treasury department of Louisiana for the year 1797.[5] Forwarded to Madrid in March, 1798, it was still under consideration there a year later. According to this report, the revenues of the province amounted to $537,869, of which $453,064 came from the Mexican subsidy, and only $68,143 from customs revenues. Expenditures amounted to $795,662, of which $74,905—almost one tenth of the total—went to the Indian department. There was thus a deficit of $257,793. What was the home government going to do about it? Something must be done, for the budget was not an abnormal one. Only $19,111 had been spent in that year for the strengthening of fortifications, although Spain was at war with England and was engaged in a controversy with the United States which threatened to bring on another war at almost any moment. The report therefore represented the normal, irreducible expenses of the colonial government, and yet they were fifty per cent in excess of its revenues.

It was evident that the government ought to increase the annual subsidy of Louisiana by the amount of the deficit. When this disturbing financial statement reached Madrid, the treasury official to whom it was referred compromised with necessity by recommending that the subsidy be increased by $100,000; but even this augmentation, inadequate though it was, seemed excessive to the harassed Secretary of the Treasury, who refused to sanction it and would do no more than instruct the Viceroy of New Spain to give Louisiana such additional assistance as he could afford.[6] The Viceroy, who had troubles enough of his own, decided that he could not do anything more for the neighboring colony. That way lay bankruptcy; and indeed the Louisiana treasury was virtually bankrupt at the end of the Spanish period. In April, 1802, the Intendant wrote the court a dolorous letter in which he complained that despite repeated requests he had been unable to obtain from the Viceroy even the insufficient annual subsidy, not to mention additional funds; that the paper currency (*certificaciones de crédito*) which he had issued to meet the emergency had lost most of its face value; and that if it were possible for him to do so he would resign the intendancy.[7]

II

Even this was only half of the story. The expenses of which we have been speaking and which wrecked the credit of the Louisiana government and were greater than either the Viceroy of New Spain or the court of Spain itself could meet, included no allowance for the adequate defense of a province which was in imminent danger of invasion. The court could not plead ignorance of the peril, for its foreign envoys and colonial officials showered it with urgent and circumstantial warnings. The projects of William Blount in 1797, of Alexander Hamilton in 1798 and 1799, of William Augustus Bowles in 1799 and 1800, and of Blount again in the latter year were communicated to Madrid by faithful servants of the crown with the most eloquent prayers that defensive measures should be taken without an instant's delay. But the court did nothing.

What indeed could have been done? If any power could have provided adequate military defenses for so vast a region as Louisiana and Florida, it was certainly not Spain. The problem was discussed by the Council of State in the presence of the King in December, 1794. If any member of the Council had come to the meeting with the hope of putting the borderlands in a proper state of defense, he did not retain it long, for the Minister of War reminded his colleagues that it cost five times as much to maintain a regiment of regulars in America as in Spain. The bearing of this fact on the question in hand was only too obvious. The Council decided to adhere to the policy already in effect, that is, to maintain enough troops and fortifications in Louisiana and Florida to hold the colonists in subjection and withstand incursions by irresponsible freebooters but not to provide against the contingency of invasion by one of the great powers.[8]

The truth is that throughout the course of the wars in which Spain was involved from 1793 to 1802, it trusted to God to protect its border provinces and assisted Him as best it could through the foreign office. Godoy summed up the situation in a pithy phrase. In 1797 it appeared that Great Britain was about to coöperate with the American cohorts of William Blount in the conquest of Louisiana, and Minister Irujo addressed an eloquent appeal to his chief for the reinforcement of the threatened province. After reading the letter,

Godoy wrote in the margin, "No es posible poner puertas al campo"—
"You can't lock up an open field." [9] That left nothing more to be
said, and little more to be done. What little could be done must
be accomplished through the slow, indirect processes of diplomacy.
This much Godoy said he would do. *Reciprocidad y maña,* concilia-
tion and caution, he told Irujo, might avert the torrent of invasion.

Events of the next few years must have convinced even the most
obtuse Spaniard that Louisiana was attached to the empire by a
thread which the puniest conqueror's sword could sever. In September, 1798, when Hamilton and the Federalist war-hawks seemed to
be on the point of getting the war with Spain which they so much
desired, Irujo wrote his government that at least one or two regi-
ments must be sent to defend St. Louis and New Madrid. Otherwise
the Americans would be able to take those posts almost without striking a blow, and then the road to New Mexico and Mexico itself
would lie open to them. Though the court knew from other sources
that he was not exaggerating the danger, it could only reply helplessly
that the troops could not be sent, and request him to prevent the invasion and keep the Spanish colonial officials informed of developments.[10] Only the hope of despair could expect the Spanish minister
at Philadelphia to defend Louisiana single-handed.

In 1800 Irujo reported that the Blount project had been revived
and that Louisiana was again threatened with invasion. The official
in America who was ultimately responsible for the defense of the
province was its Captain-General, the Marqués de Someruelos, who
was also Captain-General of Cuba. When the information reached
him, he hastened to protest to the court (April 23, 1800) that he
could not send any reinforcements to Louisiana even if it were
actually attacked, for his forces in Cuba were hardly adequate for
the mere routine service of the island.[11] Two months later he learned
that William Augustus Bowles had captured the Spanish fort at
St. Marks in West Florida. Commenting on this event, he wrote the
court on June 28, 1800: "The regrettable thing is that, as I have
already told your Excellency in my letter of April 23, Louisiana has
only the scantiest military resources; and since the same is true of
this island [Cuba], it is absolutely impossible for me to send any reinforcements there. Consequently if an Indian war breaks out and the
English support Bowles, the results may be very unfortunate." [12]

These confessions of impotence did not reach Madrid in time to
influence the negotiation at San Ildefonso, but Someruelos's informa-

tion regarding the return of Bowles to Florida was received by Urquijo on March 20, 1800, three months before he revived the Louisiana negotiation by offering to cede the province to France. Even this first news left no doubt as to the gravity of the situation. Though Bowles had not yet done Spain any material injury, it was known from the outset that he had powerful support in the British West Indies and it was feared that he was in fact, as he claimed to be, an agent of the British government itself. The despatch from Someruelos was transmitted to the Secretary of War for his advice. He did not reply until December, 1800.[13] Then he said that while the war with England had increased the dangers threatening Louisiana and Florida, it had at the same time diminished Spain's ability to give them succor, and that the consequences which might result from this situation could be averted only by the exertions of the department of foreign affairs. Though the treaty of San Ildefonso had already been signed when this letter was written, the court had abundant reason for coming to the same conclusion as the Secretary of War long before it agreed to part with Louisiana. As Godoy said in 1797, "You can't lock up an open field."

Though the cost account of Louisiana is not yet complete, the remaining items have been discussed at some length in preceding chapters.[14] A brief recapitulation of what was there said will consequently be sufficient to remind the reader of the significance of those items in relation to the retrocession of Louisiana. To begin with, Spain's whole experience with the province had proved that it would never serve the purpose for which the court intended it, and that the extraordinary privileges which Spain had granted it, reluctantly and only under the force of grinding necessity, were worse than wasted. Louisiana was a square peg in the round hole of Spanish policy. That was realized by the Spaniards soon after they acquired it, but they still hoped that even if it could not be made a genuinely Spanish colony, it might at least be made useful to Spain. In the hope of fomenting its growth and of converting it into a living barrier against British Canada and the United States, the court made several important exceptions to its colonial policy in favor of the province, inviting immigrants from foreign countries to settle there, tolerating heretics, and admitting foreign commerce to New Orleans.

Though these various measures were adopted at different times, by 1800 all of them had been in effect long enough for the success of the experiment to be judged. The results were bitterly disappointing.

The population of Louisiana did grow, but far less rapidly than that of the United States. In comparison with the nation against which it was designed to serve as a barrier, Louisiana was weaker in 1800 than in 1780. Toleration did not satisfy the Protestant immigrants, who demanded complete religious liberty; and instead of being gradually converted to Roman Catholicism, as the court had hoped, they undermined the faith of the colonists who already belonged to that church. The results of the commercial concessions were little short of disastrous to Spain, if only because they hastened the economic penetration of Louisiana by the United States and made it possible for Englishmen and Americans to carry on a large contraband trade between New Orleans and Mexico as well as other Spanish colonies in the Gulf region. Talleyrand was doubtless guilty of gross exaggeration when he asserted in 1798 that, according to documentary evidence in his possession, the annual value of this smuggling trade was two million pounds sterling; [15] but its actual volume was large enough to cause the Spanish court grave concern.

Finally, the possession of Louisiana involved Spain in serious controversies with Great Britain over the Missouri Valley fur trade [16] and with the United States over the use of the Mississippi River. Even the conclusion of the treaty of San Lorenzo did not remove the latter cause of difference. On the contrary, Spain's concession of the rights of navigation and deposit gave rise to a host of new disputes with the Americans which were almost certain to cause serious trouble sooner or later. Spain's retention of Louisiana in spite of these embarrassments would have been justified if it had been a useful colony, but that was not the case.

It is now possible to understand what Urquijo meant when he spoke of the cost of Louisiana. He erred, if at all, on the side of understatement. For Spain, Louisiana was not only an expensive luxury but a heavy liability. The evils which have been enumerated in the preceding pages were too great to be suffered, and yet so long as Spain retained the province they could not be corrected. Any effort at reform in the interests of the crown would only aggravate them. Urquijo might well congratulate himself if he could persuade France to pay for the privilege of shouldering the burden of Louisiana. If the French diplomats who conducted this long negotiation thought Spain was genuinely reluctant to part with the province, it was because they were taken in by shrewd Spaniards who knew how to drive a good bargain.

III

The retrocession of Louisiana to France was not by any means the work of Urquijo alone. It was rather the inescapable consequence of the treaty which Godoy signed with Thomas Pinckney at San Lorenzo in 1795. Godoy himself recognized this fact and on June 22, 1796, he signed a treaty with France which provided for the retrocession. Though the Directory rejected the treaty on the ground that its agent had agreed to pay too high a price for Louisiana, it was still eager to acquire the province. Until the end of 1798 it continued to press vigorously for the conclusion of the bargain on more advantageous terms. For various reasons, however, Godoy had changed his mind and was now determined not to surrender the province for the time being. First and foremost among these reasons was the inability of the Directory to pay a satisfactory price, such as an Italian kingdom for the House of Parma, or Gibraltar and Newfoundland fishing rights for the Spanish people. Among the other considerations which influenced him were a growing distrust of the Directory and the justifiable fear that, if the cession were made and news of it leaked out, the United States would seize Louisiana and perhaps other Spanish colonies in that region—for it was well known that the Federalist administration in the United States did not want to have France for a neighbor. Unable to make any headway against the stubborn resistance of Godoy and his successors in the foreign office, who continued his policy in this affair, France relaxed its efforts towards the end of 1798. From that time until June, 1800, the negotiation lay dormant.

By the latter date most of these objections had been removed, and it was then that Urquijo wrote the letter from which the passage quoted at the head of this chapter is taken. The Consulate had supplanted the Directory, and Spain was highly satisfied with the change. Napoleon was rapidly conquering Italy, thus reviving the hope of the royal family that a kingdom might after all be erected for the House of Parma. A Federalist administration still governed the United States, but the break between President Adams and the Hamiltonian Federalists, together with the arrival of the American commissioners appointed to negotiate a settlement of differences with France, greatly reduced the danger of violent opposition from that quarter, even if the secret of the retrocession should become public property.

In these circumstances and under the impulse of Urquijo's letter of June 22, the Louisiana-Parma negotiation proceeded apace. It did not encounter any serious obstacle until at the eleventh hour Napoleon injected a demand for Florida as well as Louisiana. Spain flatly refused to comply. Louisiana, said Cevallos, was more completely at the King's disposal than any of his other possessions, since it was acquired by gift from the crown of France; but he felt that he had no right to alienate Florida, which was an integral part of the empire and "the key to the Gulf of Mexico." France was unwilling to endanger the success of the whole negotiation by insistence upon this new issue, and the treaty was concluded at San Ildefonso on October 1, 1800, without any mention of Florida.[17]

It may be added that, so far as the Spanish records throw any light on the question, no part of Florida was included in the cession of Louisiana. All that Spain intended to cede was Louisiana, and that is apparently all that the French government thought it was getting.[18] Time and again France tried to persuade Spain to add the Floridas, or at least West Florida, to the cession, but Spain always refused. At one time, late in 1802, the court did offer to cede West Florida to France on condition that Lucca should be annexed to the kingdom of Etruria, as the new state of the House of Parma was called;[19] but nothing came of the proposal. In order to prevent any misunderstanding, the commissioners appointed by Spain to effect the transfer to France published a proclamation at New Orleans on May 17, 1803, which defined the eastern boundary of Louisiana.[20] The proclamation specifically stated that the territory between the Iberville River and the thirty-first parallel was not a part of Louisiana and would remain in the possession of Spain. Nevertheless the United States, after buying Louisiana, was soon to claim that region as a part of the province, and to make good its claim by force and perseverance.

None of these complications could be foreseen in 1800, and as matters stood when the treaty of San Ildefonso was signed the bargain was not a bad one for Spain, or at any rate for the royal family. If it involved the abandonment of the expansionist policy of Charles III in North America, it also involved the resumption of the far older Spanish policy of aggrandizement in Italy. In effect Charles IV was giving up a colony of 50,000 inhabitants on the Mississippi in order that his cousin, who was also his son-in-law, might have a kingdom of a million inhabitants on the Arno. To a monarch who had spent the best years of his life in Italy, Louisiana, with its miasmatic

swamps and trackless wastes, might well seem a small price to pay
in order that his daughter and her husband might rule over the smil-
ing fields and busy towns of historic Tuscany. Louisiana was only
a burden to Spain, a constant source of anxiety, a standing invitation to the invader; whereas in Tuscany the House of Parma would
have the instant protection of Napoleon, whom the hero-worshiping
king of Spain was proud to call his friend.

Two features of the treaty protected Spain. One was its provisional nature, for it was merely a preliminary treaty and it contained
the stipulation that Louisiana should not actually be transferred to
France until Napoleon had obtained the establishment and general
recognition of the kingdom of Etruria. The treaty was also a secret
one, for Spain had no desire to affront the United States prematurely
and risk the loss of Louisiana before Napoleon was ready to take
over the province and defend it against invasion.

The subsequent history of the negotiation need not detain us long.
In December, 1800, Urquijo was driven from power and his place
was taken by Pedro Cevallos. This change did not involve any substantial alteration of Spanish policy in regard to Louisiana, for
Cevallos was the kinsman and creature of Godoy, and Godoy was
committed to the retrocession. It was he who had signed the abortive
treaty of cession of 1796 on behalf of Spain, and in 1800 he had
approved of Urquijo's treaty in principle, though he had urged that
it should be altered in three respects so as to provide that the succession to the Italian kingdom should be vested in the Spanish Bourbons, that Spanish commerce with Louisiana should be placed on the
same footing as that of France, and that France would never alienate
the province.[21]

On March 21, 1801, he committed himself to the retrocession still
further by signing with Lucien Bonaparte the treaty of Aranjuez,
which confirmed the preliminary agreement of San Ildefonso.[22]
Several months later he expressed regret that Louisiana had been
ceded, but the cause of his regret was Napoleon's failure to fulfil his
pledges with regard to Parma; there is no evidence that he was re-
pining over the loss of Louisiana. However that may be, it was now
too late for Spain to retrace its steps even if it desired to do so, for
in the autumn of 1801 Napoleon began the peace negotiations with
Great Britain which were to result in the treaty of Amiens in the
spring of the following year. Up to this time France had had to proceed with some circumspection in its dealings with Spain, for there

was always the danger that the Spaniards, if pushed too far, might make a separate peace with England, as they had so often had an opportunity to do. The peace of Amiens removed this restraint and Napoleon, throwing off the disguise, gave the court to understand that Louisiana must be turned over to him at once, regardless of the state of affairs in Tuscany. He would have no more of Spain's niggardly insistence upon the terms of an inconvenient treaty.

After a brief period of resistance Spain gave in, and on July 15, 1802, Cevallos notified him that the King would deliver Louisiana to him without waiting for the fulfilment of his obligations towards the House of Parma.[23] In return he agreed through the French ambassador at Madrid that he would never alienate Louisiana without first giving Spain an opportunity to recover it.[24] After some further correspondence and conferences, Charles IV finally issued an order, dated October 15, 1802, directing the proper colonial authorities to deliver Louisiana to the accredited agent of Napoleon whenever he should present himself at New Orleans for that purpose. This was the order by virtue of which France obtained possession of Louisiana in November, 1803, after it had already sold the province to the United States.

PART FOUR

THE FLAG FOLLOWS TRADE

CHAPTER XI

THE CLOSING OF THE DEPOSIT

I

On October 18, 1802, the acting Intendant of Louisiana, Juan Ventura Morales, published a proclamation closing the American deposit at New Orleans. The measure was one of the most provocative in the whole history of international rivalry in North America. Highly offensive to the American people as a flagrant violation of a treaty right under which they had built up an extensive commerce, the measure became still more exasperating and took on a far more serious aspect when certain circumstances created the violent suspicion that it was instigated by Napoleon. Although foreign relations provided that generation of Americans with a constant succession of surprises, it is doubtful whether any event of the period—even Jay's treaty or the X Y Z affair—caused a greater sensation than the closing of the deposit. It released a stream of invective and exhortation from members of Congress, pamphleteers, newspaper editors, and their correspondents; gave the recently routed Federalists hope that they might drive the Republicans from power; and for several months kept the United States and Spain on the brink of war. If it did not revolutionize Jefferson's foreign policy, at least it forced him to adopt a course of action which was not easy to reconcile with certain of his former professions.

Mingled with the rage of the American people was wonderment. It was almost inconceivable that the Intendant should have taken such a step on his own responsibility, though the wording of the proclamation indicated that such was the case. It was hardly more credible that the Spanish court, about to surrender Louisiana to France, should have been willing to play cat's paw to Napoleon, though in their perplexity many Americans could find no other explanation. Morales's own colleagues in the colonial service were thunderstruck at what they took to be his foolhardiness; and the outburst of indignation in the United States had its counterpart in a bitter dispute among the Spanish agents in America, in which the Governor of Louisiana, the Captain-General of Cuba, and the Minister at Washington were all arrayed against the uncommunicative and unyielding Morales.

Though the controversy was terminated by the reopening of the deposit within seven months after its closure, that did not bring any nearer to solution the question of the motive which lay behind the proclamation. Henry Adams, writing more than eighty years later, drew extensively upon the secret archives of France and Spain; but the net result of his labors was only to add to the existing confusion. Even to-day, when further research in those archives has made it possible to correct Adams's account at certain points, the problem of responsibility and motive is at least as far from solution as ever.[1] We know more facts than did either Adams or his predecessors; but the more facts we accumulate, the more difficult it is to arrange them in an intelligible pattern. It could be maintained with almost equal force that the deposit was closed by Spain for the benefit of France; that it was closed by Spain in order to create difficulties for France; and that its closure was due to fiscal reasons which had no connection with diplomacy.

The starting-point of this intricate affair was a despatch sent to the court in July, 1801, by Ramón de López y Angulo, Intendant of Louisiana.[2] Two Kentucky flatboats, he said, had recently arrived at New Orleans, and their owners had declared that they were placing in the American deposit $4,300 in specie. When a suspicious customs official demanded that they produce the money so that he might count it and verify their statement, it appeared that they actually had only $140.[3] The Intendant was convinced that the purpose of the attempted fraud was to facilitate the exportation of Spanish specie, which was prohibited under severe penalties. After enlarging upon the difficulty of preventing this and many other abuses of the right of deposit, he concluded that the Americans were carrying on an extensive contraband trade with Louisiana under cover of it, and that this trade was highly detrimental to the interests of Spain.

It was not until nine months later that the Intendant's communication received the serious consideration of the Secretary of the Treasury, Soler, to whom it was addressed. By that time the treaty of Amiens had restored peace in Europe, and Spain had undertaken the Herculean task of restoring order in its far-flung dominions. Then Soler found in the despatch cause for grave concern. It revealed the existence of contraband trade; and the Spanish Bourbons sought to suppress smuggling almost as ardently as the Spanish Hapsburgs had sought to suppress heresy. The incident reported by López y Ángulo involved a particularly obnoxious form of smuggling—the exportation of specie to a foreign country. In the stress of war the court had reluctantly consented to its exportation from Louisiana on the payment of a six per cent duty; but, naturally, specie smuggled through the deposit paid no duties. A privilege which the King had graciously bestowed upon the undeserving Americans was now being used to defraud him of his just revenues and to drain the empire of gold and silver. A more flagrant abuse of the right of deposit could hardly have been imagined.

Hard on the heels of the peace of Amiens, Minister Soler called the question to the attention of the Foreign Secretary, Pedro Cevallos, who had to be consulted before the treasury department took any action in a matter involving the treaty rights of the Americans. The correspondence between the two ministers was begun in April and continued until July 11, 1802, when Cevallos informed Soler that the King disapproved of the continuance of the deposit at New Orleans beyond the three-year term stipulated in the treaty of 1795. Accordingly, on July fourteenth, Soler sent Morales (acting Intendant of Louisiana since López y Ángulo's recent summary removal) a royal order, marked "very secret," which directed him to suppress the deposit at once. However, continued the order, he must conceal the fact that he had received any communication whatever from the court and must explain his action to the public on the ground that, since the three-year term had expired, he could not tolerate the continuance of the deposit privilege until he had consulted the court and received its orders.[4]

That the French government had a hand in the framing of this order is suggested by a curious coincidence. While Cevallos was engaged in this correspondence with Soler in regard to the American deposit at New Orleans, he was also discussing with the French government the immediate delivery of Louisiana to France. Both affairs dragged on through May and June, 1802, and they were settled simultaneously in July. At the very same time that the King (through Cevallos and Soler) ordered the immediate closing of the deposit, he notified Bonaparte (through Cevallos) that he was ready to surrender Louisiana without further delay.[5] One might infer from this coincidence that the closing of the deposit was one of the conditions of the agreement with France; but there does not seem to be any evidence that the deposit question was even so much as mentioned in the negotiations between the two powers. On the contrary, the evidence indicates that the order to Morales was carefully concealed from the French government; and this fact, together with the deep-rooted hostility of Godoy to Napoleon and other circumstances, furnishes ground for a plausible argument that the order was designed to embroil France with the United States.[6] Again, there is the possibility that the order was dictated simply by a desire to correct the wholesale abuses of the right of deposit committed by the Americans. The Soler-Cevallos correspondence on the subject supports this hypothesis. Yet Cevallos's agency in the affair [7] leaves a lingering suspicion, and a very strong one, that diplomatic considerations played an important part in the making of the order; and, since Spain was so soon to free itself of the deposit problem by surrendering Louisiana, it does not seem likely that the mere desire to correct fiscal abuses at New Orleans during that brief remaining period would have induced the court to take a step which would certainly provoke a violent controversy, and perhaps war, with the United States.

II

About nine o'clock on the morning of October 14—precisely three months after its issuance—Intendant Morales received and read the momentous order.[8] Since it was the birthday of one of the Spanish princes, he had first to attend the ceremony of kissing hands. When that was over, he returned home and spent the rest of the day pondering the perplexity in which the strict injunction of secrecy had placed him. It would be easy enough for him to comply with the letter of the order by announcing that he was acting on his own responsibility in closing the deposit; but his zeal would not be satisfied unless he made the public believe him. The situation was all the more difficult since the order was endorsed not merely "secret," but "very secret," by which he understood that he must not reveal its existence to any person whatever, not even to the Governor of the province. The character of the Governor removed any lingering doubt that Morales may have had on that score for Salcedo was in such a state of physical and mental decrepitude that he could not be trusted to keep a secret. This rigorous interpretation of the court's injunction was probably correct, and yet it very nearly defeated its own purpose, for the Governor had the authority to overrule the Intendant, and three times during the course of this affair Salcedo was on the point of using his power in order to protect the deposit against Morales's meddling. At a critical period early in 1803 he was dissuaded from doing so only by the influence of Napoleon's recently arrived agent, Prefect Laussat.

After a day's cogitation, the Intendant decided that the most plausible ground on which he could base his proclamation was the termination of the privilege of trade with neutrals which had been granted by the Intendant in 1798 for the duration of the war. Every one knew that, since the war was over, the privilege must soon be withdrawn, and Morales had already had some correspondence with the Governor on the subject.[9] Salcedo had maintained that action in the matter should be postponed until the receipt of formal notification from Madrid that the war was over; and, though the conclusion of the treaty of Amiens was a matter of common knowledge, Morales had agreed to await the arrival of the July mail from the court. Now that mail had come, bringing the "very secret" order of July 14; but the expected notification from the government that peace had been restored was not among the despatches. Accordingly, on October 15, Morales wrote Salcedo that the intendancy could no longer postpone taking cognizance of the fact that the war was over. Recalling their previous correspondence on the subject, he said that neutral trade at New Orleans could no longer be permitted; and, as if it were the most natural thing in the world, he added that the American deposit also must be suppressed, inasmuch as its original three-year term had long since expired and its subsequent toleration, like that of neutral trade, had been simply a war measure.

Totally ignorant of the royal order that inspired Morales's letter, Salcedo thought—as did every other Spanish official in America whose opinion is recorded—that the suppression of the deposit at New Orleans, without the previous provision of an equivalent establishment elsewhere on the lower Mississippi, was a gross violation of the treaty of 1795. He was also offended, as Carondelet had been some years earlier, at the Intendant's meddling with an institution which, since it was guaranteed by a treaty, was of a political character and lay well within the Governor's jurisdiction. His reply to Morales was prompt and vigorous and was intended to be decisive. He not only refused the Intendant's request to coöperate in the publication of the proposed proclamation but declared that he would, if necessary, use force to prevent its publication.

Morales, one may suspect, rather enjoyed the situation. He had so often come into conflict with the governors of the province, and had so often been overruled. Now he was playing the same game; but this time he had a joker up his sleeve—the "very secret" royal order of July 14. He would have had to play it if he had been dealing with a younger and more energetic governor, such as Gayoso or Carondelet. Salcedo, however, was not the man to force his hand. His infirmity weakened his will, and he may have been awed by the Intendant's well known talent for blackening the reputation of those whom he could not openly defy. It was believed that Morales's poison pen had brought about the disgrace of his predecessor, López y Ángulo, and his own restoration to the post of acting Intendant; and as Salcedo had arrived at New Orleans in the ship which brought the royal order in Ángulo's case, there can be little doubt that the incident taught him to deal cautiously with his colleague.

At any rate, a two days' correspondence reduced the Governor to acquiescence, though he never saw the court's confidential order to Morales. To his original note forbidding the Intendant to publish the proclamation, the latter replied that he would post it with his own hands if necessary and would not yield an inch unless Salcedo used the force at his disposal and removed him from the intendancy. The Governor then tried persuasion, transmitting a royal order (endorsed "very secret," as was the order that Morales so resolutely concealed from Salcedo) in which the court announced the impending transfer of Louisiana to France. In view of this information, he argued, Morales should not take a step which would throw commerce into confusion, excite deep resentment among the colonists, and bring on an international crisis just as Spain was on the point of evacuating the province. Morales, however, held his ground, and since it appeared that neither threats nor persuasion could move him, the decrepit Governor gave in, agreeing not to prevent the publication of the proclamation, though still refusing to provide the military escort which the Intendant requested in order to lend dignity to the occasion.[10] So it was that the proclamation, though dated October 16, was not published until the eighteenth. Then, without the customary ceremonial flourishes, it was quietly posted in the usual public places by a government clerk.[11] "On similar occasions," says a contemporary account, "this ceremony has been extremely splendid and pompous; but on the present there was little more than when the governor gives an order to have the streets cleaned."[12]

This is the measure that led Henry Adams to give one of his chapters the title "The Closure of the Mississippi." The title is misleading, for the proclamation did not close the Mississippi and was not intended to do so. Neither on this nor on any other occasion after the ratification of the treaty of 1795 did Spain deny or interfere with the free navigation of the Mississippi by citizens of the United States. What the proclamation did was to close the deposit to further entries and prohibit neutral ships from trading with Louisiana. It was only the first of these two restrictions that infringed upon the rights of the United States as established by the treaty of 1795, for neutral trade with Louisiana was a matter of Spanish municipal law, and neither the United States nor any other power had the slightest legal right to demand its continuance. As for the treaty rights of the United States, they were not by any means completely destroyed, and it was still possible for the Americans to make extensive use of the right of free navigation. Though the deposit was closed to further entries, goods already entered before October 18 could still be exported duty free in American ships.[13] The latter could still ascend the river freely to any place within the territory of the United States, and the sea-going vessels that were being built in increasing numbers on the waters of the Ohio could still descend unhindered to the Gulf. Most important of all, Morales made no effort to interfere with the practice, already common, of transferring Western produce directly from flatboats to American ships anchored in the river at New Orleans.[14] This kind of operation had its drawbacks, for a flatboat might not find a ship available when it arrived, and the cargo might deteriorate while waiting for one. The difficulty can hardly have been a serious one in many cases. Flatboats that had housed produce during a six weeks' voyage down the Ohio and the Mississippi could still afford the same shelter while the owner waited for a ship at New Orleans. As it turned out, it was sea-going vessels, not flatboats, that were superabundant at New Orleans during the closure of the deposit.[15]

Morales even left open to the Americans certain channels of trade not protected by treaty. When he closed the deposit, he decided that, until the Americans had had time to learn of his proclamation, flour from the Ohio Valley and cotton from Natchez (the two most important commodities exported from the American West) should still be admitted to New Orleans on the payment of a duty of six per cent; and, since that operation nationalized them, they could then be exported in Spanish ships on paying a duty of the same amount.

On February 5, 1803, at the instance of the Governor and the Cabildo, he confirmed the privilege as to flour and extended the list to include all kinds of provisions.[16] In explaining the measure to the court, he said that if he had refused to adopt it the Governor would have humiliated him by promulgating the order on his own authority. New Orleans was faced with a serious shortage of food, and the government could not afford to be too unyielding, for, said Morales, "Hunger knows no law." [17]

Even those prohibitions and restrictions which were maintained by the Intendant could be evaded. A letter of November 22, 1802, purporting to have been written by a member of a commercial house at New Orleans to a correspondent at Philadelphia, spoke of the modifications of Morales's order by which American goods and ships were admitted to New Orleans upon the payment of duties, and added: "I know of none that has yet done so [that is, paid the duties], but somehow or other they find ways and means to discharge and get reloaded. Some [ships] they convert into Spaniards, others discharge their cargo in the river into boats for Natchez, but they [the sea-going ships] seldom go farther than New Orleans." [18] Spain's abstention from interfering with the right of free navigation, Morales's concessions to American trade with Louisiana, and the revival of familiar practices of the old, exclusive régime—such as converting American ships into "Spaniards"—saved the United States from the worst consequences of the closing of the deposit and also saved Spain from the worst consequences of American indignation at that measure.

III

It was only with the greatest difficulty that Morales maintained the principal features of the system established by his proclamation of October 16, 1802. Public opinion at New Orleans condemned the measure bitterly. The Frankfort (Kentucky) *Palladium* published an "extract of a letter from a very intelligent gentleman at New Orleans," dated January 3, 1803, in which the writer declared that all classes in the city, creoles as well as Americans, were violently agitated over the Intendant's measure, "as we are perfectly persuaded, that the prosperity of this city chiefly depends on the intercourse with the United States." [19] The Intendant himself admitted —perhaps exaggerated—in his despatches to the court the popular indignation that greeted his proclamation.

Had the colonial officials stubbornly refused to make concessions in this crisis, the Spanish régime in Louisiana might have ended, as it began, with an insurrection. It was widely believed that Spain could not much longer retain its grip on so eagerly coveted a spot as New Orleans, and the seditious could find encouragement in persistent rumors that Great Britain would never permit France to take possession of Louisiana and that the United States could easily be persuaded to seize New Orleans. There were, however, excellent reasons for the failure of the creoles to take up arms against the Intendant. Immediate success was not likely, for the seven hundred Spanish soldiers concentrated in or near New Orleans and supported by the river fleet of gunboats were a formidable force; and, even if the rebels carried everything before them at first, another "Bloody" O'Reilly might soon be expected from Havana. Most important of all, the Louisianians were satisfied with the mild rule that Spain had given them in the last generation.[20] There were no direct taxes; customs duties were lower than they were likely to be under any other government; the profitable trade with Havana would be lost if Louisiana ceased to be Spanish; and some compensation for the proclamation of October sixteenth was found in the simultaneous reopening of trade with France and the French West Indies. Before the end of the year, the creoles gave evidence that they had little desire to exchange the domination of Spain for that of France or the United States.

More formidable to Morales than the colonists—for the moment, at any rate—were his fellow officials in America. The Marqués de Casa Irujo (for that was the Castilian title of nobility which had been bestowed upon the Spanish minister to the United States) had reasons of both a public and a private nature for condemning Morales's action, and he went so far as to order him in the King's name to restore the deposit at New Orleans, or else to designate another place of deposit.[21] The American government was doing all in its power, he said, to restrain its indignant citizens from taking up arms against Spain but would fail unless the deposit were quickly reopened; and in his opinion the closing of the deposit was not only most imprudent but also a palpable violation of the treaty. This peremptory note, which was received at New Orleans in April, 1803, left the Intendant unmoved. He coolly replied that Irujo had no more right than did he himself to give orders in the name of the king, and that he saw no reason for altering the system which he had adopted in October. But Irujo had written simultaneously to Governor Salcedo, whom he ordered—again in the name of the King—to exercise his paramount authority over the Intendant to compel the reopening of the deposit. Otherwise, he declared, Salcedo would be held responsible for the calamities which would undoubtedly befall Spanish America—war, invasion, pillage, and the loss of Louisiana and Florida and perhaps of New Spain. The poor old Governor was dismayed at this portentous picture of his responsibility; and it was only with the aid of the French Prefect, Laussat, recently arrived at New Orleans, that Morales prevailed upon him to leave things as they were until the receipt of the court's reply—which might be expected any day now—to the despatch informing it of the closing of the deposit.[22]

Hardly had Morales weathered this storm when another burst over his head. The Captain-General of Louisiana and Florida, Someruelos, who resided at Havana, had received from Irujo a communication similar to those sent to Morales and Salcedo. It had filled him with indignation and alarm—indignation at the Intendant's wantonly provocative measure, alarm at the harrowing picture of American wrath that Irujo painted. Without a moment's delay he sent off an order to the Governor and Intendant at New Orleans directing them, jointly and severally, to restore the deposit at once, unless they had closed it in conformity with a royal order which left them no room whatever for the exercise of discretionary power; and he concluded with the warning that he would not tolerate the least equivocation or delay.

This was far more serious than an order from Irujo, for Someruelos's authority over the Governor of Louisiana had never been questioned, and his authority over the Intendant had been explicitly affirmed by a royal order of December, 1802. But again Morales, fortified by his "very secret" royal order, refused to budge. Again Salcedo was on the point of overruling him; and again, thanks to Prefect Laussat's advice to the Governor, Morales had his way.[23] He did not reopen the deposit, and he did not reveal to any one, not even to the Captain-General, the royal order which had induced him to close it. That seems a remarkable achievement, a proof of the Intendant's firmness of character and his high prestige in Louisiana. There can be little doubt, however, that he succeeded in keeping his secret because everybody in the creole capital was by this time morally certain that he had a secret to keep. American and French civilians and Spanish officials were all convinced that he was acting under orders from Madrid, and that the Madrid order was dictated by Napoleon.[24] It was because Spain was notoriously subservient to a foreign power that the will of the Spanish government was done in its North American province.

CHAPTER XII

Chauvinism and Incantation

I

Reports of Morales's extraordinary proclamation of October 18 were immediately despatched by land and water to various parts of the United States. On the evening of October 28 Governor Claiborne of Mississippi Territory, who resided at Natchez, was informed of it by a letter from the American Vice-Consul at New Orleans, and on the following day forwarded the information to Secretary of State Madison. As the regular mail service was not functioning at the moment, an express rider was engaged to carry the letter to Nashville for a fee of eighty dollars and deposit it in the post-office at that place. So slow was overland travel that the rider did not reach Nashville until November 18. Only four days later the *Superior,* Captain Sinclair, brought the news by sea to New York.[1] The Kentuckians, who were probably more deeply concerned than the people of any other State, were among the last to learn of Morales's order. The enterprising *Palladium* of Frankfort, the State capital, got out an "extra" on November 29, in which it published an English translation of the proclamation, together with a covering letter from a Dr. James Speed of New Orleans and another letter from an American mercantile firm at that place to the Governor of Kentucky.[2] The news was even slower in reaching Pittsburgh, where it was published on December 3.[3]

A shout of indignation went up from every quarter of the Union, and everywhere the news was met with the same comment: Morales had acted on orders from Madrid, and Madrid had acted on orders from St. Cloud. Western legislatures drew up memorials to the federal government clamoring for relief. Inflammatory articles and pamphlets appeared in the seaports on the Atlantic coast. Even remote New England, through its members of Congress, threatened to punish the arrogant Spaniards with militiamen drawn from the Southern and Western States. Some of these outbursts represented genuine concern for the honor and interests of the nation. Some were a gleeful response to a golden opportunity for playing politics. Some proceeded from the sinister designs of self-seeking adventurers.

The arrival of the startling news from Louisiana ushered in a period of paradoxes in the United States. Jefferson, whose warning against entangling alliances still rang in the ears of his countrymen, acted as if he were ready to make good his more recent threat to "marry ourselves to the British fleet and nation." The New England States, which in 1786 had voted to barter away the free navigation of the Mississippi, now posed as the protectors of the West, and supported a motion by Senator Ross of Pennsylvania authorizing the armed seizure of a part of Louisiana in order to assure the free use of the river by Americans. The Westerners, who had but recently whispered secession, talked nullification, and shouted conquest, now stoutly asserted their devotion to the Union, their respect for traditions established by Washington and Adams, and their determination to remain at peace if war could be avoided.

It may seem surprising that the posting of a notice in a Spanish colonial town by a mere government clerk, without even a squad of soldiers to lend the occasion dignity, should have created so great a sensation in the United States; but the excitement was justified. For the West, the Mississippi was, as Madison said, "the Hudson, the Delaware, the Potomac and all the navigable rivers of the atlantic States formed into one stream"; and while the Intendant's proclamation did not deny the right of free navigation, it did impair the value of that right by withdrawing the deposit privilege. Ports on the Atlantic seaboard from Savannah to New York were also injured by the proclamation, for it wiped out in a moment the profitable trade with New Orleans which they had built up since the establishment of the deposit and the opening of that place to American shipping in 1798. Moreover, any interference with Western exports down the Mississippi would inevitably reduce the volume of merchandise purchased by the people of the Ohio Valley from New York, Philadelphia, and Baltimore. As for New England, though its people had little if any direct interest in the Mississippi trade, they were nevertheless in a mood to resent any affront from Spain. Whalers and merchantmen from various New England ports had been flocking to the Plata River, the Patagonian coast, and the South Pacific, where they had time and again come into conflict with the Spanish authorities. Even those ships which were armed with passports from the

Spanish consul at Boston, John Stoughton, were not free from molestation.[4] That Stoughton had no right to issue such passports and that the colonial officials were therefore justified in their action did not lessen the indignation of the sufferers. Incidents of this nature had been the subject of frequent complaints in American newspapers in 1801 and 1802,[5] and the feeling of irritation against Spain was still keen in New England as well as in the rest of the country when news of Morales's proclamation arrived.

To make matters worse, it transpired at the same time that the King of Spain had at last issued an order directing the transfer of Louisiana to France, and that a French expedition was about to sail for New Orleans to take possession of the province. The coincidence threw a sinister shadow across Morales's action, for it was difficult to avoid the conclusion that the closing of the deposit had been dictated by France and was a foretaste of what the United States would suffer at the hands of its new and mighty neighbor.

However much they might differ as to the details of the diagnosis and the prescription of a remedy, Jefferson and Hamilton both regarded the situation as the most serious that the United States had faced since the end of the American Revolution. Hamilton professed to believe that the dismemberment of the Union impended. Jefferson tried to persuade others—and apparently persuaded himself—that the real danger lay in the realm of domestic politics and in the use Hamilton's party would make of the crisis in order to regain control of the government. He and Madison argued that the folly of secession was too obvious for the Westerners to attempt it; but Jefferson at least must have had some misgivings. It had long been axiomatic with him that the Spanish borderlands could not be in better hands than those of Spain until the United States should be ready to acquire them. As he saw the situation, Spain was cast in the rôle of trustee, to hold the border provinces until the United States came of age and was able to take over the management of the estate.

Now this comforting dream of republican expansion was shattered. Napoleon had Louisiana, and it was believed he would soon have Florida too. What that meant to Jefferson can be judged from his oft-quoted letter to Minister Livingston of April 18, 1802. It was reported at that time that both the Floridas and Louisiana had been ceded to France. Though the actual transfer appeared to be a rather remote eventuality, Jefferson declared that the cession "compleatly reverses all the political relations of the U.S. and will form a new epoch in our political course. . . . There is on the globe one single spot," he continued, "the possessor of which is our natural and habitual enemy. It is New Orleans, through which the produce of three-eighths of our territory must pass to market, and from its fertility it will ere long yield more than half of our whole produce and contain more than half our inhabitants. . . . Spain might have retained it quietly for years. Her pacific dispositions, her feeble state, would induce her to increase our facilities there, so that her possession of the place would be hardly felt by us, and it would not perhaps be very long before some circumstance might arise which might make the cession of it to us the price of something of more worth to her. Not so can it ever be in the hands of France. . . . The day that France takes possession of N. Orleans fixes the sentence which is to restrain her forever within her low water mark. . . . From that moment we must marry ourselves to the British fleet and nation." [6]

Perhaps when that letter was written not every word of it was to be taken literally. Jefferson may have been carried away by his love of phrase-making, or he may have hoped to bluff France into giving the United States the commercial facilities at New Orleans which, according to him, Spain would surely have granted. But the eventuality that was remote in April had by December become immediate. Recent reports from Europe stated that the French expedition would soon set sail for Louisiana, and Jefferson's springtime faith that Spain would "increase our facilities" at New Orleans had been shattered by Morales's proclamation. The peril feared by Republicans and Federalists alike for the last six years was now magnified tenfold. In 1798, when Spain was friendly to the United States and when France, still at war with Great Britain, was governed by the incompetent Directory, Pickering and Hamilton were ready to precipitate a war of conquest rather than have the French for neighbors in North America. Now all Europe was at peace, Napoleon was master of France, and, if the common interpretation of what had happened at New Orleans was correct, he was the master of Spain as well. The diplomatic crisis was one of the first magnitude. Yet from the administration's point of view, Jefferson was justified in believing that the most immediate danger lay in the field of domestic politics. The diplomatic crisis gave the Federalists a golden opportunity to turn their rivals out, and they were not slow to seize it. Jefferson's first task was to repulse this flank attack, for in his opinion the control of

New Orleans by France could hardly cause the United States greater injury than the control of Washington by the Federalist party.

II

Caught between the battalions of Napoleon on the one hand and Federalist snipers on the other, the sage of Monticello needed all his sagacity to avert disaster. Sagacity was not all he needed, for forces were at work the operation of which no one could foresee or control. The weakest point in his defenses seemed to lie in the West. For many years past, the question of its separation from the Union had been one of the commonplaces of American political discussion. In a period when dissatisfaction with the federal experiment was to be found in every part of the country, the West distinguished itself for the frequency and violence of its complaints;[7] and a generation accustomed to think in terms of natural law was ready to believe that the States west of the mountains were predestined to secession. The present crisis might precipitate the separation, unless something "sensible" (to use Jefferson's term) were done to quiet the clamor on the frontier; or, at the very least, the Westerners might wreck the administration by joining the Federalist opposition.

But what was that something "sensible" to be? The use of force was out of the question, since war with Spain would probably mean war with France as well, and Spain alone was vastly superior to the United States at sea. As for diplomatic representations, they would have almost precisely the force that European circumstances might give them; and no one knew better than Thomas Jefferson that as long as the great powers of Europe remained at peace with each other the infant republic could only bide its time.[8] That, however, was the one ray of hope. Few persons in Europe or America believed that peace between France and England could long be maintained. The question was whether Jefferson could stave off disaster at home and abroad until they went to war again.

Procrastination was, therefore, the keynote of his policy: but procrastination did not mean inaction. It is true that the presidential message which he sent to Congress in December, 1802, contained not a word about the closing of the deposit and spoke rather casually of the retrocession of Louisiana to France; but the lesson of this is that history should not be written from presidential messages. Jefferson was indeed doing about all that it was possible for him to do. Through his own letters and those of administration supporters and through inspired articles in the press, he endeavored to keep the West quiet while he negotiated; and the effort met with almost complete success. He also sought and obtained the intervention of the diplomatic representatives of France and Spain at Washington in favor of the restoration of the deposit. Simultaneously he made direct representations to the Spanish court through the American minister, Charles Pinckney. And, finally, he sent James Monroe to Paris on a special mission.

The domestic situation, which was a source of profound embarrassment to the administration, greatly facilitated the solution of the diplomatic problem that had produced it. Calling into conference the Spanish minister, Irujo, and the French chargé, Pichon, Jefferson painted a hair-raising picture of the American dogs of war barely held in leash by a pacific president, who would be dragged down from his high ground of peace unless France and Spain came to his aid with a prompt redress of grievances. What made Jefferson's picture lifelike was the war clamor of his sworn enemies, the Federalists. Both the envoys responded to the pull of the strings precisely as he had hoped, bombarding the colonial officials and foreign offices of their respective governments with despatches that could hardly have been more satisfactory to the administration if Jefferson himself had written them.[9]

Irujo was peculiarly obliging; and indeed he was peculiarly indebted to the Republican leaders. Incensed at his conduct during the controversy over the execution of the treaty of San Lorenzo, Timothy Pickering, Secretary of State under John Adams, had sought to obtain his recall; but Spain had avoided the issue until the election of 1800 brought the Republicans into office. They not only dropped the demand, but urged Spain to let Irujo remain at his post.[10] He had at least one very good reason for wishing to remain there, for in 1798 he had married Sally McKean, daughter of the Republican Governor of Pennsylvania, and had formed many pleasant associations in and around the Republican court. If we are to credit a weighty authority, he had another and a very special reason for wishing to remain in the United States. That authority is Valentín de Foronda, consul general of Spain in the United States, who declared in 1805 and 1806 that Irujo had been engaged in extensive contraband trade between the United States and the Spanish colonies ever since 1797, and that, though he had come to the United States penniless, these fraudulent operations had gained him "immense riches."[11]

If the charge was true, Irujo owed a heavy debt of gratitude to the administration which had made it possible for him to remain at so lucrative a post.

He certainly did everything in his power to pay off whatever debt he owed the Republicans. His official assurance to the American government that the Intendant of Louisiana had acted on his own responsibility in closing the deposit [12] strengthened the hand of the administration in dealing with its critics. His peremptory orders to the Intendant and Governor at New Orleans to reopen the deposit and the excited despatches which he addressed to the Captain-General at Havana for the same purpose were further evidences of his zeal in a cause so near to the President's heart; and he almost succeeded in forcing the Intendant's hand.[13] Most effective of all were his representations to Madrid, for a despatch which he wrote on January 9, 1803, determined the court to reverse its mysterious order of the preceding July and direct the reopening of the deposit.[14]

While Irujo was drafting the despatch that was to create such consternation at Madrid, Jefferson was formulating the plan that flowered in the Monroe mission. When the crisis first developed at the end of November, 1802, with the simultaneous arrival of news of Morales's proclamation and the impending transfer of Louisiana to France, the President had tried to disarm his critics by treating the two events as unrelated incidents and by negotiating with France and Spain through the resident ministers, Livingston and Pinckney. His message to Congress mentioned the retrocession but ignored the closing of the deposit. When John Randolph, spokesman of the administration in the House of Representatives, moved a resolution (December 17, 1802) calling on the President for papers relating to the affair at New Orleans, no reference was made to the retrocession.[15] This official interpretation was widely questioned. Even Irujo's assurance that Morales's proclamation must have been his own unauthorized act did not carry conviction, for no American had much confidence in the word of any Spaniard.[16]

The Federalists were determined to force the simultaneous discussion of the two questions. On January 4, 1803, one of their number, Griswold of Connecticut, moved a resolution in the House calling on the President for information relating to the cession of Louisiana to France. The motion was carried on the following day by a vote of 35 to 32,[17] though the administration could normally count upon a comfortable margin of some twenty or thirty votes in that body. If the decision of the House was any indication, the country was un-willing to accept Jefferson's convenient fiction that the retrocession was not related to the affair of the deposit. This vote, and perhaps Du Pont de Nemours's letters from Paris, led Jefferson to send James Monroe to Europe. On January 10, the President wrote his friend that he would "tomorrow" nominate him to the Senate for an extraordinary mission to France. On January twelfth the Senate confirmed the nomination. On the same day a committee of the House reported favorably a resolution appropriating two million dol-lars for the purchase of New Orleans and East and West Florida and volunteered the opinion that "should alliances be necessary they may be advantageously formed." Jefferson immediately notified Monroe of the Senate's action and on the following day wrote him a long and urgent letter in regard to the mission, in which he said, "Were you to decline, the chagrin would be universal. . . . I know nothing which would produce such a shock, for on the event of this mission depends the future destinies of this republic." [18]

Given the purpose that the President had in mind, the mission was a very clever stroke. By sending a special envoy to Paris at this junc-ture, he met the popular demand for a recognition of the possibility that France might have had a part in the trouble on the Mississippi. By selecting Monroe as the envoy, he gave the West eloquent assur-ance that American rights on the Mississippi would be championed with the utmost zeal; for Monroe—who owned extensive tracts of land in the West [19]—had identified himself with the "Mississippi interest" more closely than any other man of political prominence in the United States. In 1786 he was one of the leaders of the opposi-tion in Congress to Jay's proposal that the United States should sus-pend its claim to the navigation of the Mississippi for a generation. Monroe's defeat on that occasion converted him into an anti-federal-ist; and in the Virginia convention of 1788 he represented his solici-tude for the navigation of the Mississippi as one of his chief reasons for opposing the ratification of the federal constitution. While min-ister to France (1794–1796) he strove valiantly to obtain French support at Madrid for the American claim. Though his efforts did not contribute to the success of that negotiation, as he believed, they won him the gratitude of the West. "No man," wrote Congressman Fowler of Kentucky shortly after Monroe's appointment in 1803, "is better qualified, by actual knowledge of the western country, to be entrusted with this negotiation." An anonymous contributor to the

Palladium, which was published at the capital of Kentucky, said in reply to a criticism of the new minister, "The fact is, the people of Western America have always regarded Mr. Monroe as one of their best and ablest advocates." And the influential Kentucky senator, John Breckinridge, wrote: "I was much gratified at the appointment of Mr. Monroe. . . ." [20]

If the West was satisfied and for the time being placated, then Monroe's mission was a success even if he never reached Paris. That seems a fair inference from Jefferson's letter to him of January 13, 1803.[21] It was not so much what France and Spain had done as what the Western people might do that produced the roving commission of this advocate of Western interests. For the present, at least, it was less important that he should accomplish something in Europe than that the West should agree to his going there. At the very worst, though he should fail at once and utterly, it would be three months or more before his failure would be known in the United States; and by that time—it was reasonable to expect—word from Madrid would have shown whether the Intendant at New Orleans was to be supported or overruled by the court. If he should be overruled, then the war party in the United States would have no grievance to keep it alive; if supported, there would be no restraining the Westerners, whatever progress Monroe might be making in other quarters.

As for the success of the mission at Paris, the prospects there were slender at best. The special mission was already a recognized practice of American diplomacy, and fairly satisfactory results had been obtained by its use; but there was no reason to suppose that France and Spain, which had turned a deaf ear to American buyers for more than a year past, were likely to sell New Orleans to Monroe merely because his country chose to denominate him envoy extraordinary. Jefferson knew as well as any Federalist that Monroe could not succeed without the help of a fairy godmother; but in his long letter to the new minister following the Senate's confirmation of the appointment, he draped the thought in one of his inspired euphemisms. Our object of purchasing New Orleans and the Floridas, he said, was "a measure liable to assume so many shapes, that no instructions could be squared to fit them." [22] In candor, he would have said that the measure was most liable to assume no shape at all. But in order to equip Monroe for anything that might turn up, he was appointed, as the Federalists put it, "minister itinerant," with power to negotiate with France, with Spain, and, eventually, with Great Britain, and to conclude a treaty of alliance or navigation or purchase—in short, to go almost anywhere he chose and to do almost anything he could. He was given such extensive powers because it was more than half suspected that he would be powerless to do anything.

III

Before Monroe sailed from New York, another tempest broke over Jefferson's head at Washington. The immediate occasion seems to have been the publication in the United States of a Spanish order relating to the transfer of Louisiana to France, though the nervous tension was so great that the stirring of a leaf would have been enough to cause a stampede. The order in question was one of July 30, 1802, by which the court formally notified the Intendant of Louisiana of the impending transfer of the province to France. The American Vice-Consul at New Orleans had contrived to obtain a copy of it, which he sent to Secretary of State Madison. Either the Vice-Consul or some one else sent another copy to Natchez, where it was published in a newspaper; and by the middle of February, 1803, it had been reproduced in newspapers all over the country.[23] What alarmed the overwrought public was a certain passage in the order which, reciting the language of the treaty of San Ildefonso, stated that Louisiana was to be retroceded with the boundaries that it had when France possessed it—that is, before 1763. Ignoring other parts of the order which took account of subsequent treaties relating to the province, many people regarded this passage as conclusive proof of France's determination to claim that Louisiana embraced the whole Mississippi Valley, and therefore as proof of the futility of Monroe's mission as well. The opposition was further stimulated by information, received from New Orleans about the middle of February, to the effect that Irujo's intervention with Morales had proved ineffectual, and that the Intendant was determined to keep the deposit closed until he received orders from the court to reopen it.[24]

The Federalists now made their supreme effort to detach the West from the Republican party and otherwise embarrass the administration. With heads bloody but unbowed after the fierce encounter of 1800, they still had reason to hope that a skilful maneuver would wipe out the narrow margin by which they had lost control of the government in that election. Party leaders such as Fisher Ames and Gouverneur Morris were confident that victory was within their grasp.[25] Even the gloomy Hamilton, who saw no prospect of success for his party, was determined to go down with flying colors. Offered an opportunity for a rousing rally, the Federalists sounded the tocsin in Hamilton's *New York Evening Post* and the United States Senate.

Besides the restive West, the most vulnerable point in the Republican defense was the faction led by Aaron Burr. For reasons of his own, Burr was deeply interested in the Louisiana question. Almost a year before the deposit crisis developed, he was attempting to stir up the public against French possession of Louisiana. On February 2, 1802, he wrote his son-in-law, Joseph Allston, that France was apparently on the point of recovering the province. "How do you account for the apathy of the public on this subject?" he asked. "To me the arrangement appears to be pregnant with evil to the United States. I wish you to think of it, and endeavour to excite attention to it through the newspapers." [26] If we are to believe Chargé d'Affaires Pichon, he decided to "excite attention to it" himself the following winter when the deposit-retrocession crisis occurred. In December, 1802, and January, 1803, the New York *Morning Chronicle* published a series of inflammatory articles denouncing France and Spain, criticizing Jefferson's administration, and inciting the American people to attack New Orleans. Pichon declared positively that Burr was the author of the articles.[27] He was probably right, for he was well informed about the activities of the leading politicians and the tenor of the articles was suited to the game that Burr was playing at this time.

If Burr did write the articles, they bear an intimate relation to the party politics of the period. Since the presidential election of 1800–1801 Burr had been a pariah in his own party, and he faced the certainty that his career in both State and national politics was closed unless he could form new connections. Accordingly he began a flirtation with the Federalist party which met with some encouragement. Though Alexander Hamilton never wavered in his hostility to the man whom he called the "Catiline of America," many other Federalists would have welcomed an alliance with the astute politician who had won New York and the presidential election for the Republicans in 1800. Early in 1802 progress towards such a coalition had been halted by Burr's conduct in regard to the repeal of the Judiciary Act of 1801. "There was a moment," wrote Gouverneur Morris, one of the most influential and best-informed members of the party, "when the Vice-President [Burr] might have arrested the measure by his vote, and that vote would, I believe, have made him President at the next election; but there is a tide in the affairs of men which he suffered to go by." [28] This incident, however, caused only a passing coolness and did not put an end to the possibility of coöperation between Burr and the Federalists. He still needed them and, as the events of 1804 were to show, many of them were still willing to use him. In view of these facts, the Coriolanus articles seem to have been designed by Burr to soften the resentment of the Federalists at his conduct in regard to the Judiciary Act and make a place for him in their party.

For their immediate purpose, however, as well as for the ultimate good of the party, it was more important for the Federalists to concentrate their attention upon the West. Tennessee and Kentucky, already admitted to the Union, were rapidly growing in population and political strength. Ohio had just been authorized to form a constitution and was about to attain statehood. Georgia was still a frontier State and shared the Western point of view in the present crisis. If the Federalists could detach these four States from their opponents and hold in line their own following in the East, they would gain immediate control of the Senate and lay the foundation for a sweeping victory in 1804. Though their strength in the West had diminished rapidly in the last few years, they still had faithful adherents in that region around whom a rehabilitated party could rally.[29]

At the very outset Alexander Hamilton sensed the possibilities of the situation. Writing to General C. C. Pinckney of South Carolina on December 29, 1802, he admitted that Jefferson's "lullaby message" of December fifteenth had met with praise instead of the contempt it deserved; but he thought the administration had been placed in a serious dilemma. If it resorted to war, its financial system would be wrecked. On the other hand, he asked, "how is popularity to be preserved with the western partisans, if their interests are tamely sacrificed?" Hamilton believed that it was good strategy to force the issue and impale Jefferson on one of the horns of this dilemma. The line he would take was indicated by the concluding passage of his letter to Pinckney: "I have always held that the *unity of our Empire,* and the best interests of our nation, require that we shall annex to the United States all the territory east of the Mississippi, New Orleans included. Of course I infer that, on an emergency like the present, energy is wisdom." [30]

"An emergency like the present" had existed in 1798–1799, and on that occasion, too, Hamilton had held that energy was wisdom.[31] Indeed, Jefferson was now placed in much the same situation, with reference to the Hamiltonian group, as that occupied by John Adams four years earlier. In both cases the Hamiltonians sought to capitalize popular resentment against France in the interest of an assault on the dominions of Spain, and possibly also as a means of forcing an alliance with Great Britain; and in both cases the Hamiltonians strained every nerve to prevent the appointment of a special mission to France, and, when the mission was appointed, to defeat the negotiation. There was, however, an important difference, as will soon appear.

We know little about the Federalist opposition to Monroe's appointment except that it was confirmed in the Senate by a strictly partisan vote of 15 to 12.[32] The Federalists seem to have justified their resistance by attacking not the sending of a special envoy but the choice of Monroe for that post, declaring that the stone rejected by Washington should not be made the cornerstone of Jefferson's foreign policy. Their hostility to Monroe is quite comprehensible, for it was Timothy Pickering who had made him a rejected stone by recalling him from Paris in 1796. Monroe had retorted by writing a book against the Federalists and had aided in reviving charges against Hamilton which the latter took so seriously as to reply to them in the extraordinary "Reynolds pamphlet." Nevertheless, the Federalists' opposition to Monroe looked very much like opposition to the mission itself, since no other person could have served half so well the purposes that Jefferson had in mind.

The appointment was confirmed by the narrow margin of three votes, but the Federalists did not relax their efforts to sabotage the negotiation. Circumstances favored them. The public became more and more restless as week after week passed without bringing any important modification of the Intendant's order, much less its revocation. Even Irujo's intervention had failed to budge Morales, and the time was at hand for the Mississippi River fleets to make their annual descent with Western produce to New Orleans.

Only a plausible pretext was needed for reopening the question in Congress, and that was afforded by the publication of the confidential Spanish order of July 30, 1802, with its equivocal statement regarding the boundaries of Louisiana. Hamilton, thinly disguised as "Pericles," rattled the saber in the *New York Evening Post*.[33] "Since the question of independence," he began, sounding the keynote of solemnity, "none has occurred more deeply interesting to the United

States than the cession of Louisiana to France." He then struck a chord which had aroused widespread response in 1798, declaring that this cession threatened the dismemberment of a large part of the country, the safety of the Southern States, and the independence of the whole Union. The right of immediate resort to war could not be doubted: ". . . The nature of the cession to France, extending to ancient limits without respect to our rights by treaty; the direct infraction of an important article of the treaty itself, in withholding the deposit of New Orleans: either of these affords justifiable cause of war, and that they would authorize immediate hostilities, is not to be questioned by the most scrupulous mind."

Only two courses, he said, were open to the United States. The first was to negotiate for the purchase of territory at the mouth of the Mississippi, reserving a declaration of war until the negotiation failed. The second was "to seize at once on the Floridas and New Orleans, and then negotiate." The first alternative offered no hope of success. "There is not the most distant probability," he said, braving the perils of prophecy, "that the ambitious and aggrandizing views of Buonaparte will commute the territory for money." War was inevitable in any case. "The second plan is, therefore, evidently the best. First, because effectual; the acquisition easy: the preservation afterwards easy. . . . Secondly, this plan is preferable because it affords us the only chance of avoiding a long-continued war." He then urged the strengthening of the army and navy and the prosecution of negotiations with Great Britain, and concluded: "If the President would adopt this course, he might yet retrieve his character, induce the best part of the community to look favorably upon his political career, exalt himself in the eyes of Europe, save the country, and secure a permanent fame. But for this, alas! Jefferson is not destined."

In his edition of Hamilton's works, Henry Cabot Lodge makes the arresting statement that this article "shows how completely Hamilton parted with his party on the Louisiana question and how unswervingly national he was in everything." [34] Lodge would have come much nearer the truth if he had written that the article "shows how completely Hamilton agreed with his party on the Louisiana question and how unswervingly partisan he was in every thing." The partisan character of the Pericles article is really quite obvious not only in the concluding thrust at Jefferson but also in the nature of the proposal. It was simply not true that either the retrocession or the closing of the deposit, or both together, justified an immediate appeal to arms.

On the contrary, the circumstances of the case and the precedents set by Washington and Adams required the administration to exhaust the means of diplomacy before resorting to war. Nor was the war nearly so certain to be successful as Hamilton assumed. New Orleans and the Floridas could indeed have been conquered without great difficulty; but their invasion would have provoked both France and Spain to war against the United States. Both were still great naval powers, and both could have played havoc with American shipping on the high seas.

Hamilton, it is true, said that "we might count with certainty on the aid of Great Britain with her powerful navy"; but that was problematical, especially since Great Britain was at peace with both France and Spain and there was no certainty, when the Pericles articles were written, that hostilities would be resumed in the near future. In any event it would have been the sheerest folly for the United States to challenge two great naval powers to combat before the indispensable aid of Great Britain had been secured by an ironclad guarantee. Indeed, it was precisely because the United States was utterly unprepared for such a war that Hamilton so urgently advised immediate hostilities. It is scarcely credible that he really expected or desired to have his recommendations adopted. He was too intelligent and too good a patriot for that. His purpose must therefore have been to impale Jefferson on the horns of the dilemma stated in his letter to Pinckney of December 29, 1802.

Whatever his purpose may have been, Hamilton did not "part with his party," as Lodge asserted. On the contrary, he walked hand in hand with it in the crisis. The measures proposed in the Pericles article were in all essentials the same as those proposed in the Senate in February, 1803, by the Federalist James Ross of Pennsylvania, supported in debate by Gouverneur Morris and other Federalist senators, and voted for by the whole Federalist group.[35] The Pericles article was, in short, a clever and perfectly legitimate political maneuver; but there is nothing in it either to justify an encomium on Hamilton's nationalism or to warrant setting him above his fellow Federalists, whose principles and strategy were identical with his own in this crisis. The unanimity with which the party acted is what makes the episode interesting. Realizing that it was shrinking from national to sectional proportions, the leaders were apparently attempting to broaden their party's base by detaching the West from its Republican connection.

IV

Though Senator James Ross impressed even the rather critical Gallatin as a "man of talents," [36] he was chosen to lead the Federalist assault not because he was talented but because he lived in Pittsburgh. That made him technically a Westerner, and the party's strategy required that a Westerner should appear as the champion of its proposals. It was true that Ross's prestige had suffered from his defeat in a recent election in Pennsylvania, and Jefferson even averred that his unpopularity was so great that his support of a measure was enough to turn his constituents against it; but he was the only Westerner who could be persuaded to play the part of Federalist stalking-horse.

On February 14, 1803, Ross opened the drive in the Senate with a salvo which at once revealed the strategy of the attacking party. Interrupted on a point of order, he returned to the assault two days later. "I will ask honorable gentlemen," he said, "especially those from the Western country, what they will say on their return home to a people pressed by the heavy hand of this calamity, when they inquire, What has been done? You answer: 'We have provided a remedy, but it is secret; . . . by and by, you will see it operate like enchantment . . .' This idle tale may amuse children. But the men of that country will not be satisfied." [37] And so on for two hours. Senator William Plumer of New Hampshire described the speech as one of the ablest he had ever heard.[38] Perhaps that was because Plumer was a Federalist; or perhaps it was because he had taken his seat in that august body only a few weeks earlier, and was not accustomed to senatorial flights of eloquence.

In place of the Jeffersonian enchantment, Ross offered as his own remedy a set of resolutions. They began by asserting the right of free navigation of the Mississippi (it had never been questioned by Spain since 1795) and the right of deposit *on the island of New Orleans* (no such right existed), the importance of these rights to the United States, and the impropriety of their being held on so insecure a tenure as hitherto. The resolutions next authorized the President to call out fifty thousand militiamen from Georgia, South Carolina, Ohio, Kentucky, Tennessee, and the Mississippi Territory, and to use them, together with the land and naval forces of the United States, to take possession of such place or places on the island of New Orleans as he might deem fit for a place of deposit; and finally they appropriated five million dollars for the purpose.[39]

These resolutions made substantially the same proposal as that urged by Hamilton in his Pericles article. Though Hamilton advised the seizure of the Floridas as well as New Orleans, the difference is unimportant. What he desired was a war measure, and that was provided by the Ross resolutions. Yet they were so framed as to leave the impression that the Federalists did not really want war. The resolutions did not, in fact, provide for a declaration of war. They did not even direct the President to occupy any part of the island of New Orleans; they merely authorized him to do so. That was no way to get a war, for nothing was more certain than that Jefferson would refuse to exercise the authority which the Federalists sought to confer upon him. Their strategy was simply to place the responsibility for deciding between war and peace squarely upon his shoulders. If, as no one expected, he should choose war, he would thereby defeat his own pet measure, the Monroe mission, and would compel his party to abandon its vaunted program of economy. If, as could hardly be doubted, he should choose peace, the impatient Westerners might be persuaded that he had callously sacrificed their interests and might join forces with the Federalist opposition.

The debate on the resolutions, which was public, began on February twenty-third and continued for three days. White of Delaware opened for the Federalists. ". . . This business," he said, "can never be adjusted abroad; it will ultimately have to be settled upon the banks of the Mississippi. . . . I believe the only question now in our power to decide, is whether it shall be the bloodless war of a few months, or the carnage of years." That, it will be recalled, was the essence of the Periclean argument. In any case, continued White, the Westerners could not be restrained. You might as well try to dam up the Mississippi itself as to stop them. The government must lead or follow in the path of honor, or else give up the Western country.[40] Gouverneur Morris of New York, Dayton of New Jersey, Mason of Massachusetts, and Ross himself were among the leading supporters of the resolutions.[41]

The Western Senators, for whose support Ross was bidding, did not seem dismayed at the prospect of facing their constituents with only the Jeffersonian remedy for their afflictions. They knew the difficulties of warfare on the Mississippi, the deadly climate of lower Louisiana, and the ease with which a naval power could blockade the mouth of the river. A sense of ultimate strength, as well as a realization of present weakness, disinclined them from violence. James Jackson of Georgia was so sure of the future of his country that not even the prospect of a Napoleonic army on the Mississippi dismayed him: "Should Bonaparte send an army of forty thousand men here, and they should not be destroyed by our troops, within twenty years they would become Americans, and join our arms." He was an expansionist, but confidence in the outcome gave him patience: "God and nature have destined New Orleans and the Floridas to belong to this great and rising empire [the United States]. As natural bounds to the South, are the Atlantic, the Gulf of Mexico, and the Mississippi, and the world at some future day cannot hold them from us." [42] Most important of all, the Westerners were wary of the Achæans and their wooden horse. They could not forget that the Federalist party was the party of John Jay, who had proposed in 1786 to barter away the free navigation of the Mississippi for a generation. Other grievances had been added with the passing years, and by the end of the century a settled antagonism had developed between them. The result was that the Federalists' unwonted professions of solicitude for the West in the deposit crisis did not ring true. Their conversion was too sudden to be genuine, and the Western Senators said so quite bluntly in the course of the debate on the Ross resolutions.[43]

When the resolutions came to a vote on February 25, they were defeated by a vote of 15 to 11. Ross was the only Western Senator who voted for them. A mild substitute offered by Breckinridge of Kentucky, true spokesman of the West, was then adopted unanimously. This authorized the President to call out 80,000 militia when he should see fit and to enlist volunteers. The militia was to be drawn from all the States, whereas Ross had proposed to levy exclusively upon the frontier States and territories of the South and West; and, most important of all, nothing was said about seizing any part of Louisiana.[44] Simultaneously, Congress made provision for the building of fifteen gunboats for use on the Mississippi or in the Southern waters of the United States.

Such was the military demonstration with which the Monroe mission was tardily supported. Would the feeble gesture intimidate the courts of France and Spain? Such was the Western Senators' reply to the appeal of chauvinism. Would the Western people make the same response?

CHAPTER XIII

The Enchantment Works

●   I

It was only with the coöperation of the West that Jefferson's policy of palliation and endurance could succeed; for while the federal government might palliate, it was the Western people who must endure. Nothing was easier than to say that the Intendant's proclamation was unauthorized and that the precious privilege of deposit would soon be restored intact; but to believe it was a supreme act of faith,[1] and to await redress with folded arms was an example of monumental patience. As many intelligent people saw it, Jefferson's policy required the Westerners to turn a deaf ear to the counsels of common sense, and to expect relief from a government that was almost inactive and altogether impotent. Senator Ross was not unjustified in describing this policy as a species of diplomacy by incantation. If the Western people had refused to heed the wizard's voice, the spell would have been broken. By joining hands with the Federalist opposition in Congress, they would have wrecked the administration's policy at the very outset. By taking up arms and invading Louisiana, they would have embroiled the United States with two formidable powers; and if the government had then disavowed them, they might even have disrupted the Union.

Many well-informed observers feared, and others hoped, that the frontiersmen would now earn their reputation for hair-trigger impetuosity. The general expectation was expressed by an American at New Orleans, who wrote when the controversy was at its height: "The Kentuckymen have often wished for an opportunity of sacking New-Orleans, and the day may not be far distant." [2] But the "Kentuckymen" and their neighbors surprised nearly every one by choosing the path of peace. In so doing, they followed the course already plotted for them by their economic interests and political affiliations.

The quiescence of the Western people is explained in part by their attachment to the Republican administration.[3] They relied upon its good will and were convinced that the policy which it adopted was more promising than the alternative proposed by the opposition. The Senate debate on Ross's resolutions furnishes the most striking and familiar evidence that they approved of Jefferson's course. Breckinridge of Kentucky, preëminent among the frontier representatives in Congress, moved the administration's substitute for Ross's warlike resolutions, and denied that there was any danger of violence among his constituents, who, he said, "hold in too sacred regard their federal compact to sport with it." Cocke of Tennessee spoke in the same vein, and in his effort to demonstrate the satisfaction of the West with the policy of palliation, went so far as to declare that "the Spaniards, our neighbors, appear to be a friendly, candid, honest people. . . ." Even Jackson of Georgia, who had asserted and proved his independence of party ties, declared that his State, sharing the interest of Kentucky and Tennessee in the question, joined with them in approving of Jefferson's course. It has already been pointed out that when Ross's resolutions were put to a test all the Senators from the South and West who were present supported the administration by voting in the negative. They then joined in the unanimous endorsement of Breckinridge's milder substitute.[4] Party discipline alone would hardly account for their action.

In the West itself, where even the sound of the party whip could hardly be heard, support of the administration was formally pledged —indeed it was pledged even before any one could know what course would be taken. When the first news of Morales's proclamation was received in Kentucky, the legislature, already in session, adopted (December 1, 1802) a memorial to the President and Congress which concluded: "We rely with confidence on your wisdom and justice, and pledge ourselves to support, at the expense of our lives and fortunes, such measures as the honor and interest of the United States may require." Two weeks later the council of Mississippi Territory adopted a similar declaration, in which it was said that because of the "liberal indulgence" the territory had always received from Congress and especially from the present administration, "we rest with full confidence that our grievance will be redressed as speedily and effectually as possible." Subsequently word was received that the Spanish authorities at Baton Rouge had adopted measures similar to those of the Intendant at New Orleans; and, although this was no more than was to be expected, the Mississippi legislature made it the occasion of a memorial offering "our lives and fortunes in support of such measures as Congress may deem necessary, to vindicate the honor and protect the interest of the United States." The Tennessee legislature was not in session at this juncture, but the newspapers published letters from the State's representatives in Congress praising the administration's zeal for the welfare of the West and approving of its resolution to exhaust the resources of diplomacy before going to war.[5]

II

Evidence from other sources confirms the impression created by the pronouncements of Western representatives in legislative assemblies. On February 15, 1803, a correspondent in Bourbon County, Kentucky, wrote Senator Breckinridge: "Our country is in a State of perfect tranquility the confidence the people has in the president and I may add in Congress too, are so firmly fixed that they will not move in any direction but that pointed out by the General Government."[6]

One of the most interesting expressions of Western opinion occurred in connection with the publication of a letter signed "A Western American," which appeared in the Kentucky *Guardian of Freedom* early in March, 1803. The writer, as it developed later, was a certain Francis Flournoy. His advice to the West was to secede from the Union and look after its own interests. The Eastern States, he argued, feared the competition of Western produce and would never obtain justice for that long-suffering region; whereas France, which was about to occupy Louisiana, had need of what the West produced, and, as a great commercial nation, could give its commerce the needed stimulus. The *Palladium,* another Kentucky newspaper, promptly published a counterblast by "A Friend to the Union," who declared that the "Western American" was the only American in the West who held the depraved principles he professed, and that all the rest of the people were "well pleased with our present administration; and with the utmost confidence rely upon the integrity and wisdom of our beloved president." On his own account the editor added that "One general burst of indignation against the author ["A Western American"] and his principles he avowed, was heard from every mouth. . . . Sentiments more abhorrent to the feelings of the people of Kentucky, could not have been penned. They are warmly attached to the Union, and in general highly approve of the principles which pervade the present administration."[7]

A less fervid but more realistic rebuttal of the "Western American's" argument was provided by "A Freeman," whose contribution appeared in the next number of the *Palladium*. There was, he said, no truth in the assertion that the East was hostile to Western prosperity. Analyzing the exports of the Eastern States, he found that Kentucky—whose principal products were flour, tobacco and whisky—competed with only three of them—New York, Pennsylvania, and Maryland; and this rivalry was offset by the increasing supplies of goods that the merchants of Baltimore, Philadelphia, and New York sold to the Western people. Even admitting the hostility of these three Eastern States, the West could still count upon the support of the other eight. He continued: "If whilst you had but two members in each house of the national legislature, you could procure a treaty so favorable to your interests, as that with Spain [1795]; surely with ten or twelve representatives in one chamber, and six in the other, the inviolability of that treaty will be seriously and efficaciously asserted." As for a connection with a foreign power, the Western people would be lost if they were "prepared to bend the knee either to a British, to a Spanish or to a French monarch, by whatever name he may be called, or to abandon the rights of conscience and do homage to the pope or any other pretender to spiritual supremacy." [8]

It might be added that the offending Flournoy was presented by the next federal grand jury for entering into "indirect" correspondence with a foreign power in violation of "Dr. Logan's Act." [9] It was peculiarly gratifying to Republicans to be able to turn that act against a Federalist.

There were of course discordant notes in the Western symphony of confidence in the administration. Joseph H. Daveiss, at this time federal district attorney and later one of Burr's most persistent enemies, said in a public address in December, 1802: "Until we possess a tract of territory on the bank of the Mississippi, where the tide flows, that river will only tantalize our hopes and expectations as it has hitherto: but produce no real advantage. As however we are dependent on the federal government for this, it is difficult to say when or how we can get it." [10] A more outspoken critic of the administration was Thomas T. Davis, member of Congress from Kentucky, who published an open letter in May, 1803, on the occasion of his retirement from Congress. He declared that he was not satisfied with either Federalist or Republican policy in regard to the deposit question. Both parties were playing politics, and "the western people have been neglected." Monroe, he thought, would doubtless return from Europe with an order for the reopening of the deposit, but if the French ever got possession of New Orleans, there would be no security for American commerce: "I believe we have let the golden opportunity pass by, without reaping the benefits of it." [11] For all his ostensible dissatisfaction with the party's course, that was a good, sound Federalist sentiment.

There were no doubt many Westerners who were eager to seize the "golden opportunity." Senator Breckinridge was bombarded with bellicose letters from Kentucky. One of his constituents, who bore the priceless name of Achilles Sneed, wrote from Frankfort on December 30, 1802: ". . . I believe there are few (if one) who would not cheerfully give his aid in bringing Mr. Intendant [Morales] and his adherents to condine punishment. . . ." A month later William Bradford wrote that the people living on Green River, who had had their boats ready to descend the Mississippi, were now at a loss what to do with them, and that several merchants at Nashville who had collected a large supply of cotton for shipment to New York were faced with ruin. "I am certain," he concluded, "that I could raise 500 men in and have them Ready in one week if permesion was only gave." John A. Seitz, a Lexington merchant, "taking it for granted" that it would be "impossible for the U. S. to steer clear of a warr with France, provided they mean to protect the Western Country," obligingly offered (February 17, 1803) to supply the government with such military stores as Kentucky produced. Another Lexington correspondent wrote about the same time: ". . . The voice of the people becomes serious and they people of this state begin to mesure their strength by their numbers, which is found to be about 30000 strong." [12]

The *Palladium* of January 20, 1803, did measure Kentucky's strength by its numbers, reporting that according to the Adjutant-General's return for 1802 there were 26,605 officers and men in the militia, and that their arms consisted of 11,157 rifles and 2,923 muskets. "When it is considered," the report continued, "that the Western Country produces abundance of lead and materials for the manufacture of gun powder—marksmen equal to any in the world, and a hardy race of men, inferior to none in courage and activity—we see no reason to fear an appeal to arms, with any power, that has dared, or may hereafter attempt, to trample on the rights which nature has given us; and which the most solemn treaties have recognised." [13]

Among the many Westerners who believed that war was certain to come, there were doubtless some who would have welcomed it; but there can be no question that the slender chorus of chauvinism was swelled by purely partisan clamor. It was the Federalist minority in the West which raised the war-cry. Members of the same party in the East coöperated with them in the good work.[14] As stated in the preceding chapter, Aaron Burr was playing the Federalist game at this juncture and he was reputed to be the author of the inflammatory articles signed "Coriolanus" which the New York *Morning Chronicle* published in December, 1802, and January, 1803. These articles urged the immediate seizure of New Orleans as the only means of righting the wrong done by Morales, securing the commerce of the West, and preventing France from separating that region from the Union.[15] In his first letter, published December 17 and 18, Coriolanus told his readers: "All empire is travelling from East to West. Probably her last and broadest seat will be America." On December 30, he complained of the strange inaction of the federal government, and two days later he saluted the new year with a clarion call to arms concluding with the following verse, in which the Spaniards appear as a "bristly herd":

> Your danger now you know;
> Then take this time, the gods bestow;
> And hasten to the stream, set wide the door;
> March forth, and drive the bristly herd before.

Just after Burr passed through Philadelphia in January, there appeared a pamphlet, *An Address to the Government of the United States,* which developed the same thesis at great length, stressing the argument that if Louisiana were not seized at once the opportunity would soon be lost, and that "the western people will not be trifled with." [16] The pamphlet was attributed by some to Burr, but more plausibly by others to Gouverneur Morris. It was so forcefully written and contained information of so startling a character that it created a sensation.

The reception accorded the Coriolanus articles in the West is a good indication of the state of opinion there. Extracts from them were published in the Frankfort *Palladium* of January 27, 1803, and were made the subject of an interesting comment by the editor. "The attachment," he wrote, "which the citizens of this State have long felt to the Union, has often been very undeservedly questioned by

political writers in the papers of the Eastern States. When such writers as Coriolanus (who professes to be a republican) can prevail on
themselves to give currency to the idea, we think it is high time, publicly to deny, in behalf of our fellow citizens, that any Power has, or,
in all human probability, will have claims to their affection superior
to the general government of the United States. Whatever may be
the result of the present dispute with Spain—whatever may be the
privations in consequence thereof—or however great the inducements
to desert the Union,—the people of this state can never be brought
'to enroll themselves as dependent provinces of Louisiana' [a phrase
used by Coriolanus]. One sentiment only prevails on this subject, *a
perfect reliance on the justice of the Federal Government, and a determination to support its decision, let it cost what it will.*" [17]

Though the editor may have overdone it a bit in the final clause,
there can be no doubt that the Western people were willing to support the administration at least until diplomacy had had a fair trial.[18]
While the Federalist *Pittsburgh Gazette* [19] roundly declared that the
peace and security of a large part of the United States absolutely required the government to seize New Orleans, the Republican *Tree of
Liberty* of the same place gave Jefferson the most unwavering support. Even after the publication of Minister Soler's disquieting order
of July 30, 1802, relating to the retrocession of Louisiana to France,
the editor of the latter journal wrote: "We have further the happi-
ness to state that the people of the western country generally, have the
fullest confidence in the administration, and are highly pleased with
its measures, anything to the contrary notwithstanding, said, or written by the Pittsburgh junto." [20] In short, the deposit question had
taken on the character of a party controversy, and, as it happened,
most of the Western people were not Federalists but Republicans.

III

The wonderment of contemporary observers increased as month
after month passed and still the fontiersmen made no move to sack
New Orleans. So firmly rooted was the tradition of their impetuosity
that fantastic rumors gained easy credence in the East. For instance,
the *New York Evening Post* of March 4, 1803, published under the
caption "Important" a report to the effect that, on February 26, a
messenger had arrived at Washington with a memorial from the
Kentuckians stating that, though their patience was exhausted, they
would make one more appeal to the federal government, and were

holding themselves in readiness to march (against New Orleans) at a moment's notice; and that they had already raised $50,000 by subscription for the purchase of arms and ammunition, and had embodied, organized, and equipped 15,000 men, who had already been three days in camp. It was pointed out by the *Evening Post* that if the memorial had reached Washington twelve hours earlier, it would have arrived before the Senate voted on the Breckinridge resolutions.

There was apparently no truth whatever in the report; at any rate, when it came to the attention of the editor of the Kentucky *Palladium* he declared that nothing had occurred in that State which "could give even a *colour of probability* to a single assertion in it." An esteemed contemporary, the Republican *Citizen* of New York, also branded the story as a tissue of lies, and the *Evening Post* then revealed the source of the story. On a recent journey from Washington to New York, a certain William Hunter had fallen in at Baltimore with Senator Mason of Massachusetts. Mason introduced him to a merchant of Alexandria, Virginia, by the name of Herbert, who said he had talked with the messenger from Kentucky. Herbert then told Hunter the story that the messenger had told him about the memorial and about conditions in Kentucky, and Hunter passed the story on to the *Evening Post*. Though the editor must have found it rather embarrassing to be forced to admit that his sensational story had reached him at third hand and rested solely on the assertions of an anonymous "messenger," he stoutly affirmed his belief in its accuracy. When asked why the Kentucky representative Davis, a Federalist, to whom the memorial was supposed to have been addressed, had not given aid and comfort to his party by publishing it, the editor replied that Jefferson had just thrown a "sop to the Mastiff" by appointing Davis a judge in the Indiana Territory. The editor's obduracy is not surprising, for the report gave the sort of news about the West that Eastern leaders were ready to believe and that suited the partisan purposes of a Federalist newspaper.[21]

Western declamation during the last two decades had given the rest of the country reason enough to swallow such a story; but there were many good reasons why the backwoodsmen made no concerted effort either to conquer New Orleans or to secede from the Union. Even if there had been no other objection to it, the project of conquest was discredited with the jealous Republicans of the West by the support it received from Eastern Federalists; and secessionism had become outmoded since Jefferson's election put the ship of state on a Republican tack in 1801. Though once not inconsiderable, the Federalist party in the West was dwindling. Throughout the country, farmers were swinging over to the Republican party, and the West was a farming community. The simplicity and frugality of Jefferson's administration appealed to frontier tastes, and Jefferson had done what he could to cultivate their friendship by abolishing the whisky tax, modifying the territorial governments, facilitating the acquisition of more land from the Indians, and in many other ways. The majority of the Westerners came from Eastern communities where Republican sentiment was in the ascendant, and the emigrants belonged to the class which was most inclined to the Jeffersonian faith. Many of the pioneer leaders were bound to the Republicans of the East by ties of blood and friendship. To take a few random instances, James Madison's brother George was an influential Kentuckian; Senator Breckinridge was not only a political lieutenant of Thomas Jefferson, but also James Monroe's adviser in matters relating to Western lands; Andrew Jackson had formed an enduring connection with Nathaniel Macon and other Eastern Republicans a few years earlier; and Governor Claiborne of Mississippi Territory was another of Jefferson's protégés.

Moreover, the representative man of the West was no longer a George Rogers Clark, to whom the frontier meant romantic adventure, but a John Breckinridge, who had come to Kentucky with the substantial middle-class ideal of improving his law practice and getting plenty of land for his many children. Even among the frontier leaders of an earlier and more ebullient generation there were doubtless many who, like John Sevier, had lost a good deal of their exuberance under the impact of increasing years, experience, and prosperity, but still retained the prestige and influence which their former exploits had won for them. These prudent men, whose response to the closing of the deposit was conditioned by such conservatizing influences, may have been in the minority; but it was a powerful minority, occupying public office, enjoying the confidence of the people, and so able to act as a brake upon any tendency to follow irresponsible freebooters.

To such prudence the administration appealed in a variety of ways. Jefferson himself replied reassuringly to communications from the Governor of Kentucky in regard to the deposit, and his letters—as he no doubt intended—were promptly published in Kentucky newspapers. In conversation with Thomas Worthington of Ohio he confidently predicted that matters would "very soon be put in their usual train"; and Worthington passed the good news on to an influential friend at home. Secretary of State Madison wrote similarly to Governor Claiborne at Natchez.[22] Western members of Congress advised their constituents through the press that the best way to safeguard Western interests was by supporting the administration's policy of negotiation.[23] Obviously inspired articles were published in the Eastern papers and copied in the West. According to one of these, which the *Palladium* of January 6, 1803, borrowed from the *Philadelphia Gazette* of December 17, 1802, a "high official character" at Washington was authority for the statement that the government had already given "the most pointed attention" to the affair at New Orleans, and that the Intendant was expected "to revoke his late order, before any material injury can result to the western people, or to our commercial interests generally." [24]

The administration was hardly more scrupulous in its efforts to tranquilize the Western people than the Federalists were to inflame them. On March 3, 1803, the *Palladium* announced that the French minister of foreign affairs had promised that France "would respect the rights of America" under the Spanish treaty of 1795, and that an official note from the French government to this effect would soon follow. This item was communicated by John Brown, member of Congress, who said that he had received it from "the president himself" just before leaving Washington for Kentucky. The item was one which might well have been labeled "interesting if true." As a matter of fact, Jefferson had been informed by a despatch from Minister Livingston that such a promise had been made verbally by Talleyrand, but Livingston plainly showed that he did not think the promise was made in good faith, and he even warned Jefferson to strengthen the defenses of the Southwestern frontier against a French attack from Louisiana.[25]

Whether or not the Western people believed in the efficacy of Jefferson's policy of patience and persuasion, many of them had the good sense to appreciate the futility of mere violence. A Westerner wrote from Cincinnati in March 1803: "The shutting of the port of Orleans is the whole subject of conversation, from the oldest citizen to the shoe-black. You would be diverted to hear them talk on the subject. They suppose the Millitia could take Orleans, and keep it against all the Troops that could be sent. . . . But you have seen too much *service* to believe that millitia is equal to carry on a campaign at a distance of fifteen hundred miles, to any purpose, or for any length of time." [26] A mournful plaint came to Senator Breckinridge from Jessamine County, Kentucky, in a letter of December 15, 1802, from Samuel McDowell. The closing of the deposit, said McDowell, ". . . appears to us Western People an Evel. But how we are to help our Selves I know not. We could very easily take possession of New Orlenes but how could we keep it. One of the Enemy's 74s could Prevent our going out to Sea, from Orlens, and also stop other Ships from coming to N. Orlens. But I am affraid the united States are too Weake to attempt any thing by force, therefore I Suppose some other means must be used. I fear we Shall be insulted by other nations and not have it in our Power even to make an attempt to Repell the Insult. No Army No Nevy and worst of all an Empty Treasury. (O America)." [27]

Breckinridge used the argument from sea power in the Senate debate on Ross's resolutions, and it received more elaborate development in Tom Paine's sixth "Letter to the Citizens of the United States," and in a series of newspaper articles signed "Camillus," [28] which were written by Minister Irujo. The latter added an important item overlooked by even the gloomy McDowell. This was Spain's Mississippi squadron of gunboats, which the writer described with some exaggeration as "equal to any in the world" and as carrying twenty-four pounders and manned by sixty men each. Even if the Americans should defeat this formidable squadron and the reinforcements which would certainly be sent to New Orleans from Cuba and Mexico, the Spanish navy "could immediately block up the Mississippi, and not a barrel of flour would reach the ocean."

As matters stood, even with the deposit closed many a barrel of Western flour was reaching the ocean. Perhaps that was why the Western people bore the affront of the Intendant's proclamation so patiently. The Mississippi was not closed to American navigation, and a considerable export trade was carried on, during the closure of the deposit, in ways that have already been indicated.[29] To be sure, the West suffered from an economic depression at this very time; but there can be little doubt that the depression was due to the restoration of world peace rather than to the closing of the deposit. As early as January, 1802, ten months before the deposit was shut, Governor Claiborne wrote from Natchez that the approach of peace had already lessened the price of all commodities, except cotton, exported from New Orleans, and he expressed the fear that the Western people would suffer heavy losses.[30] His fears were amply justified. Before Morales posted his proclamation, even cotton had tumbled to one-half its peak price of 1801, and flour, the other great staple of Western export, had sagged to about the same level.[31] In June, 1802, the Pittsburgh *Tree of Liberty* informed its readers that the commercial situation at New Orleans was "most distressing," for prices were very low and there was no money in circulation.[32] Western Pennsylvania soon felt the full force of the depression. Early in November, four weeks before news of the closing of the deposit reached that place, the *Pittsburgh Gazette* complained: "If it can be said that we ever enjoyed commerce, it is now totally suspended. . . . We hear nothing now but the general cry of the 'scarcity of money.'" [33]

If Morales's proclamation deepened the depression, it was not so much because of the obstructions which he actually placed in the way of American commerce as because of the psychological effect of his order. Many of the Westerners were afraid to use even those privileges which he left undisturbed. If they had not been so timorous and had come on down to New Orleans as usual, they would probably have been able to dispose of their produce with no greater difficulty than they had already experienced between the end of the war and the closing of the deposit. Throughout the period of its closure, there were always more than enough ships to take off their produce, and it was always possible, though not so convenient as formerly, to transfer cargoes directly from the river craft to sea-going ships at New Orleans. Six months after the proclamation was issued, Claiborne reported that Western boats were daily arriving at Natchez, that prices were low but freight rates "not high," and that there was no difficulty in exporting Western produce to the Atlantic coast or Europe.[34] About the same time the American Vice-Consul at New Orleans stated that there were then "in the River, and in port, about one hundred and twenty vessels; about one half of which are Americans." [35] What the Westerners suffered from most of all was the loss of an oversea market, and that had been taken away from them not by Intendant Morales but by the peacemakers of Amiens.

In May, 1803, William Breckinridge wrote his brother John that the resumption of war between France and Great Britain would ease the minds of the Western people about the Mississippi trade and would probably raise the price of flour.[36] This prognostication suggests that the people of that region realized where the source of their troubles lay. The realization would not keep them from resenting

Morales's high-handed violation of their rights; but it might suggest to them the folly of trying to raise the price of flour by driving the Spaniards out of New Orleans. The attempt would really have defeated its own purpose, for the Spaniards were among their best customers and paid in gold and silver coin; and as long as they continued to enjoy the many facilities for their export trade which Morales had left undisturbed, they were much more likely to suffer than to benefit by a filibustering expedition which would throw the river traffic into utter confusion. In short, Spain had injured the Westerners enough to make them talk loudly about fighting,[37] but had left enough of their commercial privileges intact to keep them from actually beginning hostilities. Their inaction gave Jefferson an opportunity to fish in the troubled waters of European diplomacy, and their angry rhetoric provided him with the bait.

IV

By the middle of February, 1803, Pedro Cevallos, Spanish Secretary of State for Foreign Affairs, had received Minister Irujo's despatches of November 26, December 1, and December 20, 1802, warning him that the United States would not tolerate interference with any of its treaty rights on the Mississippi, and that Morales's action must be reversed. By this time too the American chargé d'affaires at Madrid had communicated the formal protest of his government and a notification that it would demand compensation for damages suffered by its citizens as a result of the closing of the deposit. This was no more than Cevallos must have foreseen when he obtained the royal order closing the deposit; and yet he capitulated immediately. On February 13, 1803, he sent a confidential note to the Secretary of the Treasury, Soler, informing him that the King wished him to order the reopening of the deposit. Soler accordingly wrote Morales on the same day directing him to tolerate the deposit, though without formally revoking his October proclamation and without letting it be known that the court had ever sent him any orders whatever on the subject. On his part, Cevallos informed Irujo of the order to Morales and instructed him to tell the American government that Spain really had the right to suppress the deposit altogether, as well as to remove it from New Orleans, and that its continuance was "a pure and gratuitous concession on the part of the king." "But," the despatch concluded, "you will say this without revealing that you have been ordered to do so and without making haste to conclude this discussion." [38]

Less than two weeks later, the court's happy system of procrastination and evasion was wrecked by the arrival of another and a thoroughly alarming communication from Irujo. This was his despatch of January 9, which was written just after the belligerent opposition in Congress had won an important victory by linking the deposit question with the retrocession of Louisiana in public discussion, and just before Jefferson, fearful that the situation would get entirely out of hand, sent Monroe to Paris in order to allay the excitement in the United States. The burden of Irujo's letter was that the war fever was mounting rapidly and that an explosion might be expected at any moment. He described "the extraordinary sensation" caused by Morales's order, "the bitter debates behind closed doors in both houses [of Congress], the fermentation that reigned in their minds, and the risk to which we have been exposed of seeing ourselves involved in war, if the moderation and virtue of the president and the preponderance of the party that now holds the reins of government had not obtained a majority in favor of trying to obtain first by conciliatory means that which they are determined to have by force if necessary." [39]

In the face of such imminent danger, procrastination must find wings and evasion must come out into the open. On March 1, 1803, a new royal order was drawn up directing Morales to reopen the deposit formally and on precisely the same conditions that existed before his closing order was posted.[40] In place of the earlier effort to conceal the agency of the King in the reopening, great pains were now taken to bring it to the attention of the American government; and in place of procrastination the court acted with a degree of celerity almost unparalleled in the history of its relations with the United States. The order to Morales was sent not by the usual route of Havana but under a covering despatch to Irujo at Washington, who was instructed to show it to the American government and then to forward it immediately to New Orleans. This procedure recommended iself as probably the quickest way of communicating with Morales [41] and certainly the quickest way of letting the Americans know that the King had graciously granted their request. The letter to Irujo, with the enclosure for Morales, was sent by special messenger from Madrid to Coruña. Arriving there at 2:30 on the afternoon of March 5, it was immediately started on its way in the packet

Casilda which, under orders despatched a few days previously by the Secretary of the Navy, the port authorities were holding in readiness to take "important despatches" to the United States.[42]

On April 19 the despatch was placed in Irujo's hands. As instructed, he immediately informed Secretary Madison of its contents and forwarded the order by express to Morales. It arrived at New Orleans on May 17, and though the Intendant could hardly believe his eyes, the order was so explicit and peremptory that within two hours after its receipt he had published a proclamation formally restoring the deposit. On the following day, precisely seven months after the withdrawal of the privilege, the Americans began to avail themselves of it again, and they continued to use it regularly until the province was transferred to the United States in December of that year.[43]

Though any attempt to discover the springs of Spanish policy in this chaotic period must be carried out with a divining-rod, we may conjecture without too great a probability of error that the abrupt decision to reopen the deposit was the result of the gathering of war clouds in Europe. When the closure order was issued (July 14, 1802), the Spanish government could not have forgotten the stubbornness with which the United States had insisted upon the grant of a place of deposit in the course of the negotiations which led up to the treaty of 1795; and it was certainly well aware that the Americans had made extensive use of the privilege. It must, therefore, have foreseen that the suppression of the privilege would provoke the United States to vehement protest. At that time, however, Europe was at peace. There was no reason to apprehend that the Americans would be able to find a European ally if they decided to fight for the maintenance of the deposit; and there was excellent reason to believe that France would support Spain. By February of the following year, the situation had changed completely. The Spanish government was now convinced that peace between France and Great Britain would not be maintained much longer, and it had no stomach for such a war as that would be. Yet Irujo's despatches from Washington made it clear that, unless Spain yielded, the United States would probably take up arms and form an alliance with Great Britain, thus involving Spain in war with a power with which it was determined to remain at peace.[44] In several respects the situation which led to the reopening of the deposit resembled the one that had first obtained the privilege for the United States in the treaty of San Lorenzo, for on both occasions pressure from the Americans, combined with European perplexities, forced

Spain to yield to the United States in order to preserve its policy of peace.

The Federalist guns, which had kept up a running fire ever since December, 1802, were not silenced even by this unexpected success of Republican diplomacy. The business of the opposition is to oppose; and the Federalists, undaunted by their failure to defeat the Monroe mission, to have the Ross resolutions adopted by the Senate, and to detach the West from the Republican party, returned to the assault with undiminished vigor after each reverse. About the beginning of March there appeared a pamphlet, *Munroe's Embassy,* which contained a slashing attack on the administration's policy in regard to the Mississippi Question.[45] The authorship of the pamphlet was attributed to Gouverneur Morris, Federalist Senator from New York, whose widely read *Address to the Government on the Cession of Louisiana* had caused a sensation two months earlier. The party newspapers also kept up the good work. A month after Monroe sailed for France, the *United States Gazette* and the *New York Evening Post* published an article drawing a parallel between the current dispute over the Mississippi and the Falkland Islands controversy between Spain and Great Britain in 1770.[46] William Pitt was quoted as saying on that occasion: "The Spaniards are as mean and crafty as they are proud and insolent. . . . We may, perhaps, be able to patch up an accommodation for the present but we shall have a Spanish war." These remarks, concluded the article, were accurately descriptive of the current crisis and might well have been delivered in the Senate during the debate on the Ross resolutions.

As might have been expected, Irujo's note to Madison announcing the reopening of the deposit found no favor with the *Evening Post.* Even the stereotyped Spanish form of valediction—"your servant, who kisses your hand"—and the signature—"Marqués de Casa-Irujo"—did not escape scornful comment. "Let us look calmly once more at this hand-kissing communication of the sweet-scented Marquis," said the editor, who then proceeded to prove to his own satisfaction that the Spanish court had made the concession with its fingers crossed. The deposit right was still altogether insecure, he declared, pointing suspiciously to a passage in the note which spoke of a future agreement to be entered into by "the two governments." "Which governments?" he asked, with more than a hint that the door was still left wide open for French meddling in the affair; and once more the Falkland Islands parallel was drawn and the reader warned of the

Spanish court's duplicity.[47] For all its partisan flavor, there was food for thought in the article; but this does not alter the fact that the Republicans had won a brilliant diplomatic and political victory. The wrong done by Morales had been righted, Jefferson's interpretation of Spanish policy had apparently been confirmed, and it was now certain that the Westerners would await quietly the outcome of the Monroe mission.

V

Monroe's work at Paris was soon done. Indeed, it was almost done before he arrived there. Napoleon, ignoring Talleyrand, had already instructed Marbois to sell Louisiana to the United States; Talleyrand, anticipating Marbois, had already broached the subject to Livingston; and Livingston, jealous of Monroe, had hastened to get the news off to Washington before his unwelcome colleague could reach Paris. After his arrival the negotiation continued to move forward at a dizzy pace and was concluded early in May.[48] The two American ministers, who had been instructed to purchase New Orleans and, if they were able, the Floridas, bought New Orleans and, since they could not help themselves, Louisiana—Louisiana, which not even the most ardent expansionist had demanded in the heated debate on Ross's resolutions, and whose acquisition, along with that of Mexico and Potosí, was mentioned on that occasion only as a *reductio ad absurdum* of the demand for Florida.[49] Livingston and Monroe, however, signed with enthusiasm, for the treaty gave them the indispensable port of New Orleans and extended to the river's mouth the territorial possessions of the United States on the eastern bank of the Mississippi. Thereby the rights of navigation and deposit guaranteed by the Spanish treaty were put beyond the reach of foreign faithlessness. That this was accomplished by Napoleon's violation of his formal promise to Spain not to alienate Louisiana was regrettable, but apparently not very important.

After the pledge had been broken and Louisiana sold to the United States, it became Talleyrand's task to explain the transaction to the Spaniards. As finally elaborated, his apologia neatly placed the responsibility for the alienation of Louisiana on the shoulders of Spain itself. By closing the deposit, he said, Spain had all but provoked the United States to war just as France, about to take possession of Louisiana, was on the point of another war with Great Britain. Even France, mighty as it was, could not defend Louisiana against such a coalition.

Moreover, Spain had then made matters still worse by suddenly reversing its position and confirming the American deposit at New Orleans. This precipitate concession, made without consulting France, had deprived the latter power of the right, which it would otherwise have enjoyed under the treaty of San Lorenzo, of removing the deposit from New Orleans to some other spot on the banks of the Mississippi where the Americans would have less abundant opportunity to carry on the fraudulent trade which they had built up in Louisiana. This ill-considered action on the part of Spain had left the French government no alternative to the sale of Louisiana.

Quite unjustifiably, Henry Adams dismisses this explanation as a transparent falsehood.[50] No one would pretend that it was a straightforward account of the transaction or that Talleyrand knew what was in Napoleon's mind when he decided to sell Louisiana. But we can at least say that Adams was wrong and Talleyrand right in regard to French concern about the deposit. France did regard that institution as highly prejudicial and did intend to remove it from New Orleans to a place where the Americans would have less opportunity for smuggling and intrigue with the people of Louisiana. Talleyrand had not, as Adams clearly implies, obligated France to respect the American rights of navigation and deposit, but had on the contrary evaded the repeated efforts of Livingston to obtain such a pledge in writing; and upon learning of Morales's proclamation closing the deposit, he had urged Spain, in the name of Napoleon, to give the Intendant vigorous support. Before it was decided to sell the province, officials in Paris were well informed of the outburst of indignation in the United States that followed the suppression of the deposit, and they were also informed from Madrid of reports that Spain had ordered the reopening of the deposit despite the urgent advice from Paris that it should be kept closed. Finally the reopening of the deposit did, as Talleyrand asserted and Adams denies, confirm the American privilege at New Orleans.

Our information on the subject is far from complete, but it is certain that, when Napoleon decided to sell Louisiana, he and Talleyrand realized the importance of the deposit question and the extreme difficulty of reaching any solution of it which would be acceptable to both the United States and France. In view of these considerations, it would seem that Talleyrand's explanation of the sale was substantially correct as far as it went. There was of course a great deal that he left unsaid—considerations relating to British sea power, French reverses in St. Domingue, and many other matters. But there can be little doubt that again in this Paris negotiation, as at Aranjuez in March of this same year and at San Lorenzo eight years earlier, the pressure of American expansion in the Mississippi Valley contributed to a notable triumph of American diplomacy in Europe.

CHAPTER XIV

A CHANGE OF MASTERS

I

In 1802 some American newspapers gave currency to rumors that Napoleon was considering the sale of Louisiana to the United States. The report was of course without foundation in fact and even the most ardent will-to-believe could not find comfort in it for long. It probably originated in an item to that effect which appeared in Duane's Philadelphia *Aurora* on March 22, 1802.[1] Western journals snapped it up with ingenuous eagerness, only to have their hopes dashed within a few weeks by the news that Napoleon was making vigorous preparations to colonize Louisiana. The Kentucky *Palladium* published an optimistic item in April of that year to the effect that "a negociation is going on between our Government and that of France, immediately connected with the above event [the retrocession of Louisiana to France], by which our citizens are likely to acquire considerable advantages," and that "the President has hinted to several gentlemen admitted to his confidence, some very pleasing information on the subject"; and in the same month "Cato" informed the readers of the *Palladium* that the United States could probably acquire not only New Orleans but the whole of Louisiana. In September, however, the same paper carried an article in which the writer, "Dewitt," said, "We have no prospects that Louisiana will ever belong to the Union."[2]

The *Pittsburgh Gazette* records a similar disillusionment. On April, 2, 1802, it clipped the *Aurora* article of March 22; but two months later it noted sadly that Louisiana was "destined for the bounty lands of the heroes of the Rhine and of Italy, who were disappointed in their town-lots in Egypt."[3] When Senator Breckinridge learned, in the summer of 1803, that Louisiana had actually been bought, he described the news as "totally unexpected by me."[4] Others in the Mississippi Valley who were quite as much interested in the fate of Louisiana as was Breckinridge were equally unprepared for the event. In the summer of 1802, Daniel Clark of New Orleans journeyed all the way to Paris to ingratiate himself with the French in the evident expectation that they would soon become and would long remain the rulers of Louisiana;[5] and as late as August, 1803, Moses Austin, now well established at his mines near St. Louis, still thought that his exports of lead down the Mississippi would have to pass through French hands at New Orleans.[6]

Since Breckinridge was a representative Westerner, it is worth while recording his reflections on the purchase in the first flush of surprise at its consummation. It was, he thought, an achievement "of which the annals of no country can furnish a parallel." The manner of its acquisition, he remarked with more justice than he realized, was as remarkable as its magnitude. A vast region had been obtained without bloodshed and virtually without cost, for New Orleans alone would repay the purchase price within fifteen years. The Floridas were still desirable, but the United States would probably get them on its own terms long before they were wanted; and certainly the proposed exchange of Louisiana for those provinces should not be made. Emigration to Louisiana should be delayed if possible, though that would be difficult if the Spanish land grants had been numerous. Previous to the receipt of letters from Jefferson (of August 12 and 18, 1803) suggesting such a step, he had already written Senators Worthington of Ohio and Cocke of Tennessee asking that they and their colleagues meet him in Washington on October 15 for an "interchange of sentiments" respecting Louisiana, since it was feared that serious opposition to the treaty might develop in Congress. The representatives of Kentucky, he concluded, would not fail to be on hand at the opening of the session, for "the public anxiety is so great that any neglect of duty at this time would be deemed treasonable."[7]

This letter probably expresses the prevailing sentiment in the Ohio Valley at that juncture. With the acquisition of New Orleans assured, the inhabitants of that region had little interest in acquiring Florida. They had not asked for Louisiana and had not expected to get it, but once the possibility of its acquisition was demonstrated, they promptly developed a hankering for it—if not for immediate settlement, then as an added protection to trade on the Mississippi. According to Henry Clay, the people of Kentucky were in agreement with their Eastern brethren that extensive settlement of the new territory was not desirable. Only such settlements should be made as were necessary to guard the navigation of the river against robbery and piracy, and this could be done by developing grants already made by previous governments of Louisiana.[8] The people of Tennessee had other ideas, if we are to believe their senator, William Cocke, who said that "you had as well pretend to inhibit the fish from swimming in the sea as to prevent the population of that country [Louisiana] after its sovereignty shall be ours." [9]

II

"There will probably be a portion of Loaves, and Fishes, to distribute," observed Governor Garrard of Kentucky, invoking Breckinridge's aid to obtain some office in Louisiana for his friend, Harry Toulmin.[10] That was the thought which was uppermost in many of the Westerners' minds when they learned of the purchase. While security for their river trade and more elbow-room than could be found in the Ohio Valley might appeal to some, others saw in the new acquisition an opportunity for land speculation and political preferment.

Among those interested in land speculation was Henry Clay. While he prepared for an early descent to New Orleans, he wrote Breckinridge asking whether persons holding lands unconditionally granted by Spain would be permitted to dispose of them by sale or to have them settled. "Be pleased to give me whatever information relative to this subject you may be possessed of, as it may be highly useful to me in case I should go to Orleans." Some weeks later, after he had decided not to make the journey, he wrote the Kentucky Senator recommending his brother, John Clay, for a subordinate post in Louisiana, on the ground that a three years' residence at New Orleans had given John some acquaintance with the inhabitants and their manners. But, he concluded, do not trouble yourself, "much less add to the perplexity of the Executive, already I learn overwhelmed by the multitude of applications." [11]

Clay was well informed on this last point, for a swarm of office-seekers had descended upon the administration and every person who might be thought to have any influence with it. One of the earliest of the applicants was James Mackay, Spanish "Captain Commander Civil and Military of the district of St. Andrew on the Missouri," who, while frankly regretting the end of the Spanish régime, felt that he could serve the United States well, and so recommended himself to Congressman Fowler of Kentucky.[12] Breckinridge was bombarded with letters from or in behalf of Harry Toulmin, George Madison, James Blair, Henry Hurst and many others, and Andrew Jackson was a candidate for the governorship of Louisiana.[13] Most of the ap-

plicants were as obligingly flexible in their requirements as the Kentuckian, James Brown, who was willing to be collector or naval officer
or attorney general.[14] Mackay asked for "some such office" as that of
chief judge or surveyor general; and Governor Garrard declared that
Toulmin was "well qualified to fill any respectable office in any of the
new governments that may be erected by Congress, either as secretary
or judge."

Such applications and recommendations from representative Westerners are interesting not so much because they show that the Western
people hungered for the loaves and fishes of Louisiana as because they
indicate the existence of a general assumption in the democratic West
that the inhabitants of the newly acquired territory would not be permitted to govern themselves. The assumption did not convict the
Westerners—or the mass of the American people, who shared it—of
insincerity or inconsistency. The revolutionary dogma that just
governments exist by consent of the governed was subject to a reserva-
tion: the people must be fit for self-government. The people of Louisiana, it was believed, were quite unfit to govern themselves, since they
had never known any but a despotic government. That view was approved by the very authors of the Declaration of Independence. John
Adams, a member of the committee that framed the Declaration, and its
foremost champion on the floor of Congress, once remarked, apropos of
Francisco de Miranda's plan for the liberation of Spanish America,
that it would be equally sensible to talk of establishing democracies
among the birds, beasts, and fishes. Jefferson, who wrote the Declaration, might well have used the same phrase to express his opinion of
the political talents of the Louisiana creoles, to whom he never had
the slightest intention of entrusting their own government. On this
as on many other occasions the Western people showed that they only
shared ideas prevalent among their countrymen of the East.

III

While the frontiersmen calculated the advantages they would derive
from the new acquisition and while Jefferson set about devising a government suitable to the peculiar needs of that foreign province, rumors
began to fly thick and fast that Spain would fight rather than give it
up. Even the Spanish minister, Irujo, was so apprehensive of a rupture that he sent off expresses by land and sea to advise the colonial
officials of Louisiana, Florida, and Cuba regarding the proper defensive measures.[15] As for Jefferson, he was at last ready to take New

Orleans by force if force were necessary. He had palliated and endured long enough. France was now at war with Great Britain, and Spain alone was not formidable. General James Wilkinson was ordered to concentrate all the available troops of the United States Army on the lower Mississippi; but as they numbered only about one thousand, the governors of Tennessee and Kentucky were requested to raise volunteers—two thousand and four thousand respectively—to aid in taking possession of Louisiana.[16]

The response to this call for volunteers lacked spontaneity. In Tennessee, personal and sectional rivalries put a damper on the enthusiasm that might otherwise have developed. John Sevier, Governor of the State and hero of many an Indian scrimmage in East Tennessee, was then engaged in a bitter dispute with Andrew Jackson, rising politician and lawyer of West Tennessee, who had recently defeated the older man in a contest for the post of major-general of the state militia. In October, 1803, the dispute reached its climax in a verbal and epistolary brawl in which both professed a desire to fight a duel and each charged the other with avoiding the contest like a poltroon and a coward. Worse epithets were exchanged, and a farcical encounter, sometimes mistakenly called a duel, furnished amusement for every one but the principals. So when the call for volunteers came from Washington in November, Governor Sevier completely ignored General Jackson in the raising and officering of the force, and Jackson's many friends in West Tennessee retaliated by discouraging enlistment. In the neighboring State of Kentucky, Henry Clay heard that Sevier had "lately become disgraced in the public estimation by an affair with Genl. Jackson" and had "made such unpopular appointments that no volunteers can be had."[17] Sevier himself, while attributing the opposition to irresponsible malcontents in West Tennessee, admitted that he had had great difficulty in raising recruits. Neither faction deserves much sympathy, and the episode is worth relating only because it shows how easily local squabbles could induce the frontiersmen to sacrifice national interests even when the welfare of the West itself was at stake.

In Kentucky too where the people had long been clamoring with the greatest energy and persistence for leave to blast the Spaniards out of New Orleans, the response to the call for volunteers was tardy and hesitant. On November 21, 1803, James Brown, who had received an appointment as aide-de-camp in the expeditionary force, wrote Breckinridge from Paris (Bourbon County) that the militia officers who had been passed over were actively and successfully opposing enlistment in the volunteer force. "I overcame my usual dislike of mob-oratory," he said, "mounted the rostrum and addressed the multitude. The attempt succeeded beyond my most sanguine expectations." But, he added, "I cannot yet assure you that a draft will not be necessary. The pay is inconsiderable, and the martial character of our people is nearly effaced." [18]

Three days later another Kentuckian declared that if Congress had only offered to pay the volunteers ten dollars a month it would have been easy to raise the requisite number, but that "the emoluments held out are not sufficient to engage men to abandon their domestic pursuites to engage in a war so far from home, and we are not suffi-ciently patriotic to make so great a sacrifice for honour only. . . ." Isaac Shelby, writing from Lincoln County on December 3, 1803, also complained that Congress had not been generous enough. In his opinion it should have offered every private 640 acres of land in the newly acquired territory, in addition to the regular pay. About the same time Caleb Wallace reported from Frankfort, the State capital, that it was doubtful whether a sufficient number of volunteers could be obtained at such a low rate of remuneration. [19]

Henry Clay, who, like Caleb Wallace, viewed the scene from the State capital, was almost the only champion of the expedition who was cheered by what he saw at this juncture. "Armies, sieges and storms," he wrote, "completely engross the public mind, and the first interrogatory put on every occasion is Do you go to New Orleans? If all who answer in the affirmative really should design to go, Govern-ment will find it necessary to restrain the public Ardor, instead of resorting to coercion to raise the 4000 called for." [20] Perhaps Clay felt more enthusiasm than most of his neighbors because he had been appointed aide-de-camp to one of the Kentucky generals. At any rate, it was not until the State legislature offered every volunteer a bounty of 150 acres of land in addition to his federal pay that other observers began to share Clay's optimism. As soon as this news was published, thirty-two men in one militia company volunteered. One third of an-other company did likewise, whereupon the remaining two thirds raised a fund of one hundred dollars as an additional bonus for them. [21]

The James Brown who had taken so gloomy a view of the pros-pect only three weeks earlier breathed a sigh of relief in a letter of December tenth to Senator Breckinridge. "On no occasion have I felt more apprehension for the honor of Kentucky than on the late call for

Volunteers," he wrote. "We had so often regretted that N. Orleans belonged to a foreign power—had so frequently wished for a just and legitimate order to take it, and had so solemnly pledged ourselves to support the measures of the President when directed towards the assertion of our rights in that quarter, that any reluctance in offering our services in the proposed expedition would have stamped indelible disgrace upon our National character. . . . Our number is ready. They are volunteers and if twice the number is wanting, a draft will be unnecessary to complete them." [22] As it turned out, the Tennessee and Kentucky contingents were not needed, for long before they could have arrived there New Orleans had already passed peacefully into the possession of the United States.

IV

While the Westerners' anxiety gave way to rejoicing at the good news from Paris and while they debated whether they would aid in securing the acquisition which they had hailed with such relief, the uneasy Louisianians watched their own political and commercial system booted from one corner to another on the field of world politics. "All is at present here anxious and dreadful suspense," wrote Consul Daniel Clark from New Orleans in March, 1803. If his conversation with his wide circle of acquaintances in that city was in the same vein as the letter to Secretary of State Madison from which we have just quoted, he contributed his share towards building up the feeling of dreadful suspense of which he spoke. "The Inhabitants," he said, "are now so alarmed, that Creoles, Spaniards and Americans would form but one body, they would now without bloodshed take the Government into their own hands and they would inseparably unite themselves to us. . . . They tremble when they see. . . themselves on the point of falling under the lash of a Government they detest . . . there is now nothing to oppose us should we think proper to take possession of the country . . . there is no energy in the Government, no money in the Treasury, no Troops, no fortifications that could withstand us for a moment and the Inhabitants call on us to redress ourselves, and assist them . . ." [23]

When Clark wrote, the chief causes of agitation were Morales's proclamation of October, 1802, and the confirmation of the oft-repeated rumor that France was very shortly to occupy Louisiana. The Intendant's proclamation had abruptly terminated a four-year period of almost unrestricted trade, which had brought Louisiana unparalleled prosperity. At New Orleans as well as in the United States it was believed that he had merely obeyed the orders of the court and that the court in turn had obeyed orders from Paris.[24] If that was true, the event augured ill for the commercial freedom of the colony. Clark was doubtless guilty of exaggeration when he represented the whole body of creoles as detesting Napoleonic France; but the prospect of passing from the loose hold of Spain to the iron grip of Napoleon was not relished by a people who, though they had been subjects of an absolute monarch from birth, had also from birth breathed the free air of the frontier. Not knowing what the future might bring, but more than half expecting it to bring something disagreeable, they awaited with tense anxiety the coming of the French.

Shortly after the date of Clark's letter, the answer to their question came with the arrival at New Orleans of Prefect Pierre Clément de Laussat, advance agent of the French occupation.[25] Instead of calming the colonists, it seemed almost as if he were bent upon increasing their agitation. His clashes with the champions of Spanish and American interests, together with a startling series of events of international significance, worked the province into a fever of excitement which reached its climax in December. Then when it was a virtual certainty that Louisiana would pass into the possession of the United States, the rivals forgot their animosities for a moment and seemingly in the best of comradeship drowned their joys and sorrows in drink.

The chief parts in this little drama were played by a Frenchman, a Spaniard, and an American. The first of these was Prefect Laussat, of whom Daniel Clark said with some justice, "Vanity and presumption are I believe leading traits in [his] Character." [26] Laussat would have found Edmond Genêt a kindred spirit. Like the French minister who threw the American people and their government into convulsion in 1793, he came of a good family, was educated in the old régime for a government career, and found a place for himself in the new order established by the Revolution; and he was likewise a passionate patriot, headstrong and overbearing.

The Spaniard was Don Sebastián Calvo de la Puerta y O'Farrill, Marqués de Casa Calvo, whom we have already met as acting military governor of Louisiana between the death of Gayoso in 1799 and Salcedo's arrival in 1801.[27] In May, 1803, Casa Calvo returned to Louisiana as one of the commissioners—Salcedo was the other—empowered by Spain to deliver Louisiana to France. Laussat found his selection for the post an ill omen, since, as a young cadet, he had taken part in "Bloody" O'Reilly's forcible pacification of Louisiana in 1769, and had subsequently given many evidences of his dislike of France.[28] Though not a man of great ability, he had a will of his own, and, unlike the superannuated Salcedo, was able to keep the presumptuous Laussat within bounds.

Daniel Clark, native of Ireland and once, according to rumor, a subject of Spain, was the American. He had just returned (February, 1803) from Paris, where he had gone to see what terms he could make with the French masters of Louisiana. Failing to make any terms he had come back to New Orleans flaming with zeal for the American cause and had signalized his return by his letter to Madison urging the American government to seize Louisiana before the French troops arrived. His long residence at New Orleans, his wealth and numerous connections, his appointment as United States consul, and his recent visit to the seats of government of both the United States and France gave his voice authority and made him the natural leader of the American faction in this crisis. As Laussat noted, he also possessed two other qualifications for leadership—uncommon perspicacity and talent for intrigue.[29] No one, however, could make a more convincing parade of indignation at the devious ways of others. Wrote this former intimate of James Wilkinson and his Spanish employers: "I am sore all over when I perceive any thing like a communication on the point of being established between the Prefect and our Western Settlements. . . . We have reason to apprehend the effect of intrigue on the people of Kentucky." [30]

Laussat had been in the province only a few days when he made his first misstep. In a proclamation to the people of Louisiana (March 26, 1803) announcing the early reëstablishment of French rule, he made a pointed allusion to O'Reilly's cruel treatment of the Louisianians in 1769 and to the Spanish court's approval of his conduct. Laussat himself wrote home as if no one but Governor Salcedo had resented the allusion; but according to Clark, it not only disgusted the Spaniards in general but "the very Creoles who had almost forgot the transaction blame the mention of it." [31] Certainly the creoles found little to praise in the proclamation or in anything else that Laussat did or said. That was not entirely, or even largely, his fault. He could not conceal the character of the régime about to be established, and he was not to blame if its leading features were repellent to the colonists. Within a month after his arrival Clark was able to write, with evident satisfaction, that the creoles feared they would "be great losers by returning to the bosom of the mother Country." Desiring freedom from taxation, which they already enjoyed under Spain, and at least a modicum of self-government, which they might reasonably expect the "heir of the French Revolution" to grant them, they found themselves faced with the expropriation of private property and the most unbridled despotism.

If Laussat was to blame at all, it was because, in giving the colonists a foretaste of Napoleonic rigor, he did not sweeten the dose. He showed no respect whatever for private property, invoking the aid of the Spanish government—which was not accorded—in commandeering what he wanted in the way of goods and labor. On one occasion he tried to force some artisans to work for him at a wage of one dollar a day, though they were accustomed to receiving from two and a half to five dollars a day. He also suffered in the colonists' estimation by his refusal to pay cash, when he paid at all; with the result, noted the unsympathetic Clark, that he had to pay eight cents a pound for beef instead of the current price of four cents, and so in proportion for other articles. His manner was highly offensive when he was crossed. ". . . The tone of authority sometimes assumed [by him]," wrote Clark, "disgusts the rich and frightens the poor." [32]

Realizing the weakness of his position, he began to cultivate the influential colony of American merchants at New Orleans; but again he was unable to conceal his real views, which were those of his government, namely, that France could not tolerate the continuance of the privileges which the Americans had enjoyed in Louisiana under Spain. Once, in the presence of some other American merchants, he promised Clark that Americans with property would receive every encouragement to settle in Louisiana. Thereupon Clark, who had heard him sing a very different tune in Paris, said with an air of perfect innocence that he was pleased to learn of Laussat's change of views. The other Americans present pricked up their ears at that phrase and became so pressing for an explanation of the "change of views" that the Frenchman was put out of countenance—as Clark had planned. [33]

Soon after this another incident occurred which left no doubt in any one's mind as to Laussat's intentions with regard to American commerce. On May 17 Morales received the royal order of March 1 directing the immediate reopening of the deposit; and, although the order was peremptory and final, [34] Laussat was unable to conceal his indignation at the Intendant's compliance with it. [35] So vehement was his protest that every one in New Orleans heard of it. Nearly every one was offended by it—the Americans, for obvious reasons; the Spaniards, because of his invective against their government; and the creoles—except a few merchants—because they benefited by the smuggling carried on under cover of the deposit.

v

Things were already going badly for the Prefect when rumors of the sale of Louisiana to the United States began to trickle in. By July nineteenth he was writing that the Americans at New Orleans had become insufferable and were openly declaring that France would never take possession of the province. "Ils s'y croient déjà chez eux," he spluttered indignantly.[36] Early in August official confirmation of the report came in the form of a letter from Secretary of State Madison to Consul Clark, who was able to report back that the news of the cession gave "general Satisfaction to the Planters and Spaniards (even in office)" and was displeasing only to the handful of colonists under Laussat's influence. The latter was indeed in an uncomfortable situation. His proclamation of March twenty-sixth returned to haunt him. In it he had pilloried the old régime in France which had abandoned its Louisiana children by the cession of 1762; now every epithet that he had hurled at Louis XV and Choiseul was turned against his own master. "The name of Bonaparte will now become odius on the Banks of the Mississippi," wrote Clark.[37]

The name had certainly become odious in official circles in the colony. Relations between Laussat and the Spaniards, which had been subjected to increasing strain for some time past, now reached the breaking point. Shortly after his arrival, his wife had been arrested by a Spanish patrol for driving to mass in her carriage on Holy Thursday; and, though she was promptly released and the patrol themselves jailed, and though it was explained that even the King of Spain went on foot on that holy day, Laussat was indignant at the affront. Then came his proclamation with its provoking reference to O'Reilly, and this was followed by a series of petty disputes over the preparations for the arrival of the French troops, the Spaniards regarding his demands as utterly unreasonable, and Laussat denouncing the Spaniards for their evident ill will towards France. With the news that Napoleon had betrayed Spain and sold Louisiana, irritation was converted into rancor. In October a public scandal was caused by Laussat's bouncing out of Casa Calvo's house in high dudgeon when he saw among the guests a certain enemy of his. When it was learned that the unwelcome individual's presence was known to Laussat beforehand and that he had gone to the reception only for the purpose of leaving it, Casa Calvo, barely restrained from challenging him to a duel, refused to have anything more to do with him even in an official capacity.[38] On his own part, the Prefect wrote his government that it should make the Spanish court punish Casa Calvo, Salcedo, and two other Spanish officials, because of their conspicuous lack of respect for France.[39]

These personal differences, added to Spain's well-known resentment at the Louisiana transaction, created the greatest uneasiness in the province. Again Laussat complicated the situation, this time by his precipitancy in taking possession of the province before it was certain that he would be able to maintain his authority in it. As early as October, 1803, Clark wrote that the Frenchman had forfeited the respect of the people and could not count upon their loyalty. The Spanish officials had formally tendered him the use of their troops, and Clark begged him to await the arrival of the American forces descending the river under the command of General James Wilkinson; but personal vanity and national pride prevented him from acceding to either proposal. Yet somehow an adequate force must be raised for his use. A popular tumult might at least make him ridiculous, and there was a distinct danger that Spain might resist the transfer. Casa Calvo maintained a haughty silence, refused to fix a date for the ceremony, saying that he must await further orders from the court, and prepared to go off on a hunting trip to Barataria, a wild region southwest of New Orleans soon made famous by the exploits of Jean Lafitte and his gang of smugglers and pirates.[40]

Faced by this double danger—that, on the one hand, Laussat might plunge the province into civil war by taking possession of it prematurely; and that, on the other hand, any day might bring orders from the Spanish court directing the Governor to resist the transfer—Clark urged the United States government to send a large body of American troops to New Orleans at once. The Spaniards, he thought, would not offer any resistance to the transfer if a show of force were made by the United States. "The guns on the works are almost buried in their ruins," he said. The gates of New Orleans could not be shut, "being incapable of turning on their hinges, and if an attempt were made to do it I can count on 300 men in the city whom you will find ready to fall on your opposers at the first signal of attack." The garrison itself consisted of only three hundred men, of whom seventy-five were in the hospital and as many more in the guard house. But, he wrote on November 23, the United States must act quickly or it would be too late, for relations between Laussat and the Spaniards were more strained than ever. Again it was Mme. Laussat who had complicated matters. Some Spanish officers had refused to attend a fête given by her on the evening of the twenty-second, and she had given vent to her rage and resentment before the whole company, denouncing the Spaniards as "sons of filth and mean slaves." "For God's sake," wrote Clark to Governor Claiborne of Natchez, one of the two American commissioners for taking possession of Louisiana, "lose no time in marching this way to put an end to the horrid situation we are in. . . . We are placed over a mine that may explode from one moment to another." In the meanwhile, he promised, he would censor the mail from the United States and see to it that the Spanish officials learned nothing from that source about Minister Irujo's protest in the King's name against the sale of Louisiana to the United States.[41]

As a matter of fact, Irujo's letter notifying the Spanish commissioners of his protest did not reach them until December seventh, and by that time they had already transferred Louisiana to France. Their decision to do so was the result of the silence of their own government and of their fear that the United States would invade Louisiana if Spain tried to keep it. Though mail was arriving regularly from Spain they had received no order from the court to resist the transfer, and Laussat was becoming more and more insistent that it should be made at once. General Wilkinson and the United States army were on their way to New Orleans. Nothing was to be gained by further delay and much might be lost. Casa Calvo and Salcedo saw only one course open to them. The royal order of October 15, 1802, which had never been revoked or altered, directed them to deliver Louisiana to the accredited representative of France, and Laussat had his credentials. Assuming the responsibility of concluding the business under the authority of that order, they notified the Prefect on November twenty-ninth that they were ready to give him immediate possession of the province.[42]

Their decision caused Consul Clark the greatest uneasiness. Fearing that Laussat's administration, however brief, might reawaken the creoles' affection for France, and still more apprehensive that the Prefect would be unable to maintain order, he was eager to postpone the transfer until the arrival of the commissioners and troops of the United States. Then Laussat would receive possession of the province only to hand it over at once to the United States. But the action taken by Casa Calvo and Salcedo made that impossible.

"The public mind," according to Clark, was thereupon thrown into "a high state of fermentation . . . all who have anything to lose look on the measure as premature and not without danger." Since the prosperous consul himself had a good deal to lose, he took the lead in organizing a volunteer company to preserve order and defend the interests of the United States during Laussat's administration. The company was formed on the morning of November thirtieth by about one hundred Americans and their sympathizers assembled at George King's coffee house. Among them was the Reuben Kemper who was later to harry the Spaniards in West Florida. The volunteers agreed to do military duty under the American flag and officers of their own choosing and elected Clark captain. Every man wore a black cockade, the distinguishing badge of the American faction. The services of the company were offered to Laussat, who "gladly accepted" them. "The most respectable people" flocked to its standard, so that within a few days the number of volunteers had grown to one hundred and eighty. Until the arrival of the American commissioners and troops three weeks later, this force was on duty night and day, furnishing "the grand guard and the city patrols," and contributing, according to Clark, "to keep up a police to which for a long time past we were strangers." [43]

Laussat also raised a force of some two hundred men, among whom were many veterans of the recent European war. Clark, however, spoke very scornfully of this company, asserting that it was neither so respectable nor so numerous as his own, and that every man in it would have welcomed an opportunity to serve the American colors. The prefect had a following in the province, but it seems to have consisted largely of creoles in the frontier settlements of Attakapas, Opelousas, and Natchitoches, who were too remote and too scattered to be of much use, and of the lower class at the capital, who were a doubtful asset in a period when it was customary to look to one's betters for leadership. [44]

VI

The American volunteer association was organized on the morning of November thirtieth. At noon of the same day Louisiana was formally transferred to the possession of France. The ceremony took place at the *cabildo* (*hôtel de ville*) facing the public square. Though a torrent of rain poured down all day long, "the principal part of the inhabitants male & female" assembled in the square. On one side of it, the regular infantry and a detachment of mounted Mexican chasseurs were drawn up and opposite them the local militia. At noon the three commissioners arrived with their French and Spanish suites. Entering the council chamber they took their seats on a platform, where three chairs had been placed. Salcedo sat in the middle, with Laussat on his right and Casa Calvo on his left. There was a brief pause. Laussat then presented his powers. Salcedo, after reading them, delivered up on a silver platter the keys of the New Orleans forts, St. Charles and St. Louis, and yielded the place of honor to the Frenchman. Casa Calvo stepped out on the balcony and released the people of Louisiana from their obedience to Spain.[45] As the Spanish flag was lowered and the French flag took its place, a salute was fired. "Except the noise of the cannon not a sound was heard," Clark tells us. "The most gloomy silence prevailed and nothing could induce the numerous spectators to express the least joy or give any sign of satisfaction on the occasion." [46] Thus did Spain divest itself of one of the largest of its American provinces and surrender control of the greatest river system in the European-American world, just at the moment when colony and river were beginning to fulfill the promise they had held out to Frenchmen, Englishmen, and Spaniards for more than a century.

As soon as these formalities were over, the Spanish commissioners withdrew. Laussat accompanied them to the head of the stairway. Old Salcedo, symbol of Spanish decrepitude, "tombait de caducité"— in Laussat's phrase—and had to be helped down the stairs; but Casa Calvo retained that calm, serene air "dont les politiques les plus secondaires de sa nation," said the Prefect, not without malice, "ne se départissent jamais."

Determined to give éclat to his brief rule, Laussat organized a "fête au drapeau français" on the following day. The merrymaking lasted all night long, and the assembled representatives of the three powers which were masters of Louisiana within as many weeks drank a toast in white champagne to the French Republic and Bonaparte, one in red champagne to Charles IV and Spain, and another in white champagne to the United States and Thomas Jefferson. A week later Casa Calvo, who was in a more expansive mood now that the controversy was settled, gave a great *fiesta* in honor of the French which was said to have cost him fifteen thousand francs. Not to be outdone,

Laussat returned the compliment with a party in Casa Calvo's honor on December fifteenth. Among the amusements, which again lasted all night, were several dances—the Spanish *bolero,* the English gavotte, the French and English quadrille, the galopade, and perhaps—as at one of the earlier fêtes—that daring innovation, the waltz. Covers were laid for more than two hundred persons, while hundreds of others ate standing. The creoles' justly famous dish, gumbo, was an important item in the menu. There was also a buffet, constantly replenished, where the guests could help themselves to tea, coffee, chocolate, consommé, and *bavaroises.* Eight gaming tables were provided for those who did not care to dance, and the whole scene was lighted by twenty lamps and two hundred and twenty candles.[47]

One writer aptly remarks that "manger, jouer, danser et s'amuser fut la grande affaire de la Louisiane pendant la domination française," [48] but not every one spent the whole of the three weeks so joyously. According to Morales, the Americans were fearful of Spanish treachery—the city was still garrisoned by several hundred Spanish soldiers—and slept on their arms the first three nights after Laussat took possession of the government.[49] That gentleman himself was busy issuing French commissions to local officials, reorganizing the cabildo, and otherwise enjoying the exercise of power so long withheld from him. As for the Spanish officials, instead of meditating treachery they were trying to find out from their government what was to become of them. Morales had been acting Intendant of Louisiana and West Florida. Was he to be Intendant of West Florida now that Louisiana had been given up? Salcedo had formerly requested permission to retire to the Canaries on a pension, but he had subsequently learned that the cession did not include West Florida, and now begged to remain as its governor, with his capital at Baton Rouge.[50]

Sooner than they were expected the American commissioners, Governor William Charles Cole Claiborne of Mississippi Territory and James Wilkinson, commanding the United States army in the West, arrived at New Orleans. Uneventfully they took possession of the province on December twentieth in a ceremony closely resembling that of November thirtieth. American observers said that the populace greeted the change of masters with enthusiasm. French and Spanish observers saw only apathy unmoved by the efforts of an American claque to stampede the crowd into a demonstration of joy.[51] Laussat, who always had his eye on the flag rather than on the crowd, noted that when the American flag was raised in place of the lowered French colors, it "resta longtemps embarrassé, malgré les efforts pour l'élever, comme s'il eût été confus de remplacer celui à qui il devait sa glorieuse indépendance." [52]

As for the creoles, the opinion of most of them is probably well expressed in the following report of their early comments on the Louisiana Purchase: "The inhabitants, tho' mortified at being put up, in this manner, at auction, are yet well pleased with being transferred to the Americans. Some of them have been calculating, at what rate they were actually sold, & make it amount to about eleven sous p[r] head, including negroes & cattle." [53]

CHAPTER XV

I

The apprehension that Spain would resist the American occupation of Louisiana was groundless, for the court had soon run the
gamut of emotions from rage to resignation. The Spaniards were of
course highly incensed at Napoleon's breach of his solemn promise
not to alienate Louisiana. Charles IV took it as a personal affront.
Cevallos met the explanations of Beurnonville, the French ambassador, with "extreme recrimination." Godoy, while less bitter than
the minister of foreign affairs, condemned Napoleon's conduct in
unequivocal terms. The King's displeasure was thought to spring
largely from wounded self-esteem. Cevallos rested his complaint
chiefly on Napoleon's broken pledge; and Beurnonville, who had not
been forearmed by Talleyrand against this objection and admitted to
his superior that the engagement did seem to be "à la vérité extrème-
ment formel," could only counter with the hackneyed admonition that
everything else must be subordinated to the "grands intérêts de la
guerre." [1] This consideration had little weight with the Spaniards,
who were not a party to the new war just begun between France and
England, and did not intend to join in it if they could help themselves.

Even the mild-mannered Godoy pointed out to Beurnonville that
the sale of Louisiana to the United States was sure to aggravate the
very danger Spain had sought to guard against by retroceding the
province to France. Referring to the recent crisis occasioned by the
closing of the deposit, he said: "If for the simple denial of the right
of having warehouses at New Orleans, it [the American govern-
ment] believed that it must vote a levy of 60,000 men, though we
[Spain] were supported by France, with what danger shall we not
be threatened later when the door to Mexico will be open to our natural enemies [the United States] and we shall have only our own
unaided forces to oppose them with?" [2]

Before many days had passed, however, Beurnonville was able to report that, though reluctantly, Spain was ready to acquiesce in the transfer of Louisiana to the United States.[3] As a matter of form it protested vigorously against the transaction to both France and the United States, citing Napoleon's pledge of 1802, which had been one of the conditions of the retrocession;[4] but it offered no resistance, and in 1804 its protest was withdrawn.[5] That it submitted tamely to so flagrant a violation of its rights would seem a monumental act of cowardice if we did not know in what low esteem Spain then held Louisiana. Resistance would have meant war with the United States, and probably a breach with France. The price was one that Spain was not willing to pay for the privilege of shouldering again the burden of Louisiana. Had not Urquijo said three years earlier that the colony "costs us more than it is worth"?[6] He was then speaking mainly in terms of budgets and contraband trade. Now the cost of a war and the alienation of an ally which, though faithless, was still indispensable to Spain, would have to be added to the debit column.

Perhaps in another generation or for another cause the Spanish government might have disregarded these prudential considerations, appealing to the god of battles in defense of its rights. The Spanish court of that generation, however, was one which seldom thought or acted in terms transcending common sense. Bred in the eighteenth century atmosphere of rationality, a Floridablanca, a Camponanes, a Godoy showed themselves in matters of statecraft true contemporaries of Franklin, Bentham, Pitt, and Vergennes, discarding all standards but that of utility. As the most recent of Spain's acquisitions in America, Louisiana offered the fairest field for the play of this new spirit; and in seeking to make Louisiana useful to the monarchy, the court had cast overboard many of its most sacrosanct principles in government, religion, and trade.[7] In the crisis of 1803 it was only natural that the habitual attitude towards the province should prevail and that, instead of flying to arms, the court should coolly strike a balance of probable profit and loss.

The result of the computation was never in doubt for a moment. Spain no longer regarded Louisiana as a valuable colony; and if it had done so, the enthusiastic approval with which the American people welcomed the Purchase would have made the court think twice before taking that transaction as a cause for war. During the first twenty years after the birth of the new republic gave rise to the controversy over conflicting claims in the Mississippi Valley, it had been a fundamental principle of Spanish policy to capitalize sectional rivalry in the United States, playing off the commercial States of the North Atlantic region against the agricultural States of the South and West. For several years this policy was carried out with a considerable measure of success, for it was based upon a correct analysis of the situation in the United States; but in 1803 sectional rivalry, while at least as sharp as ever in relation to other subjects, no longer had much significance for the Mississippi question. Two forces were at work, one economic and the other political, which cut across sectional lines and assured Jefferson's administration of virtually nationwide support in its effort to get and keep Louisiana.

In the first place, as pointed out in an earlier chapter,[8] the Mississippi Question had ceased to be the exclusive concern of the South and West. Largely because of the development of commerce on the Mississippi it had become a genuinely national interest. In the second place, two national parties had grown up in the United States—national, that is to say, in the sense that both of them found support in every part of the Union. Of these two parties the Republican had the more widely distributed following; and, as it happened, the administration which bought Louisiana was Republican. As a result of these changes the Louisiana Purchase met with a warmth of commendation in most parts of the country which would have been inconceivable fifteen years earlier. Northern Republicans supported it as a party measure whether they had a direct interest in the Mississippi trade or not. There were Northern merchants and shipowners who approved of it regardless of party affiliations, for it meant money in their pockets. Federalists of the South and West could hardly condemn a measure so peculiarly gratifying to the people of their section.

This is not to say that the Purchase was received with universal acclamation, for many Northern Federalists opposed it with every ounce of strength they possessed, fearing that the acquisition of this immense inland empire would give the "agricultural interest" an overwhelming preponderance in the Union. Their opposition, however, became hopeless when they were deserted by Hamilton. His defection is not surprising. How indeed could he have condemned Jefferson for buying territory which he himself had been willing to fight a war to obtain? After having urged annexation by conquest, he could hardly join the irreconcilable Federalists in their assertion that acquisition by purchase was unconstitutional. Whether it was because he was more consistent or more sincere than many members of his party who had once professed views similar to his own, he now gave the Louisiana Purchase his blessing. Hereafter organized opposition was confined to a group of New Englanders whose scanty numbers made their cause hopeless.

Besides alleging its unconstitutionality, the critics of the Purchase employed an argument which might have been expected to win many converts. This was the assertion that the Purchase was illegal and immoral, since Napoleon had not fulfilled the conditions under which Louisiana was ceded to France, had formally promised Spain that he would never alienate the province, and had concluded the sale of it to the United States without the consent or even the knowledge of the Spanish court, which had protested energetically when it learned of the transaction. There are at least two good reasons why the argument might have been expected to win a host of converts. In the first place, a long series of controversies—before independence, over the English constitution; after independence, over the federal constitution; and in both periods, over countless titles to land—had given a legalistic turn to American thought and had taught the people the importance of ascertaining the legal validity of a claim before undertaking to establish it. In the second place, their assumption of moral superiority to the nations of the Old World obviously placed them under an obligation to justify themselves by the most scrupulous conduct.

Why then did the appeal to their prudence and their consciences fail to move them? Even if we admit that the appeal was fully warranted by the facts, the question can be answered without much difficulty. Its legal aspect offers no difficulty whatever, for while the keenly sharpened legal perceptions of the American people told them that the purchase of Louisiana under a clouded title involved a certain amount of risk, willingness to take a chance was a fundamental trait of their character, and generations of frontier experience had rendered them adept in the art of perfecting imperfect titles.

The apparent moral callousness of a people who freely admitted that they were the best in the world may seem puzzling, but in reality it is not hard to explain. Spain was the victim in this affair, and it was difficult for any one brought up in the English tradition, as were the American people, to sympathize with the Spaniards or even to do them justice. The tradition of Spanish bigotry, faithlessness, and cruelty, which Spanish writers resentfully call the "Black Legend," had taken root in Europe during the religious wars of the sixteenth century, when the power of Catholic Spain was at its height. In Protestant England, which was first the maritime and then the colonial rival of Spain, the tradition fell on fertile soil. Transplanted to the English colonies in the seventeenth century, it was kept alive there through the next two centuries by the incessant hostility of Spain to the Anglo-Americans. From the time when Spain tried to wipe out the infant colony at Jamestown until it suppressed the deposit at New Orleans in 1802, hardly a year passed without giving the Americans some fresh proof of the ill will or bad faith of Spain.

If the people of the United States had ever had any confidence in the good faith of the Dons, it would have been destroyed by the tortuous course which the court followed during the American Revolution and the subsequent controversies over the navigation of the Mississippi River and the Florida boundary, the execution of the treaty of San Lorenzo, and the closing of the deposit. By 1803 Spanish duplicity was a byword throughout the whole country, regardless of party, creed, occupation, or locality. In 1797 even John Quincy Adams, who was remote from the scene of conflict, could write that Spain "performs not even like a Jew, she does not perform at all"; and early in 1803 Federalist newspapers quoted with approval the elder Pitt's charge that "the Spaniards are as mean and crafty as they are proud and insolent." Even that most sensitive of moral instruments, the Puritan conscience, would register not compunction but rejoicing if these Philistines were smitten hip and thigh. The mainspring of New England opposition to the Purchase was solicitude for the interests of New England, not regard for the rights of Spain. Piety itself could easily become the handmaiden of imperialism. When in 1797 Spain seemed bent upon provoking a war with the United States, William Cobbett, one of the most prolific and widely read Federalist writers, declared: "Everything seems to be working together for good. As Cromwell said, when the Scots were coming down upon him, 'the Lord hath delivered them into my hands.' May we treat them [the Spaniards] as they deserve." Cobbett urged the United States to take advantage of the coöperation of the Lord and seize the Spanish colonies, justly observing that they would be "the cream of the war." [9]

This long, unbroken tradition of Spanish faithlessness would have blinded the American people to the moral short-comings of the

Louisiana Purchase even if they had been much more flagrant than in fact they were. The Americans believed that Spain's cession of the province to France had been dictated by hostility to the United States, knew that Spain had denied the fact of the cession long after it had taken place, and suspected that Spain had tried to help France and injure them by suppressing the New Orleans deposit on the eve of the transfer to France. If in the course of the transaction Napoleon double-crossed his confederate by selling Louisiana to the United States, the treacherous Spaniards only got the treatment they richly deserved.

Channing characterizes the rôle of the United States in the Louisiana Purchase as that of an accomplice of the greatest highwayman in modern history and a receiver of stolen goods.[10] The facts do not altogether justify his harsh judgment, but for our purpose, which is to understand the behavior of the American people in the affair, it would be idle to insist upon the narrowly legal aspects of the Purchase. Some of the facts that are most favorable to the legality of the transaction were unknown to the American people when they set the seal of their approval upon it. They felt they had ample moral justification for taking Louisiana, and that consideration was powerful enough to override all others. When William Seward, defending his anti-slavery position half a century later, appealed to a "higher law," he struck a chord to which the American people had long been responsive. If law conflicted with right, law, not right, must yield. This seems to have been the attitude of most of them in regard to the Louisiana Purchase. Even if they had been thoroughly convinced, as was Channing, that they were receiving stolen goods, it is not likely that they would have hesitated to accept the loot, for the "mean and crafty" Spaniards had forfeited all claim to the protection afforded by legal forms. They themselves were the chosen people, and they were performing a pious act when they spoiled the Egyptians.

The acquisition of one of Spain's border colonies met with such widespread approval because it came as the fulfilment of a wish which many Americans had long entertained but which they had not expected to realize quite so soon. The early stages of the expansion of the United States are sometimes described as if they had been more or less fortuitous and certainly not planned by the American people. This is not altogether true. The phrase "manifest destiny" did not come into use until forty years after the Louisiana Purchase, but the desire for territorial expansion is almost as old as the American republic. Though it was not precisely formulated and though there was no agreement as to the extent the United States should or would ultimately have, by the end of the eighteenth century there was a widespread belief that some day it would make large accessions of territory at the expense of Spain. The Virginia Republican, Thomas Jefferson, hoped Spain would be able to retain possession of its border colonies until the United States was ready to take them. The New York Federalist, Alexander Hamilton, was eager to fight a war of conquest for Louisiana and Florida, and suggested that we might even "squint at South America." The eagerness with which in 1802 American newspapers snapped up the rumor that Napoleon was about to sell Louisiana to the United States suggests that the wish was father to the thought. While some people, especially among those who lived on the Atlantic seaboard and in New England, thought that the United States was already too large, it is probable that many if not most Americans shared the expansionist enthusiasm of Hamilton and Jefferson. It was doubly fortunate for them that the power which stood in their path was Spain, for Spain's feebleness made their onward march comparatively easy and the tradition of Spain's wickedness enabled them to rationalize their predatory instincts.[11]

II

Only in defense of one of the most precious jewels of his crown would the King of Spain have gone to war with the United States in 1803; and the crisis caused by the Louisiana Purchase only added to the already abundant proof of the disesteem in which the province was held by the maker of Spanish policy, Manuel de Godoy. Married to a princess of the blood, he had now completely recovered his ascendancy at court. His position was so eminent that he did not, as formerly, confine himself to the direction of one department of the government but occupied a newly created post of general superintendence over the army and navy, with the august title of generalissimo of the Spanish forces on land and sea. Since, as his commission stated, this appointment vested Godoy with the amplest powers and the control of everything relating to the "military, political and economic government" of the royal army and navy,[12] there was hardly any matter of importance that did not come within his jurisdiction. He was, in short, a kind of viceroy for the whole empire. His opinion on any subject must therefore be respectfully attended to, and the Louisiana question was no exception. Both in its local and international aspects, it was a subject about which he was probably as well informed as any Spaniard. For several years he had followed carefully the correspondence of the Governor of Louisiana and West Florida; he had conducted in person the negotiation of the American treaty in 1795; and he had had innumerable conferences with French agents during the long-drawn-out preliminaries of the retrocession.

No matter how much Godoy might complain to Beurnonville of the sale of Louisiana, he was not in reality greatly distressed at losing it. On July 8, 1803, the "Board of Colonial Fortifications and Defences" submitted to him its reflections on the alienation of the province by Napoleon. "If," wrote that body. "Louisiana passes into the hands of the United States, the loss of New Spain within a few years may be regarded as inevitable. . . . In order to avert so great a peril, the board is of the opinion . . . that the best and perhaps the only recourse is to persuade the Americans to exchange Louisiana for the Floridas, with the Mississippi serving as a precise and fixed boundary and its navigation free to both nations; and an effort should be made to have New Orleans remain in the possession of his Majesty." Such an arrangement would not only restore a much needed barrier between the greedy Americans and the silver mines of Mexico: it would also forestall the dangerous boundary controversies which, as the Board warned Godoy, were sure to arise if the United States retained Louisiana.[13]

At that time there was reason to believe that the United States would consent to such an arrangement. The Spanish court was well aware that the American government had sought to acquire not New Orleans and Louisiana, but New Orleans and Florida, and that Monroe was daily expected to proceed from Paris to Madrid in quest of Florida.[14] Since the United States had not yet laid claim to West Florida and Texas as part of Louisiana, there seemed to be no insuperable obstacle to an agreement along the lines indicated by the Board. There was, of course, no prospect that its recommendation with regard to the recovery of New Orleans could be carried out; but since that recommendation was only a suggestion and was not an integral part of the plan, its impracticability could not be urged as an objection to the plan as a whole.

Yet, though the proposal was supported by weighty arguments and was—for all he knew at the time—entirely feasible, Godoy dismissed it with the cool observation that "there is a diversity of opinion on these subjects, and not everyone gives the same preference [as the Board] to the province of Louisiana." [15] Perhaps the Board's report genuinely expressed the reaction of the military mind to the threat of an American invasion of New Spain from the Louisiana border. Perhaps, again, it was inspired by Godoy's enemies; for powerful as he was, he still had enemies at court, and one of the most prominent of them was Jerónimo Caballero, the head of the war department, of which the Board was a part. At any rate, whether the report was submitted in good faith or not, it represented a narrow view of the problem; and Godoy always prided himself on his breadth of vision.

The system preferred by him was to let the United States keep Louisiana and to concentrate on the defense of the adjoining provinces of Florida and Texas. [16] There he would establish military colonies to contain the American frontiersmen while prudent diplomacy avoided any serious misunderstanding with their government. [17] If Spain remained aloof from the conflict between Great Britain and France, as the court was then resolved that it should, it might still hope to keep the Americans within bounds. The uninhabited stretches of Louisiana would divert pressure from the Florida-Texas frontier for many years to come, and New Orleans would provide the Americans with that commercial outlet which, as Spain had learned to its cost, they were determined to have. Under the new system, the problem of defense would be simplified, for both Florida and Texas were more accessible than Louisiana from the sea, and Spain was still a great naval power. In West Florida, it would have the Baton Rouge salient, [18] which would enable it in time of peace to compete with New Orleans and in time of war to cut American communications on the Mississippi; Mobile, which effectively bottled up the American settlements on the extensive river system emptying into Mobile Bay; and Pensacola, with a harbor which was regarded as one of the best naval bases in the whole Gulf region. Texas, while less defensible than Florida at that time, was also less likely to be attacked. The strengthening of its eastern frontier would render highly improbable any American attempt to reach Mexico across its plains and in the face of its many tribes of warlike Indians.

This plan of flanking Louisiana with Spanish military colonies sustained by the still respectable sea-power of Spain was an attractive one, and Godoy can hardly be blamed for his failure to foresee the developments which were soon to defeat it. He could not be expected to anticipate that the United States, having acquired Louisiana with an imperfect title, would claim that it embraced the very regions he was planning to fortify; or that Spain, dragged against its will into the Anglo-French war, would see its navy go down with the French at Trafalgar, its treasure ships cut off by the British, its dynasty expelled by Napoleon, and the empire brought to the verge of dissolution—all within the space of five years after the loss of Louisiana. He did know from the outset that it would require a considerable expenditure of energy to put Florida and Texas in a proper state of defense. A report submitted to him in January, 1804,[19] showed that there was not a single fortified post on the whole frontier between New Spain and the United States. The only thing remotely resembling a fortification was a handful of adobe enclosures built for defense against Indian marauders. In Florida there were four fortified posts (Mobile, Pensacola, St. Marks, and St. Augustine), but not one of these was capable of withstanding a siege. The regular troops in West Florida consisted of the third battalion of the "Fixed Regiment of Louisiana," which had a paper strength of 479 men, but at the latest report (July, 1803) was reduced by unfilled vacancies to an actual strength of 282 men. In East Florida there was the third battalion of the "Infantry Regiment of Cuba," with a paper strength of 396, but only 315 effectives; and a detachment of seventeen dragoons. Even after the arrival of the rest of the Louisiana regiment, which was transferred to West Florida in 1804, the two Floridas together could muster less than two thousand Spanish regulars; and Kentucky alone had 30,000 men enrolled in its militia.

III

In one respect the Spanish defenses of Florida were weaker than ever before, for both the ability and the desire of Panton, Leslie and Company to serve Spain had diminished sharply since 1795. Before that date the firm was largely instrumental in building up the wall of Indian alliances with which Spain sought to protect Florida, but the treaty of San Lorenzo destroyed this system and threatened the firm's business with utter ruin. Though, as we have seen,[20] the canny William Panton salvaged a good deal from the wreck, he had learned his lesson. He abandoned his efforts to turn the Indians against the United States, and henceforth stuck strictly to business. In the next few years Spain declined rapidly in the scale of nations, while the United States increased correspondingly in wealth, numbers, and stability. It was the part of prudence to conciliate so powerful a neighbor, and Panton, Leslie and Company never lacked business acumen.

There was one purpose for which the friendship of the United States government was of great importance to the firm, and that was the collection of the debts due to it from the Southern Indians, most of whom lived within the limits of the United States. Perennially in debt, they often had no other means of satisfying their creditors than to make a cession of part of their lands. In 1803 they owed Panton, Leslie and Company the very tidy sum of $173,000, according to a statement made by its agent.[21] In 1802, probably because of the current rumor that Spain was about to cede Florida as well as Louisiana to France, the company sought to obtain the approval of the United States government for such a cession of land by the Choctaw Indians in payment of their part of this debt. Colonel John McKee supported the application in a letter to the War Department recalling the promise made through him by the Federalist administration on the occasion of his mysterious visit to Pensacola in 1797, to the effect that the firm "might reasonably look forward to such indulgences as would greatly facilitate the effectual and prompt collection" of its debts among the Southern Indians. But Secretary Dearborn vetoed the proposal, pointing out "the extreme impropriety of permitting foreigners to possess large tracts of country among any of our Indian Nations." [22]

Hard on the heels of the Louisiana Purchase came another sign that the company's thoughts were turning fondly towards the United States. On a trip to Florida late in 1803, General James Wilkinson met John Forbes, head of the company since Panton's death in 1802, and the two were soon apparently on very friendly terms with each other. Learning that Forbes was about to visit the United States, Wilkinson wrote Alexander Hamilton introducing him in the following terms : "Although you can have no motive for desiring to extend the circle of your acquaintance, yet I am persuaded your Hand & your Heart will ever be free, to the Honourable, the amiable, & the erudite of whatever clime or country ; under this impression I have presumed to introduce to you Mr. John Forbes of Pensacola, the principal Caportace [*capotaz,* manager] in America, of the opulent & respectable House of Pa[n]ton & Leslie, in whom you will find sound Intelligence & sterling worth, and therefore I beg leave to recommend Him to your attentions." [23]

The scanty sources at our disposal hardly justify even a conjecture as to the object of Forbes's journey. It may have been for some perfectly legitimate and commonplace business affair or to make friendly overtures directly to the American government, as he had for some time past been doing to its Indian agent, Benjamin Hawkins. But the possibility that some sinister purpose carried Forbes to the United States is suggested by other passages in Wilkinson's letter to Hamilton, especially when they are interpreted in the light of the former's inveterate habit of intrigue, his close association with Hamilton in the projected assault on Spanish America a few years previously, and the Federalist overtures to William Panton on that occasion. ". . . With military Eyes," wrote Wilkinson, "I have explored every critical pass, every direct route, & every devious way between the Mexican Gulph & the Tenessee River; I have extended my capacities for utility, but not my sphere of action, & in the present moment my destination is extremely precarious. To divorce my sword is to rend a strong ligament of my affections & to wear it without active service is becoming disreputable." Drawn to the neighborhood of Pensacola by official duties, he had gone there and paid his respects to the Spanish commandant; but not, he assured Hamilton, out of courtesy alone. "The site is a good one & the Harbour divine." "The geographical relation of this place, to the Indians & American Estates of the European powers," he continued, "renders it in my conception immeasurably valuable; and the acquisition of the Floridas, is rendered additionally important, by the luxuriant soil" along the watercourses.

It is curious that this letter, which obviously has a place in the literature of the Burr conspiracy, should have been addressed to Alexander Hamilton; but at the same time it was quite fitting. If Burr's career went off at a tangent while Hamilton's described a majestic circle about the center of patriotism, at least they converged at one point: both men at different times were deeply concerned in plans for the conquest of Spain's American dominions.

Forbes carried out his intention of visiting the United States and was there in 1804. Perhaps to disarm suspicion, or perhaps in good faith, he called on the Spanish minister and wrote for him a lengthy memoir on West Florida.[24] What other employment he found for his time, the present writer cannot say. At any rate, the episode shows how far the world had moved since the troublous times of the Confederation—when William Panton gleefully predicted the partition of the United States by Spain, France, and Great Britain—and since 1793—when he promised his Spanish patrons to let loose on the

American frontier such an Indian fury as it had not known for thirty years.

In the winter of 1803–1804, however, it was reasonable for Godoy to believe that the defenses of Florida could be repaired; and as long as it seemed possible to find an alternative course, it would have been sheer insanity for Spain to go to war with the United States over Louisiana. Such an act of insanity was not likely to be committed by Godoy, who was well aware that his treaty of 1795 with Thomas Pinckney had written "finis" to the Spanish domination in Louisiana. Though disconcerted at its falling into the hands of the United States, he shed no tears over the loss of the province. Rather, its loss fitted in with his policy, foreshadowed as early as 1795, of shortening the Spanish lines of defense in North America. Abandoning the ambitious schemes of expansion entertained—and to a considerable extent executed—by Charles III and his ministers, Godoy had prepared for a strategic retreat from the Mississippi Valley. If the operation was not carried out in the way he had planned and if the retreat was turned into a rout, he still found himself at the end of 1803 in the position to which he had intended to retire.

"You can't lock up an open field." With that phrase of 1797, which distilled the essence of his four-years' experience in North American affairs, Godoy dismissed the possibility of fortifying the great inland province of Louisiana against attack from the United States and Canada.[25] The incredibly rapid growth of the American settlements in the Mississippi Valley had destroyed every premise on which the expansionist policy of Charles III was based. The time had come to revise that policy, frankly recognizing accomplished facts. The port of New Orleans had offered Spain the only opportunity for fencing in, so to speak, a part of the "open field." Now that New Orleans was gone beyond recall, the rest of Louisiana, vast as it was—or perhaps because it was so vast—was worth nothing to Spain.

For the United States, the Louisiana Purchase was only the beginning of an imperial progress to the Pacific Ocean. Both the first and last stages of that progress had their origin in the Mississippi Question, for in January, 1803, a few days after he nominated James Monroe envoy extraordinary to Paris, Jefferson sent a secret message to Congress proposing the expedition that we associate with the names of Meriwether Lewis and William Clark.[26] The Monroe mission obtained Louisiana; the Lewis and Clark expedition contributed to the acquisition of the Oregon Country. Well might Gouverneur Morris write in November, 1803, "I knew as well then [1787] as I do now that all North America must at length be annexed to us—happy, indeed, if the lust of dominion stop there." [27]

BIBLIOGRAPHICAL NOTE

It has not seemed necessary to list the printed works consulted in the preparation of this study. Those cited in the foot-notes are accompanied, in the first instance in each case, by the place and date of publication; comments of a bibliographical nature are inserted in some cases. Authors' names, with reference to page and note containing the first citation, are given in the Index of Authors.

Extensive use was made of government archives of Spain (Archivo Histórico Nacional, Archivo General de Indias, and Archivo General de Simancas), France (Archives du Ministère des Affaires Étrangères), and the United States (State Department and Interior Department). The nature of this material is amply indicated in the foot-notes, and abbreviations there used are explained in the "List of Abbreviations."

Manuscript collections of the correspondence of individuals cited in the notes are to be found in the following places:

Breckinridge Papers	Library of Congress
Clay Papers	" " "
Draper Mss.	Library of the State Historical Society of Wisconsin
Samuel S. Forman Correspondence	New York Public Library
Alexander Hamilton Papers	Library of Congress
Innes Papers	" " "
Jefferson Papers	" " "
Monroe Papers	" " "
Monroe Papers	New York Public Library
Madison Papers	Library of Congress
Pickering Papers	Massachusetts Historical Society
James Ross Papers	Western Pennsylvania Historical Society
Sevier Papers	Archives of the State of Tennessee, Nashville

The following newspapers were consulted:

The Aurora, Philadelphia (1802, Library of Vanderbilt University).

The Daily Advertiser, New York (1801–1803, Library of Congress).

The Kentucky Gazette, Lexington (1795–1800, Western Reserve Historical Society, photostat copy).

Le Moniteur de la Louisiane, New Orleans (miscellaneous numbers in AE).

The Morning Chronicle, New York (1802–1803, New York Historical Society).

The New York Evening Post (1801–1803, New York Historical Society).
The Palladium, Frankfort, Kentucky (1798–1803, Library of the State Historical Society of Wisconsin).
The Pittsburgh Gazette (1798–1803, Carnegie Library, Pittsburgh).
The Tree of Liberty, Pittsburgh (1800–1803, Carnegie Library, Pittsburgh).

LIST OF ABBREVIATIONS

AE: Archives du Ministère des Affaires Étrangères, Paris. (See below.)
AGS: Archivo General de Simancas.
AHN: Archivo Histórico Nacional, Madrid.
AI: Archivo General de Indias, Seville.
Am. Hist. Rev.: American Historical Review.
AME: Archivo del Ministerio de Estado, Madrid.
ANC: Archivo Nacional de Cuba.
ASP: *American State Papers.*
Cor. Dip.: Correspondencia Diplomática (AME).
EU: États-Unis (AE).
Esp: Espagne (AE).
Est: Estado (AHN).
exp.: *expediente.*
FR: *Foreign Relations* (ASP).
IA: *Indian Affairs* (ASP).
LC: Library of Congress, Washington.
leg.: *legajo.*
M. V. H. R.: *Mississippi Valley Historical Review.*
mod.: *moderno.*
res.: *reservado, reservada.*
PC: Papeles de Cuba (AI).
Sto. Dom.: Audiencia de Santo Domingo (AI).
Sup.: Supplément (AE, EU).

(Note: In citations of documents in AE, the words "volume" and "folio" have been omitted. Thus, "55: 123" means "volume 55, folio 123.")

NOTES

Chapter I. The American Vanguard

¹ Randolph C. Downes, "Trade in Frontier Ohio," M. V. H. R., XVI, 483–487.

² Quoted in *ibid.*, p. 481.

³ Francis Baily, *Journal of a Tour* (London, 1856), p. 228; Simon Gratz, "Thomas Rodney," *Pennsylvania Mag. Hist. and Biog.*, XLIII, 130.

⁴ *Ibid.*, LII, 202–204.

⁵ *Ibid.*, XLIII, 120–125; F. A. Michaux in Thwaites, *Early Western Travels*, III, 157–159; Thaddeus M. Harris in *ibid.*, III, 342–344.

⁶ Jedidiah Morse, *The American Geography* (Boston, 1797), art. "Pittsburg"; Zadok Cramer, *The Navigator* (Pittsburgh, 1811), p. 55. But Victor Collot wrote in 1797 that at Pittsburgh "neither boats nor men are found, except at exorbitant prices, and an incalculable loss of time": *A Journey in North America* (reprint, Firenze, 1924), I, 33, 34.

⁷ Thwaites, *op. cit.*, III, 342–343; Baily, *op. cit.*, pp. 146–149.

⁸ "A Memorandum of M. Austin's Journey . . . ," *Am. Hist. Rev.*, V, 523–542.

⁹ *Kentucky Gazette*, May 7, 1796, item dated Lexington, May 7.

¹⁰ Breckinridge Papers, "1793," copy of a letter from John Breckinridge to J. Cabell, Jr., Lexington, July 23, 1793. There is an excellent sketch of Breckinridge in the *Dictionary of American Biography*.

¹¹ Breckinridge Papers, "1799," ms. volume containing notes on these books.

¹² *Tennessee Gazette*, Jan. 7, 1801, item dated Nashville, Jan. 7; Breckinridge Papers, "Jan.–Dec., 1802," M. Lejon to Breckinridge, Eddyville, March 19, 1802.

¹³ *Ibid.*, "1794," paper endorsed "Written for the press . . . ," dated May 6, 1794.

¹⁴ *Am. Hist. Rev.*, V, 527.

¹⁵ Samuel S. Forman Correspondence, "Reminiscences of Maj. Samuel S. Forman." In slightly different form, this has been published, with notes by Lyman C. Draper, as *Narrative of a Journey down the Ohio and Mississippi in 1789–90* (Cincinnati, 1888).

¹⁶ *Kentucky Gazette*, Jan. 23, 1796, advertisement signed by E. Winters and J. Winters, dated Lexington, Dec. 24, 1795. In 1790 Elisha Winters visited New Orleans "with commercial views," as James Wilkinson said in a letter introducing him to Governor Miró (AI, PC, leg. 2374, letter dated Lexington, April 22, 1790); but Wilkinson apparently regarded him as one of the many "impostors" to whom he had, as a mere matter of "form

and policy," given such letters (*ibid.*, Wilkinson to Gayoso, May 4, 1790). Nevertheless, Winters won the favor of the Spanish officials at New Orleans, and with their permission established a rope-walk at that place (*ibid.*, leg. 1447, Carondelet to Las Casas, April 23, 1796, No. 159 res.).

[17] See below, Chs. V and VIII.

[18] Robert Barr, writing Breckinridge from Locust Grove, Ky., Nov. 22, 1803, spoke of this trade, and said he believed the horses, cattle, and pork sent out of Kentucky by land would be worth twenty times the produce exported by water if good roads were provided (Breckinridge Papers).

[19] Account book of Howell Tatum, Nashville merchant, for 1793-1798 (Ms., Tennessee Hist. Soc., Nashville).

[20] J. S. Bassett, ed., *Correspondence of Andrew Jackson* (Washington, 1926-) I, 94, 95. Jackson used the same route for the same purpose in 1795 (*ibid.*, p. 15).

[21] Downes, "Trade in Frontier Ohio," *loc. cit.*, pp. 478, 486.

[22] Account book cited above, note 19.

[23] *Palladium,* Jan. 1, 1802, item dated Lexington, Dec. 25.

[24] *Correspondence of Andrew Jackson,* I, 14, 15; cf. *ibid.*, p. 45.

[25] "Correspondence of General James Robertson," *Am. Hist. Mag.,* III, 282, Blount to Robertson, Jan. 19, 1794.

[26] *Correspondence of Andrew Jackson,* I, 21, 22.

[27] *Palladium,* July 7, 1801, item dated Frankfort, July 7.

[28] *Ibid.,* Aug. 25, 1801, communication addressed to "Fellow Citizens," dated Aug. 16, 1801.

[29] *Ibid.,* Sept. 15, 22 and 29, 1803, "Reflections on Political Economy and the Prospect before us," by Aristides. A similar criticism of Kentucky's economy was made in 1798 (evidently for communication to the Spanish authorities at New Orleans) by Judge Harry Innes, Thomas Todd, and (presumably) Benjamin Sebastian. They declared the system was ruinous to the State, draining it of specie and leaving the people with immense quantities of produce on their hands without the prospect of finding a market for it, thus "making the people miserable in the midst of plenty." They authorized Samuel Montgomery Brown, who was about to go to New Orleans, to act for them, subject to their final approval, in organizing a company which would exchange Kentucky produce for articles imported by way of New Orleans. Brown submitted the proposals to Governor Gayoso, but as one of them called for a loan of $200,000 from Spain, no progress was made in the negotiation (AI, PC, leg. 2371, Innes and Todd to Brown, Frankfort, April 15, 1798; Brown to Gayoso, New Orleans, June 23, 1798.) See Part III, Ch. VII.

[30] Breckinridge Papers, "Jan.–Dec., 1801," Elijah Craig to Breckinridge, Georgetown, Ky., Dec. 30, 1801. See ASP, *Finance,* I, 732.

[31] Breckinridge Papers, "Jan.–Dec., 1802," Robert Barr to Breckinridge, Locust Grove, Feb. 4, 1802.

[32] T. H. Benton, *Abridgement of the Debates in Congress,* II, 302.

[33] Nov. 5, 1802, under "Ohio Company."

[34] Zadok Cramer, *The Pittsburgh Magazine Almanac* (Pittsburgh, 1804), p. 18.

[35] Victor S. Clark, *History of Manufactures in the United States* (Washington, 1916), p. 230.

[36] See below, Ch. IV, note 19.

[37] "Correspondence of General James Robertson," *loc. cit.*, IV, 343. For Sevier, see Ch. VII, note 29.

[38] Clark, *op. cit.*, p. 342.

[39] *Ibid.*, pp. 340–342.

[40] Thwaites, *op. cit.*, III, 343.

[41] *Palladium*, March 13, 1800. Other arguments in favor of domestic manufactures appeared in the *Palladium* of July 28, 1801 (letter signed "Cato," reprinted from the *Aurora*) and Aug. 4, 1801 (letter from "A Citizen of Kentucky").

[42] See the discussion of this subject in Ch. VIII.

[43] Among the most useful works on this subject are Catherine C. Cleveland, *The Great Revival in the West* (Chicago, 1916); William W. Sweet, *The Baptists, 1783–1830* (New York, c. 1931, a collection of sources relating to one of the most energetic of the sects); Bishop Francis Asbury's *Journal* (3 vols., New York, n.d.), and Walter B. Posey, *The Development of Methodism in the Old Southwest, 1783–1824* (Tuscaloosa, Ala., 1933).

[44] R. G. Thwaites, *The Ohio Valley Press before the War of 1812–15* (Worcester, 1909, reprinted from the *Proceedings* of the American Antiquarian Society, 1909); William H. Perrin, *The Pioneer Press of Kentucky* (Filson Club Publications, No. 3, Louisville, 1888), pp. 9–22; Clarence S. Brigham, "Bibliography of American Newspapers," Am. Antiquarian Soc., *Proceedings,* 1914 (Kentucky), 1919 (Ohio), 1920 and 1922 (Pennsylvania), and 1925 (Tennessee).

[45] *Correspondence of Andrew Jackson,* I, 13, 17, 18, 27, 28; Sevier Papers, Sevier to Jackson, March 28, 1798, and same to Jackson, Anderson, and Claiborne, Jan. 22, 1798. Political and social developments in Tennessee in this period and subsequently are ably discussed in Thomas P. Abernethy, *From Frontier to Plantation in Tennessee* (Chapel Hill, 1932).

[46] *Kentucky Gazette,* Sept. 26, 1795, item under the caption "The Political Creed of a Western American."

[47] Breckinridge Papers, "1795," paper headed "Toasts," and dated Aug. 28, 1795.

[48] *Kentucky Gazette,* March 26, 1796.

[49] "A Letter from George Nicholas to his Friend in Virginia," Lexington, 1798, in Temple Bodley, ed., *Reprints of Littell's Political Transactions . . .* (Louisville, 1926), p. 123.

[50] "Correspondence of General James Robertson," *loc. cit.*, IV, 370, Robertson to ——, Oct. 20, 1798. See below Ch. VII.

[51] Breckinridge Papers, "1799," Sam Hopkins to John Breckinridge, City of Henderson, Feb. 4, 1799.

Chapter II. The Spanish Fringe

[1] See the suggestive discussion of this subject in Herbert E. Bolton, *The Spanish Borderlands* (New Haven, 1921), pp. 251–256.

[2] See below, Ch. V.

[3] To go no further back, the project was urged by Governor Carondelet and supported by Captain-General Las Casas of Havana, who was Carondelet's brother-in-law. It was also recommended by Diego de Gardoqui (Secretary of the Treasury, 1792–1796) in order to cut off communications and contraband trade between Louisiana and other Spanish colonies. In 1795, Godoy was authorized by the King to erect Louisiana and the Floridas into a commandancy (*comandancia*) whenever he should see fit to do so. Under special authorization from Las Casas, Carondelet did act as *comandante general interino* of Louisiana and West Florida from December, 1796, to the eve of his departure for Quito in August, 1797; but Las Casas's order was immediately reversed by the court, so that from July, 1797, to the end of the Spanish régime Louisiana was again under the authority of the Captain-General residing at Havana. Captain-General Someruelos renewed Carondelet's proposal in 1801 but, because of the retrocession of Louisiana to France, no action was taken on his recommendation. The chief authorities for the foregoing statement are as follows: AGS, Guerra, leg. 6929 *mod.*, memorandum beginning "Señor. La Capitanía gral de la Provincia de la Luisiana y Florida . . . ," no date or signature; *ibid.*, Someruelos to Cornel, April 26, 1801, No. 136; AI, Sto. Dom., leg. 2565, Carondelet to Azanza, December 1, 1796, No. 1; *ibid.*, leg. 2566, Santa Clara to Álvarez, June 23, 1797, No. 1; *ibid.*, Carondelet to Álvarez (day?) July, 1797, No. 43.

[4] Arthur P. Whitaker, *Spanish-American Frontier* (Boston, 1927), pp. 17, 18.

[5] The annual subsidy (*situado*) of Louisiana was fixed by an ordinance of 1785. In 1799 it amounted to 537,869 *pesos fuertes* (AI, Sto. Dom., leg. 2616, Morales to Soler, April 30, 1799, No. 288 and enclosed *noticia*). A *peso fuerte* was worth about one dollar in United States money.

[6] The intendancy in Louisiana was established in 1780 and the office conferred on Martín Navarro. His commission subordinated him to the governor and expressly withheld Indian affairs from his control (*ibid.*, leg. 2606, draft of Navarro's commission as Intendant, dated El Pardo, Feb. 24, 1780). Studies dealing with the Spanish colonial intendancy are W. W. Pierson, "The Establishment and Early Functioning of the *Intendencia* of Cuba," *James Sprunt Historical Studies*, XIX, No. 2, 74–133; and Lillian E. Fisher, *The Intendant System in Spanish America* (Berkeley, 1929).

[7] This is expressly stated in a memorandum prepared for the King by Gardoqui on May 25, 1793 (AI, Sto. Dom., leg. 2606). Rendón's commission as Intendant was dated Oct. 25, 1793 (*ibid.*).

[8] For further information about Morales, consult the index.

⁹ For Berquin-Duvallon's account of the judicial system, see below, note 43. Another description is in Jefferson's "Account of Louisiana," ASP, *Misc.*, I, 351–353.

¹⁰ The notation in question was made by Tomás Portell, commandant of New Madrid, on a representation in English by James Rayen, New Madrid, July 2, 1794: "Hable esta parte en Castellano respecto a que estamos en Castilla, y se le oira" (AI, PC, leg. 196). Portell's difficulties, for lack of an interpreter and for other reasons, were described by Gayoso in a letter of Dec. 10, 1795, to Carondelet (AI, PC, leg. 43). Partell was transferred to St. Marks, where misfortune still dogged his footsteps (see below, Ch. IX).

¹¹ This was the case of the ship *Noah's Ark*. See Arthur P. Whitaker, *Documents Relating to the Commercial Policy of Spain in the Floridas* (Deland, Florida, 1931), p. 242, note 173.

¹² Translation in James A. Robertson, *Louisiana under the Rule of Spain, France and the United States* (Cleveland, 1911), I, 207. Prefect Laussat also wrote that Vidal "sells his decisions almost publicly" (Marc de Villiers du Terrage, *Les Dernières Années de la Louisiane Française*, Paris, n.d., p. 410).

¹³ *Ibid.*

¹⁴ AI, 87–3–21, *expediente* on the case of the ship *San Francisco de Paula*, endorsed on wrapper: "Consejo de Indias en sala 1ª. á 7. de Dizᵣᵉ. de 1785." The case was decided against Navarro.

¹⁵ AHN, Consejos, Consejo de Indias, *residencia* of Miró.

¹⁶ AI, Sto. Dom., leg. 2615, Morales to Soler, March 31, 1799, No. 23 res.

¹⁷ *Ibid.*, 86–5–24, *extracto* beginning with a despatch from Rendón dated Aug. 22, 1795, signed at the end by Aparici. Orue had been retired on half pay as the result of recommendations by Rendón.

¹⁸ See below, Ch. X, note 9.

¹⁹ AHN, Est. leg. 3899, Campo de Alange to the Prince of the Peace, San Lorenzo, Dec. 2, 1795.

²⁰ AGS, Guerra, leg. 7292 mod., "Estado del Regimiento Fixo de la Luisiana," Dec. 31, 1796. The full strength of the regiment was 1856, but there were 470 vacancies. Slightly different figures were given in Carondelet's despatch to Minister Azanza, Dec. 1, 1796, No. 2 res. (AI, Sto. Dom., leg. 2565 *mod.*). A battalion of Mexican infantry of 215 effectives was also temporarily stationed in Louisiana at that juncture.

²¹ *Ibid.*, leg. 2615, Morales to Soler, May 31, 1799, No. 27 res., enclosing a statement from Gayoso, dated May 15, 1799, showing the strength of the river fleet ("Esquadra de galeras") of Louisiana. The total number of officers and men in the fleet was 295. The smallest boat (the gunboat *Socorro*) carried eighteen men, the largest (the galley *La Leal*), forty. Information about the range of the fleet's activities is contained in despatch No. 356 from Morales to Soler, Dec. 22, 1799 (*ibid.*, leg. 2638).

²² State Department, Consular Letters, New Orleans, Daniel Clark to Pickering, Nov. 18, 1799.

[23] On Dec. 1, 1796, Carondelet wrote that St. Louis was defended by a "fuertecito de estacas guarnecido con 28. hombres" (AI, Sto. Dom., leg. 2565, to Azanza, No. 1 res.).

[24] In a despatch of Jan. 24, 1794, containing a comprehensive report on the religious situation in Louisiana, Carondelet stated that there were 44,116 souls in Louisiana and West Florida (despatch extracted in the last *expediente* cited in note 42, below). In 1797, the Bishop of Louisiana gave the population of lower Louisiana and Natchez District as 43,087 (AI, Sto. Dom., 86–7–25, Luis, Bishop of Louisiana, to Llaguno, New Orleans, Feb. 16, 1797, enclosing an "estado de los curatos" dated Feb. 15, 1797). This excluded upper Louisiana and the Floridas. According to a census of 1799, upper Louisiana had a population of 6,028 (Gayarré, *History of Louisiana*, III, 406). In 1791, West Florida was said to contain 2,236 inhabitants, distributed as follows: Pensacola, 572; Mobile, 733; Fort Apalache (St. Marks), 90; Tombekbé, 348; Tenzas, 493 (report of the Suffragan Bishop after a visitation to West Florida, dated New Orleans, May 28, 1791: AI, Sto. Dom., leg. 2531, *expediente* on schools and churches in Mobile and Pensacola). There is no reason to believe that the population of West Florida increased greatly between 1791 and 1796 (except in the Baton Rouge district, which was included in the Louisiana enumeration). Putting this information together and deducting the Bishop's figures for Natchez (4,556), since that district passed into the possession of the United States early in 1798, it appears that upper and lower Louisiana and West Florida had a population of some 46,000 in 1797. By 1800 the population of upper Louisiana had grown to 6,911 according to a general census given in Louis Houck, *The Spanish Régime in Missouri* (Chicago, 1909), II, 414. A census furnished by Daniel Clark in 1803 showed a total population of 42,375 for Louisiana and West Florida, but he said that the Spanish government was confident that their population was actually over 50,000 since the census was based upon district returns some of which were as much as seven years old (State Department, Consular Letters, New Orleans, Clark to Madison, Aug. 17, 1803).

[25] See preceding note. In a most interesting article ("Population and Extent of Settlement in Missouri before 1804," *Missouri Hist. Rev.*, V, 189–213), Professor Jonas Viles maintains that even as late as 1804 the Americanization of upper Louisiana had hardly begun, despite the fact that by this time more than half of the inhabitants were Americans (that is, immigrants from the United States). He attributes the Americans' relative lack of influence to the fact that most of them lived on detached farms, leaving the villages, trade, and industry in the hands of the French.

[26] *Am. Hist. Rev.*, V, 535. See Ch. IX, note 2.

[27] A. P. Nasatir, "The Anglo-Spanish Frontier on the Upper Mississippi, 1786–1796," *Iowa Journal of History and Politics*, April, 1931, and "Anglo-Spanish Rivalry on the Upper Missouri," M. V. H. R., XVI, No. 4, and XVII, No. 1.

[28] For instance, in reinforcing the determination of the Spanish government (May, 1796) to execute the treaty of San Lorenzo faithfully and

to cultivate friendly relations with the United States (AI, Sto. Dom., 87–3–22, Montarco to Gardoqui, May 29, 1796). British aggression in this region was cited as a cause of war in the Spanish declaration of war of Oct. 5, 1796. See Ch. X.

[29] In 1787 the population of East Florida was 1,390; in 1804, 4,445 (Whitaker, *Documents Relating to Spanish Commercial Policy in the Floridas*, pp. liii, 55). Since most of the increase occurred after 1793, the estimate in the text seems quite liberal enough for the period about 1795.

[30] AI, Sto. Dom., leg. 2589, Folch to Caballero, Pensacola, April 1, 1799, No. 1. This letter also contains information about the "wreckers," with a reference to Bernard Romans's work on Florida. As for the Florida Indians, Folch said that they were in fact among the best behaved he had ever seen.

[31] For 1788, Gayarré, *Louisiana*, III, 215. In 1803, according to Daniel Clark, the population of New Orleans was 8,056, consisting of 3,948 whites, 1,335 free Negroes, and 2,773 slaves (State Department, Consular Letters, New Orleans, Clark to Madison, Aug. 17, 1803).

[32] There were thirteen watchmen (*serenos*) and eighty lights. The cost was met by a chimney tax. Protests from the inhabitants induced Governor Gayoso to replace this by a tax on meat and bread. He argued that the meat tax would come out of the excessive profits of the butchers, and that the bread tax would not fall on the poor people of New Orleans, since they did not eat bread (except on special occasions), but rice and corn. Moreover, he said that this tax would levy a contribution on visitors to New Orleans (AI, Sto. Dom., 86–5–24, royal order to the Governor of Louisiana, May 19, 1801).

[33] Edward L. Tinker, "Bibliography of the French Newspapers and Periodicals of Louisiana," Am. Antiquarian Soc., *Proceedings*, XLII, 250; John S. Kendall, "Early New Orleans Newspapers," *La. Hist. Quarterly*, X, 384, 385. The first number was probably published in January, 1794. The paper appeared weekly and consisted of four small pages (five by seven inches), with two columns to the page.

[34] Berquin-Duvallon, *Vue*, pp. 30, 31 (see below, note 43).

[35] AI, Sto. Dom., leg. 2589, the Bishop of Havana to Bajamar, Havana, June 20, 1791.

[36] *Ibid.*, leg. 2531, *expediente* on the pious works of Andrés Almonester y Roxas, and his petitions for privileges, 1786–1798.

[37] Grace King, *Creole Families of New Orleans* (New York, 1921), pp. 98, 99, quoting letter-journal of Pontalba.

[38] AI, Sto. Dom., leg. 2531, *expediente* on the schools of East Florida; *ibid.*, leg. 2537, *extracto*, with *nota*, of despatch from Miró to Valdés, Oct. 8, 1788, No. 121; *ibid.*, leg. 2531, *expediente* on schools and churches in Mobile and Pensacola.

[39] Dunbar Rowland, ed., *Official Letter Books of W. C. C. Claiborne* (Jackson, Miss., 1917), I, 315.

[40] Robertson's *Louisiana*, cited above, note 12, is a most useful compendium of information for the period covered (1785–1807). Besides

documents, it contains notes quoting liberally from the many books of travel of the period; and the whole is elaborately indexed. The most critical traveler was Berquin-Duvallon, whose *Vue de la Colonie espagnole du Mississippi* was published at Paris in 1803 (see below, note 43). Others are L. N. Baudry des Lozières, *Voyage à la Louisiane* (Paris, 1802), and F. M. Perrin du Lac, *Voyage dans les deux Louisianes . . . en 1801, 1802 et 1803* (Paris, 1805). Amos Stoddard, *Sketches of Louisiana* (Philadelphia, 1812), pp. 151–158, describes New Orleans at the end of the Spanish period.

[41] Grace King, *op. cit.*, p. 99. quoting Pontalba.

[42] This and the preceding paragraph are based on the following documents: AI, Sto. Dom., leg. 2531, *expediente* on the founding of a *seminario conciliar* at New Orleans, 1795–1800; *ibid.*, leg. 2589, Luis (de Peñalvert y Cardenas), Bishop of Louisiana, to Caballero, New Orleans, July 21, 1799; *ibid.*, *expediente* relative to the sending to Florida of three Irish priests and a Franciscan, 1791–1798. This last *expediente* is much more comprehensive than its title indicates, and in fact deals largely with Natchez and Louisiana. See also Gayarré, *Louisiana,* III, 407–409, and Robertson, *Louisiana,* I, 209–211.

[43] See especially Berquin-Duvallon, *op. cit.*, 207. He was a very severe critic. Prefect Laussat, who came to New Orleans about the same time and remained there longer, said that the only good chapter in his compatriot's book was the one on the judicial system and Vidal, and that otherwise it was the work of an "esprit étroit et mal tourné," who saw only the swamps and snakes of Louisiana (Marc de Villiers du Terrage, *op. cit.*, p. 402, note).

[44] "William Johnson's Journal," *La. Hist. Quarterly,* V. 36–38.

[45] *Palladium,* June 23, 1801, letter dated New Orleans, March 2, 1801, and addressed to his "friend in Burlington," whether New Jersey, Vermont, Massachusetts, Connecticut, or Kentucky does not appear.

[46] ASP, *Miscellaneous,* I, 351. It was stated in 1803 that there was another suitable tract in the Attakapas country; but it was apparently not in use and its extent was not known.

[47] Under royal orders of 1792 and 1793, as interpreted in 1794, slaves could be imported into Louisiana duty free, either from foreign colonies or direct from Africa; but the specie and goods exported to pay for African slaves were duty free, while those exported to pay for slaves from foreign colonies were subject to a duty of six per cent. Governor Carondelet prohibited the importation of slaves from the French West Indies on account of the insurrection there. This cut off the chief source of supply. In 1800 the acting Civil-Governor, Casa Calvo, wrote that Louisiana was badly in need of more slaves. The shortage was then accentuated by a royal order of the same year granting a monopoly of the Louisiana slave trade to a French company. As late as May, 1802, according to acting Intendant Morales, the company had made no use of its privilege and Louisiana was languishing for lack of hands (Whitaker, *Documents Relating to Spanish Commercial Policy in the Floridas,* p. 177 and note 172; AI, Sto. Dom., leg. 2589, Casa Calvo to Caballero, Oct. 18, 1800, No.

1; leg. 2619, Morales to Soler, May 31, 1802, No. 97). There was, however, some local opposition to the slave trade. In a report of Aug. 8, 1800, enclosed in Casa Calvo's despatch (cited above), the *síndico procurador general*, Barran, declared that the embers of the servile insurrection which occurred in Louisiana in 1795 were still glowing; that the proposed reopening of the slave trade was a project conceived by foreigners for their own profit; and that, if the planters themselves were consulted, they would raise a "terrible clamor" against the measure, and would paint a "fearful picture of the disorders to which the colony is a prey because of the insubordination of the slaves." In 1803, Daniel Clark called attention to the fact that the slave population of Louisiana was proportionately less then than in 1785 and attributed the decline to restrictions on the slave trade since 1792, to the ravages of smallpox, and to the want of an adequate number of females to keep up the stock (State Department, Consular Letters, New Orleans, Clark to Madison, Aug. 17, 1803).

[48] Robertson, *Louisiana,* I, 214. See Barran's report of 1800, summarized in the preceding note.

[49] W. C. C. Claiborne, one of the United States commissioners to take possession of Louisiana, wrote Madison from New Orleans on December 27, 1803, that he was "not a little indebted" to Prefect Laussat for having abolished the *cabildo,* and continued: *"This body was created on principles altogether incongruous with those of our government"* (*Official Letter Books,* I, 313).

Chapter III. The Border Posts

[1] The conflict terminated by the treaty of San Lorenzo is discussed in A. P. Whitaker, *Spanish-American Frontier, 1783–1795.*

[2] F. L. Riley, "Spanish Policy in Mississippi after the Treaty of San Lorenzo," Am. Hist. Assn., *Report,* 1897, p. 178; B. A. Hinsdale, "The Establishment of the First Southern Boundary of the United States," *ibid.,* 1893, p. 349; F. P. Renaut, *La Question de la Louisiane* (Paris, 1918?), p. 135.

[3] This subject is discussed more fully, with references, in an article by the present writer, "The Retrocession of Louisiana in Spanish Policy," in the *American Historical Review,* April, 1934.

[4] AHN, Est., "Actas del Consejo de Estado," May 27, 1796; AI, PC, leg. 1447, the Prince of the Peace to Carondelet, Aranjuez, June 1, 1796, copy certified by Carondelet (LC transcript); *ibid.,* leg. 2354, Carondelet to Gayoso, New Orleans, March 5, 1797, states the contents of the order of Aug. 27, 1796, which is also discussed in Carondelet's despatch to Azanza cited below, note 7.

[5] *Memoirs of Don Manuel de Godoy* (2 vols., London, 1836), II, 402.

[6] AI, PC, leg. 1447, Carondelet to Las Casas, April 15, 1796, No. 158 res.; leg. 2354, same to same, June 18, 1796, No. 161 res.; leg. 1447, same to same, Nov. 1, 1796, No. 163 res. The last of these despatches relates to the arrival of General Collot at New Orleans after his tour of the

upper Mississippi Valley. A new turn to Carondelet's thoughts was given by Collot's assertion that the retrocession of Louisiana to France was an accomplished fact. Carondelet wrote that, in that case, the revolutionizing of both the American West and Mexico was a certainty.

[7] AI, Sto. Dom., leg. 2565 *mod.*, Carondelet to Azanza, Dec. 1, 1796, No. 1 res. An English translation of this despatch is in Louis Houck, *The Spanish Régime in Missouri,* II, 133–138.

[8] AI, PC, leg. 2365, Carondelet to Gayoso, Feb. 13, 1797 (LC transcript) ; leg. 2354, same to same, Feb. 11, 1797, official (see below, note 9).

[9] *Ibid.* Carondelet to Gayoso, Feb. 11, 1797, personal: "Veo las dudas que Vm tiene de la verificacion del tratado, pero puedo asegurar que no estan fundadas. . . ."

[10] The principal source of information about this affair is Carondelet's despatch to the Prince of the Peace of March 29, 1797, No. 91 res., and enclosures (LC film). According to Intendant Morales, the last Spanish troops left Chickasaw Bluffs on March 16, 1797, and the troops from Fort Confederation arrived at Fort St. Stephen on March 18 (AI, 87–1–24, Morales to Gardoqui, March 31, 1797, No. 9 res., LC film.) The original letter to Wayne was returned to Carondelet by Lieutenant Colonel Carlos Howard from Chickasaw Bluffs (AI, PC, leg. 2354, Carondelet to Gayoso, April 27, 1797, personal). A draft of the letter, addressed to "Excelentísimo Señor Don Antonio Wayne," is in PC, leg. 212. See the following note.

[11] There seems to be some discrepancy in Carondelet's statement regarding the date of receipt of the order of Oct. 29, 1796. In his despatch No. 91 res. (cited above, note 10), he said the order reached him on Feb. 24, and that he immediately sent off couriers with orders to stop evacuation; but his letter to Gayoso containing that order is dated March 5 (copy enclosed in No. 91 res.).

[12] Daniel Clark, *Proofs of the Corruption of General James Wilkinson* (Philadelphia, 1809), p. 70, Ellicott to Wilkinson, Jan. 21, 1808. J. F. H. Claiborne, *Mississippi* (Jackson, 1880), gives no quarter in his attack on Ellicott.

[13] Andrew Ellicott, *Journal* (Philadelphia, 1803), pp. 29, 30.

[14] *Ibid.*, p. 45. In his despatch No. 91 res. (cited above, note 10), Carondelet said that Ellicott had with him thirty laborers and twenty-five soldiers.

[15] Ellicott, *Journal*, p. 45.

[16] *Ibid.*, pp. 65–67.

[17] *Ibid.*, Appendix, p. 17.

[18] State Department, Bureau of Rolls and Library, "Southern Boundary, United States and Spain, 1796–1804" (three bound vols., ms.), Ellicott to the Secretary of State, Natchez, April 14, 1797. Shortly after receiving the royal order of Oct. 29, 1796, Carondelet wrote Godoy that the inclination of the majority of the people of the district to take Ellicott's side was one of the chief obstacles to the execution of the order (AHN, Est, leg. 3900, despatch No. 92 res., April 19, 1797: LC film).

[19] A. P. Whitaker, *Spanish-American Frontier,* pp. 102–107, 157–162.

²⁰ AI, PC, leg. 200, "A return of the district of the Natchez," signed by Carlos Grand-pré, Natchez, Jan. 18, 1787; leg. 1441, report by Gayoso, June 14, 1792, enclosed in a despatch of July 20, 1792, from Carondelet to Las Casas.

²¹ AI, PC, leg. 2354, Gayoso to the Duke de la Alcudia (Godoy), Natchez, March 31, 1795, draft.

²² Ellicott, *Journal*, pp. 115, 116; John Pope, *A Tour* . . . (Richmond, 1792), p. 29.

²³ This consideration was mentioned by Gayoso in a despatch of June 2, 1796, as one that was already causing great uneasiness in the district (AI, PC, leg. 2371, to Carondelet, draft). His proclamation of March 22, 1797, played on this fear.

²⁴ *Ibid.*, leg. 202, Ebenezer Dayton to Gayoso, Aug. 3, 1795.

²⁵ Whitaker, *op. cit.*, pp. 159–160.

²⁶ The "return" of 1787, cited above, note 20, states that the tobacco crop of Natchez district (presumably for the year 1786) was 589,920 pounds. Ten years later, in response to an emergency call from the home government for tobacco, Gayoso wrote that the district no longer exported tobacco, producing barely enough for its own needs. (AI, Sto. Dom., leg. 2614, Gayoso to Morales, Dec. 29, 1796, copy, enclosed in Morales to Gardoqui, Jan. 21, 1797, No. 81).

²⁷ See Ch. VIII.

²⁸ Bruin's case is particularly interesting since he was one of those select Roman Catholic immigrants who were admitted to Spanish territory under the more rigorous laws in effect before the royal order of Dec. 1, 1788, was received in Louisiana. He served in the Virginia troops during the American Revolution, got in touch with Gardoqui in 1788, and emigrated to Louisiana with about one hundred other persons. In 1792 he was appointed commander of the volunteers of Natchez district at a salary of $1,200 per annum; but in 1796 he complained that he had never received but two months' pay from Spain. In May, 1797, he wrote that he was deep in debt, and he attributed his misfortunes to Spain's failure to keep promises made by Gardoqui in 1788 with respect to the support of himself and the others in his party of immigrants (AI, PC, leg. 2371, memorial of Peter Bryan Bruin to Carondelet, New Orleans, June 16, 1796; leg. 197, same to same, Natchez, May 18, 1797). An account of Bruin's emigration to Natchez and of his financial difficulties, especially with Daniel Clark, is contained in despatch No. 4 *muy res.* from Gayoso to Carondelet, May 16, 1792: *ibid.*, leg. 2353). Bruin was one of the committee of nine whose election by the planters in July, 1797, "put the finishing stroke to the Spanish authority and jurisdiction in the district" (Ellicott, *Journal*, p. 117).

²⁹ There were two proclamations, one of May 24, the other of May 31, 1797. The former justified the retention of the posts on the ground of the threatened invasion by Great Britain; the latter emphasized the menace of an invasion by the United States. According to Morales, Carondelet had 100 copies of the latter printed at a cost of twelve and a half pesos (AI, Sto. Dom., leg. 2614 *mod.*, Morales to Varela, June 30, 1797, printed

copy of the proclamation enclosed). Carondelet seems to have been convinced that an invasion down the Mississippi actually was impending. He prepared to assemble 2,500 militia at Baton Rouge, and bought 1,000 guns from the Indian trader, William Panton, at seven dollars each (*ibid.*, same to same, same date, Nos. 134 and 139).

[30] State Department, Bureau of Rolls and Library, "Southern Boundary," I, Ellicott to the Secretary of State, June 27, 1797; Ellicott, *Journal,* pp. 99 ff., describes these events in minute detail.

[31] Gayoso took possession of the government of Louisiana and West Florida on Aug. 5, 1797 (AI, Sto. Dom., leg. 2566, Santa Clara to Álvarez, Havana, Sept. 3, 1797, No. 17).

[32] AI, PC leg. 2371, Stephen Minor to Gayoso, Natchez, Oct. 14 and 18 and Nov. 21, 1797.

[33] *Ibid.,* same to same, Oct. 14, 1797. Minor described Mathews as "an old bauld headed half Irishman fond of talking very loud and saying a great deal about nothing.—no great depth of understanding, but appears to be very open and candid" (letter of Oct. 9, 1797, item dated Oct. 12).

[34] Mathews told Minor as much at the outset but was not believed. He brought a letter of introduction from Secretary of State Pickering to Ellicott (*Historical Index to the Pickering Papers,* in *Collections* of the Massachusetts Hist. Soc., 6 ser., VIII [Boston, 1896], 128). He had good reason to expect the appointment as Governor of Mississippi Territory, for he was actually President Adams's first nomination for the post (*ibid.,* p. 443); but the nomination was withdrawn—according to Jefferson—because it scandalized the Senate, which was well informed of Mathews's connection with the notorious Yazoo grants (Jefferson, *Writings,* ed. Ford, VII, 248).

[35] AI, PC, leg. 2371, James White to Gayoso, Natchez, Jan. 30, 1798.

[36] AI, Sto. Dom., leg. 2619, Morales to Soler, May 31, 1802, No. 105, enclosing a "Relación de gastos extraordinarios," stating that the salary, amounting to 2,500 pesos a year, was still being paid as a permanent charge.

[37] The order was dated Sept. 22, 1797: AI, PC, leg. 1501A, Gayoso to Santa Clara, Jan. 23, 1798, No. 99 (LC film).

[38] AHN, Est., leg. 3902, Gayoso to the Prince of the Peace, Natchez, June 25, 1797, with marginal note by the latter, dated Oct. 28, 1797: "muy buen medio p[ra]. tranquilizarlos y proceda a la entrega en la forma prevenida." This is followed by an endorsement in another hand: "fho en 19. de Nov[bre]. de dho sin minuta."

[39] See below, Ch. VII.

[40] See the article mentioned above, note 3.

[41] Ellicott, *Journal,* p. 176.

Chapter IV. The Indian Country

[1] See estimates for the Creek, Choctaw, and Chickasaw in John R. Swanton, *Early History of the Creek Indians* (Washington, 1922), pp.

437–449. It is of course impossible to ascertain precisely the numbers of any of these tribes. See the following note.

² John Forbes, successor to William Panton as head of the house of Panton, Leslie and Company, made a statement in regard to the Creek Indians which shows how little confidence should be placed in any estimate of their numbers. Writing in 1803, he expressed the opinion that Colonel Benjamin Hawkins's recent estimate of 3,500 "gunsmen" for the Creek towns within the limits of the United States was far too low, for, adding 1,000 for the "Semanolies & Creeks included within the Spanish limits," this would give only 4,500 as the effective fighting force of the whole Creek Confederacy. Alexander McGillivray, said Forbes, had once estimated the number of Creek fighting men at 15,000, and never at less than 10,000, while Olivier (Pedro—or Pierre—Olivier, Spain's agent among the Creek in 1792) placed the number at 9,700 after a careful investigation. Forbes himself was inclined to regard Olivier's estimate as the most accurate (Florida Hist. Soc. *Quarterly,* IX, 279, "A Journal of John Forbes," entry conjecturally dated May 11, 1803). The best account of the Creek at this juncture is Benjamin Hawkins, *A Sketch of the Creek Country in 1798 and 1799* (New York, 1848). Milfort's *Mémoire . . . sur . . . mon séjour dans la nation Crëck* (Paris, 1802), is useful, but must be used with meticulous care.

³ *Letters of Benjamin Hawkins* (Georgia Hist. Soc. *Publications,* vol. IX, Savannah, 1916), p. 293, Hawkins to the Secretary of War, Feb. 23, 1798. For information about Hawkins, see note 22, this chapter.

⁴ An excellent account of earlier rivalries in this region is contained in Verner W. Crane, *The Southern Frontier, 1670–1732* (Durham, N. C., 1928). Spanish interests and claims are admirably developed in H. E. Bolton and Mary Ross, *The Debatable Land* (Berkeley, 1925).

⁵ This is a very conservative estimate. See above, note 2.

⁶ When Carondelet received the royal order of Oct. 29, 1796, directing him to suspend the evacuation of the posts in question (see Ch. III), he wrote: "When I received the confidential order of his Majesty [of Oct. 29] . . . everything had been arranged previously and secretly so that the destruction and evacuation of the posts of San Fernando de Barrancas [Chickasaw Bluffs], Confederation, Tombecbé, Nogales [Walnut Hills] and Natchez should take place simultaneously and before the American troops could arrive and demand their delivery,—a thing which could not have failed to compromise us with the powerful savage nations who, under the influence of these same Americans, suspected us of the perfidious intention of placing them [the forts] at the disposition of their [the Indians'] enemies, putting the latter in possession of the lands which they [the Indians] had given us under the influence of the promise, which we made them, that we would build on those lands forts which would serve as a protection and defence against their [the Americans'] usurpations." (ᴀʜɴ, Est., leg. 3900, Carondelet to the Prince of the Peace, New Orleans, March 29, 1797, No. 91 res., ʟᴄ film). The bearing of the treaty of San Lorenzo on Spain's Indian relations was a source of great anxiety to Carondelet. Most of the despatches which he sent to Havana and

Madrid in 1796 and 1797 allude directly or indirectly to the question.

⁷ Thus Gayoso wrote in 1797: "I know positively that the greatest desire of the Americans is that the Indians may oppose it [the execution of the treaty of San Lorenzo], so that they may have a pretext for declaring war on them [the Indians] and seizing their lands" (AI, PC, leg. 2365, Gayoso to Carondelet, Natchez, Feb. 25, 1797. The LC transcript of this letter is erroneously dated 1798). After he became Governor-General of Louisiana, he was equally alarmed at the efforts of the United States government to win the Indians' friendship (*ibid.*, leg. 1502 B, Gayoso to Santa Clara, New Orleans, Nov. 30, 1797, No. 7, LC film).

⁸ Even after the treaty of San Lorenzo, Panton hoped to extend his trade west of the Mississippi, proposing that he should be indemnified for losses in the service of Spain by the permission to establish a trading post in that region. In support of the proposal he argued that the Chickasaw and Choctaw, two of the three nations with which he traded, were now doing most of their hunting west of the river. Intendant Morales advised against granting the request, preferring one of two alternative proposals made by Panton (AI, Sto. Dom., leg. 2670, Morales to the Secretary of State, Dec. 31, 1801, No. 4).

⁹ The growth of Panton's company and its relations with the Spanish authorities are discussed in detail in A. P. Whitaker, *Documents Relating to the Commercial Policy of Spain in the Floridas* (Deland, Fla., 1931), Historical Introduction, pp. xxx–xxxix.

¹⁰ ANC, Florida, leg. 1, *expediente* 5, No. 65, Panton to Carondelet, July 25, 1796, LC transcript. Italics inserted.

¹¹ A royal order of June 21, 1797, stated that his Majesty desired that, in order to satisfy the Indians and preserve their friendship, the means indicated in the treaty of San Lorenzo should be employed and that offers might be made without involving Spain in heavy expenses, since that was the evil which it had been the King's desire to abate (by the treaty) (AHN, Est., leg. 3902, Morales to the Prince of the Peace, New Orleans, Jan. 20, 1798, No. 2, reciting the royal order).

¹² AI, PC, leg. 212, Carondelet to Juan de la Villebeuvre, Aug. 19, 1796. "La ligne" refers to the boundary between the Spanish possessions and the United States. Italics inserted.

¹³ AHN, Est., leg. 3902, Morales to the Prince of the Peace, Jan. 20, 1798, No. 2, enclosure No. 3.

¹⁴ ANC, Florida, leg. 9, Carondelet to Morales, Jan. 30, 1797. In AI, Sto. Dom., leg. 2670, is a collection of seventy-five orders and other documents relating to Panton, Leslie and Company in the period 1785–1807. Made at Pensacola in 1809, it is apparently complete and is accompanied by an extract of the documents.

¹⁵ ASP, IA, I, 583, 643, 646, 653. In the Interior Department (Washington), Indian Office, "Letters Received," there are dozens of letters from Indian agents and others denouncing the factory system. Professor R. S. Cotterill, who is preparing a study of government control of Indian trade in the South, very generously placed his notes on the subject at my disposal. Since the preceding was written, he has published an article,

"Federal Indian Management in the South, 1789–1825", in M.V.H.R., XX, 333.

[16] Many references to Panton's traders are contained in *Letters of Benjamin Hawkins,* cited above, note 3.

[17] Archives of the State of Tennessee (Nashville), Sevier Papers, Sevier to Jackson, Anderson, and Claiborne, Jan. 22, 1798; same to Blount, Claiborne, and Jackson, Jan. 29, 1797.

[18] ASP, IA, I, 646.

[19] Interior Department, Indian Office, Letter Book A, Secretary of War to Israel Whelen, War Department, June 5, 1802; "Letters Received," William Cocke to Jonathan R. Meggs (*sic*: Return Jonathan Meigs?), Carter Iron Works, Feb. 17, 1803.

[20] Sevier Papers, Sevier to Joseph Evans, May 5, 1796.

[21] Carl S. Driver, *Life of John Sevier* (Chapel Hill, 1932), pp. 141–144.

[22] Interior Department, Indian Office, Letter Book A, Secretary of War to Hawkins, War Department, Feb. 22, 1803, stating that when Hawkins was appointed it was contemplated that his agency should extend to all the Indian nations within the United States east of the Mississippi River, but that, because of the establishment of a territorial government at Natchez and other subsequent developments, it had been decided to restrict his agency henceforth to the Creek and Seminole Indians within the limits of the United States.

[23] ASP, IA, I, 646–648. See also *Letters of Benjamin Hawkins,* p. 385.

Chapter V. The Opening of the Mississippi

[1] A. P. Whitaker, *Documents Relating to the Commercial Policy of Spain in the Floridas,* Historical Introduction.

[2] AI, PC, leg. 11, Bouligny to Miró, Natchez, Aug. 9, 1785, No. 25. The well-known case of Thomas Amis is probably the one referred to in a letter of the Intendant which speaks of the condemnation of 90 barrels of flour illegally brought to Louisiana in a boat belonging to "Tomas Ormis" and "José Calvert" (leg. 573, Navarro to Orué, New Orleans, Oct. 3, 1787).

[3] AI, Sto. Dom., 86–6–16, Miró to Valdés, Oct. 25, 1787, No. 4; 87–3–19, Navarro to Sonora, June 7, 1787, No. 498. Miró enclosed evidence to show that Philadelphia flour was cheaper and better than flour obtained from Spanish and French sources. Navarro told how Spanish restrictions were evaded by ships bringing flour from Philadelphia to New Orleans via St. Domingue.

[4] Baron Pontalba, who was engaged in business at New Orleans for several years, stated in a memoir of 1800 addressed to the French government that the whole of the *situado,* or subsidy, found its way into the coffers of the merchants (Gayarré, *Louisiana,* III, 440). According to Intendant Rendón, about $400,000 in specie was smuggled out of the province every year (AI, Sto. Dom., leg. 2580, Aparici to Soler, Madrid, Aug. 29, 1799, *informe* on Rendón's despatch No. 123 to Gardoqui). A

valuable account of the exportation of specie from Louisiana by way of St. Domingue is contained in a despatch from Manuel de las Heras, Spanish consul at Bordeaux, to José de Gálvez: AI, Sto. Dom., 87-3-21.

[5] Unless otherwise noted, all statements in the text regarding arrivals and sailings of vessels (sea-going ships or river craft) at New Orleans are based on tables compiled under my supervision from the port records in the Archives of the Indies, Seville.

[6] *Hispanic American Hist. Rev.,* I, 179-180, "Reflexiones acerca de la prov^a de Texas," presented by James Wilkinson to Iturbide, dated Mexico, Nov. 18, 1822.

[7] A. P. Whitaker, *Spanish-American Frontier,* pp. 102, 103.

[8] *Annals Cong.,* 10 Cong., 1 Sess., 2735, 2736, statement made by Daniel Clark in 1798. According to the Intendant, the nominal duty of six per cent was thus reduced in practice to about four per cent (AI, Sto. Dom., leg. 2670, Morales to the Secretary of State, Dec. 31, 1801, No. 4).

[9] *Pennsylvania Mag. Hist. and Biog.,* LII, 202-204.

[10] See above, note 5. For various reasons I have not studied the American export trade to Natchez in the same detail as that to New Orleans. The former was by no means insignificant. For instance, in a single day in May, 1790, seven flatboats arrived at Natchez from Kentucky with forty persons aboard (among them Ezekiel Forman) and cargoes of tobacco, pork, whisky, deerskins, and other articles (AI, PC, leg. 41, Gayoso to Miró, May 16, 1790, No. 103).

[11] See the work cited above, note 1.

[12] AHN, Est. leg. 3899, Carondelet to Alcudia, March 27, 1794, No. 30 res., Gardoqui, Secretary of the Treasury, had sent Carondelet an order, dated Sept. 27, 1793, which was intended to cut off all trade between Louisiana and the United States. Carondelet protested that the enforcement of this order would entail the ruin of Louisiana or its loss to Spain. Gardoqui, who was then engaged in the negotiation with the American envoys, Carmichael and Short, over the navigation of the Mississippi, argued that the illegal trade with the United States permitted by Carondelet made his negotiation more difficult, and also deprived Spain of one of its chief means of attracting immigrants from the United States to Louisiana. Carondelet had his way, but his resistance to Gardoqui cost him the intendancy. He continued as Governor of Louisiana until 1797.

[13] AI, Sto. Dom., leg. 2614, Morales to Gardoqui, New Orleans, Jan. 21, 1797, No. 85.

[14] *Am. Hist. Rev.,* XXXII, 809, Evan Jones, United States consul at New Orleans, to the Secretary of State, May 15, 1801. The conduct of the pilots had already occasioned a heated controversy between Governor Gayoso and acting Intendant Morales long before Jones wrote the letter just cited. In 1799 an American vessel, the *Star,* ran aground while under the orders of the Spanish pilot. Thereupon Gayoso, whose patronage of American commerce won praise from Andrew Ellicott, summarily arrested the offending pilot and removed the chief pilot from office. In the course of the ensuing controversy with Morales, two interesting state-

ments were made by the chief pilot: first, that the channel at the Balize was so clear that ships could safely sail in and out without the services of a pilot; secondly, that the frequency with which American ships entering and leaving the Mississippi came to grief was due to the impatience of their captains, who would not await the proper conjunction of wind and tide (AI, Sto. Dom., leg. 2615, Morales to Soler, May 31, 1799, No. 28 res., and July 10, 1799, No. 31, res.).

¹⁵ State Department, Consular Letters, New Orleans, Gayoso to Clark, New Orleans, Aug. 6, 1798, copy in Spanish.

¹⁶ *Am. Hist. Rev.*, XXXII, 810. This regulation, too, led to a controversy among the Spanish officials concerned: AGS, Guerra, leg. 6929 mod., Someruelos to Caballero, Havana, May 12, 1802, No. 247.

¹⁷ AHN, Est., leg. 3900, Carondelet to the Prince of the Peace, March 29, 1797, No. 91 res., LC film.

¹⁸ AI, PC, leg. 2343, letter book of Morales, Morales to Saavedra, July 31, 1798, No. 237. In 1802 Morales wrote that he was changing the regulations because of the overwhelming flood of goods deposited. Henceforth, the government officials would no longer keep one of the keys. Instead, the New Orleans merchants who were agents for the American owners of the goods would be held responsible for the proper use of the deposit privilege, and persons unknown to the customs officials would be required to give bond (AI, Sto. Dom., 87-1-29, Morales to Soler, May 31, 1802, No. 101). Daniel Clark, United States consul at New Orleans, described the way in which these new regulations affected the American owner, and regarded them as "burdensome" and "unjust" (*Am. Hist. Rev.*, XXXII, 816).

¹⁹ As recently as 1931, Professor C. H. Ambler wrote: "When the period of the Spanish concession [the deposit] finally expired in 1798 and a request for renewal was denied, American frontiersmen demanded war and induced Congress to prepare for the emergency" (*A History of Transportation in the Ohio Valley*, p. 84). So far as I am aware, no such request was made by the United States government in 1798. Certainly Spain cannot have refused compliance, for it was in April of this year that the deposit was formally established at New Orleans. Moreover, the Spanish records of the deposit (cited below, note 20) show that the right of deposit at New Orleans was uninterruptedly exercised by American citizens from April 17, 1798, to October 18, 1802. Finally, the speeches of Western members of Congress in June, 1798, show that they knew the Mississippi was open to their export trade. In the course of the discussion, Samuel Smith asserted that "the spring trade this year from Kentucky by the Mississippi has been both great and profitable," and no one contradicted the assertion (T. H. Benton, *Abridgement of Debates*, II, 298, 302, 303). As for the statement that "the American frontiersmen demanded war," see Ch. VII, notes 30 and 31.

²⁰ AI, PC, leg. 631, two bound volumes, ms., one for 1798–1802, the other for 1803. All figures in the text relating to the deposit were obtained from these volumes.

²¹ There is a very good sketch of Clark in the *Dictionary of American Biography*. For further information about him, see below, Ch. XIV, notes 5 and 30.

²² Clark's *Proofs of the Corruption of General James Wilkinson* gives a remarkably accurate account of Wilkinson's dealings with the Spaniards. All the book lacks is what the title claims to give—the proofs. These were in the Spanish archives, and are still there.

²³ A copy of the memorial was enclosed in Morales's despatch No. 238, cited below, note 28.

²⁴ Clark explained that Commissioner Andrew Ellicott and Captain Isaac Guion, commanding the United States troops at Natchez, had persuaded him to assume the character of Vice-Consul (State Department, Consular Letters, New Orleans, Daniel Clark to the Secretary of State, March 17, 1798, enclosing a copy of a letter from Ellicott and Guion, dated Natchez, March 2, 1798). Clark added: ". . . I conceive that Governor Gayoso has gone too far in acknowledging me as Vice Consul for the U. S. . . ." The Captain-General was of the same opinion.

²⁵ *Ibid.*, Clark to the Secretary of State, April 18, 1798. Clark said that, after discussing the matter with Intendant Morales, he was preparing the memorial at the latter's request.

²⁶ This was probably true during the first year the deposit was open, for a large part of the articles deposited came from Natchez district and consisted of cotton; but as the volume and variety of deposits increased, it must have become much easier to make up a suitable cargo from that source alone. See below, Ch. VIII.

²⁷ See above, note 25.

²⁸ AI, PC, leg. 2343, letter book of Morales, No. 3, Morales to Saavedra, New Orleans, July 31, 1798, No. 238. Kentuckians were informed of the Intendant's action by the *Palladium* of Aug. 14, 1798.

²⁹ AI, Sto. Dom., leg. 2616, Morales to Soler, Oct. 15, 1799, Nos. 333, 334 and 335; and same to same, Nov. 30, 1799, No. 354. These despatches show that, in obedience to a royal order of April 20, 1799 (which cancelled all previous concessions to neutral trade, whether they had been made by colonial officials or by the King himself, and directed that the Laws of the Indies should be enforced), neutral trade was prohibited at New Orleans on Sept. 19, 1799; but that on Oct. 17 it was again permitted pending the receipt of the King's reply to Morales's despatch No. 238 (cited above, note 28). Perhaps it was this incident which gave rise to the mistaken belief that the deposit was closed in 1798 or 1799 (see above, note 19); but as a matter of fact, the right of deposit remained unimpaired during the brief period when New Orleans was closed to neutral trade. In reporting the decision of Sept. 17, 1799, to exclude neutral ships, Morales informed the court that he had decided not to disturb the trade with Kentucky, the commerce of Panton, Leslie and Company, the American deposit, or the free navigation of the Mississippi by American citizens.

An interesting survey of Spanish regulations concerning colonial commerce is contained in a communication from the Council of the Indies to the King, Aug. 22, 1818. A royal order of 1797 opened most of the colonies (but not, apparently, Louisiana and the Floridas) to neutral trade. Abuses led to the rescinding of the order in 1799 and the adoption of a system of restricted neutral trade under special license (AI, América en General, leg. 1, LC transcript).

[30] See Ch. VIII.

[31] See Ch. VIII. The Spaniards may also have hoped that the application of steam-power to navigation would aid them. In 1785, Gardoqui noted a conversation with John Fitch of Kentucky regarding the latter's device for propelling a boat up-stream by horse power (AHN, Est., leg. 3886, exp. No. 1, Gardoqui to Floridablanca, New York, Oct. 21, 1785, No. 30). On Dec. 17, 1790, James Wilkinson wrote Governor Miró introducing a "Mr. Ford," who, he said, was connected with "the inventor of the steamboat" and would show Miró how a vessel loaded with two hundred barrels of flour could be propelled against the strongest current. He added that Ford would undertake at once to build such a vessel at New Orleans (AI, PC, leg. 2374).

[32] See Ch. XI.

[33] When the case came to the attention of the court, with the information that the United States desired to have a consul at Havana as well as at New Orleans, Minister Urquijo instructed Irujo to inform that government "that such consuls will by no means be received in his Majesty's colonial dominions" (AME, Cor. Dip., leg. 207, Urquijo to Irujo, Aranjuez, March 5, 1800, No. 15, LC transcript). See also *Am. Hist. Rev.*, XXXII, 805–808 (unsuccessful efforts of United States consular agents to obtain formal recognition) and 808–810 (a statement of "inconveniences" and "oppressions" suffered by American citizens at New Orleans and on the lower Mississippi, drawn up by Evan Jones in 1801).

[34] *Ibid.*, pp. 802–808.

[35] State Department, Consular Letters, New Orleans, Daniel Clark to Andrew Ellicott, New Orleans, Aug. 7, 1798, copy. On May 20, 1799, Captain-General Someruelos informed Saavedra that he had permitted the establishment at New Orleans of a "Receptor de los derechos de Presas de la Republica Francesa" (AI, Estado, Sto. Dom., leg. 2, exp. 6).

Chapter VI. The Shadow of France in the West: I

[1] "Correspondence of General James Robertson," *Am. Hist. Mag.*, IV, 349; *Correspondence of Andrew Jackson*, I, 22, 44.

[2] Ellicott, *Journal*, pp. 173–175, 182, 183.

[3] State Department, "Southern Boundary," Vol. I, Ellicott to the Secretary of State, Natchez, May 27, 1797; *Historical Index to the Pickering Papers*, p. 127, Ellicott to Pickering, Nov. 17, 1797. In the earlier letter, Ellicott said that in case of a rupture (with the United States), Spain would count largely on intrigues with the Westerners. "That such intrigues have been carried on I think there can be little doubt." The chief suspects, he said, were General James Wilkinson, Judge (Benjamin) Se-

bastian, and a Mr. (William) Murray, a Kentucky lawyer. In the second letter Ellicott gave information tending to implicate Wilkinson in the plot. In his *Journal*, pp. 182, 183, Ellicott says he also sent to the State Department a cipher letter dated Nov. 8, 1798, containing the most unequivocal proofs that such an intrigue was on foot. Compare Ellicott's letter to James Wilkinson, Jan. 21, 1808, in Clark's *Proofs of the Corruption of General James Wilkinson*, pp. 69–72.

⁴ Charles Francis Adams, *The Works of John Adams* (Boston, 1856), VIII, 563, 564, Adams to Wilkinson, Feb. 4, 1798. It was, of course, only fair that Adams should refuse to accept as proof positive the vague and anonymous charges against Wilkinson. The remarkable thing is that he did not feel it incumbent on him to start an inquiry, for, as he himself said, "scarcely any man arrives from that neighborhood [the West] who does not bring that report along with him." The letter was decidedly flattering to Wilkinson.

⁵ See Isaac J. Cox, "Wilkinson's First Break with the Spaniards," *Proceedings* of the eighth annual meeting of the Ohio Valley Historical Association, pp. 49–56 (published as an appendix to the Biennial Report of the Department of Archives and History of West Virginia, 1911–1914, Charleston, W. Va., 1914).

⁶ Frederick J. Turner, "Documents on the Blount Conspiracy," *Am. Hist. Rev.*, X, 574–606. Among more recent discussions of the conspiracy may be mentioned: Isaac J. Cox, article cited in preceding note; the same writer's *West Florida Controversy* (Baltimore, 1918), pp. 37, 38, 52, 53; W. B. Posey, "The Blount Conspiracy," in Birmingham-Southern College *Studies in History* (Birmingham, 1929); and Isabel Thompson, "The Blount Conspiracy," East Tennessee Hist. Soc., *Publications*, No. 2, 3–21.

⁷ ASP, FR, II, 87–96.

⁸ *Annals Cong.*, 7 Cong., 2 Sess., 245, Feb. 25, 1803.

⁹ Pickering Papers, XXI, Arthur Campbell to Pickering, Washington (County), V(irginia), July 29, Aug. 7, Oct. 7, 1797. Many other persons besides those mentioned at this point and subsequently in the text were said to have been implicated. It was even charged that Senator Humphrey Marshall of Kentucky was a party to the conspiracy (Innes Papers, vol. 19, Thomas Todd to (Innes), Richmond, Sept. 23, 1807).

¹⁰ H. M. Wagstaff, ed., *The Papers of John Steele* (Raleigh, 1924), I, 57, Blount to Steele, April 18, 1790. Arthur Campbell wrote of Blount: "That man, possesses considerable abilities, a restless ambition, griping avarice, much vanity and pride; and as he seem'd to have a prospect to gratify his favourite pursuits, he was a republican or an admirer of royalty" (Pickering Papers, XXI, Campbell to Pickering, Oct. 7, 1797).

¹¹ Hist. Soc. of Pennsylvania, Dreer Collection, Letters of Members of the Federal Convention, p. 77, Blount to Major J. C. Mountflorence, Washington (Southwest Territory), Nov. 1, 1791; Monroe Papers (NYPL), Mountflorence to (Monroe), torn, undated, endorsed in pencil "Feb?"; and same to same, March 9, 1795.

¹² In November, 1795, Romayne, who was in London selling Western lands, was presented by Count de Moustier to the Spanish ambassador,

Simón de Las Casas, to whom he gave a map "of the American conti-
nent" and a pamphlet explaining his business (AGS, Est., leg. 2361 *mod.*,
contains several letters relating to this affair).

[13] A. P. Whitaker, "The Muscle Shoals Speculation," M. V. H. R., XIII,
365.

[14] Three days after the date of his letter to Carey (see text at note 29),
Blount wrote James Robertson: "You will have heard probably that I am
much embarrassed by my security paper for David Allison which is un-
fortunately too true . . ." (*Am. Hist. Mag.*, IV, 343, letter dated Beaver
Creek Iron Works, April 24, 1797). For the Allison business, see *Correspondence of Andrew Jackson*, I, 22, note 2.

[15] AI, PC, leg. 177, John McDonald to (Carondelet), Cherokees, Dec.
31, 1795.

[16] *Am. Hist. Rev.*, X, 595–597.

[17] AI, PC, leg. 178, Gayoso to Irujo, Oct. 20, 1797, copy.

[18] Chief among these was Anthony Hutchins. On Oct. 18, 1797, Stephen
Minor wrote Gayoso from Natchez that since the exposure of Blount's
conspiracy "Hutchins' plan has entirely changed which convinces me he
had a hand in it" (*ibid.*, leg. 2371). Ellicott also suspected Hutchins of
complicity (*Journal*, pp. 64, 73, 74).

[19] Arthur Campbell charged that Mathews was implicated in the conspiracy, and said that, after its exposure, he accompanied Blount in the
latter's flight to Tennessee (see below, note 22). Curiously enough,
Mathews had with him a letter of introduction to Andrew Ellicott from
Secretary Pickering, who was trying to intercept Blount and have him
arrested (see below, note 34).

[20] AI, PC, leg. 1502, Gayoso to Santa Clara, Sept. 24, 1797, No. 22 res.;
Ellicott, *Journal*, pp. 64, 73, 74.

[21] For information regarding the plan, see Isaac J. Cox, "Documents
Relating to Zachariah Cox," *Quarterly Publications of the Hist. and Phil.
Soc. of Ohio*, Vol. VIII, Nos. 2 and 3.

[22] Arthur Campbell wrote Pickering from southwestern Virginia on
July 29, 1797, that Blount had just passed that way with McIntosh,
former Governor Mathews of Georgia, and others on the road to Tennessee (Pickering Papers, XXI). On March 12, 1798, Blount wrote to
James Robertson introducing "Major McIntosh," late of Georgia, as
"my particular friend," whom he had known for about fourteen years,
and who had been living with him for the past three or four months
(*Am. Hist. Mag.*, IV, 351–353). Blount denied that McIntosh was a
member of the Muscle Shoals company, but admitted that he had appeared
at Philadelphia as "attorney in fact" for Cox, the head of the company.
Irujo was also informed that McIntosh was implicated in the conspiracy
(letter cited below, note 40).

[23] Report of the House Committee on the Impeachment of William
Blount, p. xiv, Romayne to Blount, March 22, 1797, and p. lii, same
to same, May 13, 1797, mentions discussing the land scheme between
"you and me" with Burr.

[24] *Ibid.*, pp. xxxvii, xxxix.

[25] *Ibid.,* pp. 1, li.

[26] *Am. Hist. Rev.,* X, 600, 601, statement made before Rufus King, United States minister to Great Britain, about Nov. 29, 1797, and sworn to by Chisholm Dec. 9, 1797. Mitchell's statement (*ibid.,* 585) is of little value.

[27] AHN, Est., leg. 3998, the Marqués del Campo to the Prince of the Peace, Paris, Dec. 16, 1796, No. 2. Godoy's autograph note on the despatch, dated Dec. 27, 1796, reads: "This is an old scheme, and the late treaty [*i.e.,* with the United States?] was made with this in mind, but let him inform me of whatever he finds out."

[28] ASP, FR, II, 87; *Am. Hist. Rev.,* X, 585–587, 591. On Feb. 23, 1797, the Spanish consul at Charleston, Diego Morphy, warned Governor White of East Florida that, according to information received from a trustworthy person, the British consul "of these states" had just sent an express to the frontiers of Georgia to organize an expedition against Spanish Florida (AHN, Est., leg. 3891).

[29] ASP, FR, II, 76, 77, letter dated April 21, 1797.

[30] *Report* cited above, note 23, deposition of James Grant; *Letters of Benjamin Hawkins,* pp. 254–257.

[31] *Am. Hist. Rev.,* X, 590, 593. Liston also argued that, if the affair were given publicity, it would afford Spain a pretext for retaining the Southwest posts. He thought he had made a convert of Pickering and attributed the determination to publish the letter to President Adams himself.

[32] According to Liston, Pickering was convinced that France was about to recover Louisiana and that the Blount conspiracy was promoted by France for the purpose of separating the Southwestern "territories" from the Union (*ibid.,* pp. 589, 590). See Ch. VII.

[33] Though the charge that Jefferson had a hand in the conspiracy rested on the flimsiest kind of evidence, it was persistently repeated by the Federalists. The only thing in the nature of evidence was a far-fetched conjecture made by Chisholm in his statement of November, 1797, to Minister Rufus King, who was a Federalist. It should be noted that, when asked the direct question, "Do you know whether Blount communicated the Plan to any person but Romaine?" Chisholm replied, "I don't know that he did" (*ibid.,* 602).

[34] Pickering Papers, VI, Pickering to Archibald Stewart, Esqr., Counsellor at Law, in or near Staunton, Va., dated Department of State, Philadelphia, July 28, 1797, transmitting evidence to secure Blount's arrest as he passed through Staunton.

[35] Washington, *Writings* (ed. Ford), XIII, 400, Washington to McHenry, July 7, 1797; Pickering Papers, XXI, Washington to Pickering, July 3, 1797; *Am. Hist. Mag.,* IV, 343–345, Sevier to Robertson, July 15 and Aug. 17, 1797. See also Sevier to Colonel David Henley, Aug. 16, 1797, in "Executive Journal of Gov. John Sevier," East Tennessee Hist. Soc., *Publications,* II, 142.

[36] *Am. Hist. Mag.,* IV, 344, Robertson to Cocke, Aug. 1, 1797.

[37] Arthur Campbell wrote Pickering on Oct. 1, 1797: "The final trial

took place last Week, and Judge Anderson and Mr. [Andrew] Jackson, was easily elected Senators in room of Blount and Cocke— This is considered, as a fatal overthrow to the ci-divant Governor [Blount] and his plans in Tennessee" (Pickering Papers, XXI).

³⁸ *Am. Hist. Mag.*, IV, 351–353.

³⁹ I. J. Cox, "Documents relating to Zachariah Cox," *loc. cit.;* Sevier Papers, Sevier to Jackson, Anderson, and Claiborne, Jan. 22, 1798; Bernard C. Steiner, *Life and Correspondence of James McHenry* (Cleveland, 1907), p. 267.

⁴⁰ AHN, Est., leg. 3889 *bis*, Irujo to Urquijo, Philadelphia, March 6, 1800, No. 152, postscript dated March 10.

⁴¹ Frederick J. Turner, "The Policy of France toward the Mississippi Valley," *Am. Hist. Rev.*, X, 275.

⁴² See especially ASP, FR, II, 87–96.

⁴³ See Ch. XII, note 10.

Chapter VII. The Shadow of France in the West: II

¹ Jefferson, *Writings* (ed. Ford), VII, 207.

² Some of the most important documents relating to this affair are in Charles R. King, *Life and Correspondence of Rufus King* (New York, 1894), II, 649–666. Others are cited in the following notes. No adequate study of the episode has yet been made, but there are useful accounts in William S. Robertson, *Life of Miranda* (Chapel Hill, 1929), I, 176–187, and the same writer's "Francisco de Miranda and the Revolutionizing of Spanish America," in Am. Hist. Assn., *Report*, 1907, I, 321–336. Robertson's account of the parts played by Adams and Pickering seems open to question. Adams's subsequent explanation of his course (*Works*, X, 134–152) deserves serious consideration, especially in view of his letter cited below, note 32.

³ On May 31, 1798, Irujo wrote an urgent letter in cipher to Godoy advising the court not to let Spain become involved in the impending war between the United States and France. A French war would not be popular in the United States, he said, nor could the United States do France much harm; but war with Spain would be popular because of the prospect of rich prizes and conquests, and Spain would lose at least Louisiana and Florida (AHN, Est., leg. 3897, No. 103).

⁴ Bernard C. Steiner, *Life and Correspondence of James McHenry*, pp. 291–295.

⁵ J. C. Hamilton, *Works of Alexander Hamilton* (New York, 1851), VI, 275, 276.

⁶ *Historical Index to the Pickering Papers*, p. 135. The two despatches by Fauchet were written on Feb. 4 and Feb. 16, 1795. In 1804 Thornton said that, about four years before, he put a despatch from Fauchet in Pickering's hands. According to this statement, Pickering did not receive the despatch until about 1800. It is very probable, however, that Thorn-

ton's memory betrayed him as to the date and that he actually gave Pickering the despatch at a much earlier date, perhaps as early as 1797. In the first place, Thornton's memory of details was not very accurate, for he says that the despatch was written in 1794, whereas it was written in 1795, and he speaks of giving Pickering one despatch, whereas he very probably gave him both of the despatches mentioned above. In the second place, the circumstances which Thornton mentions as justifying his action fit the year 1797, or even 1796, better than 1800. There was no very good reason for Thornton's giving Pickering the intercepted despatch or despatches in 1800; there was excellent reason for his doing so in the period 1796–1798. In this connection see J. Q. Adams, *Writings* (ed. Ford), II, 211.

[7] W. H. Smith, ed., *The St. Clair Papers* (Cincinnati, 1882), II, 395–396, James McHenry to Arthur St. Clair, War Office, May, 1796; James Ross Papers, bundle endorsed "Secret Service Papers," containing a draft of a letter from Ross to H. H. Brackenridge, June 10, 1802, and Brackenridge's two replies, dated June 28 and July 2, 1802. The Ross Papers were in the temporary possession of the Western Pennsylvania Historical Society when the writer examined them, as he was able to do through the courtesy of the director, Professor Solon J. Buck.

[8] James D. Richardson, *Messages and Papers of the Presidents* (Washington, 1896), I, 216. Then follows the allusion to the treaty of San Lorenzo mentioned in Ch. I. After my manuscript had been sent to the printer, there appeared an article by Samuel F. Bemis, "Washington's Farewell Address," *Am. Hist. Rev.,* XXXIX, 250.

[9] *Am. Hist. Rev.,* X, 589, 590.

[10] *Porcupine's Works,* VI (London, 1801), 270, 273, July, 1797. As a result of the publication of these and similar passages by Cobbett, Irujo brought suit for libel against him in the courts of Pennsylvania after first protesting to Pickering and being informed that the executive department of the government could not take any action in the matter.

[11] J. Q. Adams, *Writings,* II, 217, Adams to William Vans Murray, Hamburg, Oct. 26, 1797.

[12] *Porcupine's Works,* VI, 123, note (July, 1797).

[13] J. Q. Adams, *Writings,* II, 211, Adams to John Adams, London, Sept. 21, 1797.

[14] AHN, Est., leg. 3889 *bis,* Irujo to the Prince of the Peace, July 20, 1797, No. 66.

[15] J. C. Hamilton, *Works of Alexander Hamilton,* VI, 278. "I am against going immediately into alliance with Great Britain," wrote Hamilton. "If *Spain* would cede Louisiana to the United States, I would accept it absolutely, if obtainable absolutely; or with an engagement to *restore,* if it cannot be obtained absolutely."

[16] *Ibid.,* p. 279, Pickering to Hamilton, April 9, 1798, stating that he had never received the promised letter.

[17] Henry Cabot Lodge, *Works of Alexander Hamilton,* V, 417. The article was published in the New York *Commercial Advertiser* on April

12, 1798. It is signed "Titus Manlius" and is the fourth in a series entitled "The Stand."

[18] J. C. Hamilton, *Works of Alexander Hamilton*, VI, 551, 552. See Ch. XII.

[19] King, *Correspondence of Rufus King*, II, 658, 659, Hamilton to Rufus King, Aug. 22, 1798. King was the United States Minister to England and was very active in this affair. On the same day Hamilton wrote Miranda himself in King's care, saying: "It was my wish that matters had been ripened for a co-operation in the course of this Fall on the part of this Country. But this can now scarcely be the case. The Winter however may mature the project and an effectual co-operation by the U States may take place" (*ibid.*, pp. 659, 660).

[20] Hamilton, *Works of Alexander Hamilton*, V, 184.

[21] Lodge, *Works of Alexander Hamilton*, VI, 153–156.

[22] Wilkinson, *Memoirs*, I, 437–438.

[23] Lodge, *Works of Alexander Hamilton*, VI, 163, 164.

[24] Wilkinson, *Memoirs*, I, 440–458, II, 157–159.

[25] Hamilton, *Works of Alexander Hamilton*, V, 199–208, 211; Lodge, *Works of Alexander Hamilton*, VI, 149.

[26] *Historical Index to the Pickering Papers*, p. 128, Pickering to Ellicott, Aug. 30, 1798.

[27] Interior Department, Indian Office, Letter Book A, Secretary of War to W. C. C. Claiborne, June 11, 1802, quoting from McKee's letter to the War Department of May 6, 1802. For biographical data about McKee, see *Correspondence of Andrew Jackson*, I, 12, note 1.

[28] In 1803 the debts still amounted to $173,000 (Interior Department, Indian Office, Letters Received, "General Abstract of the Debts due to the House of Panton, Leslie & Co. by the Creek, Cherokee, Chickasaw, and Chactaw Nations," dated Aug. 20, 1803, and signed by the agent of the company). For Panton's estimate in 1796, see Ch. IV.

[29] Driver, *Life of John Sevier*, p. 131, note 57. Washington also asked, "By what circuitous route did you come at Severe in the wilderness?" (*Writings*, XIV, 48, 49). Timothy Pickering was apparently the "circuitous route" by which Hamilton and McHenry "came at" Sevier, for Pickering suggested that the appointment would have a salutary effect on public opinion in Tennessee (Steiner, *McHenry*, pp. 313, 314).

[30] A different view is taken by Charles H. Ambler, who says in his *History of Transportation in the Ohio Valley*, p. 84, that in 1798, when Spain refused to renew the deposit concession (on this point, see above, Ch. V, note 19) the "American frontiersmen demanded war and induced Congress to prepare for that contingency."

[31] T. H. Benton, *Abridgement of Debates*, II, 294. Claiborne of Tennessee and Davis of Kentucky as well as Gallatin spoke in opposition to war. Claiborne was even more outspoken than Gallatin. He said he was opposed to any measure tending to war with France, "for the moment war is declared with France, we shall also be at war with Spain and Holland. her allies. And when a war with Spain shall take place, the commerce

of the Southern States and Western country will be immediately gone" (*ibid.,* p. 298). On the third reading of the bill to authorize the President to raise a provisional army, Claiborne, Davis, and Fowler (also of Kentucky) voted in the negative (*ibid.,* p. 276).

[32] C. F. Adams, *Works of John Adams,* VIII, 600.

[33] *Ibid.,* X, 134–152.

[34] *Ibid.,* I, 532.

[35] Hamilton, *Works of Alexander Hamilton,* V, 283.

[36] Adams, *Works of John Adams,* I, 554–559; George Gibbs, *Memoirs of the Administrations of Washington and John Adams* (New York, 1846), II, 267–268.

[37] Henry Adams, *History of the United States,* I, 404; Jefferson, *Writings* (ed. Ford), VIII, 33, 34.

Chapter VIII. Trade on the Mississippi, 1799–1802

[1] For the measures of 1798 at New Orleans, see Ch. V. The royal order of 1797 was revoked in 1799, but the authorities at Havana (like those of New Orleans) kept the port open to neutral trade in spite of the second order (AI, América en General, leg. 1, Council of the Indies to the King, Aug. 22, 1818, LC tr.).

[2] AI, Sto. Dom., leg. 2565 mod., Carondelet to Llaguno, May 31, 1796, No. 20; AE, Mém. et Doc., EU, 10:180–291, "Mémoire sur la Louisiane," by Victor Collot, Part II, Ch. 6. This *mémoire* is conjecturally dated "(ca. 1800)" by Surrey, *Calendar of Manuscript Materials in Paris Archives,* but it was unquestionably written in 1797. Collot's printed *Voyage* seems to be identical with it in most respects, although the present writer has not made a careful comparison of the two.

[3] Channing, *History of the United States,* IV, 311, note 2, gives statistics compiled from the Spanish archives and ASP, *Finance,* II, 56. As early as 1797, 154,872 *arrobas* of ginned cotton and 552,050 pounds of sugar were exported from New Orleans to foreign ports (AI, Sto. Dom., leg. 2668, "Estado" transmitted by the Intendant of Louisiana to the Secretary of the Treasury in despatch No. 222, April 27, 1798). Morales described the rise of cotton and sugar cultivation, supplanting rice and tobacco, in the despatch cited below, note 6.

[4] Gayarré, *Louisiana,* III, 347–350. As pointed out in the text, what distinguishes Boré's effort is not originality but persistency. *De Bow's Review,* XXII, 617–619, reprints an article from the New Orleans *Delta* by a "Mr. Avequin" which gives some interesting details in a convincing way. According to this account, Solís revived the planting of sugar cane in Louisiana; Méndez bought him out and by 1792 had succeeded in producing refined sugar. He was aided by a man of practical experience from "St. Domingo," Morin by name. His sugar, however, was regarded as a mere curiosity until Boré took up the idea, employed this same Morin, and made a commercial success of sugar refining in 1795 and 1796. If Avequin stated the facts correctly, Louisiana owes its sugar industry to the technical

proficiency of Morin of "St. Domingo" as well as to the capital and courage of Boré. See also the account in Lewis C. Gray, *History of Agriculture in the Southern United States to 1860* (Washington, 1933), II, 739–740.

⁵ Part II, Ch. VI of Collot's *Mémoire* cited above, note 2.

⁶ AI, Sto. Dom., leg. 2619, Morales to Soler, May 31, 1802, No. 96. Boré is not mentioned by name. Morales speaks simply of the *dueño* of the first crop of cane.

⁷ *Ibid.*, Morales to Soler, May 31, 1802, No. 95. Morales said that he would permit the exportation of specie only in case of emergency and on his own written order in each case. The merchants of New Orleans protested vigorously but ineffectually against his decision.

⁸ A. P. Whitaker, *Documents Relating to the Commercial Policy of Spain in the Floridas*, p. 242, note 173.

⁹ See Ch. V, note 4. The figures in the text for 1787 are taken from a letter from Navarro to Valdés, No. 1, Jan. 15, 1788 (AI, Sto. Dom., 87–3–19) ; for 1803, from ASP, *Misc.*, I, 354–356, Jefferson's "Account of Louisiana." It is probable that the latter information was furnished by Daniel Clark and applied to the year 1802.

¹⁰ See Ch. V.

¹¹ *Am. Hist. Rev.*, XXXII, 814.

¹² *Ibid.*

¹³ AI, Sto. Dom., 87–1–27, López y Ángulo to Soler, New Orleans, July 13, 1801, No. 65. This despatch started the correspondence at the Spanish court which led to the order of July 14, 1802, directing the Intendant to close the deposit (see Ch. XI). López y Ángulo mentioned many other abuses of the right of deposit by the Americans, declaring that "under cover of it one may say they carry on an import and export trade [with Louisiana] entirely free from the payment of duties." The remedy which he attempted to apply was ineffectual, according to his successor, Morales, who wrote, in 1802, that the Americans evaded it by taking specie on board a league or so above New Orleans. Morales accordingly required the Americans to bring with them a statement of their cargo (including money and all other articles) certified by the proper United States customs official (*ibid.*, 87–1–29, Morales to Soler, New Orleans, Feb. 28, 1802, No. 66). Consul Clark protested in vain against the three per cent fee charged for the handling of specie deposited by American citizens (*Am. Hist. Rev.*, XXXII, 816).

¹⁴ ASP, *Misc.*, I, 356, table of sailings from New Orleans in 1802:

Nationality	Number of Ships	Tonnage
American	158	21,383
Spanish	104	9,753
French	3	105
Total	265	31,241

The Spanish records for this year (AI, PC, leg. 519) show only 211 sailings, and list only 90 of these ships as American. The discrepancy as to total number is explained in the text; as to nationality, by the incompleteness of the Spanish records.

¹⁵ Even in the period 1798–1802 there were doubtless American vessels which masqueraded as Spaniards in order to trade between New Orleans and other Spanish colonial ports, or else, arriving at New Orleans, as Americans, were transferred to Spanish registry. In the latter category belongs the ship which arrived at New Orleans on Jan. 26, 1801, as the American *Donaldson* and sailed on March 9 for Cadiz as the Spanish *San Francisco de Asis* (AI, PC, leg. 519).

¹⁶ Figures in the text are based on tables compiled under my direction from the customs records in AI, PC, legs. 2320 (1793), 2318 (1794), 513 (1795), 620 (1796), 654 (1797), 519 (1798 and 1799), 503 (1800), and 519 (1801, 1802, and 1803).

¹⁷ See above, note 14.

¹⁸ State Department, Consular Letters, New Orleans, Hulings to the Secretary of State, New Orleans, May 7, 1802.

¹⁹ See Ch. XI.

²⁰ *Official Letter Books of W. C. C. Claiborne,* I, 28, Claiborne to Madison, Natchez, Dec. 20, 1801.

²¹ Unless otherwise indicated, statistics of importations from the American West at New Orleans were drawn from the sources indicated above, note 16.

²² Statistics relating to the deposit were taken from the two bound volumes (ms.) of deposit records in AI, PC, leg. 631.

²³ *Palladium,* April 22, 1802, a list communicated to the House of Representatives by Gallatin, and to the *Palladium* by Representative Davis. This list differs in several respects from the one given in J. W. Monette, "The Progress of Navigation and Commerce on the Mississippi River," Mississippi Hist. Soc., *Publications,* VII, 487.

²⁴ AI, Sto. Dom., leg. 2669, López y Ángulo to Soler, July 13, 1801, No. 117.

²⁵ *Tree of Liberty,* June 26, 1802, communication signed "A Farmer."

²⁶ *Ibid.,* March 12, 1803.

²⁷ *Mémoire* cited above, note 2.

²⁸ AI, PC, leg. 2373, unsigned and undated memorial on Kentucky commerce, in English, with two enclosures. It may have been drawn up in 1798 by Samuel Montgomery Brown, agent for Innes, Sebastian and Todd (see Ch. I, note 29). Enclosure No. 1 contains the estimate given in the text.

²⁹ *Tennessee Gazette,* Feb. 18, 1801, item dated Nashville, Feb. 18.

³⁰ *Palladium,* June 23, 1801, unsigned letter dated New Orleans, March 2, 1801.

³¹ *Tennessee Gazette,* June 24, 1801, item dated Nashville, June 24.

³² *Pittsburgh Gazette,* May 21, 1802, Frankfort, Ky., item. In 1802 Governor Claiborne complained of a band at Walnut Hills, "sons of rapine and murder," who were plundering travelers (*Official Letter Books,* I, 91; see also *ibid.,* pp. 10, 11, 44–46, 60–62). Other information is given in J. F. H. Claiborne, *Mississippi,* pp. 225, 226.

[33] Breckinridge Papers, "Jan.–Dec., 1802," Robert Barr (? torn) to Breckinridge, Locust Grove, Feb. 4, 1802. Cf. Michaux's statement in Thwaites, *Early Western Travels*, III, 159.

[34] State Department, Consular Letters, New Orleans, Jones to Pickering, New Orleans, April 15, 1800, and Clark to Gallatin, New Orleans, Sept. 29, 1803; *Palladium*, Nov. 25, 1802, letter from Thomas T. Davis dated June 2, 1802; *Daily Advertiser* (New York), Nov. 2, 1801, "Spanish Inhumanity."

[35] *The Navigator* (Pittsburgh, 1811), 38.

[36] Innes Papers, Vol. 23A (Vol. I of the Wilkinson Papers), copy of instructions from James Wilkinson to Hugh McIlvain, Frankfort, March 17, 1791; articles of agreement, same date, "it being the Anniversary of St. Patrick"; invoice dated March 19, 1791. The tobacco was to be carried in flatboats named the *Union,* the *Royal Oak,* and the *Dreadnaught.* In a letter of Dec. 15, 1791, probably to Peyton Short, Wilkinson said this shipment had proved fatal to his interests.

[37] Michaux in Thwaites, *Early Western Travels*, III, 159.

[38] *Pittsburgh Gazette*, Nov. 5, 1802, "Ohio Company."

[39] Deposit records cited above, note 22.

[40] State Department, Consular Letters, New Orleans, Clark to Madison, June 22, 1802.

[41] James Ross Papers (see above, Ch. VII, note 7), bundle marked "Spanish Spoliation Claims."

[42] Mrs. Dunbar Rowland, *Life, Letters and Papers of William Dunbar*, pp. 114–117, 120.

[43] "William Johnson's Journal," *Louisiana Hist. Quarterly*, V, 34–50 (reprinted from the *New Jersey Hist. Quarterly*).

[44] The New Orleans customs records do not confirm all these details. There were two ships named the *Ocean* at New Orleans at this time. One cleared on May 12, the other on May 22. The *Neptune* is not mentioned at all; but that is probably to be explained on the ground that it obtained its cargo from the American deposit and sailed for an American port (New York). The other *Ocean*, Captain Robert Harrison, though ostensibly American, was suspected of being British; and it also came to grief at the mouth of the Mississippi (AI, Sto. Dom., leg. 2669, López y Ángulo to Soler, July 13, 1801, No. 118).

[45] AI, PC, leg. 177, Miró to Valdés, Aug. 28, 1788; invoice of the *Speedwell's* cargo. The cargo, consisting of wine, brandy, window glass, cotton goods, Barlow penknives, hair powder, and other articles, cost $18,246.60, and the cost of shipment to Kentucky was $2,810.50. It was sent in a boat with twenty oarsmen. The Spaniards hoped that the venture would promote the separatist intrigue.

[46] Breckinridge Papers, "Jan.–Dec., 1802," G. J. Johnston to Breckinridge, Louisville, Aug. 19, 1802. In October, 1802, a keelboat with a crew of fourteen men brought a cargo worth $30,000 from New Orleans to Kentucky (*New York Evening Post*, Nov. 12, 1802). In 1797, Victor Collot asserted that freight rates from Philadelphia to the Illinois country amounted to twelves *piastres* a hundred pounds, English measure, as

against only five *piastres* from New Orleans for one hundred pounds, French measure (*Mémoire* cited above, note 2; cf. Collot's *Journey,* I, 118). Minister Pichon, however, wrote from Washington in 1803 that the cost of transportation from Philadelphia to Kentucky was one-third less than that from New Orleans. In regard to the difficulties of up-stream navigation, it has been said that it was necessary for the boat to keep close to the sheltered bank and consequently to cross the river at every bend. In doing so it was usually carried back downstream about half a mile; and a boat going from New Orleans to St. Louis had to cross the river 390 times in this fashion (U. S., House of Reps., Exec. Docs., 50 Cong., 2 Sess., Vol. XX, No. 6, Part II, p. 185).

47 J. W. Monette, *op. et loc. cit.,* 485, 486. See also *Magazine of Western History,* II, 260.

48 *Pittsburgh Gazette,* April 3, 1801, report by the commandant of Fort Massac.

49 Breckinridge Papers, "Jan.–Sept. 1803," "Statement of duties collected at Fort Adams in the Mississippi District from the establishment of the office to 30 September 1803."

50 *Ibid.* The receipts from import duties are stated in round numbers in the text.

51 See above, note 14.

52 Henry Adams, *History of the United States,* I, 443.

53 *Tennessee Gazette,* March 17, 1802, extract of a letter from Lexington dated Feb. 20.

54 *Daily Advertiser* (New York), Oct. 28, 1802; *Pittsburgh Gazette,* Oct. 8 and 22 and Nov. 5, 1802; *Tree of Liberty,* Oct. 9, 1802, and Feb. 26, 1803.

55 Mann Butler, *History of the Commonwealth of Kentucky* (Cincinnati, 1836), p. 300.

56 Randolph C. Downes, "Trade in Frontier Ohio," *loc. cit.,* pp. 489–490.

57 Mary Verhoeff, *The Kentucky River Navigation* (Filson Club Publications, No. 28, Louisville, 1917), p. 83, note B, quoting an item from the *Kentucky Gazette* of May 5, 1792, to the effect that the sloop *Western Experiment,* built on the Monongahela and bound for Philadelphia, passed Limestone on April 20 (1792). This may be the case which Ambler, on the authority of a report written by Gallatin in 1807, mentions as having occurred in 1793 (*A History of Transportation in the Ohio Valley,* p. 83). Governor Carondelet, informed that the Westerners had sent the ship as a challenge to Spain (which did not yet permit the free navigation of the river by citizens of the United States), wisely refrained from interfering with its passage down the Mississippi.

58 *Palladium,* Aug. 31, 1801, "Extract of a letter from New-Orleans, dated June 17, 1801." *Ibid.,* May 12 and Aug. 18, 1803. Recent accounts of the subject are in Archer B. Hulbert, "Western Shipbuilding," *Am. Hist. Rev.,* XXI, 720, and Charles H. Ambler, *A History of Transportation in the Ohio Valley,* 83–101. Before the final revision of the present work was completed, the writer had the privilege of reading in manu-

script *The Keelboat Age on Western Waters,* by Dr. Leland D. Baldwin of the Western Pennsylvania Historical Society. It is the most thorough study of the physical aspects of river transportation that has yet been written. He has subsequently published some of the results of his study in "Shipbuilding on the Western Waters, 1793–1817," M. V. H. R., XX, 29–44.

59 Table in Baldwin, *The Keelboat Age* (cited in the preceding note).

60 "Extract of a letter" cited above, note 58.

61 Chargé d'Affaires Pichon wrote Talleyrand on March 18, 1803, giving a rather full account of Western shipbuilding (AE, EU, 55:36). Ambler, *op. cit.,* pp. 98–101, maintains that the influence of the embargo on the decline of Western shipbuilding has been exaggerated. It might also be noted in this connection that Zadok Cramer, writing in 1811, said that the frequency of the accidents suffered by these sea-going ships in descending the Ohio had "given a damp to shipbuilding at present." (*The Navigator* [Pittsburgh, 1811], p. 69; cf. *ibid.,* p. 26.)

62 ASP, FR, II, 523. The dependence of Louisiana on the commerce of the United States was freely admitted by the Spanish officials. For instance, Governor Salcedo wrote Morales on Oct. 29, 1801, that but for the Americans, "the inhabitants of these provinces would literally have not even a shirt to their backs," since there was no one else to take the cotton and sugar produced in Louisiana (AI, Sto. Dom., leg. 2669, Morales to Soler, Nov. 30, 1801, No. 46, enclosing a copy of Salcedo's letter).

The American infiltration into Louisiana has been discussed from different points of view by Louis Pelzer, "Economic Factors in the Acquisition of Louisiana," in Mississippi Valley Hist. Assn., *Proceedings,* VI, 11, and Lawrence Kinnaird, "American Penetration into Spanish Louisiana," in *New Spain and the Anglo-American West,* Vol. II (Los Angeles, 1932). The latter deals mainly with American immigration into Louisiana and Florida, and has little to say about trade. My own discussion of the subject is based on the conviction that a faithful account of the American infiltration must embrace both points of view, but that trade was a more important factor than immigration. Additional information in regard to immigration will be found in Chs. II and IX.

63 *Palladium,* April 1, 1802, extract of a letter from Evan Jones to the Secretary of State, New Orleans, Aug. 10, 1801, enclosed in a presidential message to Congress of Feb. 24, 1802, suggesting that steps be taken to provide hospital accommodations at New Orleans for American seamen and boatmen. Daniel Clark had received a recess appointment as United States consul at New Orleans just before Jones's letter was written (see Ch. XIV, note 30).

64 Gaillard Hunt, ed., *The Writings of James Madison,* VI, 462.

65 See table on p. 137, this chapter.

66 Breckinridge Papers, "1799," Samuel Hopkins to Breckinridge, Henderson (Ky.), May 3, 1799.

Chapter IX. Fin de Siècle

[1] A. P. Whitaker, *Spanish-American Frontier, passim,* especially Chs. XIII and XIV.

[2] AI, Sto. Dom., leg. 2617, Carondelet to Morales, June 11, 1797, enclosed in López y Ángulo to Soler, July 13, 1801, No. 102. About 1806 Moses Austin wrote an interesting account of the immigration of Americans to upper Louisiana (Am. Hist. Assn., *Report,* 1919, Vol. II, "Austin Papers," Part I, pp. 115–116). The *Palladium* of Sept. 26, 1799, printed what purported to be a copy of instructions to post commanders in upper Louisiana regulating the admission of settlers from foreign countries (item dated Lexington, Sept. 19).

[3] AI, Sto. Dom., leg. 2565, Carondelet to Azanza, Dec. 1, 1796, No. 1 res. In May, 1797, Lieutenant William Henry Harrison reported the presence at Cincinnati of a man named Hamilton, who was trying to persuade people there to settle in Spanish territory west of the Mississippi (B. C. Steiner, *McHenry,* p. 263).

[4] *Official Letter Books of W. C. C. Claiborne,* I, 47.

[5] AI, Sto. Dom., leg. 2580, *expediente* on Bastrop's Ouachita grant; leg. 2617 mod., López y Ángulo to Soler, July 13, 1801, Nos. 102 and 103; AHN, Est., "Actas del Supremo Consejo de Estado," Nov. 9, 1792; Gayarré, *Louisiana,* III, 353, 354.

[6] AI, Sto. Dom., leg. 2617, letters cited above, note 5. Ángulo stated that throughout the province the immigrants were generally Americans and Englishmen, who either settled without asking permission from anybody or else obtained permission from the local authorities, though the latter knew they were exceeding their powers in granting it.

[7] AI, Sto. Dom., 87–1–26, Morales to Soler, July 25, 1799, No. 321. The royal order was dated Oct. 22, 1798. The regulations drawn up and promulgated by Morales are in Gayarré, *Louisiana,* III, 632–640. Morales had three hundred copies of the new regulations printed at a cost of $150 by the only printer in New Orleans.

[8] Letters cited above, note 5.

[9] AI, PC, leg. 2371, Michel Lacassagne to (Gayoso), Louisville, Dec. 14, 1795.

[10] Among the most important despatches relating to the intrigue at this time are: AI, PC, leg. 178, Carondelet to the Prince of the Peace, June 15, 1797, No. 96 res.; Gayoso to same, Dec. 18, 1797, No. 10 res., and June 5, 1798, No. 20 *sumamente reservada.* See Isaac J. Cox, *West Florida Controversy,* pp. 33, 34, 46–49. Temple Bodley, *Reprints of Littell's Political Transactions,* Introduction, makes a heroic defense of Harry Innes and George Nicholas. For a different view as to Innes, see A. P. Whitaker, "Harry Innes and the Spanish Intrigue, 1794–1795," M. V. H. R., XV, 236.

[11] AI, PC, leg. 2375, Wilkinson to Carondelet, Ft. Washington, Sept. 22, 1796 (original cipher letter and deciphered copy).

[12] *Ibid.,* Wilkinson to Gayoso, Nov. 19, 1798 (place of writing not given), in which occurs the thoroughly Wilkinsonian phrase: "You per-

ceive my Dear Sir I prattle away without disguise"; *ibid.,* same to same, Loftus Heights, Jan. 30, 1799.

[13] Gayoso to Morales, July 1, 1799, enclosure No. 5 in despatch No. 102 cited above, note 5.

[14] State Department, Consular Letters, New Orleans, Clark to Pickering, Nov. 18, 1799. Casa Calvo returned to New Orleans in 1803 (see below, Ch. XIV).

[15] See the biographical sketch of Morales in A. P. Whitaker, *Documents Relating to the Commercial Policy of Spain in the Floridas,* p. 244, note 187.

[16] Letter cited above, note 14.

[17] See above, Ch. II.

[18] AI, Sto. Dom., leg. 2569, Salcedo to the king, New Orleans, Oct. 3, 1801, original, enclosed in Someruelos to Caballero, Havana, Feb. 17, 1802, No. 200, asking for an increase in salary and stating that he left the Canaries Aug. 5, 1800, and arrived at New Orleans July 13, 1801; Marc de Villiers du Terrage, *Dernières Années de la Louisiane Française,* p. 410, letter from Laussat to the minister, July 19, 1803; AI, PC, leg. 1574, Salcedo to Someruelos, June 9, 1803, No. 407; Folch to Someruelos, Pensacola, June 26, 1803, No. 29. In an *instancia* to the king, dated March 14, 1802, Salcedo asked certain favors for his two sons. The Captain-General, forwarding the *instancia,* described it as "disonante en todas sus partes," and said it proved, as he had already reported, that Salcedo "no está en la aptitud correspondiente para aquel mando" (*ibid.,* Sto. Dom., leg. 2569, Someruelos to Caballero, May 12, 1802, No. 248).

[19] *Ibid.,* leg. 2607, Ramón de López y Ángulo to Soler, May 23, 1803, enclosing a representation to the King, dated May 29, 1803, and a personal letter to Soler, dated San Sebastián, June 4, 1803; *ibid.,* summary of letters from López y Ángulo to Soler, New Orleans, April 25 and Aug. 12, 1801, with marginal notations; the Bishop of Louisiana to Caballero, New Orleans, July 31, 1801, No. 27 (referring to another letter of the Bishop's of June 13, 1800); representation by López y Ángulo to the Prince of the Peace, San Sebastián, Jan. 17, 1803; the acting Intendant of Havana to Soler, Havana, Jan. 11, 1805, No. 582.

[20] Ellicott, *Journal,* p. 191.

[21] Robertson, *Louisiana,* I, 355. In 1797 Carondelet reported that seditious disturbances had been created at Natchitoches by the curate, Father Jean Delvaux. When Carondelet sent Antonio Argote to pacify the people, the emissary was threatened by a band of "ghosts" ("revenants ó apareci-dos": AI, Sto. Dom., leg. 2566, Carondelet to Llaguno, Jan. 9, 1797, No. 23).

[22] *Ibid.,* leg. 2617, López y Ángulo to Soler, July 13, 1801, No. 77 and No. 95. See I. J. Cox in *Quarterly of the Texas State Historical Association,* X, 53–55.

[23] *Palladium,* June 9, 1801, "Extract of a letter from Doctor Latimore of Natchez," dated May 6, 1801.

[24] See the sketch of Bowles in *Dictionary of American Biography.* A somewhat different view from that stated in the text is contained in Law-

rence Kinnaird, "The Significance of William Augustus Bowles's Seizure of Panton's Apalachee Store in 1792," *Florida Hist. Soc. Quarterly*, IX, 156–192. It is understood that Professor Kinnaird plans to publish a life of Bowles.

[25] Article cited above, note 24, pp. 158, 159.

[26] See above, Ch. IV. In 1801 Morales attributed Bowles's attack on Panton's company to the jealousy of John Miller, "formerly an inhabitant of Pensacola, and now of Nassau" (AI, Sto. Dom., leg. 2670, Morales to the Secretary of State, Dec. 31, 1801, No. 4).

[27] Whitaker, *Documents Relating to the Commercial Policy of Spain in the Floridas,* pp. xl, 89, 95. In a report of Aug. 22, 1791, on William Short's memorial on the navigation of the Mississippi, Gardoqui suggested the cession of the Floridas to England; and Floridablanca, commenting on the suggestion, remarked that England would not consider the proposal (AHN, Est., leg. 3889 *bis,* exp. No. 4).

[28] AHN, Est., leg. 3889 *bis,* exp. No. 10, especially: (1) opinion of the *fiscal* of the Council of the Indies, Madrid, Aug. 30, 1798, (2) another opinion of the *fiscal,* Madrid, Dec. 31, 1798, and (3) letter from Francisco Cerdá to Urquijo, Madrid, March 8, 1799; AI, PC, leg. 2371, Bowles to the Duke de la Alcudia, Madrid, "Carcel de la Villa," July 14, 1793, duplicate, signed; fragment (first four pages) of a letter in Bowles's handwriting, undated; Bowles to Lord Grenville, Sierra Leone, June 5, 1798, draft or copy, signed.

[29] ANC, "Florida," leg. 1, exp. 5, No. 92, Panton to Gayoso, Pensacola, Jan. 24, 1799, LC transcript.

[30] *Ibid.,* leg. 1, exp. 24, No. 10, "Issue of T. H. Ferguson's adventure to the Muskogie nation (as collector of a Town not yet built on the Okelochnee)," in English, signed "Thomas Hugh Ferguson," Pensacola, June 16, 1800.

[31] Ellicott, *Journal* (ed. 1814), pp. 226–233. If Ellicott recorded it faithfully, Bowles gave him a garbled story of his life. For one thing, he failed to mention his Philippine exile.

[32] AHN, Est., leg. 3889 *bis,* exp. No. 10, Irujo to Urquijo, Philadelphia, April 22, 1800, No. 157, LC transcript.

[33] ANC, "Florida," leg. 1, exp. 24, No. 7, "Inventario de los efectos tomados al Aventurero Bowls en el dia 3 del corriente," Feb. 5, 1800, LC transcript.

[34] *Expediente* cited above, note 32, autograph note by Urquijo, dated March 20, 1800, on a despatch of Sept. 24, 1799, from Someruelos.

[35] Facts stated by the *fiscal* at Portell's court martial (see below, note 36).

[36] ANC, "Florida," leg. 4, exp. 1, "Expediente de Vitrian," especially the "conclusión fiscal" by Francisco Xavier de Lamadriz, and the sentence of the *consejo de guerra,* Havana, Sept. 28, 1805.

[37] *Palladium,* Aug. 4, 1801, item on p. 3 relating to approaching treaty with the Indians in Tennessee; *Letters of Benjamin Hawkins,* p. 385.

[38] AHN, Est., leg. 3889 *bis,* exp. 10, Irujo to Urquijo, Philadelphia, June 3, 1800, No. 168, and June 17, 1800, No. 170.

NOTES 305

[39] ANC, "Florida," leg. 1, exp. 5, No. 92, Panton to Casa Calvo, Pensacola, July 24, 1800, LC transcript.

[40] *Ibid.*, leg. 2, exp. 21, "Relación de la reconquista q⁰ del Fuerte de Apalache hace dⁿ Manuel Garcia" (LC transcript), covering the period from June 16, 1800, when the expedition left Pensacola, to July 11, 1800, when it was on the point of returning to that place. García commanded the *Leal,* one of the galleys. His letter of transmission (*ibid.,* García to Casa Calvo, July 11, 1800) gives further information about the "reconquest."

[41] This account is based on the "Relación" cited in the preceding note, and on Folch's report of July 15, 1800, to Casa Calvo (enclosure No. 8 in Someruelos to Caballero, Havana, Aug. 18, 1802, No. 289: AI, Sto. Dom., leg. 2569).

[42] *Ibid.,* leg. 2639, Morales to Soler, Dec. 31, 1801, No. 63.

[43] AHN, Est., leg. 3889 *bis,* exp. No. 10, Irujo to Cevallos, Philadelphia, June 29, 1801, No. 232.

[44] *Letters of Benjamin Hawkins,* pp. 418, 419.

[45] AME, Cor. Dip., leg. 207, Urquijo to Irujo, Aranjuez, Feb. 14, 1800, No. 6, LC transcript.

[46] Interior Department, Indian Office, Letter Book A.

[47] AI, PC, leg. 1574, Salcedo to Someruelos, June 9, 1803, No. 407.

[48] But in regard to the reward, see *Letters of Benjamin Hawkins,* p. 418.

[49] The principal sources of this account are: (1) AI, PC, leg. 1574, Folch to Someruelos, Pensacola, June 26, 1803, No. 29 and enclosures, especially No. 11 (letter from Benjamin Hawkins to Folch, Creek Agency, May 29, 1803), and No. 12 (letter from John Forbes to Folch, Hickory Ground, May 28, 1803); (2) Salcedo's despatch cited above, note 47; (3) "A Journal of John Forbes, May, 1803," Florida Hist. Soc. *Quarterly,* IX, 279–289. The writer made a careful search for Hawkins's report of the affair to his own government, but did not find it in the regular file of his correspondence (Interior Department, Indian Office, Letters Received).

[50] Hawkins to Folch, cited above, note 47, and "A Journal of John Forbes, May, 1803," *loc. cit.,* pp. 280, 285, 288, 289.

[51] Despatches of Folch and Salcedo cited above, notes 47 and 49.

Chapter X. The Retrocession of Louisiana

[1] AHN, Est., leg. 3963, copy of a confidential letter from Urquijo to Hervas, Aranjuez, June 22, 1800, enclosed in a copy of a despatch from Urquijo to Múzquiz of the same date. The whole passage relating to Louisiana is given in English translation in the present writer's article, "Spanish Policy towards the Retrocession of Louisiana," which was published in the *American Historical Review* in April, 1934. The reader is referred to that article for a more detailed discussion of the question and for many citations of authorities which it is not necessary to repeat here. The present chapter contains additional information regarding the cost of Louisiana to Spain and the eastern boundary of Louisiana.

[2] *History of the United States,* I, 363–365. Adams was apparently un-

aware of the existence of Urquijo's letter to Hervas of June 22, 1800. Five years after his book appeared, the existence of the letter was made known and excerpts from it published in Andrés Muriel, *Historia de Carlos IV* (Madrid, 1894), VI, 69, 70. Though Muriel properly points out that Napoleon encountered little resistance on the part of Spain to the retrocession, he makes the mistake of attempting to controvert Urquijo's assertion that Louisiana cost Spain more than it was worth. The best Spanish account of the Louisiana negotiation is contained in Jerónimo Bécker, *Historia de las Relaciones Exteriores de España en el Siglo XIX* (Madrid, 1922–24), Vol. I, but Bécker throws no new light on the negotiation at San Ildefonso.

[3] AHN, Est., bound volume, ms., entitled "Actas del Supremo Consejo de Estado," entry for May 27, 1796.

[4] AI, PC, leg. 1737, Urquijo to the Captain-General of Louisiana and the Floridas, San Lorenzo, Nov. 7, 1800.

[5] AI, Sto. Dom., leg. 2368, Morales to the Marqués de las Hormazas, New Orleans, March 3, 1798, No. 6.

[6] *Ibid.*, Casas to Vega, undated (*ca.* March 19, 1799); Vega to Casas, March 20, 1799; Soler to the acting Intendant of Louisiana, Aranjuez, March 24, 1799, draft.

[7] *Ibid.*, leg. 2619, Morales to Soler, New Orleans, April 30, 1802, No. 80.

[8] AHN, Est., "Actas del Supremo Consejo de Estado," entry for Dec. 29, 1794.

[9] *Ibid.*, leg. 3891, exp. No. 23, Irujo to the Prince of the Peace, Philadelphia, Aug. 5, 1797, No. 73, with an autograph note in the margin by Godoy dated Oct. 20, 1797; Godoy to Irujo, San Lorenzo, Nov. 19, 1797, draft.

[10] *Ibid.*, leg. 3897, Irujo to the Prince of the Peace, Philadelphia, Sept. 17, 1798, not numbered; (Urquijo) to Irujo, Madrid, Dec. 31, 1798, draft. The latter despatch was sent in cipher.

[11] AI, PC, leg. 1737, Someruelos to the Secretary of State, Havana, April 23, 1800, draft.

[12] *Ibid.*, Someruelos to the Secretary of State, Havana, June 28, 1800, res., draft.

[13] AHN, Est., leg. 3889 *bis*, exp. No. 10, Someruelos to Urquijo, Havana, Sept. 24, 1799, with an autograph note in the margin by Urquijo dated March 20, 1800; the Secretary of War to Cevallos, Dec. 31, 1800.

[14] See especially Chs. II, V, VIII, and IX. The formulation and results of Spanish policy towards Louisiana in the period 1783–1795 are discussed in A. P. Whitaker, *The Spanish-American Frontier;* the commercial aspects of Spanish policy in the same writer's *Documents Relating to Spanish Commercial Policy in the Floridas, 1778–1808*, Historical Introduction.

[15] AHN, Est., leg. 4018, Azara to Saavedra, Paris, May 27, 1798, No. 2, reporting a conversation with Talleyrand.

[16] Since this matter has been dealt with very briefly in preceding chapters, it might be well to remind the reader that British intrusions into the Missouri Valley injured Spain in two ways: first, by the economic loss which it caused Spanish subjects, and secondly, by the political embarrassments in which it involved the court—for instance, it was partly responsible for the surrender of Spain to the United States in the treaty of San

Lorenzo (Whitaker, *Spanish-American Frontier*, pp. 219, 220). See above, Ch. II, note 27, for a reference to the recent work of A. P. Nasatir in this field.

[17] For a more detailed discussion and citation of authorities, see the article cited above, note 1.

[18] On Sept. 19, 1800, Talleyrand wrote Ambassador Alquier at Madrid that he was authorizing Berthier, the special envoy who was conducting the negotiation at San Ildefonso, to conclude the treaty on the terms to which the King of Spain had agreed (that is, the cession of Louisiana without Florida). Talleyrand added that he agreed with Alquier that the eastern boundary of Louisiana would still remain a subject for negotiation, and that the sensitiveness of the King on that subject (the cession of Florida) prevented France from insisting upon the extension of Louisiana to the Mobile River. It seems clear from this letter that when the treaty of San Ildefonso was signed the French government understood that it was getting Spanish Louisiana alone without any part of Spanish West Florida—in other words, that the Iberville River and the Lakes formed the eastern boundary of Louisiana. The same conclusion is indicated by a letter which Decrès, minister for the colonies, wrote to Talleyrand on Oct. 4, 1802, when France was preparing to take possession of Louisiana. Asking for a conference with Talleyrand and his most skilful *délimitateur*, Decrès inquired whether France was going to keep within the boundaries of 1763 or whether it was going to occupy the territory as far east as Mobile. In the former case, he said, the boundary would be the Iberville River and the Lakes, and France would not possess Mobile. "Pensez-y bien !" he added. After "thinking that over," Talleyrand evidently decided two things. The first was that, since the basic treaty of San Ildefonso stipulated the boundaries of 1763, the territory now ceded by Spain was, as Decrès said, limited on the east by the Iberville River and the lakes, and therefore did not include Mobile; the second was that France must contrive to get Mobile. At any rate just two weeks after the date of Decrès's note, Talleyrand offered to add Parma to the kingdom of Etruria on condition that Spain should "round out the cession of Louisiana by adding the Floridas thereto"; and Ambassador Beurnonville was sent to Spain posthaste to press this offer on the court. It was not accepted, however, and no change was made in the description of the boundaries of Louisiana contained in the treaty of San Ildefonso. (AE, Esp., 659:494, Talleyrand to Alquier, Sept. 19, 1800, draft; AE, EU, Sup., 7:225, Decrès to Talleyrand, Oct. 4, 1802; AHN, Est., leg. 5207, Azara to Cevallos, Paris, Oct. 17, 1802, No. 476, endorsed "By special messenger"; same to same, Oct. 18, 1802, No. 480, enclosing a note from Talleyrand dated 26 Vendémiaire—Oct. 17). For the Spanish government's understanding of the extent of the ceded territory, see below, note 20. The view here stated is supported by Talleyrand's report to Napoleon, dated Nov. 19, 1804 (text in Renaut, *op. et loc. cit.*, pp. 468–474), as well as by the instructions of Nov. 26, 1802, to General Victor (Henry Adams, *op. cit.*, II, 6–7).

[19] AE, EU, Sup., 7:285, memorandum by the Prince of the Peace, Tarragona, Nov. 13, 1802, copy in Spanish.

[20] AI, PC, leg. 2368, printed proclamation endorsed in longhand, "Es copia de su original. Andres Lopez Armesto." Armesto was secretary to the commissioners. This proclamation may have been issued in response to a letter from Cevallos to the Captain-General of Louisiana and the Floridas, dated Aranjuez, Jan. 18, 1803 (*ibid.*). In this letter, which was written in reply to an inquiry regarding the boundaries of Louisiana, Cevallos said: ". . . Tratandose de una *retrocesión* de lo que nos cedio la Francia, de ningun modo puede concedersele mas, ni ella exigir lo que nosotros hemos descubierto, conquistado, ó cedido por convenios particulares à otras Potencias." Since West Florida was obtained by Spain through conquest from Great Britain during the American Revolution, it is obvious that the Spanish court regarded the Iberville River and Lakes Pontchartrain and Maurepas as forming the eastern boundary of the ceded territory below the junction of the Iberville with the Mississippi. Cevallos's statement is all the more important because it was made before France either occupied Louisiana or sold it to the United States.

[21] Godoy, *Cuenta Dada de su Vida Política* (Madrid, 1909), III, 53–62. Godoy says that he once advised the King to erect Louisiana into a liberal monarchy with one of the Spanish *infantes* (princes of the blood) as king (*ibid., pp.* 32–52).

[22] André Fugier, *Napoléon et l'Espagne, 1799–1808* (Paris, 1930), I, 129. This is a work of capital importance for the study of diplomatic relations between France and Spain, but there are several inaccuracies in the account of the Louisiana negotiation.

[23] AE, Esp., Sup., 19:67, Cevallos to the French ambassador, Palacio, July 15, 1802 (original in Spanish).

[24] ASP, FR, II, 569, note dated July 12, 1802. This was in reply to a note from Cevallos, dated May 26, 1802, in which he stated the conditions upon which Charles IV would agree to the immediate delivery of Louisiana to France (AE, Esp., Sup., 19:44).

Chapter XI. The Closing of the Deposit

[1] A. P. Whitaker, "France and the American Deposit at New Orleans," *Hispanic Am. Hist. Rev.*, XI, 488–491, especially note 11. In 1922, Jerónimo Bécker published two important documents (notes exchanged by Ministers Soler and Cevallos in July, 1802), which, in his opinion, settled the question by showing that the deposit was closed solely because of the abuses committed by the Americans (*Historia de las Relaciones Exteriores de España*, I, 76–82). Without reference to Bécker, Professor E. Wilson Lyon later reached the same conclusion on the basis of a document summarizing the two notes published by Bécker and other related correspondence (*Am. Hist. Rev.*, XXXVII, 280–286). As I have shown, however, in the article just cited, the question is not so simple as they make it appear.

[2] AHN, Est., leg. 5538, exp. No. 16, "Sobre el derecho que pretenden tener los Americanos para comerciar á su sombra sin pagar ningunos

derechos," including despatch No. 65, July 13, 1801, from López y Ángulo to Soler.

3 This incident, together with other instances of abuses of the right of deposit by the Americans, is mentioned above, Ch. VIII.

4 The order of July 14, 1802, is in AI, PC, leg. 2317B, endorsed "muy reservado" (*i.e.*, "very secret"). A translation of the most important portion is printed in Channing, *History of the United States,* IV, 326, 327. It was little more than a repetition, *mutatis mutandis,* of the note from Cevallos to Soler of July 11, 1802, printed in Bécker, *op. cit.,* I, note on pp. 77-79. It is very doubtful whether Lyon is justified in saying that a despatch from Morales, dated May 31, 1802, was responsible for the court's decision to "discontinue the right of deposit altogether, instead of allocating an alternate place, according to the treaty of 1795" (*Am. Hist. Rev.,* XXXVII, 282). There is no evidence to show that this despatch was considered by the court in framing the order of July 14, or that the despatch had even been received when that order was issued.

5 On July 15, 1802, Cevallos informed the French ambassador that the King had consented to cede Louisiana to France without awaiting the fulfilment of the conditions prescribed by treaty (AE, Esp., Sup., 19:67, original in Spanish). See *Hispanic Am. Hist. Rev.,* XI, 489, note 11.

6 According to M. André Fugier, who is the best authority on relations between France and Spain at this period, Cevallos was Godoy's submissive creature; Godoy was at the height of his power in the summer of 1802; and he and Napoleon, despite their apparent reconciliation, were still deeply suspicious of each other (*Napoléon et l'Espagne,* I, 119, 183, 184).

7 See above, note 4.

8 Morales's account of the affair is contained in his despatch No. I "very secret" to Soler, dated Oct. 21, 1802 (AI, Sto. Dom., leg. 2619). In the interest of perfect secrecy, he wrote this despatch with his own hand, and on the same day, in order to forestall suspicion on the part of his clerks, he had drafted a despatch, not secret, giving another account of the affair, without mentioning the "very secret" royal order of July 14, 1802 (*ibid.,* leg. 2618, No. 151). The precaution was a wise one, for leaks were frequent. For instance, Daniel Clark often obtained important information from subordinates in the government offices.

9 Despatches cited in preceding note. The discussion began in February, 1802 (*ibid.,* leg. 2619, Morales to Soler, Feb. 28, 1802, No. 75).

10 At an earlier stage of their correspondence on the exclusion of neutral trade, Morales had written Salcedo that a military escort was all the more necessary because there were no "deputies of the merchants through whom this news may [officially] come to their attention," and because "there had already been a case in which, since [a proclamation] had been made simply through the town crier, it was argued that the publication lacked force, and it was compared to those that are daily made for negro and mulatto dances, auctions, and other matters of small consequence" (Morales to Salcedo, Sept. 10, 1803, enclosed in despatch No. 151, cited above, note 8).

11 A copy of the proclamation is in AI, PC, leg. 2317B. An English translation of part of it is in ASP, FR, II, 470.

[12] New York *Morning Chronicle*, Nov. 27, 1802, letter dated New Orleans, Oct. 17.

[13] Despatch No. 1 "very secret," cited above, note 8.

[14] This was stated in a letter from Morales to Irujo (copy enclosed in Morales to Soler, April 13, 1803, No. 6 "very secret": AI, PC, leg. 594, copy). The fact was well known to the people of the United States (*Aurora*, Dec. 22, 1802, extract of a letter from New Orleans to a gentleman in Lexington, dated Oct. 28, 1802; *Official Letter Books of W. C. C. Claiborne*, I, 250, 251, Claiborne to Madison, Dec. 21, 1802; *Tennessee Gazette*, Jan. 29, 1803, item dated Philadelphia, Dec. 16, 1802; *Palladium*, Jan. 20, 1803, item dated Philadelphia, Dec. 28, 1802). At the same time, it is true that many reports were circulated in the United States about the rigor with which Morales enforced such restrictions as he did adopt. The commonest of these stories related to an American whose cotton fell into the river at New Orleans, and who, when he hauled it up on the shore to dry, was peremptorily ordered by Morales to take it off on pain of confiscation. What is apparently the same case is very differently described by Morales in despatch No. 174 to Soler, dated Dec. 31, 1802: AI, Sto. Dom., leg. 2669.

[15] *Official Letter Books of W. C. C. Claiborne*, I, 277, Claiborne to Madison, March 5, 1803, stating that many vessels were still lying opposite New Orleans waiting for return cargoes. On March 25, 1803, Stephen Zacharie wrote Pichon from New Orleans that, as he wrote, there were more than 120 ships in the river at that place waiting for cargoes (AE, EU, Sup., 28:220). In Jefferson's "Account of Louisiana," it is stated that in the first six months of 1803, 173 merchantmen entered the Mississippi and 156 left it. Of these, 93 and 68 respectively were American (ASP, *Misc.*, I, 356). Allowing for the inevitable reduction of the volume of commerce at New Orleans with the return of peace, these figures compare not unfavorably with those for 1802 (see Ch. VIII). When the deposit was closed, Vice Consul Hulings wrote that the flat boats were too frail to serve as "floating stores" while awaiting "the arrival of sea vessels to carry away their cargoes"; but after the deposit had been closed five months, he wrote that there were "upwards of 100 sail of vessels in port," half of them American, "waiting for the produce to come down" (State Department, Consular Letters, New Orleans, Hulings to Madison, Oct. 18, 1802, and Feb. 25, 1803, postscript dated March 23, 1803). For a discussion of this subject in relation to Western opinion during the deposit crisis, see Ch. XIII.

[16] Information about this decision was transmitted through General James Wilkinson to Governor Claiborne, and by him to Madison (*Official Letter Books of W. C. C. Claiborne*, I, 275, March 3, 1803). It was published in the *Palladium* of March 24, 1803, and in the Pittsburgh *Tree of Liberty*, March 26, 1803.

[17] AI, Sto. Dom., leg. 2669, Morales to Soler, Feb. 16, 1803, No. 186 and enclosures.

[18] *Palladium*, Jan. 20, 1803, item dated Philadelphia, Dec. 28.

[19] *Ibid.*, extract of a letter from New Orleans.

[20] On June 1, 1803, Morales wrote Soler that it would be a day of rejoicing for the greater part of the people of Louisiana, including the most respectable inhabitants, if they learnd that Spain was to remain permanently in possession of the province (AI, PC, leg. 594, No. 10 "very secret"). It is true that the deposit had been reopened when Morales wrote and that he was not an unbiassed observer; but see *Official Letter Books of W. C. C. Claiborne*, I, 47.

[21] AI, PC, leg. 594, Irujo to Morales, Washington, March 11, 1803, duplicate enclosed in Morales to Soler, April 13, 1803, No. 6 "very secret." Irujo had already written (Nov. 26, 1802) asking Morales for information about the reasons for the closing of the deposit, which, he said, seemed contrary to the treaty of San Lorenzo. Having received Morales's reply of Jan. 15, 1803, Irujo wrote the despatch of March 11.

[22] *Ibid.*, Morales to Soler, April 15, 1803, No. 7 "very secret."

[23] *Ibid.*, No. 8 in the same series. According to Morales, the Governor was all the more disposed to overrule him since his eldest son, Manuel María Salcedo, just returned to New Orleans, disapproved very strongly of his failure to obey Irujo's order. Young Salcedo was universally regarded as having an extraordinary ascendancy over his father; but in this controversy, it appears, two other persons who had great influence with the Governor (his secretary, Armesto, and the *auditor de guerra,* Vidal) joined with Laussat in persuading him not to interfere with Morales.

[24] On March 8, 1803, Daniel Clark wrote Madison from New Orleans: "On the subject of the authority on which the Intendant has acted, there is among well informed People but one Opinion, which is, that he merely executes the order received from his Government. He is too rich, too sensible, and too cautious to take such a responsability on himself . . ." (*Am. Hist. Rev.,* XXXII, 331).

Chapter XII. Chauvinism and Incantation

[1] *Official Letter Books of W. C. C. Claiborne*, I, 210, 211, 222; *Tennessee Gazette,* Nov. 20, 1802; New York *Daily Advertiser,* Nov. 23 and 26, 1802; *New York Evening Post,* Nov. 25 and 26, 1802; Philadelphia *Aurora,* Nov. 24, 1802; State Department, Consular Letters, New Orleans, Hulings to Madison, Oct. 18, 1802. The first information concerning the closing of the deposit was brought to New York on Nov. 22 by the ship *Superior,* Captain Sinclair, thirty-eight days from New Orleans. The news from this source was published in New York on Nov. 23, and in Philadelphia the following day. The text of Morales's proclamation (or rather, that portion of it which relates to the deposit) was apparently first received in the duplicate of Hulings's despatch of Oct. 18, which came to Baltimore in the brig *Charlotte,* Captain Diamond. An English translation of this extract appeared in the New York newspapers on Nov. 26. Hulings sent his despatch in quadruplicate—the original and duplicate in a schooner and a brig to Baltimore, the triplicate by an express rider, and

the quadruplicate in the post via Natchez. It is the last named that is preserved in the State Department.

[2] *Palladium,* Thursday, Dec. 2, 1802, reprinting from "the extra of
Monday last" a summary of Speed's letter, an English translation of
Morales's proclamation (enclosed by Speed), and a letter of Oct. 18, 1802,
from Messrs. Meeker, Williamson and Patton at New Orleans to Governor Garrard of Kentucky. An unsigned letter endorsed "James Speed to
Col. Shelby," dated New Orleans, Oct. 18, 1802, is in Draper MSS., 54 J
39. Together with this is a copy of Morales's order, which Speed calls
"a prescription for old age" (*ibid.,* 59 J 37).

[3] *Pittsburgh Gazette,* Dec. 3, 1802, item dated Philadelphia, Nov. 23;
Tree of Liberty, Dec. 4, 1802, item dated Baltimore, Nov. 23.

[4] AME, Cor. Dip., leg. 209, Cevallos to Irujo, Cartagena, Dec. 24, 1802;
leg. 210, same to same, Aranjuez, Feb. 3, 1803; leg. 211, same to same,
Aranjuez, Jan. 14, 1804, LC transcripts.

[5] *New York Evening Post,* Nov. 16, 1801, under "Spanish and French
Amity"; *ibid.,* Nov. 20, 1801, letter dated "Algeziras, Sept. 18"; New
York *Daily Advertiser,* Dec. 2, 1802, extract of a letter dated Buenos
Aires, June 26; *Pittsburgh Gazette,* Nov. 27, 1801, "Spanish Atrocity,"
and July 9, 1802, item from Buenos Aires.

[6] Jefferson, *Writings,* VIII, 144, 145. As early as 1797 Jefferson was
disturbed by the prospect of Louisiana's becoming a "Gallo-American
colony" (Randolph, *Memoirs of Jefferson,* III, 358).

[7] Washington, who was no alarmist, wrote in 1794 that the Western
people showed a "predisposition to be dissatisfied," and, as stated in Ch.
VII, he devoted a considerable portion of his Farewell Address to persuading them of the value of the Union. The excitement in Kentucky
over the resolutions of 1798 and 1799 and in Tennessee over Indian relations and Zachariah Cox's Muscle Shoals project seemed to many Easterners a proof that the West was in a dangerous state of fermentation.
Pickering regarded the Blount conspiracy as a manifestation of secessionist tendencies under French influence; and in 1798 President Adams
wrote: " . . . I have been tortured for a greater part of the year past
with written anonymous insinuations against several persons in conspicuous public stations [in the West], that they had formed improper
connections with Spain . . ." In the Senate debate of February, 1803,
on the deposit question, a great deal was said in regard to the danger of
foreign intrigue in the West. Consult the Index for discussions of these
matters.

[8] Jefferson, *Writings,* VIII, 295.

[9] What Irujo did is stated in the text. Pichon wrote Talleyrand on
Dec. 22, 1802, urging him to follow a course friendly to the United States
and warning him that public opinion in the United States held France
responsible for Morales's proclamation. France, he said, could not exclude
the Americans from the Mississippi, and should not if it could (AE, EU,
55:125). He also wrote Prefect Laussat and the Spanish Governor and
Intendant at New Orleans in favor of the American privilege (*ibid.,*
55:274, Pichon to Talleyrand, Georgetown, Feb. 12, 1803, No. 35. His

letter to the Governor was published in the *Palladium*, March 31, 1803).

[10] Jefferson, *Writings*, VIII, 33, 34. On May 8, 1798, Minister David Humphreys presented an urgent request on behalf of his Government for Irujo's immediate recall. On May 28 of the following year Urquijo replied that the request must come directly from the President. Humphreys complained vigorously against such a reply after so long a delay, but Urquijo would not yield. In 1800 provision was finally made for Irujo's recall; but, pleading the danger of travel on the high seas in war time, Spain delayed the sending of a successor until Jefferson came into office; and then Irujo's recall was not necessary (AHN, Est., leg. 3891, exp. No. 22). The Republicans charged that Federalist hostility to Irujo was due to the latter's exposure of the Blount conspiracy, in which Pickering was implicated (*Tree of Liberty*, Oct. 24, 1801, item clipped from the Philadelphia *Aurora*).

[11] AI, 146-3-8, Foronda to Soler, Philadelphia, July 2, 1805, and June 16 and Sept. 3, 1806, LC transcript. It may not be without significance that in 1800 Irujo sought and obtained permission to remain at Philadelphia instead of transferring his residence to the new capital at Washington (AME, Cor. Dip., leg. 207, Urquijo to Irujo, Aranjuez, May 18, 1800, No. 21, LC transcript).

[12] Gaillard Hunt, ed., *Writings of James Madison*, VII, 36; *Tree of Liberty*, March 26, 1803. Irujo pointed out that the extract of Morales's proclamation circulated in the United States did not contain the preamble, which represented the closing of the deposit as taken on Morales's own responsibility.

[13] See above, Ch. XI.

[14] See below, Ch. XIII.

[15] *Annals Cong.*, 7 Cong., 2 Sess., 280, 281.

[16] Thus in the Senate debate of February, 1803, Dayton said he did not believe the "artful insinuation" that the closing of the deposit was the unauthorized act of the Intendant.

[17] *Annals Cong.*, 7 Cong., 2 Sess., 312-314.

[18] Jefferson, *Writings*, VIII, 190, 191. See below, note 20.

[19] When Monroe was preparing for the trip to Paris, he required his attorney to follow Breckinridge's advice in the handling of his Kentucky lands. The letter shows that Monroe owned one tract of 20,000 acres in Kentucky (Breckinridge Papers, "Jan.–Sept., 1803," Monroe to Breckinridge, New York, March 4, 1803).

[20] *Palladium*, March 31, 1803, circular letter dated Feb. 28, 1803; March 17, 1803, contribution signed "A Freeman"; Feb. 10, 1803, letter from John Breckinridge, dated Washington, Jan. 20, 1803. Another expression of approval was contained in a letter from W. Lewis to Breckinridge, dated Campbell, Jan. 27, 1803 (Breckinridge Papers, "Jan.–Sept., 1803").

[21] Channing's explanation of Monroe's appointment is surprising in a historian of such keen insight as Channing usually displayed. He suggests that Monroe was prying into Jefferson's private affairs, and that the President welcomed the chance to get him out of the way by sending him to Paris (*History of the United States*, IV, 314, 315). This explanation

is open to two objections, which are as formidable as they are obvious. The first is that it rests upon a conjectural interpretation of circumstantial evidence. The second is that it is superfluous, since the appointment is adequately explained by the considerations which I have mentioned in the text and since these considerations are based upon direct evidence drawn from documents. One of the chief reasons for Monroe's choice was well stated by Jefferson when he told Pichon that "Mr. Monroe was so well known as the friend of the western people that his mission would contribute more than anything else to tranquilize them and prevent irritating incidents" (AE, EU, 55:192, Pichon to Talleyrand, Georgetown, Jan. 23, 1803).

[22] Jefferson, *Writings*, VIII, 190.

[23] On Dec. 24, 1802, Vice Consul Hulings of New Orleans sent Governor Claiborne an English translation of the order, which was addressed by Soler to the Intendant of Louisiana. Hulings said he had procured a copy from "a Friend," though the order had not yet been "communicated publicly by government" (*Official Letter Books of W. C. C. Claiborne*, I, 257; Hulings also sent a copy of the order to Madison: *Am. Hist. Rev.*, XXXII, 823). On Jan. 11, 1803, the order was printed in the *Constitutional Conservator* of Natchez, from which it was clipped by the *Palladium* (Frankfort, Ky.), Feb. 17, 1803. It had been published in Philadelphia by Jan. 29, 1803 (clipping enclosed in letter from Daniel W. Coxe to the Secretary of State, Philadelphia, Jan. 29, 1803: State Department, Consular Letters, New Orleans). The *Aurora* denounced it as a forgery. On Feb. 12, 1803, Chargé d'Affaires Pichon wrote his government that the publication of the order in the United States had created a very unfavorable impression, that even the administration newspapers were beginning to write in a less pacific tone, and that the situation had taken a very serious turn (AE, EU, 55:274, Pichon to the Minister, Georgetown, Feb. 12, 1803, No. 35). It was probably this order that Hamilton referred to in his "Pericles" letter to the *Evening Post* (cited in note 33). Other factors which probably added to the war spirit at this time were the pamphlet mentioned in note 16, p. 316, and the growing conviction that Great Britain would soon go to war with France and would therefore be willing to aid the United States.

[24] *New York Evening Post*, Feb. 16, 1803.

[25] Seth Ames, ed., *Works of Fisher Ames* (Boston, 1854), I, 295, 296, 298, 313–316; *Diary and Letters of Gouverneur Morris*, II, 415, 421, 427.

[26] Matthew L. Davis, *Memoirs of Aaron Burr* (New York, 1852), II, 171.

[27] AE, EU, 55 : 119, 125, 153, Pichon to Talleyrand, Georgetown, Dec. 21 and 23, 1802, and Jan. 1, 1803. Irujo wrote Cevallos to much the same effect (AHN, Est., leg. 5538, Dec. 20, 1802, No. 317, and Jan. 9, 1803, No. 318). See below, Ch. XIII, note 15.

[28] *Diary and Letters of Gouverneur Morris*, II, 423, 426.

[29] Homer C. Hockett, *Western Influences on Political Parties to 1825* (Columbus, 1917), pp. 51–68; Robert M. McElroy, *Kentucky in the Nation's History* (New York, 1909), Chs. VII and VIII.

[30] J. C. Hamilton, ed., *Works of Alexander Hamilton*, VI, 551, 552.

[31] See above, Ch. VII.

[32] William Plumer, Jr., *Life of William Plumer* (Boston, 1857), p. 249.

[33] Feb. 8, 1803, with an introductory paragraph deploring the cooling of the zeal for vigorous action formerly shown by Coriolanus. The "Pericles" letter can be consulted most conveniently in H. C. Lodge, *Works of Alexander Hamilton*, V, 464–467. Mr. Allan Nevins, in *The Evening Post* (New York, 1922), pp. 27, 28, does not include the Pericles article among those which he regards as unquestionably written by Hamilton; but, on the other hand, he does not deny that Hamilton wrote it. Both J. C. Hamilton and Lodge attribute it to Hamilton.

[34] Lodge, *Works of Alexander Hamilton*, V, 464.

[35] Hamilton's *Evening Post* said in its issue of March 2, 1803: "We desire, therefore, that it may be distinctly remembered, that the resolutions of Mr. Ross were supported by the Federal Senators . . ."

[36] Henry Adams, *Life of Gallatin*, p. 122.

[37] *Annals Cong.*, 7 Cong., 2 Sess., 94. Ross's speech of Feb. 14 is on pp. 83–88.

[38] Plumer, *Life of William Plumer*, pp. 252, 253.

[39] *Annals Cong.*, *loc. cit.*, pp. 95, 96.

[40] *Ibid.*, 107–115.

[41] Subsequent proceedings are in *ibid.*, 115–256. The debates were published by William Duane at Philadelphia in 1803 in a pamphlet entitled "Mississippi Question." The report in the *Annals of Congress* is substantially identical with Duane's.

[42] *Annals Cong.*, *loc. cit.*, pp. 150, 151.

[43] *Ibid.*, 140, 141, 212. The inconsistency was most circumstantially exposed by Senator Mason of Virginia, who hinted that one explanation of the change might be recent speculation in Western lands by Federalist Senators (*ibid.*, 223, 224). Perhaps he had Dayton and Gouverneur Morris in mind.

[44] *Ibid.*, 119.

Chapter XIII. The Enchantment Works

[1] Speaking of the Monroe mission, Gouverneur Morris said: "These are his [Jefferson's] works, and for his faith, it is not as a grain of mustard but the full size of a pumpkin; . . . He believes in . . . defence of territory by reduction of armies, and in vindication of rights by appointment of ambassadors" (*Diary and Letters of Gouverneur Morris*, II, 431).

[2] *Palladium*, Jan. 20, 1803, "Extract of a letter from a very intelligent gentleman at New Orleans, dated the third instant."

[3] See above, Ch. I.

[4] *Annals Cong.*, 7 Cong., 2 Sess., 115–119 (Breckinridge), 139–142 (Cocke), 146 (Jackson). See above, Ch. XII.

[5] *Palladium*, Dec. 2, 1802, item dated Frankfort, Dec. 2, including reso-

lutions and a memorial of the legislature on Morales's order; *Official Letter Books of W. C. C. Claiborne*, I, 246, 247, the legislative council of Mississippi Territory; *Palladium*, Feb. 3, 1803, resolutions and memorial of Mississippi territorial legislature; *Tennessee Gazette*, Feb. 9, 1803, and April 13, 1803, letters from Representative William Dickson; ibid., Feb. 16, 1803, Jefferson's message to Congress and extracts of letters from Senators Cocke and Anderson.

[6] Breckinridge Papers, "Jan.-Sept., 1803," John Allen to Breckinridge, Bourbon, Feb. 15, 1803.

[7] *Palladium*, March 10, 1803, letter signed "A friend to the Union," and editorial comment under the caption "Frankfort, March 10."

[8] *Ibid.*, March 17, letter signed "A Freeman."

[9] *Ibid.*, item dated Frankfort, March 17. "A Western American" replied to "A Friend to the Union" in a letter filled with personal abuse (*ibid.*, March 24, 1803).

[10] *Ibid.*, Dec. 25, 1802, address by Daveiss, dated Dec. 13, 1802. It appears that, whether maliciously or not, Daveiss spread false news of a kind that would inflame the Kentuckians. On Jan. 12, 1803, Benjamin Howard wrote Breckinridge from Lexington, Ky., that the people of the State would doubtless be grateful for a recent letter of reassurance from the Senator, adding, "but Mr. Davies has informed us that the port of Orleans is *blockaded* which appeared yesterday [in the *Kentucky Herald*] with the extract from your letter" (Breckinridge Papers, "Jan.-Sept., 1803").

[11] *Palladium*, May 26, 1803.

[12] Breckinridge Papers, "Jan.–Sept. 1803," letters to Breckinridge from Achilles Sneed, Dec. 20, 1802; William Bradford, Frankfort, Jan. 29, 1803; John A. Seitz, Lexington, Feb. 17, 1803; William Stevenson, Lexington, (Jan.?) 29, 1803.

[13] *Palladium*, Jan. 20, 1803, item dated Frankfort, Jan. 20.

[14] Most of the Republican leaders in the West actively opposed an immediate resort to arms, and so far as I know, not one of them supported it. The partisan character of the controversy was pungently described by "Cato," writing in the *Palladium* of April 28, 1803. He urged the people not to vote in the approaching election for any candidate who was even suspected of having supported the Adams administration. The Federalists in Congress, he said, had recently pretended great friendship for the West, "but they have always been a dishonest, rotten-hearted crew, full of deceit and dissimulation." Their only desire was to plunge the Republican administration into a war for which it was totally unprepared, and discredit it so as to get themselves back into power.

[15] The first of the Coriolanus articles appeared in the New York *Morning Chronicle* of Dec. 17 and 18, 1802. An inflammatory article, unsigned, appeared in the paper on Dec. 3. Irujo merely said that the *Chronicle* was under Burr's "immediate patronage," but Pichon declared unequivocally that Burr was the author of the articles. Both agreed that he was actively stirring up the war spirit in the United States. Pichon said that in private Burr was doing his best to imbue certain agents of France with a desire

for Louisiana, and that he himself regretted to see France playing so completely the game of this man "whose ambition and principles, I believe, are dangerous both to his own country and to France" (AHN, Est., leg. 5538, exp. No. 16, Irujo to Cevallos, Dec. 20, 1802, No. 317, and Jan. 9, 1803, No. 318; AE, EU, 55:119, 125, 153, Pichon to Talleyrand, 2 Nivose, An XI, enclosing an extract from the *Morning Chronicle* article of Dec. 5, 1802, and same to same, Jan. 1, 1803). For Burr's relations with the Federalists, see above, Ch. XII.

¹⁶ AE, EU, 55 : 199, Fourcroy to Talleyrand, Philadelphia, Jan. 24, 1803, saying that the pamphlet had caused a great sensation; *ibid.*, 55:249, Pichon to Talleyrand, Georgetown, 8 Pluviose, An XI, No. 31, saying that the pamphlet was attributed to Gouverneur Morris, that either Morris or Burr was the author, and that it was probably the work of both. A copy of the pamphlet is in *ibid.*, fol. 200 ff. It includes a translation of a "Memorial . . . drawn up by a French Counsellor of State," which has been erroneously attributed to Vergennes and which the writer of the *Address* itself used to show the designs of France in regard to Louisiana. The first printing of the pamphlet was soon sold out and in February the publishers made a second and "large impression, on a more convenient and cheap scale," which sold for twenty-five cents (*New York Evening Post,* Feb. 24 and March 17, 1803).

¹⁷ *Palladium,* Jan. 27, 1803.

¹⁸ Breckinridge Papers, "Jan.–Sept., 1803," Breckinridge to Madison, July 9, 1803, copy: "We are all here [Kentucky] in a state of perfect tranquility, awaiting with patience & good temper the result of the mission [Monroe's]. The present prospects in Europe have greatly heightened our Expectations; & our disappointment in case of failure, will consequently be much keener. We have set our Hearts strongly on the Island of Orleans." In the same bundle of papers is an interesting letter of the same date from Breckinridge to Monroe.

¹⁹ Dec. 31, 1802, and Jan. 21, 1803.

²⁰ *Tree of Liberty,* Feb. 26, 1803. Senator James Ross was one of the "Pittsburgh Junto."

²¹ *New York Evening Post,* March 4, 5, and 9, 1803; *Palladium,* March 24, 1803; *ibid.,* April 14, 1803, item from the *American Literary Advertiser.*

²² *Palladium,* Jan. 6, 1803, Jefferson to Governor Garrard, Dec. 16, 1802; *ibid.,* Feb. 10, 1803, same to same, Jan. 18, 1803; David M. Massie, *Nathaniel Massie* (Cincinnati, 1896), pp. 220, 221; *Official Letter Books of W. C. C. Claiborne,* I, 273, Madison to Claiborne, Jan. 17, 1803. On Jan. 7, 1803, Madison wrote Breckinridge that the Kentuckians seemed "ready for the last resort," that the President "discovers a sympathy with you, which, perhaps, goes a little further than was absolutely necessary," that negotiation must by all means be tried first, and that it would be better to buy West Florida from poverty-stricken Spain and cut a canal from the Tennessee River to the Mobile than to fight (Breckinridge Papers, "Jan.–Sept., 1803"). For Breckinridge's own letters on the crisis, see above, note 18, and below, note 23.

²³ On Jan. 20, 1803, the *Palladium* published a letter from Senator Breckinridge approving of Monroe's appointment. Should New Orleans remain shut until the result of the mission was known, he said, the West would suffer considerably, "but we must submit to it," for this was the course chosen by the President, and it "seems to promise ultimately the greatest and most lasting good." But if the mission should fail, "I have confidence that the general government will resort not only to those measures which will completely invest us with, but as completely protect us in, its enjoyment"—that is, in the rights of free navigation and deposit. We shall not rest, he concluded, until we get the territory on the eastern bank of the Mississippi. For other communications by members of Congress, see above, note 5.

²⁴ *Palladium,* Jan. 6, 1803.

²⁵ *Ibid.,* March 3, 1803, item dated Frankfort, March 3; ASP, FR, II, 526, 527.

²⁶ Isaac J. Cox, "Selections from the Torrence Papers," *Quarterly Publications of the Hist. and Phil. Soc. of Ohio,* IV, 98, 99.

²⁷ Breckinridge Papers, "Jan.–Dec., 1802."

²⁸ *Annals Cong.,* 7 Cong., 2 Sess., 118; *Palladium,* May 26, 1803, extract from "the masterly letters of Camillus," communicated by a subscriber; *ibid.,* June 9, 1803, Thomas Paine's letter. The latter will be found more conveniently in Moncure Daniel Conway, ed., *The Writings of Thomas Paine* (New York, 1895), III, 409–412. It was first published in the Philadelphia *Aurora.* Under the title "The Mississippi Question Fairly Stated," the Camillus letters were published in pamphlet form as well as serially in Republican newspapers (*e.g.,* in the *Tree of Liberty,* April 2, 9, 23, 30, and May 14, 1803; Nos. 3 and 6 are missing from the file consulted). Minister Irujo, almost from the moment of his arrival in the United States, took kindly to the American custom of paper warfare.

²⁹ See above, Ch. XI. On April 13, 1803, Morales wrote Irujo that the Kentuckians were not so wrought up as the minister thought they were. "They arrive daily [at New Orleans] with their cargoes of foodstuffs, which are admitted in consequence of the decision of February 5, and they withdraw satisfied with what they receive," declared Morales. "The people of Natchez, who come down with cotton and other products the entry of which is not permitted, transfer them to the ships that are waiting for them . . ." (AI, PC, leg. 594, copy, enclosed in Morales to Soler, April 13, 1803, No. 6 *muy res.*)

³⁰ *Official Letter Books of W. C. C. Claiborne,* I, 35, Claiborne to Madison, Jan. 20, 1802. Early in 1802 the people of Kentucky were already complaining that peace had reduced the price of flour and tobacco (ASP, *Finance,* I, 732).

³¹ Mrs. Dunbar Rowland, *Life, Letters and Papers of William Dunbar,* p. 115, Dunbar to Bird and Co., Natchez, July 5, 1802, saying, "The great depression of cotton since the peace is dis[coura]ging." From this letter it appears that in the early part of 1802 the price of cotton fell from 32

to 16 cents a pound. As for flour, Harry Innes wrote Breckinridge from Kentucky on Jan. 14, 1802: "The most moderate winter I have ever known & the late moist weather have set all the mills in motion—great preperations are now going forward on the Kentucky River & wheat is at the moderate price of three shillings p^r bushel—a dull sale" (Breckinridge Papers, "Jan.–Dec., 1802"). On Oct. 30, 1802, a full month before news of the closing of the deposit reached Kentucky, Benjamin Howard wrote Breckinridge from Lexington, Ky., "As to our prospect of selling wheat it is extremely gloomy indeed in short no one offers to buy at any price; but however I believe it is pretty well disposed of by the weevil already" (*ibid.*). Ordinarily the price of flour at both Natchez and New Orleans was lowest from March to June, when the bulk of the Western exports came down the river on the spring floods, and began to rise again in the late summer and early autumn; but on March 17, 1802, flour was quoted at five dollars a barrel in Natchez, and on Sept. 21, 1802, it had fallen to three and a half and four dollars (*Palladium,* May 16 and Nov. 18, 1802, quoting prices current at Natchez). Writing from New Orleans on May 7, 1802, Vice Consul Hulings said, "The markets are exceedingly dull & cash very scarce" (State Department, Consular Letters, New Orleans).

[32] June 5, 1802, under caption "Summary."

[33] Nov. 5, 1802, under caption "Ohio Company."

[34] *Official Letter Books of W. C. C. Claiborne,* I, 277.

[35] State Department, Consular Letters, New Orleans, Hulings to Madison, March 30, 1803.

[36] Breckinridge Papers, "Jan.–Sept., 1803," letter dated Staunton, May 16, 1803. Cf. Michaux's statement in Thwaites, *Early Western Travels,* III, 205.

[37] It is of course impossible to determine the extent of the losses suffered by citizens of the United States as a result of the closure of the deposit. Daniel Clark thought the losses were heavy. On June 20, 1803, answering an inquiry from Madison, he said that the Americans had suffered in two ways: first, by the Spaniards' withdrawal of the landing privilege, which forced the Americans either to pay *douceurs* to the revenue officers, or else, as happened "more than once," see "whole cargoes" lost because they could not be landed. The second and greater injury resulted from "the loss of a market & fall in value of our Commodities," which, he alleged, the owners had to sell at any price offered, despite the fact that numbers of ships were in port. This latter assertion seems rather dubious, since, during most of the period of closure, there were about one hundred ships in the river waiting for cargoes, and half of them were American. Clark however supported his assertion by the statement that the price of cotton and flour rose immediately upon the reopening of the deposit—in the former case from thirteen and fourteen to seventeen and eighteen cents a pound; in the latter, from four to six dollars per barrel. As for the total amount of the loss, Clark advised that the United States demand of Spain at least one half the value of the exports from the West

for a whole year, that is, a million dollars. There can be little doubt that this figure was far in excess of the loss actually suffered. Clark's letter is in State Department, Consular Letters, New Orleans.

38 AHN, Est., leg. 5538, exp. No. 16; AME, Cor. Dip., leg. 210, Cevallos to Irujo, Feb. 16, 1803, *muy res.*, LC transcript.

39 *Expediente* cited in the preceding note.

40 AME, Cor. Dip., leg. 210, Cevallos to Irujo, March 1, 1803, enclosing a copy of the order of the same date to Morales.

41 As a matter of fact it was the quickest way. The order of March 1, sent via Washington, was received by Morales on May 17, two weeks before he received the order of Feb. 16, which had been sent via Havana (the usual way) and reached him on June 2 (AI, PC, leg. 594, Morales to Soler, No. 11 *muy res.*, June 3, 1803; see below, note 43). A translation of Irujo's letter of April 19, informing Madison of the reopening of the deposit, was published in the *Palladium* (Frankfort, Ky.) on May 12. The *Tree of Liberty* announced the good news to the people of Pittsburgh in an extra on April 29.

42 AHN, Est., leg. 5538, exp. No. 16, Cevallos to the Secretary of the Navy, Feb. 28, 1803; *ibid.*, the *comandante militar de marina* of Coruña to Cevallos, March 5, 1803. Charles Pinckney, the United States Minister to Spain, was so completely taken in by Cevallos and Godoy that he was convinced that the court had no prior knowledge of Morales's proclamation and would pay damages to the United States on that account (State Department, Spain, Pinckney to Madison, Feb. 22 and March 28, 1803).

43 AI, PC, leg. 594, Morales to Soler, May 18, 1803, No. 9 *muy res.* The order was forwarded from Washington under cover to Consul Daniel Clark, who wrote Madison on May 17 that he received it at 11 A. M. on that day and delivered it immediately, and that by 2 P. M. the Intendant had posted a notice of the revocation of his proclamation of Oct. 16, 1802. Clark added that on the following day, May 18, the Governor would proclaim the restoration of the deposit with the usual formalities (*Am. Hist. Rev.*, XXXIII, 344). The Spanish records of the deposit show that the first entry in 1803 was made on May 18 (AI, PC, leg. 631, bound volume, ms.).

44 On the peace policy of Spain at this period, see Fugier, *Napoléon et l'Espagne*, I, 189, where he says, " . . . En vertu du traité d'alliance de Saint-Ildefonse elle [Spain] risquait fort d'être entrainée dans les hostilités, et de cela elle ne voulait à aucun prix."

45 *New York Evening Post*, March 8, 10, 11, and 12, 1803, reviewing the pamphlet and quoting extensively from it.

46 *Ibid.*, April 19, 1803.

47 *Ibid.*, April 22, 1803.

48 The best accounts of the Louisiana Purchase are contained in Channing's *History of the United States*, IV, 315–320, and Adams's *History of the United States*, II, 25–50. The works, already cited, of Fugier, Renaut, and Bécker make no important addition to our knowledge of the subject.

49 Senator Mason of Virginia, speaking of Gouverneur Morris's clamor

for Florida, said, "Presently we shall be told we must have Louisiana, then the gold mines of Mexico . . . then Potosi—then St. Domingo" (*Annals Cong.*, 7 Cong., 2 Sess., 218).

[50] For a detailed discussion of this question, see A. P. Whitaker, "France and the American Deposit at New Orleans," *Hispanic Am. Hist. Rev.*, XI, 493–501.

Chapter XIV. A Change of Masters

[1] Daniel Clark, then at Philadelphia, wrote Madison on March 22, 1802, that he had recently heard a variety of reports about the cession of Louisiana to the United States, that Duane had assured him two days previously that the cession had certainly taken place, and that the *Aurora* had "this morning" mentioned an arrangement having been made about it (State Department, Consular Letters, New Orleans). Cf. Archer B. Hulbert, "Western Shipbuilding," *Am. Hist. Rev.*, XXI, 731, note 22.

[2] *Palladium*, April 15 and 28 and Sept. 16, 1802.

[3] *Pittsburgh Gazette*, April 2 and June 11, 1802.

[4] Breckinridge Papers, "Jan.–Sept., 1803," Breckinridge to Jefferson, Lexington, Ky., Sept. 10 (1803).

[5] This seems a fair inference from what Clark himself wrote about a conversation he had with Laussat in Paris (*Am. Hist. Rev.*, XXXIII, 338); and Laussat's account of the conversation leaves no room for reasonable doubt. According to Laussat, he and Clark met in Paris in December, 1802. Finding "somehow" where Laussat lived, Clark came to call on him, accompanied by M. de Pontalba, "a Louisianian worthy of great consideration," and fortified with a letter of introduction from an intimate friend of Laussat. Laussat says that Clark impressed him as being very supple, witty, and ambitious; was apparently on intimate terms with the Spanish officials; and, having made a good thing of the intimacy, wished to establish the same relation with the incoming French government. Laussat says that he replied to Clark in a friendly but noncommittal way, and there the colloquy ended (AE, EU, Sup, 28: 251, Laussat to Pichon, New Orleans, Aug. 24, 1803). It was probably in November, not December, that the meeting in Paris occurred (see below, note 30).

[6] E. C. Barker, ed., "The Austin Papers" (Am. Hist. Assn., *Report*, 1919, Vol. II), Part 1, p. 85, Austin to Richardson, Mine a Burton, Aug. 2, 1803.

[7] Letter cited above, note 4.

[8] Breckinridge Papers, "Oct.–Dec., 1803," Clay to Breckinridge, Lexington, Dec. 30, 1803.

[9] T. H. Benton, *Abridgement of Debates*, III, 10, Senator White quoting Cocke.

[10] Breckinridge Papers, "Oct.–Dec., 1803," James Garrard to Breckinridge, Frankfort, Nov. (day?), 1803.

[11] *Ibid.*, Clay to Breckinridge, Frankfort, Nov. 21, 1803, and Lexington, Dec. 30, 1803.

[12] *Ibid.*, "Jan.–Sept., 1803," James Mackay to John Fowler, St. Louis, Sept. 24, 1803. Mackay was appointed in 1798 by Governor Gayoso (Houck, *Spanish Régime in Missouri*, II, 245).

[13] The Breckinridge Papers contain many letters similar to those cited above, note 10, and below, note 14. Andrew Jackson's candidacy for the governorship of Orleans Territory (lower Louisiana) is noted in J. S. Bassett, *Life of Andrew Jackson*, I, 33, and in *Am. Hist. Rev.*, III, 285–287.

[14] Breckinridge Papers, "Jan.–Sept., 1803," James Brown to John Breckinridge, Lexington, Jan. 13, 1803 (*sic*, 1804).

[15] J. A. Robertson, *Louisiana*, II, 111; East Florida Papers, LC, Box 105 A 9, Irujo to the Governor of Louisiana, Washington, Nov. 1, 1803; Jerónimo Bécker, *Historia de las Relaciones Exteriores de España*, I, 97.

[16] Jefferson, *Writings*, VIII, 274, 275, Jefferson to Gallatin, Oct. 29, 1803. Jefferson planned to send 500 regulars and 1,000 militia from Mississippi Territory, as well as to have Tennessee and Kentucky volunteers held in readiness. He also suggested "including [*sic*: inducing?] Laussat, with the aid of [Daniel] Clark, to raise an insurrectionary force of the inhabitants [of Louisiana], to which ours might be only auxiliary," so that "all this should be made as much as possible the act of France."

[17] Letter cited above, note 8. A letter of Nov. 8, 1803, from Sevier to James Robertson gives some information regarding the selection of officers for the expeditionary force (*Am. Hist. Mag.*, IV, 374). Driver, *Life of John Sevier*, pp. 190–194.

[18] Breckinridge Papers, "Oct.–Dec., 1803."

[19] *Ibid.*, William Stevenson to Breckinridge, Nov. 24, 1803; Isaac Shelby to Breckinridge, Dec. 3, 1803; Caleb Wallace to Breckinridge, Dec. 2, 1803.

[20] *Ibid.*, Clay to Breckinridge, Nov. 21, 1803.

[21] *Ibid.*, James Blair to Breckinridge, Frankfort, Nov. 25, 1803, and William Stevenson to Breckinridge, Nov. 27, 1803.

[22] *Ibid.*, James Brown to Breckinridge, Frankfort, Dec. 10, 1803.

[23] *Am. Hist. Rev.*, XXXIII, 332, Clark to Madison, March 8, 1803; *cf.* I. J. Cox, "Selections from the Torrence Papers," *loc. cit.*, IV, 101. Clark had just returned (Feb. 25) from Paris to New Orleans (see below, note 30). He did not exaggerate the helplessness of the Louisiana authorities. Morales himself had just informed the court that the Louisiana government was "without troops, without money, and, for lack of money, without everything that is needed in order to oppose force to force" (AI, PC, leg. 594, Morales to Soler, Jan. 15, 1803, No. 2 "very secret").

[24] See above, Ch. XI, note 24.

[25] Laussat arrived at New Orleans on March 26, 1803 (Robertson, *Louisiana*, II, 30).

[26] *Am. Hist. Rev.*, XXXIII, 337. A sympathetic account of Laussat's New Orleans mission is in Marc de Villiers du Terrage, *Les Dernières Années de la Louisiane Française*. Several of Laussat's despatches have been published in Robertson, *Louisiana*.

[27] See above, Ch. IX. In a memorial (dated Mexico, Jan. 4, 1802) reviewing his military career and requesting promotion to the rank of *mariscal de campo,* Casa Calvo stated that he had served the king for thirty-eight years and nine months (AI, Sto. Dom., leg. 2569 mod., Someruelos to Caballero, Havana, May 13, 1802, No. 250, enclosing the memorial with his approval). A biographical sketch of Casa Calvo is in Jacobo de la Pezuela, *Diccionario . . . de la Isla de Cuba* (Madrid, 1863), I, 344.

[28] Villiers du Terrage, *op. cit.,* p. 411.

[29] *Ibid.,* p. 419. Laussat said Clark was decidedly pro-English and Federalist in sentiment, and expressed surprise that Jefferson preferred him to the Vice-Consul, Hulings, who was so different from Clark and so superior to him—was indeed a man of transparent honesty and evident patriotism, a Republican and friendly to France (see Laussat's letter cited above, note 5).

[30] *Am. Hist. Rev.,* XXXIII, 339–340. Clark received a recess appointment as United States Consul at New Orleans on July 26, 1801, and his appointment was confirmed by the Senate on Jan. 26, 1802 (*ibid.,* XXXII, 807, 808). His consular duties do not seem to have weighed heavily upon him. He left New Orleans Nov. 7, 1801, and remained in the United States (at Philadelphia and Washington, apparently) until the end of April, 1802. He returned to New Orleans in time to write Madison a despatch from that place on June 22, 1802; but five days later he had already departed again. In July and August he was in the United States; early in October he passed through England; arrived at Paris, he remained there until the end of November, returning thence to England; he sailed from Liverpool Dec. 24, and arrived at New Orleans Feb. 25, 1803 (*ibid.,* pp. 808 and 822, note 48. See above, note 5. Minister Livingston mentioned his presence at Paris: ASP, FR, II, 526, 527). In other words, in the nineteen months which elapsed between his recess appointment as Consul in July, 1801, and his return to New Orleans in February, 1803, he spent not more than four months at his post. For information regarding his earlier career, see above, Ch. V.

[31] Villiers du Terrage, *op. cit.,* p. 403; *Am. Hist. Rev.,* XXXIII, 335–336.

[32] *Ibid.,* pp. 336, 337.

[33] *Ibid.,* p. 338.

[34] See above, Ch. XIII.

[35] *Am. Hist. Rev.,* XXXIII, 345, 346; Robertson, *Louisiana,* II, 38, Laussat to Decrès, May 17, 1803.

[36] Villiers du Terrage, *op. cit.,* p. 412.

[37] *Am. Hist. Rev.,* XXXIII, 346.

[38] *Ibid.,* p. 347; Robertson, *Louisiana,* II, 41–50; letter cited below, note 39.

[39] AE, EU, Sup., 8: 40, Laussat to Decrès, Oct. 4, 1803.

[40] *Am. Hist. Rev.,* XXXIII, 346, 351.

[41] State Department, Consular Letters, New Orleans, Clark to Claiborne, Nov. 22 and 23, 1803 (copies).

[42] AI, PC, leg. 176B, Casa Calvo to Cevallos, New Orleans, Dec. 12, 1803, draft. Cevallos acknowledged the receipt of this despatch on April 2, 1804 (*ibid.*).

[43] State Department, Consular Letters, New Orleans, Clark to Madison, Dec. 3, 1803; *Am. Hist. Rev.*, XXXIII, 355, 356, note 43; *Tree of Liberty*, Jan. 21, 1804, extract of a letter from a commercial house at New Orleans, dated Dec. 6.

[44] *Am. Hist. Rev.*, XXXIII, 353–55; Villiers du Terrage, *op. cit.*, pp. 418, 419.

[45] *Ibid.*, pp. 423–25. A joint report of the transaction by Casa Calvo and Salcedo was sent to Godoy Dec. 12, 1803 (AI, Sto. Dom., leg. 2599). Intendant Morales's report stated that there was no jubilation at all when the French flag was raised, but that many tears were shed when the flag of Spain was lowered. He also said that, in arranging for the celebration of the mass, the French had to use one of their own priests in order to have the French Republic substituted for the King of Spain in the prayers (*ibid.*, Morales to Soler, Dec. 5, 1803, No. 260).

[46] Letter cited above, note 43.

[47] Villiers du Terrage, *op. cit.*, pp. 426–428.

[48] *Ibid.*, p. 428.

[49] AI, Sto. Dom., leg. 2599, Morales to Soler, Dec. 31, 1803, No. 266. The Americans' uneasiness was attributed to the arrival of a ship from Baltimore with despatches from Irujo for Casa Calvo and Salcedo.

[50] *Ibid.*, Morales to Soler, cited above, note 45; Salcedo to the Prince of the Peace, Dec. 14, 1803. Morales was also engaged in one of his innumerable controversies with his fellow officials, this time with Casa Calvo, denying the latter's claim to authority in matters concerning the treasury (*ibid.*, *informe* of Pedro Aparici to Soler, Madrid, May 6, 1804).

[51] Morales said the Americans manifested a satisfaction and jubilation not shared by the French and Spaniards present (letter cited above, note 49). C. C. Robin, an eye-witness, testified to the sorrow of the French and Spaniards at the transfer of Louisiana to the United States (*Voyages dans l'Intérieur de la Louisiane*, Paris, 1807, II, 138, 139).

[52] Villiers du Terrage, *op. cit.*, p. 432.

[53] Alexander Hamilton Papers (LC), Vol. 84, Abr. R. Ellery to Hamilton, "Deer Park, near Natchez," Oct. 25, 1803.

Chapter XV. Retreat

[1] AE, Esp., 664:61, Beurnonville to Talleyrand, Aranjuez, June 13, 1803.

[2] AE, EU, Sup, 7:377, Beurnonville to Talleyrand, June 2, 1803.

[3] AE, Esp., 664:85, same to same, June 16, 1803, cipher despatch, decoded.

[4] AME, Cor. Dip., leg. 210, Cevallos to Irujo, Aranjuez, June 1, 1803, enclosing an extract of the note from Gouvion St. Cyr of July 22, 1802, promising that France would never alienate Louisiana (see ASP, FR, II, 569); *ibid.*, Cevallos to Irujo, June 25, 1803, rebutting Talleyrand's argu-

ments in defense of the sale of Louisiana; AE, EU, Sup., 8: 5, Azara to Tal-leyrand, Paris, June 5, 1803.

[5] Bécker, *Historia de las Relaciones Exteriores de España*, I, 98. This information was communicated to the United States minister at Madrid on Feb. 10, 1804, and to Madison (by Irujo) on May 15, 1804.

[6] See above, Ch. X, note 1.

[7] See above, Chs. I and X.

[8] Ch. VIII.

[9] For the statements of Adams and Cobbett, see above, Ch. VII; for that of Pitt, Ch. XIII.

[10] *The Jeffersonian System* (New York, 1906), p. 79.

[11] On Nov. 25, 1803, Gouverneur Morris, writing about the Louisiana Purchase and referring to the opinion regarding the future territorial expansion of the United States that he held at the time of the Philadelphia Convention of 1787, said: "I knew as well then as I do now that all North America must at length be annexed to us—happy, indeed, if the lust of dominion stop there. It would therefore have been perfectly utopian to oppose a paper restriction to the violence of popular sentiment in a popular government" (*Diary and Letters of Gouverneur Morris,* II, 442).

[12] AME, Cor. Dip., leg. 214, Cevallos to Irujo, Aranjuez, Jan. 16, 1807, reciting the royal decrees of Aug. 6 and Oct. 4, 1801. Fugier, *Napoléon et l'Espagne,* I, 117–119, describes Godoy's return to power. Except for a brief period of "demi-disgrâce" at the end of 1798 and the beginning of 1799, Godoy was very influential at court throughout the period covered in the present work; but he was more powerful than ever after he obtained the removal of Urquijo from the ministry of foreign affairs (Dec. 13, 1800), and the appointment of his creature, Cevallos, to that post. Thenceforth Godoy was the absolute master of both the foreign and the domestic policy of the government.

[13] AI, Sto. Dom., leg. 2599 mod., *consulta* drawn up by the "Junta de Fortificaciones de Indias," Madrid, July 8, 1803, and covering letter from F. Francisco Gil to the Prince of the Peace, Madrid, July 8, 1803 (see below, note 14). On Aug. 8, 1803, a similar recommendation was made to Godoy by Casa Calvo and Salcedo, the Spanish commissioners for the transfer of Louisiana to France. Bécker prints Godoy's reply, which is perhaps not so obscure as he thinks (*op. cit.,* I, 95, 96).

[14] On July 7, 1803, Ambassador Buernonville wrote from Madrid that, despite the pretended regret of the Spanish cabinet over the sale of Louisiana, he would guarantee that Monroe would have no difficulty in obtaining the Floridas, if that was the object of his mission to Madrid, as had been reported (AE, Esp, 664:161). Beurnonville was of course mistaken, for Spain was not ready to give up Florida, but the letter shows that Monroe was expected to come to Madrid, and that the purpose of the mission was understood there prior to the submission of the Board's report to Godoy (see above, note 12). Perhaps it was by information from the Board or some related source that Beurnonville was deceived into thinking that Spain was ready to let the United States have the Floridas. The sale of those provinces to the United States was under consideration for some months after the Louisiana Purchase, but (presum-

ably through Godoy's influence) it was decided not to part with them. On Dec. 14, 1803, Cevallos wrote Irujo that the latter's reflections on the new importance of the Floridas had been kept in mind and that his Majesty had made the "positive decision" not to alienate them—a decision of which Irujo was to inform the United States government (AME, Cor. Dip., leg. 210, LC transcript).

[15] Autograph note by Godoy (dated July 9, 1803) on the *consulta* cited above, note 12: "Puede pasarse [al Ministerio de Estado] pues en el punto de limites podrá ser de importancia la noticia ó juicio de la Junta bien q^e sobre estas materias se opina con variedad y no todos dan igual preferencia a la Prov^a de la Luisiana." *Ibid.*, draft of a letter to this effect to Caballero (Secretary of War), Madrid, July 22, 1803, and reply from Caballero to the Prince of the Peace, San Ildefonso, Sept. 5, 1803, stating that he has transmitted the *consulta* to the Ministry of State.

[16] The boundary controversies arising out of the Louisiana Purchase lie far beyond the scope of the present work. They are dealt with in the general works of Henry Adams and Edward Channing, and in special studies by Thomas M. Marshall (*A History of the Western Boundary of the Louisiana Purchase*, Berkeley, 1914), and Isaac J. Cox (*The West Florida Controversy*, and "The Louisiana-Texas Frontier," Texas State Hist. Assn., *Quarterly*, X, 1–75). An important work now in course of publication is *Pichardo's Treatise on the Limits of Louisiana and Texas*, edited by Charles W. Hackett (Vol. I, Austin, 1931).

[17] AI, Sto. Dom., leg. 2599, the Prince of the Peace (Godoy) to Cevallos, Madrid, April 22, 1804, rebutting the American claim to Texas and part of West Florida, citing Andrew Ellicott's journal in support of Spain's contention, and continuing: "Y este mismo deberá sostenerse con aquella energía y decoro que corresponden a la dignidad de nuestro Soberano, sin necesidad de apelar a la fuerza armada como propone neustro Ministro por no adaptarse a las actuales circunstancias de la Europa, que exigen mas bien el prudente Sistema de fomentar la Poblacion de nuestras poseciones por medio de Colonias Militares Milicianas segun el Plan q^e con esta fha y por los Gefes de Estado Mayor paso al Ministerio de Guerra p^{ra} que insensiblemente aumenten nuestras fuerzas como se va á practicar en la Provincia de Texas que debe constituirse barrera de defensa de las Provincias internas por la parte Occidental del Rio Misisipi; y succesivamente se hirán reforzando los demás puntos de la parte Oriental en ambas Floridas y poniendo antemurales capaces de contrarrestar á toda hostilidad que se intente de parte de los Anglo-Americanos contra los respetables drechos de la propiedad y posecion de nuestros establecimientos confirmados y ratificados por los mas solemnes tratados, evitando por este medio al parecer pacivo y Economico el ruidoso efecto q^e pudiera causar en aquellas Provincias el movimi^{to} de tropas armadas especialm^{te} aora q^e la Ynglaterra fomenta contra nosotros los animos de aquellos avitantes."

[18] What is here called the Baton Rouge salient, commonly known as Baton Rouge district, was the westernmost tip of West Florida, touching the Mississippi River on a frontage of about fifty miles. After the Louisiana Purchase it was hemmed in by United States territory on three sides:

on the north, along the thirty-first parallel, by the Mississippi Territory, which was occupied by the United States under the treaty of San Lorenzo; on the south, below the Iberville River and Lakes Maurepas, Pontchartrain, and Borgne, by the island of New Orleans, which the United States acquired as a part of Louisiana; and to the west, across the Mississippi, by Louisiana itself. The district took its name from its principal town, Baton Rouge, which is situated on the Mississippi. Spain claimed that West Florida, including this district, was not a part of the Louisiana ceded by Spain to France and sold by France to the United States; but the United States government thought otherwise. After several years of controversy and a local uprising in 1810, the district was incorporated in the Orleans Territory, which was admitted to the Union in 1812 as the State of Louisiana. Spain relinquished its claim to the district in the treaty of 1819. This subject is discussed at length in I. J. Cox, *The West Florida Controversy*.

[19] AI, Sto. Dom., leg. 2599 mod., Caballero to the Prince of the Peace, Aranjuez, Jan. 20, 1804, enclosing a report of the same date on the defenses of East and West Florida. As for Texas, Caballero stated that the "Gefes del Estado Maior de Artillería e Ingenieros" had, upon inquiry, learned that there were no "plazas ni puestos fortificados" in New Spain, New Mexico, or the *Provincias Internas* so far as they bordered on the United States, and that the region contained only "unos cercados de adobes" for defense against the Indians.

[20] Ch. IV.

[21] Interior Department, Indian Office, Letters Received, "General Abstract of the Debts due to the House of Panton, Leslie & Co. . . . ," signed by Wm. Simpson, "Agt. for Panton, Leslie & Co.," and dated Aug. 20, 1803.

[22] *Ibid.*, Letter Book A, the Secretary of War to W. C. C. Claiborne, June 11, 1802. Dearborn also said that the United States government itself might take the lands in question and pay the debt, but was under no obligation in the matter.

[23] Alexander Hamilton Papers, Vol. 84, Wilkinson to Hamilton, Mobile, Nov. 15, 1803.

[24] The memoir is dated Georgetown, April 28, 1804, and a Spanish translation of it was sent to the court by Irujo in June (AI, Sto. Dom., leg. 2599, Irujo to Cevallos, Philadelphia, June 24, 1804, No. 426, copy).

[25] See above, Ch. X, note 9.

[26] Since the secret message was sent under the circumstances mentioned in the text, it has been suggested by other historians that Jefferson planned to use the expedition for an attack on Louisiana. That may well be true, but I have not thought it necessary to discuss the question. Jefferson was apparently not in a hurry to use the expedition for that purpose. Preparations progressed slowly and the instructions were not drawn up until June 20, 1803. In other words, a military expedition to Louisiana, like alliance with Great Britain, was something to fall back on in case direct negotiations with France and Spain should fail to bring about a peaceful settlement of the Mississippi Question.

[27] See above, note 11.

INDEX OF AUTHORS

GENERAL INDEX

(1)